EMDR AND CRI
ARTS THERAₚᵢₑₛ

This book guides therapists trained in EMDR in the successful integration of the creative arts therapies to make the healing potential of EMDR safer and more accessible for patients who present with complex trauma.

Contributors from the respective fields of creative and expressive arts therapies offer their best ideas on how to combine EMDR with these therapies for maximum benefit for people from diverse backgrounds, orientations, and vulnerable populations. Chapters offer detailed case studies and images, insightful theoretical approaches, and how-to instructions to creatively enhance clinical work. Additionally, the book addresses current critical issues in the field, including the importance of an integrative and open approach when addressing cultural, racial, and diversity issues, and creative interventions with clients through teletherapy.

Creative arts therapy practitioners such as art therapists, play therapists, and dance/movement therapists will find this a compelling introductory guide to EMDR.

Elizabeth Davis, MFA, MS, ATR-BC, LCAT, is a board-certified, state licensed art therapist, EMDR consultant and trainer, and Director at Trauma Institute and Child Trauma Institute.

Jocelyn Fitzgerald, LMFT, MA, ATR-BC, is a board-certified art therapist, EMDR consultant, a supervisor and in private practice in Vancouver, WA.

Sherri Jacobs, MS, LCMFT, MA, ATR, is a registered art therapist, licensed clinical marriage and family therapist, and founder of Heartland Art Therapy.

Jennifer Marchand, MA, CATA, CCC, is a registered Canadian art therapist and EMDRIA-approved consultant based in Addis Ababa, Ethiopia and specializes in conflict-related trauma, sexualized violence, and intercultural exchange.

"When treating trauma, the empowerment embedded in the healing approach must counter the intricacies and nuances of trauma's complexity. EMDR and the expressive arts each have their own histories of support for successfully accomplishing this goal. Now, this curated group of talented clinicians lend their voices to articulating creative integrations of these modalities in a manner that dramatically extends their effectiveness and reach."

Marshall Lyles, LMFT-S, LPC-S, RPT-S,
EMDRIA-approved consultant

"Building on the interdisciplinary foundations of the expressive arts therapies, this text offers practical applications for integrating theory and practice strategies within an EMDR framework to improve clinical care for the treatment of psychological trauma. Collectively, the authors spearhead an inclusive approach that promotes service accessibility in a wider social-cultural context. The first of its kind, this book will bolster the utility of expressive therapies-informed EMDR practices and promote an awareness of complementary approaches to person-centered care."

Juliet L. King (ABD), ATR-BC, LPC, LMHC, *Associate Professor Art Therapy; The George Washington University, Adjunct Associate Professor Neurology; Indiana University School of Medicine*

"Offering a well-integrated approach to understanding the complexities in trauma recovery, this book provides an incredible resource for integrating two powerful, evidence-based treatments to promote healing from trauma. Using a socio-political and culturally humble lens, the authors explore how integrated Art Therapy and EMDR facilitate recovery from interpersonal and community traumas in our global society."

Amy Backos, PhD, ATR-BC, *Founder: Art Therapy Center of San Francisco, Author: Post-Traumatic Stress Disorder and Art Therapy*

EMDR AND CREATIVE ARTS THERAPIES

Edited by:

Elizabeth Davis
Jocelyn Fitzgerald
Sherri Jacobs
Jennifer Marchand

Routledge
Taylor & Francis Group

NEW YORK AND LONDON

Cover image by Elizabeth Davis, Jocelyn Fitzgerald, Sherri Jacobs, and Jennifer Marchand

First published 2023
by Routledge
605 Third Avenue, New York, NY 10158

and by Routledge
4 Park Square, Milton Park, Abingdon, Oxon, OX14 4RN

Routledge is an imprint of the Taylor & Francis Group, an informa business

Library of Congress Cataloging-in-Publication Data
Names: Davis, Elizabeth Anne, 1974– editor. | Fitzgerald, Jocelyn, editor. | Jacobs, Sherri, editor.
Title: EMDR and creative arts therapies / edited by Elizabeth Davis, MFA, MS, ATR-BC, LCAT, Jocelyn Fitzgerald, LMFT, ATR-BC, Sherri Jacobs, MS, LCMFT, MA, ATR, Jennifer Marchand, MA, CCC, RCAT.
Description: New York, NY: Routledge, 2023. |
Includes bibliographical references and index. |
Identifiers: LCCN 2022020028 (print) | LCCN 2022020029 (ebook) |
ISBN 9780367742850 (hardback) | ISBN 9780367742836 (paperback) |
ISBN 9781003156932 (ebook)
Subjects: LCSH: Eye movement desensitization and reprocessing—Treatment. | Arts—Therapeutic use.
Classification: LCC RC489.E98 E46 2023 (print) | LCC RC489.E98 (ebook) |
DDC 616.89/1656—dc23/eng/20220722
LC record available at https://lccn.loc.gov/2022020028
LC ebook record available at https://lccn.loc.gov/2022020029

ISBN: 978-0-367-74285-0 (hbk)
ISBN: 978-0-367-74283-6 (pbk)
ISBN: 978-1-003-15693-2 (ebk)

DOI: 10.4324/9781003156932

Typeset in Baskerville
by codeMantra

CONTENTS

CONTRIBUTORS

Erin Bastow, MS, LPC, NCC, is the Clinical Director at Harborcreek Youth Services in Erie, PA, USA, an EMDRIA-Approved Consultant, and a contributing author to multiple professional counseling journal articles.

Isabel Beland, MACP, RP, CCC, is a Registered Psychotherapist and EMDR clinician working at a community mental health agency supporting survivors of sexual violence, as well as in private practice in Ontario, Canada.

Barbara Collins, MA, RP, RCAT, is a Registered Psychotherapist and Registered Art Therapist working at a forensic adolescent mental health facility supporting youth with complex mental health needs, as well as in private practice in Ontario, Canada.

Elizabeth Davis, MFA, MS, ATR-BC, LCAT, is an EMDR consultant, trainer, and creative arts therapist in New York. She is also Director of the Trauma Institute and Child Trauma Institute in Buffalo, New York.

Jocelyn Fitzgerald, LMFT, ATR-BC, is a licensed marriage and family therapist, a board-certified art therapist, and an EMDR consultant. Jocelyn's work with refugees in the USA and in Africa has inspired her work for this book. Her private practice in Vancouver, Washington, includes issues with complex trauma, with teens, families, and adults.

Sherri Jacobs, MS, LCMFT, MA, ATR, is a registered art therapist, licensed clinical marriage and family therapist, mediator, and founder of Heartland Art Therapy in Overland Park, KS, USA.

Peggy Kolodny, MA ATR-BC LCPAT, is a Licensed Clinical Professional Art Therapist and founder of the Art Therapy Collective in Owings Mills, Maryland, USA with 40 years of clinical experience, integrating both IFS and EMDR into trauma-informed art therapy; and is currently adjunct faculty for the George Washington University Art Therapy Graduate program and the University of Maryland School of Social Work.

Jennifer Marchand, MA, CCC, RCAT, is a Registered Canadian Art Therapist, Certified Canadian Counsellor, and EMDRIA-Approved Consultant based in Addis Ababa, Ethiopia and specialized in conflict-related trauma, sexualized violence, and intercultural exchange.

Jamie Marich, PhD, LPCC-S, LICDC-CS, REAT, RYT-500, is the founder and director of the Institute for Creative Mindfulness, an educational company that offers trainings in both EMDR therapy and expressive arts therapy. She is also the author of over ten books and monographs on trauma recovery and healing and is the developer of the Dancing Mindfulness approach to expressive arts therapy.

Salicia Mazero, MA, LPC, ATR, CEDS-S, is a licensed professional counselor, registered art therapist, and certified eating disorder specialist and supervisor in private practice in St. Louis, MO, USA.

Annie Monaco, LCSW, RPT, is an EMDR trainer and Licensed Clinical Social Worker in private practice in Buffalo, NY and is the co-editor and contributing author of *EMDR with Children in the Play Room* (2020).

Irene Rodriguez, MS, LMHC, REAT, CAP, CCTP, is the founder of Mindful Journey Center in Fort Lauderdale, Florida, USA and an EMDRIA Certified Therapist/ Approved Consultant/Trainer.

Hannah Rothschild, MSW, RSW, DTATI, is a Registered Clinical Social Worker, Art Therapist, and EMDR clinician working in private practice as well as an artivist and curator presenting in Canada and Israel.

Michelli Simpson, LMHC, BC-TMH, NCC, CDVS-I, is a mental health provider and EMDRIA-Approved Consultant based in the USA and UK, and one of the pioneers of online EMDR.

Tally Tripp, MA, MSW, ATR-BC, is an art therapist, psychotherapist, educator, and consultant in VA, USA who brings over 35 years' experience to her practice integrating experiential, expressive, and body-based tools for the treatment of trauma-related disorders.

FOREWORD

EMDR has been around for over 30 years now, and has become recognized as the most efficient of the well-established trauma therapies (Mavrenzouli et al., 2020). It is also well tolerated and can be used even with young children (Greenwald, 1999; Lovett, 1999). Art therapy has been around for about half a century longer, and has become an entire mental health discipline. While art therapy cannot compete with EMDR's efficiency in resolving traumatic memories, art therapy does bring a lot to the table—or canvas, or sand tray—in engaging clients and facilitating their ability to do the work.

Much of the innovative work in the EMDR community is not focused on the EMDR protocol, but rather on how to get clients to be ready, willing, and able to do EMDR successfully. We keep coming up with variations—for different populations and treatment challenges—on the spoonful of sugar that will make the EMDR medicine go down. Art therapy can be such a spoonful, and art therapy is already well developed and versatile. This is why integrating art therapy with EMDR is such a good idea.

The question is: how? That's where this book comes in. Most of the leading experts in integrating art therapy with EMDR are contributors here. They've figured out various ways of doing it, and they're here to teach you. I know most of these authors personally, I know their work, and I can tell you that you're in good hands.

Many artists and expressive arts-inclined therapists are creative types who may be leery of manualized treatment protocols. Even so, it is important to have a foundation of skills and strategies/frameworks for approaching one's work, whether as an artist or a therapist. This book teaches skills and strategies/frameworks, but don't worry, these won't tie you down. After mastering this book's material, you can still be your creative self—but better.

Ricky Greenwald, PsyD
October, 2021

REFERENCES

Greenwald, R. (1999). *Eye movement desensitization and reprocessing (EMDR) in child and adolescent psychotherapy.* Jason Aronson.

Lovett, J. (1999). *Small wonders: Healing childhood trauma with EMDR.* Free Press.

Mavranezouli, I., Megnin-Viggars, O., Grey, N., Bhutani, G., Leach, J., Daly, C., Dias, S., Welton, N. J., Katona, C., El-Leithy, S., Greenberg, N., Stockton, S., & Pilling, S. (2020). Cost-effectiveness of psychological treatments for post-traumatic stress disorder in adults. *PLOS One, 15*(4), Article e0232245. https://doi.org/10.1371/journal.pone.0232245

ACKNOWLEDGMENTS

We would like to thank the pioneers of both the field of art therapy and the field of EMDR.

We would like to acknowledge the founders of art therapy, namely Edith Kramer, Margaret Naumburg, and Judith Rubin, who cultivated an entire field by formally infusing art and the creative process into psychotherapy. Many of us were fortunate to attend a graduate art therapy school run by one of the founding pioneers of art therapy. We are so grateful for their wisdom, creativity, inspiration, and for their personal invitations to us, the new generation of art therapists, to continue to expand this dynamic field.

In the EMDR field, we would like to acknowledge the founder and true pioneer of our era, Dr. Francine Shapiro. Through her steadfast dedication to the model, she built a global community of EMDR therapists and gifted us all with an incredibly powerful tool to help relieve suffering in this world. We hope that this book honors that gift and helps us to pass it to the next generation of trauma therapists.

We would also like to thank the "behind the scenes" helpers in our process of launching this book. Thanks go to R. Gina Renee and Dana Greyson for their excellent editing skills and patience. They truly helped us fine-tune our voices and interpret our clinical case work and ideas into this comprehensive book.

We would also like to express our gratitude to Routledge which supports creativity and mental health, comes to our conferences, and constantly publishes books by our creative colleagues across the world.

We applied an Equal Contribution (EC) approach for the sequence of our names to speak to the shared collaboration and equal dedication throughout this process.

INTRODUCTION

Integrating creative arts therapies into the already well-established and researched framework of Eye Movement Desensitization and Reprocessing (EMDR) therapy provides an effective and accessible approach to complex trauma recovery which can reach across populations, cultures, languages, and developmental phases. In this book, we aim to demonstrate the effectiveness of this integrative approach through the expertise of innovators in the field who offer comprehensive models, theoretical perspectives, and case examples that highlight the value of creative arts therapies in trauma recovery. Contributing authors have expertise in both EMDR therapy and the creative arts therapies—such as art therapy, play therapy, dance therapy, creative writing, and body-based practices such as yoga—and are eager to share their hands-on and collaborative methods using many kinds of expressive media with different populations and in various cultural contexts.

Art therapists and creative arts therapists have published decades of mostly qualitative research demonstrating that clients can arrive at insight, meaning-making, and resolution much faster than in traditional talk therapy, but they often lacked the empirical data to prove their work, such as the use of small sample sizes. As the mental health field shifts to a neurobiological discipline with technological advancements such as functional brain imaging, parallel fields have started validating the essential role that creative engagement can have in the therapeutic process. The conversation between the worlds of psychology, neuroscience, attachment, and art continues to converge on topics such as the role of sensory-level information processing and the non-verbal nature of trauma memories. The inevitable outcome is that trauma therapists are beginning to adopt a more dynamic and "bottom-up" style which has been shown to be more conducive to trauma resolution (Grabbe & Miller-Karas, 2018). The work that art therapists have cultivated for decades is now emerging as a 21st century model of therapy for successfully accessing traumatic material and enhancing psychological and emotional safety during the reprocessing of memories, supporting clients in maintaining regulation, relational attunement, and present-moment orientation.

The overarching theme of this book is how the creative arts therapies compliment EMDR for complex trauma treatment. Since the World Health Organization's (2020) *International Statistical Classification of Diseases and Related Health Problems* (11th ed.; *ICD-11*) recently added complex trauma to its list of global diagnoses, therapists have become increasingly aware of the need to expand their toolbox to meet the needs of clients with complex trauma. The recent global crisis of COVID-19 has also dramatically increased this urgency with rates of post-traumatic stress disorder (PTSD) increasing in the general population as well as among health-care professionals (Yunitri et al., 2021). The impacts of COVID-19 measures alone, such as lockdowns, isolation, school closures, and work disruptions, have led to depression, anxiety, increased intimate partner violence, substance abuse, and suicide rates, all drastically increasing the need for accessible and effective trauma treatment for children, youth, and adults. Mental health professionals are first responders in the COVID-19

DOI: 10.4324/9781003156932-1

crisis, and many are treating clients through telehealth beyond their previous borders, both nationally and internationally. Now, more than ever before, therapists are seeking creative and expansive approaches to help meet the complex demands they are faced with.

The innovative EMDR therapists featured in this book bring together new developments in the field of neuroscience, attachment, and developmental psychology to support using creative arts therapies for complex trauma treatment. Their contributions will offer unique perspectives on the effective integration of EMDR and creative arts therapies while also providing practical, how-to advice to new and seasoned trauma therapists alike.

ADDRESSING THE LIMITS OF EMDR THROUGH ART

Eye Movement Desensitization and Reprocessing (EMDR) revolutionized the possibilities for treating the impacts of trauma; however, as effective as EMDR has been, it has some limitations as a standalone therapy model. The implementation challenges of EMDR are often seen when treating adults and children with histories of developmental and complex trauma due to the far-reaching impacts this has on functioning and skill development, such as difficulties with affect regulation, present-moment orientation, negative self-concept, and lack of trust due to the ramifications of interpersonal trauma and betrayal. Art therapy shows promise as a trauma treatment for clients who are unable to benefit from evidence-based trauma treatment, including EMDR, due to its experiential, non-verbal, and visual components which fit with the way trauma memories are encoded (Schouten et al., 2019).

A major goal of this book is to assist therapists in meeting the needs of clients who currently cannot access the healing potential of EMDR. Contributors come together to offer their best ideas on how to combine these two approaches for maximin benefit. Through detailed case studies and images, insightful theoretical approaches, as well as how-to instructions, EMDR therapists will be equipped with the knowledge and tools to apply the material presented to their clinical practice and into the framework of EMDR. This book speaks to creative arts therapists working with trauma and complex populations, as it may offer a direction to their work and guide them toward training in EMDR as a trauma treatment modality that compliments their skills and theoretical orientation.

Additionally, this book addresses current critical issues in the field, namely the importance of an integrative and responsive approach when addressing cultural, racial, and diversity issues.

As new collective trauma emerges from the impact of COVID-19, demand will increase for cross-culturally effective trauma treatments. While language barriers and specific training requirements limit the cultural applicability of most current trauma therapies, EMDR and creative arts therapies are less affected by those issues. EMDR integrated with creative arts therapies has the potential to expand the reach of EMDR and become a worldwide trauma treatment approach of choice for mental health practitioners. As the first book published in the field, it will provide a solid foundation to support a growing trend of interest in combining creative therapies and EMDR.

SECTION I

In Section I, the editors each present a comprehensive model for combining creative arts therapies and EMDR with different populations. In Chapter 1, Elizabeth Davis presents a comprehensive and innovative model that strategically aligns the creative arts therapies with EMDR therapy to effectively navigate each phase of treatment when working with complex trauma. She explores the role of art therapy in the treatment of interpersonal trauma through the theoretical framework of mentalization, highlighting how the creative arts provide clients with the mentalization skills needed to reprocess attachment trauma. This chapter will include specific art directives and illustrative case examples.

In Chapter 2, Jennifer Marchand and Michelli Simpson address the emerging need to enhance the cross-cultural applications of EMDR over telehealth to effectively respond to the COVID-19 crisis. This chapter aims to provide therapists with the skills to expand Phase Two of EMDR treatment to increase safety and readiness for online trauma reprocessing. The authors will present The COME BACK Tool, a set of eight stabilization practices that integrates movement and the creative arts, as a comprehensive framework for Phase Two of EMDR. The authors discuss the benefits of using body-based practices when working with complex trauma and dissociation as well as its application to intercultural work. A case example of using yoga to facilitate dual attention during trauma reprocessing in Phase Four of EMDR over telehealth will be presented. The authors then outline the eight COME BACK Tool scripts, one practice for each letter, so that readers can easily and immediately begin offering these practices to clients and even applying them to their own self-care routine.

In Chapter 3, Jocelyn Fitzgerald presents a model for group work with refugees and displaced youth. She outlines effective techniques to integrate EMDR and art therapy when working with adolescents who experienced immigration and displacement, using her art therapy groups from the United States and Ethiopia as illustrative case examples. The community-based and trauma-focused interventions presented emphasize developmentally and culturally appropriate art materials and methods with a strength-based and collective approach. The chapter also discusses the importance of cultural humility in intercultural work.

In Chapter 4, Sherri Jacobs presents a model for combining EMDR and art therapy for the Gen Z population (young people born in the United States between 1997 and 2007). Adolescents and young adults have increased rates of depression, anxiety, addiction, reports of loneliness, and suicide attempts compared to previous generations of adolescents and young adults. The COVID-19 pandemic has exacerbated these worrisome trends. This timely chapter identifies creative interventions to enhance each of the eight phases of EMDR therapy for a robust and powerful therapeutic experience that meets the needs of this complex generation. Art prompts, scripts, and case studies for the art directives offer readers a comprehensive understanding for creative case conceptualization using EMDR with adolescents and young adults.

SECTION II

In Section II, contributing authors provide new tools and perspectives for integrating creative arts therapies with EMDR through detailed descriptions of techniques and case studies. The authors will demonstrate how this integrative approach increases sensitivity to clients' needs and treatment goals following the eight phases of EMDR therapy and offers more options navigating complex trauma treatment phases.

In Chapter 5, Tally Tripp describes a unique approach to incorporating art therapy, EMDR, and sensorimotor psychotherapy using bilateral drawing to facilitate brain-based interhemispheric activity and promote adaptive information processing. This chapter connects the literature of neuroscience underlying EMDR therapy to art therapy practice and its application within the expressive therapies continuum (ETC), a widely accepted tool used by creative arts therapists (Hinz, 2019). The approach will help therapists support their clients in managing, accessing, and reprocessing disturbing memories using cognition, emotion, and the body. Case examples will serve as illustrations throughout the chapter.

Authors Peggy Kolodny and Salicia Mazero explore their approach to integrating art therapy, EMDR, and Internal Family Systems (IFS) therapy in Chapter 6. They offer a theoretical overview of each model and use diverse case material to provide foundational reasoning for the interweave of these approaches. The six Fs of the IFS model (Schwartz, 1995) are applied to art-making interventions which fit into the phases of EMDR treatment. Bilateral art interventions are presented as alternatives to tapping/eye movements in EMDR as well as interventions to create parts of self using clay sculpturing, body mapping, bilateral scribbling, and collage. A chart will summarize the overlapping of the phases of trauma treatment, EMDR, and IFS with correlating art interventions.

In Chapter 7, Erin Bastow illuminates various methods to effectively integrate creative writing techniques into the phases of EMDR therapy. An overview of the research and practice demonstrating the benefits of therapeutic writing is explored, making the case for how creative writing can enhance EMDR's effectiveness in overcoming common stuck points. Bastow emphasizes how writing may benefit clients who get "stuck" with the standard protocol, including clients who have difficulty with visualization or have a history of dissociation and/or complex trauma. This chapter provides the reader with practical guidelines for implementing therapeutic writing exercises within the standard protocol, including prescribed poetry, personification, letter writing, scripting dialogue, and general expressive writing. It also includes the first publication of *The Three Letters* writing intervention, which was developed to assist clients with attachment trauma, interpersonal trauma, and/or complicated grief.

Chapter 8 builds on the theory and research within the field of dissociation by introducing a novel approach to exploring parts of self with clients who present high levels of dissociation. Authors Hannah Rothschild, Barbara Collins, and Isabel Beland present the Three-Dimensional Parts of Self Tool (3-D PoST), an art therapy intervention using clay sculptures that helps clients identify and work with daily living and emotional parts of self. The authors align their tool with Martin's *Readiness Checklist for Phase 4 in Complex PTSD* (2016) to enhance the application of 3-D PoST in Phase Two of EMDR treatment. The negative, physical, and emotional impacts of complex trauma, as well as structural dissociation theory (van der Hart et al., 2006) will be discussed followed by a case vignette to illustrate the use of 3-D PoS Tool, coupled with Martin's checklist, in clinical practice.

In Chapter 9, Dr. Jamie Marich shares her passion for combining mindful movement with EMDR therapy. Marich provides context for how her work with *Dancing Mindfulness* was informed by her experience as an innovative EMDR therapist. She offers strategies for integrating creative movement into EMDR therapy from Phases Two to Seven, and for working with abreaction or other special scenarios in reprocessing. Practical tools for therapists incorporating movement into their own clinical self-care and healing practices are also provided.

Annie Monaco presents Future Self, a creative adaptation of Dr. Greenwald's Future Movies intervention (2015), in Chapter 10. Future Self is a Resource Development and

Installation (RDI) intervention designed to provide a creative format for teens and adults to generate hope, a vision, and a step-by-step plan to achieve their future self. It integrates various creative arts and somatic opportunities for the client to deepen a felt sense of their future self as a resource in Phase Two of EMDR therapy. Monaco discusses the importance of focusing on the future during treatment planning, the first phase of EMDR, while outlining the challenges of engaging clients with histories of complex trauma in future-oriented goal setting. She presents helpful strategies to aid therapists in guiding clients to find what they passionately care about or want to work toward as a way to increase motivation and readiness for trauma reprocessing.

In Chapter 11, Irene Rodriguez and Jamie Marich emphasize the power of *process* in the healing journey using the expressive arts therapy as a multi-modal approach. This chapter offers resources and applications for EMDR therapists seeking to work with complex trauma and dissociation in a more embodied and expressive way, including through dance/movement, visual arts, writing, drama, and music. The authors empower therapists and their clients to explore expressive possibilities that can help them overcome therapeutic blocks. Four case studies are presented alongside practical skills that EMDR therapists can implement in their work with clients. Culturally adaptive approaches are also presented, especially with Spanish-speaking populations.

WEBSITE AND SUPPLEMENTAL MATERIAL

Readers can access supplemental material and content related to the integration of EMDR and the creative arts therapies at our website www.emdrcat.com, including worksheets, scripts, video demonstrations of creative directives, workshops, and opportunities for further learning and collaboration.

You can access our website by scanning the QR code below:

REFERENCES

Grabbe, L., & Miller-Karas, E. (2018). The trauma resiliency model: A "bottom-up" intervention for trauma psychotherapy. *Journal of the American Psychiatric Nurses Association, 24*(1), 76–84. https://doi.org/10.1177/1078390317745133

Greenwald, R. (2015). *Treating problem behaviors: A trauma-informed approach*. Routledge.

Hinz, L. D. (2019). *Expressive therapies continuum: A framework for using art in therapy*. Taylor & Francis.

Martin, K. (2016). *Readiness checklist for phase 4 in complex PTSD* [Measurement instrument]. https://warrentechnologiesgroup.com/index.php/ct-menu-item-24/downloads/category/6-edmr-week-01?download=77:edmr-week-01

Schouten, K., van Hooren, S., Knipscheer, J. W., Kleber, R. J., & Hutschemaekers, G. (2019). Trauma-focused art therapy in the treatment of posttraumatic stress disorder: A pilot study. *Journal of trauma & dissociation: The official journal of the International Society for the Study of Dissociation (ISSD)*, *20*(1), 114–130. https://doi.org/10.1080/15299732.2018.1502712

Schwartz, R. C. (1995). *Internal Family Systems Therapy*. Guilford Press.

van der Hart, O., Nijenhuis, E., & Steele, K. (2006). *The haunted self: Structural dissociation and the treatment of chronic traumatization* (Norton Series on Interpersonal Neurobiology). WW Norton & Company.

World Health Organization. (2020). *International statistical classification of diseases and related health problems* (11th ed.). https://icd.who.int/

Yunitri, N., Chu, H., Kang, X. L., Jen, H. J., Pien, L. C., Tsai, H. T., Kamil, A. R., & Chou, K. R. (2022). Global prevalence and associated risk factors of posttraumatic stress disorder during COVID-19 pandemic: A meta-analysis. *International journal of nursing studies*, *126*, 104136. https://doi.org/10.1016/j.ijnurstu

CHAPTER 1

A MODEL FOR SUPPORTING COMPLEX TRAUMA TREATMENT INTEGRATING THE POWER OF CREATIVE ARTS THERAPIES

Elizabeth Davis

Knowing where the art therapies best fit in complex trauma treatment requires an understanding of complex trauma and conceptualizing treatment. In the following sections, I will discuss complex trauma, identify the best practice treatment approaches, and explore challenges that impede progress in treatment. Following this section, I will offer a visual tool and approach that exemplifies how I conceptualize treatment and integrate EMDR and creative arts therapies to bolster client's resources and skills. The final section offers examples and hands on directives for integrating art therapy mindfully and effectively to meet the goals of the phases of complex trauma treatment.

DEFINING COMPLEX TRAUMA

In 2012 the International Society for Traumatic Stress Studies (ISTSS) assembled a team of experts to define complex trauma. The term needed clarity as complex trauma has historically often been referred to interchangeably by other terms such as relational trauma, developmental trauma, or attachment trauma (Farina et al., 2018). The committee also set out to identify effective treatment approaches and create a guide for clinicians. In defining complex trauma, the committee affirmed the definition offered by Judith Herman in her groundbreaking book *Trauma and Recovery* (1992). Herman was the first to propose the diagnosis of Complex Post Traumatic Stress Disorder (PTSD), as distinct from PTSD. Complex PTSD (CPTSD), as defined by ISTSS, includes the symptoms that comprise PTSD (reexperiencing, avoidance/numbing, and hyper-arousal) as well as "(a) emotion regulation difficulties, (b) disturbances in relational capacities, (c) alterations in attention and consciousness (e.g., dissociation), (d) adversely affected belief systems, and (e) somatic distress or disorganization" (Cloitre et al., 2012, p. 3).

According to Judith Herman and the ISTSS committee, CPTSD results from interpersonal trauma (as opposed to natural events, accidents of fate, etc.) particularly occurring within relationships where a power differential prevents the victim from escape or the capacity to manage their physical and emotional boundaries effectively. This most often occurs between children and caregivers where the child is developmentally and physically vulnerable as well as dependent on the caregiver for survival. However, CPTSD can result from abuse between adults (as in cases of interpersonal violence), in the sex trade and organized crime, gangs, cults and religious institutions, and war and displacement. Any relationships where one party is dependent or vulnerable on the other for emotional and physical safety can be potentially a relationship vulnerable to relational trauma.

Individuals with CPTSD come to therapy naturally struggling with relationships. They struggle with trusting providers, often lack family or social support, experience dissociation from early or chronic interpersonal trauma, and evidence ineffective or destructive interpersonal behaviors which often block the maintenance of new supports and create chaotic life situations.

DOI: 10.4324/9781003156932-2

ISTSS committee proposed three phases of treatment for CPTSD. Phases comprise three basic sets of goals and follow sequentially. Below is a description of the three phases of complex trauma treatment.

TREATMENT GOALS OF PHASE-ORIENTED THERAPY (AS PROPOSED BY ISTSS TASK FORCE)

Phase One: Stabilization Symptom Reduction, and Skill Building

In Phase One the clinician introduces psychoeducation, works on strategies to improve self-management skills, and increase patient safety, helps the client build emotion regulation and stress management skills, improves social and relational skills and support. The clinician will also work on establishing a therapeutic alliance and addressing cognitive restructuring to increase executive functioning and reflective capacities.

Phase Two: Treatment of Traumatic Memory

Review and reappraisal of trauma memories in a safe environment, in order to realize, reorganize, and integrate traumatic memories into "autobiographical memory in a way that yields a more positive, compassionate, coherent and continuous sense of self and relatedness to others" (Cloitre et al., 2012, p. 9).

Phase Three: Personality Re/integration and Re/habilitation

Here the task is to address the behaviors, habits, and defenses that formed around traumatic experiences and subsequent trauma reminders (triggers) that are no longer adaptive (at least after the actual traumatic experiences are over), and limit future growth. Shifting behaviors and responses to trauma reminders may only be possible after having stabilized life situations and reprocessed trauma memories. With stability and the adaptive working through of trauma memories, new behavioral approaches are easier to conceptualize and apply toward life goals. This phase may also include learning more skills, psychoeducation, and improving self-care habits, as well as relapse prevention and maintenance of the knowledge and skills gained from Phases One and Two.

Following these phases is not typically a linear process, with one phase happening right after the other. Treatment routinely returns to Phase One after work in Phases Two and Three (van der Hart et al., 2006). The back-and-forth reflects the complexity of interpersonal trauma and can prove frustrating for providers and clients when needing to return to earlier phases. Therefore, understanding the process and progression, along with the goals of each phase, can help clinicians pace treatment and help set appropriate expectations for their clients and themselves.

COMPLEX PTSD AND EMDR

From early in the development of EMDR therapy, one major criticism of EMDR was the protocols' potential to destabilize clients with CPTSD. Debra Korn and Andrew Leeds addressed these concerns when creating Resource Development Installation (RDI) (2002) and expanded the understanding in the EMDR community around complex trauma. Joan Twombly (2000) also wrote about the use of EMDR with clients who present with dissociation in the *Journal of Traumatic Studies*, where she cautioned against the use of EMDR without a thorough understanding of dissociation.

Practitioners and researchers in the field of both complex trauma and EMDR therapy have since proposed the integration of the recommendations set out by ISTSS for treating CPTSD within the eight phases of EMDR therapy (van der Hart et al., 2013). However, the integration of the models has been conceptually left up to individual practitioners, who must learn both systems and often express confusion. EMDR is an eight-phase, three-prong (past, present, and future), trauma resolution model proposed by Francine Shapiro. The EMDR protocol alone comprises Phases Three through Six. As a result, the three phases of complex trauma do not necessarily neatly align with the eight phases of EMDR; they are independent models meant to guide clinical treatment strategies. So, with two sets of phases as well as the overall complexity of the work, a conceptualization of CPTSD treatment can be confusing for many clinicians trained only in EMDR therapy.

Add to the confusion of treatment approaches the fact that CPTSD is a rapidly growing problem (Karatzias et al., 2018). Researchers in fact have confirmed what many trauma therapists have long suspected: CPTSD is more common than PTSD. Studying the clinical samples, researchers also point out that it is not only more common, but also more debilitating and difficult to treat due to trust factors and issues inherent to interpersonal trauma. With childhood abuse, and the developmental impact on interpersonal skills and trusting others being at the core of most cases of CPTSD, effective treatments need to begin to address not only effective trauma resolution methods (such as the EMDR protocol) but how to help clients navigate to a point in treatment where they can experience a functional benefit from them. As mentioned above, too quickly addressing trauma resolution can result in a client's potential destabilization, or just prove ineffective and frustrating for both clinicians and clients. Therefore, helping clients manage to stay in treatment long enough to be ready for reprocessing trauma should be conceptualized as an important part of the process.

Below are the eight phases of EMDR to compare with the three phase of complex trauma treatment listed above. Note the emphasis in the eight phases on the EMDR reprocessing protocol and less on the tasks of preparation.

THE EIGHT PHASES OF EMDR THERAPY

Phase One: Client History and Treatment Planning

In Phase One the clinician evaluates the client for safety concerns, takes a full history, evaluates symptoms and behaviors, and develops goals with the client. The clinician then develops a case conceptualization and presents this to the client along with psychoeducation around trauma and EMDR processing.

Phase Two: Preparation

In Phase Two the clinician establishes a therapeutic alliance, introduces the client to EMDR procedures, establishes expectations, and continues with psychoeducation. The client engages in learning skills for emotional regulation as needed for managing life circumstances until they are ready for trauma reprocessing.

Phase Three: Assessment

Phase Three begins the use of the EMDR protocol specifically. The clinician sets up the EMDR target by guiding the client to identify the components of the target memory: the image, the negative belief, positive desired belief, feeling, and body sensation associated with the memory. The clinician also gets a baseline disturbance response using the Subjective Units of Distress Scale (SUD), where the client assesses their level of distress on a scale of 0 to 10. Also measured is the Validity of Cognition (VOC), where the client assesses how true their positive cognition feels on a scale of 1 to 7 while thinking of the target memory.

Phase Four: Desensitization

In Phase Four the client is asked to concentrate on the target memory: what they feel, where they feel it, and the negative belief. They are then instructed to "go with that" as they follow the associations that pop up/emerge around the target memory. Simultaneously, the clinician guides the client in sets of eye movements, tapping bilaterally, or some type of bilateral stimulation (BLS). The clinician task is to track the client's progress, helping them with cognitive interweaves if they get stuck, and supporting the client's progress generally through the memory until there is no remaining distress associated with the target memory. This is assessed using the SUD scale periodically. By the end of this phase, the client should have declared that the disturbing memory is no longer disturbing or has a SUD of 0.

Phase Five: Installation

In Phase Five, the clinician asks the client to focus on the positive desired belief and again rate how true it feels on a scale of 1 to 7, with 7 being all the way true. The goal in this phase is to increase the connection to an adaptive belief to replace the negative/maladaptive belief that was originally dominant for the memory. Bilateral stimulation is continued while the client focuses on the positive belief and the memory until the positive belief is rated at a 7 on the VOC scale by the client.

Phase Six: Body Scan

Following installation of the positive belief, the clinician invites the client to check all through their body for any residual sensations associated with the memory. The clinician addresses any residual body tension by having the client focus on them while doing more sets of BLS. This phase is complete when the client can think of the memory and the positive cognition and remain free of any associated distressful sensations in their body.

Phase Seven: Closure

Phase Seven entails the process of closure to an EMDR session. If the target memory reprocessing was incomplete and there is distress, the clinician will help the client contain the memory, ensuring that the client is regulated and stabilized. Phase Seven also involves general debriefing including discussion with the client about what might happen following the session, how to reach out for help if needed, and what to do if new material comes up.

Phase Eight: Re-Evaluation

The re-evaluation phase includes a checking in on the memory that was reprocessed to determine if more processing is necessary or if the memory reprocessing was complete. The implications of the reprocessing are also addressed at this time. This may include problem-solving of difficult behavioral patterns, and as part of relapse prevention and harm reduction, the clinician evaluates the potential, future risks.

EMDR PHASES AND COMPLEX TRAUMA

The above phase model, when originally proposed by Francine Shapiro, did not address distinct levels or types of traumatization. In the last decade, discerning the differences between types of traumas has made its way into the mainstay of EMDR therapy trainings, primarily understanding the spectrum of noncomplex to complex trauma. In the 2018 edition of *Eye Movement Desensitization and Reprocessing (EMDR) Therapy: Basic Principles, Protocols, and Procedures*, for example, Francine Shapiro acknowledges the difficulties with EMDR and complex trauma, and she discusses the necessary conditions for reprocessing. Shapiro states,

> The Preparation Phase should be customized to the client's needs by assessing their current ability to stay present, to shift from a state of distress to one of calm, and to tolerate a high level of distress without negative consequences.
>
> (p. 290)

Additionally, Shapiro states that the client must be able to use positive emotional regulation skills to "shift out of distress" (p. 291), to maintain emotional stability, and to manage life between sessions. She contends that "Processing can generally begin at the point that the client can utilize an affect regulation technique in the office and stay present with the clinician when a disturbing memory is accessed" (p. 291). Complex clients further need the ability to notice and orient "both affectively and somatically" (Shapiro, 2018, p. 291) around memories, with the motivation to approach trauma material instead of avoiding, while noticing that their capacities and choices in the present are different than those of the past.

As outlined above, Shapiro (2018) identifies the core skills needed to reprocess trauma: enough emotional regulation to get through a disturbing memory, the ability to manage life circumstances between sessions, the ability to orient emotionally and somatically to maintain *dual attention* (a sense of the present moment is maintained while thinking of the past trauma memory), the ability to evoke a calm state and shift out of distress, and the ability to reflect on changes between then-and-now perspective-taking. Shapiro does not distinguish between the nature of interpersonal complex trauma and noncomplex trauma, but rather identifies the core skills for reprocessing any trauma. She acknowledges that with complex trauma capacities may be too limited initially for reprocessing to be safe and successful.

In the following section, I will outline how art therapy can address these needs stated above by Shapiro to best support readiness for Phase Four of EMDR therapy as well as the goals and phases of complex trauma treatment set out by the ISTSS Task Force. I will propose a visualization of treatment which is based on both sets of phases. My hope is that the visual tool will help guide the clinician when conceptualizing the two models together and help the client see the path ahead with more clarity, realistic expectations, and hopefulness.

VISUALIZING A MODEL FOR HEALING COMPLEX TRAUMA

One advantage that creative therapy can bring to the field of trauma treatment is the ability to conceptualize models and provide visual tools for both client and clinician through graphic representation. Clients can discern meaning through using and concretely interacting with visual treatment tools that help to hold the unseen aspects of a conceptual understanding. Just think of Maslow's pyramid and how this helps to frame an understanding of human needs. In treatment, visual tools can provide the client with an anchoring presence to help ground future problem-solving and clinical case conceptualization. Complex trauma treatment can be challenging because of the length of treatment, the multiplicity of tasks, and the rigidity of trauma-related defenses that block access to trauma material, and the back-and-forth process. Having a good visual tool to reference can help hold to the path and light the way forward.

The visual tool below is a two-dimensional representation of the *domains of treatment* (here after referred to as DOT) that I use for conceptualizing complex trauma treatment. It shows how all DOT are sets of overlapping tasks and depicts the non-linear flow that is experienced in complex trauma treatment. The outer circle refers to the overall *container of treatment*, which includes managing life stressors for the DOT work to be successful (Figure 1.1).

Below is a description of the visual tool I share with clients and consultees.

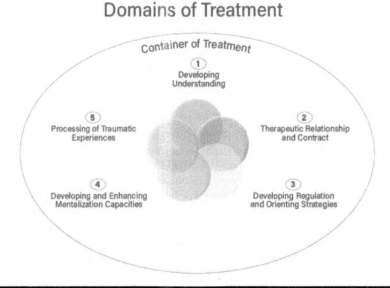

Figure 1.1 Domains of treatment.

THE CONTAINER OF TREATMENT AND FIVE DOMAINS OF TREATMENT (DOT)

Container of Treatment

The outside circle holding the inner "flower" shape refers to the work of managing the challenges of life that can impede progression in treatment. The management of daily life for clients with complex trauma can be one of the most progress-inhibiting factors due to both the needs for external regulation strategies (such as avoidance distractions and addictive and compulsive behaviors), and the ongoing impact of interpersonal issues played out through revictimization and reenactments (Bateman & Fonagy, 2019). A client's motivation for coming to therapy may in fact be based on their current life feeling unmanageable, but they may feel locked into addictive behaviors or a chaotic life structure. Ricky Greenwald (2005), in his *Fairy-Tale Model of Trauma Treatment*, proposed the concept of *fence around* as a metaphor for addressing this aspect of treatment. *Fence around* refers to the need for protection surrounding the client's progression in therapy, so that treatment can progress safely and effectively. As Greenwald points out, clinicians often believe their clients are resistant due to the perceived secondary gains of what often seems like unnecessary chaos and poor behavioral choices. However, Greenwald (2005) states, "If a client is resisting, it's probably for a good reason, and it's the therapist's job to find the reason, respect it and address it" (p. 89). The container of treatment, like the metaphor of *fence around*, depicts the ongoing task in therapy of addressing barriers and secondary gains to regulate and manage life. Without commitment to the *container of treatment* the client often has little energy or capacity for the DOT tasks held within.

DOT One: Developing Understanding

Goals in this domain involve evaluating safety, understanding symptoms and behaviors, gathering client history, developing an understanding of the client's emotional and behavioral tolerance and capacity, understanding the client's dissociative symptoms, developing goals, understanding the client's daily living and how this might impact treatment tasks, and offering psychoeducation in a way that supports a shared vision of the work and a language for understanding and communicating effectively. This phase begins in Phases One and Two of EMDR and Phase One of complex trauma treatment but continues throughout therapy. Ongoing assessment is a part of the process of evaluating what has worked, what has not worked, and problem-solving the next strategies to help treatment progress. Psychoeducation also continues as needs for understanding expand.

DOT Two: Therapeutic Relationship and Contract

With complex trauma treatment an effective working relationship is foundational for successful treatment (Courtois et al., 2015). This begins in Phase One of both complex trauma and EMDR and anchors all the tasks of treatment throughout the process. The therapeutic relationship addresses the task of arriving at shared beliefs about the nature of the problems and the treatment path forward toward goals. Additionally, the clinician models a corrective experience, good boundaries, and mitigates conflicts that arise as a part of triggered relational trauma in the form of reenactments in the therapeutic relationship. The clinician must also attend to their own countertransference, hold the vision of the way forward, and provide adequate support and structure for the treatment to be tolerated.

DOT Three: Developing Regulation and Orienting Strategies

Building skills and capacities such as problem-solving, grounding skills, mindfulness, emotional literacy, emotional tolerance, self-care, and interpersonal skills are all tasks within this domain. The work begins in Phase One of complex trauma treatment and Phase Two of EMDR but continues throughout treatment as needed. With complex trauma, skills for regulation may be compromised due to the developmental impacts of trauma early in life. Or the symptoms of trauma may be impeding the use of skills that need to be reinforced. Processing trauma can be risky and destabilizing for the client if they lack effective regulation skills.

DOT Four: Developing and Enhancing Mentalization Capacities

Overlapping the skills development work above is the task of building self and other knowledge and insight capacities. With complex trauma often comes compromised mentalization capacity, low insight into self and other, due to the developmental impact in early childhood of chronic and overwhelming stress. This can leave the client without good perspective-taking capacities that are critical for the digestion of interpersonal experiences. Peter Fonagy and his colleague Anthony Bateman, of the Ana Freud Center for Children and Families in London (referred to as "the London School"), are researchers in the field of Theory of Mind and attachment in children. Bateman and Fonagy (2019) state:

> Trauma disrupts the capacity to represent subjective experience…. This generates the problems commonly encountered in PTSD, … addressing mentalizing problems more specifically in PTSD may improve outcomes.
>
> (p. 2019)

To the point, mentalizing is necessary for effective perspective-taking which in turn is necessary for the full digestion of interpersonal trauma. Batemen and Fonagy (2019) write, "…attachment trauma typically impairs the capacity to frame and particularly to reframe overwhelming experiences" (p. 2019). This domain, therefore, is tasked with building/rebuilding mentalization skills and the client's capacity to gain a larger perspective in relation to the trauma experiences.

DOT Five: Processing of Traumatic Experiences

Reprocessing traumatic memories through trauma resolution approaches such as EMDR is the task in this domain. Trauma reprocessing begins in Phase Two of the complex trauma treatment and Phases Three through Six of EMDR. However, parts of trauma experience may emerge on the first day of treatment, particularly when taking a history, and any time throughout treatment. The clinician should therefore keep in mind that while the goal is to keep trauma reprocessing contained and carefully planned, the client's system may offer up trauma memories at any time.

THE UPWARD SPIRAL—VISUALIZING THE TRAJECTORY OF TREATMENT PROGRESS

The 3D upward spiral below adds a dimension of movement and progression for the clinician and client working within the DOT. The upward spiral helps visualize a process of revisiting all the DOT as a journey upward toward greater and even greater clarity. When returning to assessment and skill building, clients and even clinicians may become discouraged even though progress has been made on the journey. The spiral reminds client and clinician that returning to the domains first visited in treatment does not mean regression but rather progression. In fact, the metaphor of the upward spiral has been used in the treatment of mental health often to denote the pathway of progress. For example, Alex Korb in his book *The Upward Spiral* (New Harbinger, 2015) aptly describes the journey of recovery from depression as an upward spiral, and the downward spiral as "caught in the habits" of depression. Korb's book builds off the earlier research of Barbara Fredrickson (2001, on the upward spiral form and the *broaden-and-build theory* of positive emotions in positive psychology. In fact, this concept of the spiral can be traced in the field back to Carl Jung (1929) who stated, "The spiral in psychology means that when you make a spiral you always come over the same point where you have been before, but never really the same, it is above or below, inside, outside, so it means growth" (p. 21) (Figure 1.2).

With the above visual tools of treatment as a foundational reference for treating complex trauma, I will now go through each domain and discuss the ways in which I integrate the use of art and creativity within treatment to support an upward shaped spiral of treatment progression.

Figure 1.2 Spiral of treatment progression.

THE ROLE OF ART THERAPIES INTO DOT ONE: DEVELOPING UNDERSTANDING

The beginning of treatment can be very stressful. Clients have taken a risk, often moving away from avoidance strategies, or stepping out of their silo of holding their symptoms alone, and toward opening to another and dealing with painful issues. This risk comes with feeling vulnerable, and many clients have a low threshold for vulnerability. The clinician also can feel pressure initially to get the client through assessments that are invasive and painful for the client, with multitudes of questions that their agency may require. When CPTSD is suspected, the clinician is advised to take care and caution when gathering historical information. The risk is triggering the client into defensive states, such as dissociation, avoidance (possibly resulting in not coming to the next appointment), and flashbacks. With CPTSD, even discussing goals can provoke shame, fear, or thoughts that the problems are hopeless. A creative approach to the process can become a welcoming and regulating advantage at this beginning stage.

Art therapies introduced early on invite creative problem-solving from the beginning and set up the expectation that therapy can involve activities that are enjoyable, distracting, containing, and concrete. The use of art materials at this stage can also add a sensory soothing dimension that clients will then be able to experiment with and utilize outside of therapy. Additionally, inviting the client to touch and manipulate art materials and focus on an art creation task invites dual attention and distraction that is often stabilizing for history taking, and it allows the client freedom to look away and engage in an exploring way while doing what might feel otherwise exhausting interpersonally.

However, the clinician should be mindful of art activities offered at this stage before they have much information about their client. Creative arts therapists undertake training to understand the nature of the experience of utilizing a particular media and directive. This training allows for safety and attunement to be held with clients, as the trained therapist can account for the possible pitfalls as well as hold the experiential mirroring. Clinicians without art or expressive therapy training, who choose to take advantage of the potential of art therapies, need training in a media to safely administer to complex clients. Those untrained run the risk of not holding attunement while offering what might be to the client a challenging or risky directive. Clinicians who naively offer paint, for example, without knowing the potential risks (such as triggering a regressive state, frustration for not meeting internal expectations, or potential sensory flashbacks), may destabilize their client. All media present the client with unique technical, sensory, and emotional experiences. The untrained therapist would be well advised to seek training and consultation from an art or expressive therapist to use art materials safe and effectively.

With this caution in mind, below I offer an approach to the task of history taking and psychoeducation that can increase a client's satisfaction and capacity to tolerate the tasks in this DOT. As with all activities, the client is offered choices and is not just directed to perform. The process of creative expression also is interactive, not a recipe that is meant to be the same every time. These activities below represent the interplay between both the therapist and the client's creativity, curiosity, knowledge, openness, playfulness, and willingness to explore.

CREATIVE HISTORY—DOT ONE

History taking can be challenging. Every exposure to traumatic memories has the potential to retraumatize, and it may trigger states from which the client with CPTSD may find it difficult to emerge. When taking a history, I like to invite the client into the creative process in a collaborative way. Being spontaneous and creative with your client from the beginning helps promote a mindful, open, and playful engagement that can be a useful precedent when trauma work begins in earnest. This stance also is consistent with a mentalizing approach that helps maintain collaboration and encourage agency (Mitchell et al., 2020).

Creative Timelines

One approach to history taking is creating timelines. Timelines have the advantage of an external reference that holds time's progression symbolically and delineates now from then, creating increased safety for clients who lose time orientation and potentially go into a mode of reliving, rather than reviewing. With complex trauma, clients often lack time-orienting capacities, particularly around trauma memories, and orienting strategies should be used frequently (Martin, 2016).

Timelines can be done in all kinds of ways, including traditionally on paper using a ruler to draw a line from beginning or birth to present while marking significant events and time periods in between. History taking is more manageable and more engaging for the client when the clinician works creatively beyond the traditional practice. Inviting increased creative engagement allows clients to manipulate the line itself in order to express the highs and lows in life, to create color codes for specific themes or events, or to use various metaphors, like trees, to show their growth upward. Clients can add any elements that feel relevant to their life story using drawings, symbols, color or words, and many clients choose to include their artistic talents or preferences.

Ideas and approaches to this directive are as endless as the imagination. One idea that improves client engagement when they make their timeline is to use a thread instead of paper to denote the actual timeline and then attach memories written on slips of paper (such as with tape or small clips). Another easy modification is taping multiple pieces of paper together end to end, with each piece of paper representing one decade (or specific period) of the client's life. The pages of the timeline can then be folded, like an accordion, in order to explore and develop one section at a time. In this case, the client can only see one page while the others are folded away, helping to contain the exposure to the whole history. The timeline can also be spread out for the client to view and make cross-connections between life periods while the whole history is on view or even with certain decades folded away. The accordion format provides a form of concrete titration to trauma material during history taking, offering the client control over how much of their past they address at a time.

Below I use case examples to better illustrate the process of creating timelines with clients based on their needs in the moment and their ability to tolerate the past. These examples are meant to relay the collaborative innovation and problem-solving that can occur when the creative arts are integrated into the goals of trauma treatment.

Envelope Timeline

This timeline approach uses envelopes as containers for trauma memories. The envelopes are attached to a large vertical timeline taped to the wall, which is numbered based on ages or time periods. The envelopes correspond to each age or time period. The client can then write the headline descriptions of specific events or themes on colored sticky notes to place them into the envelopes corresponding to the chronological time of the events.

The approach can help the client with containment and an internal sense of organization, not only in the beginning of therapy, but also during the reprocessing of trauma memories in Phase Four of EMDR; the envelopes can be used to concretely and metaphorically keep other memories contained in order to maintain focus on the target memory. Managing levels of exposure in this way can be particularly useful for some complex trauma clients who feel overwhelmed by the memories from the past or the idea recalling their history.

CASE EXAMPLE: ENVELOPE TIMELINE

The envelope timeline is an approach born out of a collaboration with a client, whom I will call Clara, who expressed the need to manage the history taking carefully to prevent overwhelm. Together we discussed various ways to keep containment a priority so that Clara could move through the process feeling regulated and calm. Using a six-foot sheet of block paper on the wall and drawing a traditional timeline vertically with numbers on the right, the process took shape. Working on the wall seemed advantageous for Clara as it helped her stay engaged in a concrete present-oriented task. Keeping her awareness in the room was especially important as she struggled with dissociation and shutting down.

We settled on using envelopes as mini containers out of practicality and availability. Envelopes seemed easy to work with and the perfect size containers for the job. Clara wrote out headlines of her trauma memories on colored sticky notes, the colors denoting different themes of her history, and placed them in the envelopes, then placed them on the timeline from earliest to most recent on the top. The envelopes then held the memories behind their flaps but also provided a way to cluster periods of time together. Clara used the flaps of the envelopes to label the overarching themes contained, which also helped her define and name in an empowering way what the contents meant to her.

The use of the timeline in this case worked with many of the goals in other DOT. Clara was encouraged to perspective take from the present moment, looking back on her past from where she now stands; as she said, "I have been through a lot and come a long way". The external format on the wall also encouraged Clara to stay in the larger space helping with grounding. The creative process encouraged problem-solving capacities, and the naming and labeling engaged the identification of emotions and validating them in a reflective way. Additionally, the entire activity was collaborative and engaged Clara's agency (Figure 1.3).

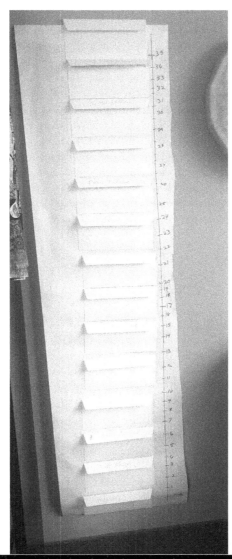

Figure 1.3 Envelope timeline.

Scroll of Life Timeline

In this approach to creating timelines, a long sheet of paper is rolled up like a scroll. A numbered timeline is drawn vertically down the length of the paper denoting the years in the client's life. The client then, beginning at the bottom of the scroll, writes down their recalled memories (both positive and distressing) in headline form along the timeline. The scroll is rolled up as the client goes so that only a few years are visible at once.

This metaphor may be especially appealing for children and teens, but also for clients who have positive associations with scrolls from fantasy, books, movies, or history. The scroll as an object allows for any amount of the timeline to be hidden from sight which may work well for clients who feel overwhelmed with the process of remembering. The client is encouraged to make creative additions to the scroll, such as making it appear ancient (for example, staining it with black tea), or any elements that add meaning for the client. This same concept can be applied using other materials, such as dowls and fabric, where the clients can use fabric markers to draw and write events along their timeline.

CASE EXAMPLE: SCROLL OF LIFE TIMELINE

In collaboration with my 13-year-old client, "Sarah", and her mother the idea of the *timeline scroll* was born. Sarah expressed liking the idea because it reminded her of what Dumbledor may have held in the Harry Potter movies. She also dreaded the idea of thinking about her history and was struggling with even being in therapy.

Sarah filled out The Scroll of Life, as it came to be known, year by year, from birth to the future. Each year Sarah and her mom identified positive experiences as well as the traumatic ones, giving only the headlines to limit activating trauma memories. This titrated approach helped Sarah to balance out the stress that she was experiencing, making history taking more tolerable. At times a good memory was discussed in full while taking the history. By the end of this process, the client had successfully created an object, The Scroll of Life, that could function as a concrete and metaphorical container for distressing memories, could increase reflective self-understanding, and could simultaneously hold positive and magical associations.

This scroll aptly demonstrates the power of a metaphor in therapy to help hold meaning and structure. Because the scroll could easily and neatly hide large amounts of the client's history, she expressed feeling more comfortable with the process. We were also able to talk about the magical qualities that go along with a wizard's scroll and how she was, in this case, the wizard!

The use of a scroll encouraged the use and development of containment skills, as well as preforming the function of history taking. The scroll metaphor also invited playfulness into a process that may otherwise be experienced as overwhelming. In addition, the collaborative problem-solving encouraged the client to become actively involved and invested in the activity, allowing the clinician to gather the information necessary to guide trauma treatment without dysregulating the client (Figure 1.4).

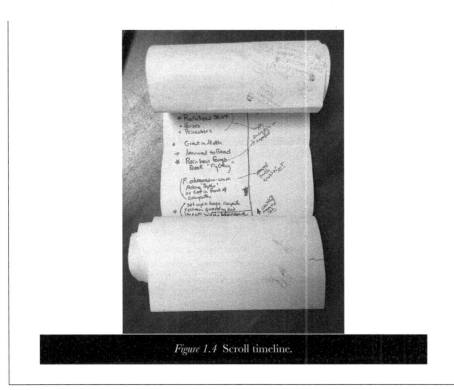

Figure 1.4 Scroll timeline.

Time Capsule Timeline

As the name implies, this timeline directive uses containers to hold memories. I typically use condiment cups but really any containers can be used. When doing a timeline with this metaphor, I like to use a container for every period in the client's history that contains developmental significance or holds a theme of memories to be worked through. The containers can also be assigned a designated number of years, such as three or five for each container (depending on the client's age and history), or hold a cluster of related memories. I have often lined up containers or arranged them in a way to replicate the progression of time, as with a timeline.

One open approach to using this directive that is especially helpful with clients who struggle remembering their past is to have scrapbooking or collage material available for them to free associate when they think about their history (with caution for clients who display severe reactions to visual reminders). Using scrapbooking and collage materials are a playful and effective way for helping the client free associate with memories that are hard to recall. The idea is not to delve into the worst memories in this approach but to encourage a playful experience of recalling the past where resource memories can be identified and some more information may emerge to help guide understanding. The use of containers allows for built-in containment options that may help the client feel safe in a concrete way just in case too much emerges.

One benefit of using this activity with complex trauma is that it provides an abundance of distraction when engaging in history taking that can help the client stay open and curious. The containers can feel satisfying for the client to open and close. As with any art activity used in therapy, the clinician should be mindful when using collage material that some collage bits and images may also ignite trauma memories.

CASE EXAMPLE: TIME CAPSULE TIMELINE

I often choose this timeline directive when working with children with complex trauma. In one such case an eight-year-old, "Amanda", expressed excitement to explore her history this way. For children with a history of foster care, exploration of the past can be intensely overwhelming, and children may outright resist the very idea. As a trauma therapist I never want a child to feel pressured to talk about the past when it feels unsafe for them. Instead, I want to create conditions for a playful and distracting experience where the child can modulate their own exposure to the task through distraction.

With a variety of random collage materials on the table as well as sand, paper, markers, and some party favors, Amanda began to fill the containers, basically one for every year of her young life. She sorted through the bits which included scrapbooking stickers, sequins, and images while discussing what would need to be in each capsule. She was able to, at times, write a word or two that denoted a big event, like having to leave her mom. Within each capsule, Amanda was invited to also include a comfort image or item for herself at that age. In Amanda's case, she chose feathers as a playful gift for herself.

Because the task is very open, Amanda could engage in curious discovery about her life which she found resourceful for the future. Additionally, the containers kept memories put away, and Amanda expressed enjoying closing away some memories in the containers. This can be very comforting and useful for clients who are concrete or have aspects of themselves that operate in concrete modes (Figure 1.5).

Figure 1.5 Container timeline.

CREATIVE PSYCHOEDUCATION—DOT ONE

In the domain of developing understanding, the therapist also has the task of helping the client understand their presenting issues and behaviors. The therapist uses psychoeducation to offer the client a new lens to make sense of their symptoms and behaviors, normalizing responses to overwhelm, and helping the client to feel seen and recognized by the therapist (Lorenzini et al., 2019). This approach to psychoeducation should be offered with attunement, and in a way that relates directly to the client's circumstances.

Understanding the impact of trauma on development, thinking, and behavior allows the client to begin to make sense of their experiences with compassion and build hope with a vision for recovery. Additionally, increasing awareness helps the client separate their identity from the impacts of trauma, increasing the hope that recovery is possible. Janina Fisher, an international expert, teacher, and writer on complex trauma and dissociation, has been a vocal advocate of psychoeducation in the case of complex trauma expressing the need to help clients understand the origin of their shame-based self-beliefs. She states, "For clients with shame-related cognitive schemas, psychoeducation becomes imperative to help them disidentify from the self-defeating story of failure and inadequacy" (Fisher, 2017, p. 54).

Psychoeducation also reinforces a collaborative stance with clients. Collaboration, as stated earlier, is a stance that encourages and reinforces the client's agency (Steele et al., 2017). Very often clients with CPTSD have suffered their traumatic experiences at the hands of others who had authority or control over them. This dynamic can easily reenact between a client and a therapist. The collaborative model encourages the dynamic of a partnership rather than a hierarchy, where the clinician openly offers their knowledge and resources, plans with the client (not for the client), and promotes open dialogue. This not only encourages trust but also models a relational experience that can be a template for the client outside of therapy.

Integrating the creative process into psychoeducation can greatly enhance learning. When working with CPTSD, the client's ability to take in information cognitively and integrate the information meaningfully is often compromised. In consultation, clinicians often express how they have repeatedly offered information to their clients who then do not seem to remember. This is to be expected when clients experience frequent triggers, dissociation, and generally have low trust in others. Additionally, when clients have developmental impacts from trauma they may think very concretely from a teleological stance. With this type of reasoning, as Anthony Bateman and Peter Fonagy (2013) note, "things have to happen or be done to be meaningful" (p. 598). Thus, offering a theory of complex trauma may not be accessible or be integrated as new learning without concrete correlates to help understanding. A concrete and metaphorical approach may scaffold a client who thinks from a teleological stance into a more elevated and objective perspective.

With appropriate psychoeducation, the client can feel that their symptoms are not their fault and, importantly, not who they are. It helps the client feel understood and in a collaborative relationship with their therapist. The education that I often offer clients with CPTSD covers many topics based on what the client's needs are. I often cover attachment patterns, shame, survival brain thinking, and emotional literacy. However, the list of subjects that may be useful for a client can be long and topics added ad hoc.

In addition to the case conceptualization tool described above, I routinely use two conceptual tools. The Window of Tolerance, proposed by Dan Siegel (1999) and adopted by many other scholars and experts in the field, explains trauma, triggers, and the nervous system to clients. Also, Daniel Nathanson's Compass of Shame (1992) that can help clients see their shame reactions patterns as separate from their identity.

Below I describe these two tools as well as a few examples of integrating a creative approach to psychoeducation. However, the possibilities for exploring hands on approaches to psychoeducation are endless. The primary idea is to invite the client to explore the new information or concepts, what these concepts means to them, and how they might experience them in their lives. I often offer a variety of art media, such as markers, paint, collage, and clay, but sand tray and sand tray figures can also be a powerful medium to help clients engage with these concepts on a personal level.

Window of Tolerance Psychoeducation

Window of Tolerance (WOT) is a metaphor proposed by neurobiologist and psychiatrist Dr. Daniel Siegel (1999) to help explain the way the brain and nervous system reacts to stress. This concept has become a highly effective teaching tool in trauma treatment to help clients reflect on their tolerance for distress and resulting behaviors and experiences. I use this psychoeducation tool paired with drawing a Window of Tolerance on a whiteboard and discussing how the brain reacts under threat.

Window of Tolerance: Facilitation Steps and Script

Below I offer a script to use as a guide for this directive. First introduce the concept of Window of Tolerance:

> We all react to stress a little differently and have our own comfort zone, or Window of Tolerance, where we feel safe and secure. When we are too stressed, frightened, or threatened, however, we can go out of our WOT. When this happens our brain switches gears and tunes out the smart thinking part, (Pre-frontal Cortex, PFC), and tunes into our emotional brain more, (limbic brain and brain stem). At this point your smart thinking brain is no longer fully online and you may feel strong emotions, like fear, anger, or panic that take over or take control.
>
> When our emotional brain takes over, we are only concerned with survival. In survival mode our brain and body acts to save us from perceived immediate danger. It tells us to either fight, flee, freeze, fawn, cry out, or in some cases shut down all together. It helps us survive when overwhelming, life-threatening events occur. Going into survival mode is often triggered by real danger but sometimes by reminders of past stress and danger we have experienced

Examples from the client's experience should be offered here, or something general such as describing the typical reactions many have after a car accident.

> If we have experienced a lot of stressful and overwhelming events in our lives, we can become overly sensitive to threat. This happens because reminders of overwhelming events that have not been fully worked through are signaling survival mode and signaling for us to withdraw and take caution. These reminders, called triggers, are not actually life threatening, but are perceived by our brains as being too similar to the stuff from the past. These

triggers cause us to overreact and keep us in survival mode longer than necessary. As a result, we may avoid more and more places and experiences that might remotely remind us of past trauma and stress.

Examples from the client's experience should be offered here, or something general.

Triggers can get larger over time if we do not work through the overwhelming experiences from our past. This is because the more we go into survival mode the more our brains tell us we are in danger and need to be on alert. Like a snowball getting bigger and bigger as it rolls downhill, our triggers can get bigger and bigger the more they misfire and send us into survival mode. Depending on the past, some people are triggered into shutting down, others into freeze, flight, fawn, crying out, or withdrawing. Still others may get angry in a flash and go into fight. Triggers seem to have a pattern of setting off a particular response in our systems. Knowing how your triggers send you into survival mode can help you become aware of how to calm down and bring your whole brain back online and back into the WOT.

Following an explanation of survival mode and the WOT, like the one above, I offer clients an opportunity to explore their WOT visually. Here is a sample script I use.

I have a fun way to explore your WOT. Do you want to give it a try? [If yes] Recall a recent situation where you struggled to keep calm or stay present. This may have been a situation where you think you may have been triggered and felt your body and brain go out of your WOT.

Often an issue that the client came in with is a good option here. The clinician should make sure the issue is not currently too big, or still out of the WOT so that the client can remain curious and open to exploring.

How did your body react to the past experience? What emotions did you notice? What thoughts did you have about yourself and others?

At this point the clinician can invite the client to draw how they experienced their WOT.

Now draw the way you felt in this situation. You may want to draw a body outline, an actual window like the one I showed you, or represent this in any way that makes sense to you.

Some clients may need a menu of ideas to choose from. Offer one up if necessary, so that the client feels a direction and does not become frustrated.

You may have your own symbol or image that portrays how you experienced this triggering situation. There is no right or wrong way to do this. Whatever you come up with is ok.

Following the client depicting their WOT the clinician offers a second part which focuses on how they managed their experience. The clinician should be careful not to critique the client for choices made here but to rather encourage with an open curious approach. Often clients may have concerning behaviors, such as binging, cutting, and drinking, that the clinician and client may be trying to manage. In this directive the objective is not to address the behaviors, but to notice how the WOT can function as a tool for self-awareness.

Now add to your drawing or create another one. What did you do to try to bring yourself back into your WOT? You can use words, colors, or symbols.

Below I offer a case example of how teaching the WOT in this way made a compelling impact.

CASE EXAMPLE: WINDOW OF TOLERANCE

My client, "Kelly", is 30 years old with a history of anorexia, and a diagnosis of PTSD and BPD. Kelly often engages in therapy concretely, from a teleological stance. For example, Kelly expresses often only feeling safe in my office if she is crouched in a corner or even under my desk. When she comes into my office, she has a place against the wall and on the floor where she typically sits. She has a history of cutting which she states helps her to feel and she continues to work with a nutritionist to keep weight on due to body dysmorphia.

I described WOT to Kelly using a whiteboard and marker while discussing a story she offered at the beginning of the session. Using her experience as an example to help illustrate the Window of Tolerance I discussed with her when and how she felt as she became upset and felt overwhelmed by emotions. Kelly expressed having felt triggered the previous week when going to a new church with her friend. She described walking into the church where many people came up to her and greeted her, even tried to touch her. Kelly expressed that she became overwhelmed and ran out of the church, got in her friend's car, and hid on the floor of the backseat. We discussed her reactions: how she felt panic, thought she was not safe, and wanted to run. After I provided the explanation of Window of Tolerance, Kelly followed the art directive. Her initial drawing appeared to follow the structure of the one I presented on the white board. She then added small pictures depicting how she reacted, such as wanting to cut, send emails to me, and hide (Figure 1.6).

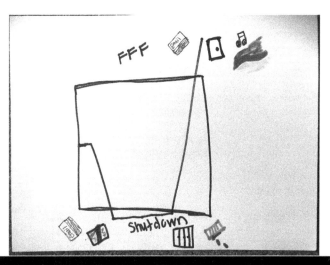

Figure 1.6 Window of tolerance: part one.

Later that evening I received an email from Kelly with a new WOT image she had created after the session. In her email Kelly discussed how she had changed her drawing to reflect her WOT differently (Figure 1.7).

Figure 1.7 Window of tolerance: part two.

I got a WOT for my own image now. I couldn't stop thinking about the Window of Tolerance and I came up with my own idea for me because it makes more sense to me. It may not make sense to you though at all but I swear it makes sense in my head. And like even if you don't understand I'll get it and that's good for me to know.

So, my window of tolerance is like a teacup. Whatever can fit in the cup is the amount of stuff I can handle. Sometimes too much comes into my window of tolerance, and I do all those… and my cup overflows and now I've got to clean up the mess.

For example: Let's say I'm anxious because of the church thing. There's A LOT of factors going on that make me feel that way. So I'm out of my WOT aka my cup of tea is now overflowing with tea all over.

What now? Well, I have a mess so I gotta think of what I can do to help clean this up, AKA time for coping skills to help bring me back into my window of tolerance. Obviously imaginary like for a real cup maybe I'd need paper towels, maybe I'd dump some out, maybe I'd put a plate under it. Just like coping skills there's a few different things I can do.

And like my WOT doesn't always overflow and I can always use coping skills too to help balance me in my WOT before I overflow. Like help keep me in my range but sometime life just fucks you up and you react. It's a thing.

Kelly's words above illustrate the proverbial "Aha!" moment that we like to see when teaching psychoeducation; a concept comes together in our client's language, and they take ownership over it, as Kelly states, "...like even if u don't understand I'll get it and that's good for me to know". Having a hands-on, concrete metaphor allowed for more options of understanding a concept that can be quite abstract. Kelly's upgraded WOT worked for her and sparked problem-solving strategies for future triggers to take place.

SHAME PSYCHOEDUCATION—DOT ONE

Toxic shame and working with CPTSD go together, as relational trauma leaves the imprint of shame beliefs, feelings, and behaviors in its wake. Patrician DeYoung (2015) wrote, "Shame is an experience of one's felt sense of self disintegrating in relation to a dysregulating other" (p. 18). This definition, from her book *Understanding and Treating Chronic Shame: A Relational/Neurobiological Approach*, deeply informed my work it captures the essential feeling and relational aspect of shame, "disintegration in relation to dysregulating other". At the core of complex trauma symptoms lie the vulnerable, shamed aspects of the self, feelings of disconnection, and often extreme loneliness. Shame holds a kind of emotional wedge internally, segregating the vulnerable self from full inclusion in life. Because shame creates such fear of reexperiencing the pain of vulnerability, clients often fail to talk about shame. But it is through interpersonal sharing with a "regulating other/s" that shame can be treated, and fear reduced. The clinician's stance toward shame should be a mentalizing one, where they hold their client's experience in mind in a curious, accepting, and authentic way.

Compass of Shame

Compass of Shame is a visual model created by Daniel Nathanson (1992, pp. 305–378) to explore emotional and behavioral reactions to shame. The compass is composed of four poles: *avoidance, withdrawal, attack self,* and *attack others*. By exploring reactions to feelings of shame on the compass, the client may increase awareness of their patterns and gain a more objective distance from shame. For example, a client may gain new insight that they typically withdraw following an experience that induces shame, or they may react by finding ways to avoid inner experience, such as by using drugs, alcohol, fantasy, binge-watching tv, or some other external distraction. These reaction patterns can be understood through the nervous system's survival responses, for example, they may move into fight mode (*attack others*) which can manifest as raging, being critical, passive aggression, or overt aggression. Or the individual may notice that they most often go inward with their fight response (*attack self*) which can manifest as self-criticism, aggression toward themself, self-harm, and even attempting suicide.

   This tool is enormously useful to many clients as it helps them see shame as an emotion that operates when they are on survival mode. For clients, this may open up an objective, meta-view of shame that can help clients separate their identity from the shame by which they feel so defined. This approach also supports the goals of DOT three, to increase mentalization skills, particularly perspective-taking capacities.

One way I like to teach Compass of Shame is using sand in a tray or container. Sand acts as a sensory medium that is both soothing and allows for containment and layering of possibilities.

Compass of Shame in the Sand

The Compass of Shame in the sand directive can be done in a sand tray or (if unavailable) a container that can hold sand. I have found paper plates, for example, to be ideal in size and shape for this activity because they are small, disposable, and the same shape as a compass. When using a plate with sand, I label the four points *avoid, withdrawal, attack self,* and *attack other,* at opposite ends on the rim of the plate. I use rocks to explore with clients the poles of the compass (Figure 1.8).

Following set up of a plate or container with sand and some objects such as rocks to explore the poles, I begin providing psychoeducation about shame, using the sand Compass of Shame to discuss and normalize different reactions. Because shame can be a difficult subject for many clients, I talk about shame experiences with care to my client's WOT. Even the word "shame" may need to be substituted with "vulnerable" or "hurt" for some clients. My approach is often laced with a bit of humor and some sharing of shame experiences I have

Figure 1.8 Shame compass in the sand.

had, to normalize the experience. Additionally, I like to discuss the difference between shame and guilt, with guilt relating to an action or behavior and shame referring to the identity of self (guilt—"I did something bad", shame—"I am something bad"). Sometimes I use a list of negative beliefs to point out ones that directly invoke internal shame scripts, such as being unworthy, unlovable, or broken.

Following the discussion, I then invite the client to explore a memory using the Compass of Shame. Below is the approach I use in a simple script. I use the rocks for clients to place at the four corners of the compass to "weigh in" with how they feel they reacted to shame in the past. In addition, I supply sand tray figures for the client to use if desired for resourcing.

Compass of Shame in Sand: Facilitation Steps and Script

Below is a script and description of how I use Compass of the Shame in the sand. First always invite the client before proceeding with the activity.

> Would you like to explore a memory to see how the Compass of Shame works? [If "yes", continue]
> Recall a memory where you felt hurt, vulnerable, or angry in reaction to the words or actions of another person.

Clinical judgment should be used, again, here to stay inside the WOT. A previously discussed memory, that is comfortable enough for the client, is a good choice. Alternatively, you can also tell the client that it is not important for them to reveal the experience at all, just think about it.

The client is then invited to write down the experience on a small piece of paper and then they are invited to bury the paper under the sand.

> Draw a quick image or write down what the memory is on the paper provided, and then fold it. Place the paper in the middle of the compass. Now pour sand over the paper or bury it.

After they bury the note, invite them to explore their reactions.

> Now reflect on how you reacted to the experience. When you felt vulnerable or hurt, did you withdraw, avoid, get angry or critical of others, or get angry or critical of yourself?

After a few moments of contemplation, invite the client to use rocks to "weigh in" on how they responded. Rocks have a weight in the hands that seems to fit the feeling of heaviness that goes with shame. Ideally the client will go with their felt sense of how they reacted, and the rocks will help to define and externalize this felt sense.

> Use as many rocks as you like to stand in for how you reacted, placing them at the four poles of the compass.

I then discuss and reflect with the client on their feelings and beliefs about the experience of the four poles of the compass.

Following discussion, I invite the client to address what they would like to do with the note in the middle.

> Now retrieve the note from the middle if you would like. What would you like to do with this for now?

Provide options of closure as needed for the activated memory. I recommend offering the client the option of exploring what they needed at the time, to identify a resource, or put the note in a container. When exploring what resources were needed, I like to use sand tray figures (but they could also draw their resource on drawing paper) and invite the client to put the figures in the center of the compass (Figure 1.9).

Figure 1.9 Shame compass in the sand with figures.

CASE EXAMPLE: COMPASS OF SHAME IN THE SAND

Cathy is a 55-year-old mother of four children, working part time at her own business. She came to therapy expressing social anxiety and fear to leave her home. Cathy disclosed having experienced feeling symptoms most of her life but had not come in for counseling until she was confronted with the story of her childhood sexual abuse being made public. She expressed feeling extreme shame and self-loathing beyond what she could manage. In the past Cathy expressed she had used drinking and acting out sexually to manage her anxiety. She had also withdrawn into her art studio where she felt inadequate to make progress but at least felt safe. Even walking in her yard ignited feelings of shame, fearing her neighbors would be judging her.

Cathy was invited to write a note on a recent experience of feeling shame and bury it in the center of the plate under the sand. After burying the note, Cathy was invited to use the basket of rocks to "weigh in" on how she reacted to the experience. Cathy placed most of the rocks on the *attack self* and *withdrawal* poles, but also some on all the other points. She pointed out she also was snippy with her kids and binged on sweets after the incident. Cathy and I discussed shame as a feeling with a purpose, to get her away from something that feels like a threat to her. We discussed how shame has worked to keep her safe from the terror of the sexual abuse, even though self-blame, hiding out, and addiction are not the best long-term solution. Understanding the protective functions of shame seemed very helpful to Cathy who could appreciate that this reaction may have been the only way she could deal with her abuse in her childhood, when she was overwhelmed, confused, and alone.

The above case example illustrates ways of integrating creative activities and expression into psychoeducation to help the client connect on a more concrete, experiential level. Inviting simple creative activities can deepen the connection and create more impact for the client. Whether the clinician is teaching one of the above concepts or about a host of other topics, the directives need not be complicated. A simple art or expressive response can be added to any psychoeducation.

THE ROLE OF ART THERAPY IN DOT TWO: THERAPEUTIC RELATIONSHIP AND CONTRACT

The value and the challenge of the therapeutic relationship cannot be overstated with CPTSD, as clients with complex trauma most often have insecure attachment. Relationships that traumatized the client (in childhood or adulthood) have likely impacted their capacity to trust and left the client feeling that relationships are a scary undertaking requiring vigilance to stay safe. In therapy this can mean the client is triggered by the very source of where they are seeking help. However, the therapeutic relationship for CPTSD is vitally important for healing relational trauma and it has the potential for providing an experience of witnessing an other person who can provide a model of compassion, offer a corrective experience, work through conflict, rework and revise their self-beliefs, and help the client practice the skills to manage life. However, the challenge of the relationship for many clients overrides the eventual advantages that therapy promises to offer. This is where art and expressive therapies can be valuable approaches.

When I was working in a residential setting with youth who had been placed in the system due to behavior and severe mental health issues, one advantage I had as the resident art therapist was the ability to engage them in therapy indirectly. Art and creativity seemed to function for these youth as a focus away from the direct confrontation of the relationship with a choice of levels of engagement with the therapist. Youth could focus solely on their art projects or engage interactively with me giving them a sense of control over the interpersonal sphere that lowered the threat of connection. Additionally, the youth could choose to communicate indirectly through their artwork, which allowed for connection while decreasing the risk of feeling too vulnerable.

Art therapy can be viewed as an interactive approach rather than a set of art activities that have a standalone impact. Neil Springham and Val Huet (2018) assert that what is known from attachment theory and relational neurobiology informs what is most effective in the exchange between therapist and client. Through their work at the Oxford College of Arts and Therapies, they have developed a biopsychosocial model of art therapy that may help to explain the benefits of using creative arts therapies, especially with attachment and complex trauma (2018). In their publication *Art as relational encounter: Ostensive Communication theory of art therapy*, they propose that art therapy provides a form of "ostensive communication" or marked mirroring through the creation of the art form. For example, a client creates an artwork in the presence of the therapist. The therapist acts with joint attention to the art as the client creates it. The attuned attention of the therapist "marks" the creative form, mirroring back to the client a sense of knowing of the form. This indirect approach allows more space for the relationally phobic client to manage the intensity that may be felt in a therapy session. It also offers another avenue for communication that might not otherwise happen, given that the client does not have to talk about it or identify experiences.

As an "ostensive communication" therapy, here are some guidelines to keep in mind when using art and expressive therapy with CPTSD so that attunement is maintained and effective. First, it is vitally important that art materials be offered and used with the client in mind. Offering creative options that exceed a client's own perceived capacity to manage emotionally, technically, or otherwise can result in a relational rupture. As stated earlier, art and expressive therapists are trained to feel fluid among the media options, giving the advantage of knowing how to meet the client with the creative art options that are in attunement with the client's needs.

Second, a common mistake therapists may make is offering the perfectionistic client a difficult media to work with. Paint, for example, may ignite self-critical thinking as it is hard to control for the client who is not trained to use it. While a skilled art therapist may be able to work with a self-critical client to help them gain insight into their self-critique, too often the opposite happens: the client becomes overwhelmed by their critical thoughts about their art performance and then "trashes" their art.

Alternatively, the media offered in sessions may reflect more about the clinician's comfort zone than the client's. In the case where the clinician finds some materials intimidating or intolerable, the expressive potential of the client may be constrained by the clinician's preferences. Many survivors of interpersonal trauma have learned to hyper-attune to the feelings and states of others in order to stay safe in relationships, including the therapeutic relationship. The client may feel inclined to use media that pleases their therapist rather than exploring their own preferences, therefore limiting the client's expression options and the opportunity for an attuned relational exchange.

The third point for clinicians to keep in mind is the importance of accurately gauging how much or how little to watch a client while they work, as doing too much or too little can lead to mis-attunement. The skilled art therapist can gauge how welcome their observation is from the client and work toward a greater and greater comfort level of connection. Even simply asking the client what feels comfortable can be a solution here. However, fearing they will inhibit their client or be perceived as intrusive, there are many therapists who are not comfortable observing their client's creative process. In some cases, clinicians have admitted to doing their own art alongside their client, which can be problematic when understood through the lens of attunement; for example, the therapist's focus on their own creative process may cause them to lose "joint attention" on the client's unfolding art form, or the client may become curious about what the therapist is creating or even inhibit their own expressiveness.

Reversely, the clinician may watch their client too intensely triggering a feeling of being on stage, or performance anxiety. In this case doodling on the side might be a good idea for the clinician as long as they are mindful that this is about helping their client feel comfortable.

With the above guidance in mind for approaching art and expression in therapy one additional dimension of creative arts therapies to highlight is the experience of creative collaboration and the resulting transitional object. While in traditional talk therapy many actions and experiences can happen, in the art therapy process actual forms are created that include a shared memory and experience of their production. The process of creating together involves multiple shared experiences—such as joining in a vision, joint problem-solving, taking concrete actions together—leading to the creation of objects. The objects can make the relational encounter more real and the experience of creating together adds a dimension of shared experience. For clients with teleological thinking, carrying home a work of art from session can act as a concrete reminder of their collaborative connection to the therapist and highlights the creative experience that is associated with the object.

THE ROLE OF ART THERAPY IN DOT THREE: DEVELOPING EMOTIONAL REGULATION

In cases of CPTSD, emotional regulation strategies in the form of avoidance and *quick relief behaviors* (Greenwald, 2013) are partly the problem that increases a client's symptoms over time. Avoidance behaviors, which developed to help manage overwhelming feelings from traumatic experience, are activated when trauma triggers/reminders are present. Avoidance behaviors operate to help the person get away from danger perceived by any reminders/ triggers around trauma. Reminders/triggers have the capacity to ignite overreactions to situations and send the client into distressing states of fight, flight, freeze, faint, and attachment cry (Fisher, 2017). Over time avoidance behaviors can become so effective in the short term at helping the client escape triggers/reminders that the client can lose a tolerance for normal life stress. The more the behavior is engaged around triggers/reminders and associated emotions, the more the client may experience a relief from avoidance that increases the felt sense of having escaped from the trigger/reminder. This can increasingly impact the capacity to deal with conflict, take appropriate risks, emotionally engage with others, and live fully. The use of avoidance behaviors can lead to a smaller and smaller tolerance of emotions and experiences generally. Under these conditions the person with CPTSD may struggle to regulate generally in their life and may engage in quick relief behaviors increasingly often like addictions, compulsions, isolation, and dissociation. Or they may swing between feeling too much and feeling too little: alternating between states of numbness and dissociated, to reactive and flooded. Over time the ability to digest and integrate new experiences is diminished due to the habitual use of avoidance behaviors and/or the swing between too much and too little feeling, which is exhausting for the person to endure. Symptoms of CPTSD increase over time and can become increasingly impactful and debilitating in all areas of life.

For this reason, many structured approaches have been created to help clients with CPTSD identify their emotions and build tolerance for them so that they can reduce the need to avoid and find unhealthy forms of relief. Many of these approaches emphasize sensory grounding, emotional literacy, use of tools for managing stress such as containment, reframing, relaxation, invoking positive feeling states, and mindfulness. But as Janina Fisher points out in *Healing the Fragmented Selves of Trauma Survivors*, much of the skills training done with complex trauma clients fails to penetrate to the aspects of the client that are acting out (Fisher, 2017). Perhaps due to the effects of trauma on focus and learning, as well as the interference of dissociation on reaching aspects of self that are dissociated, many therapeutic skill development sessions may fail to impact the client's emotional regulation capacity. This is often the topic in consultations where clinicians complain of feeling frustrated at the lack of progress, wondering, "Why don't my clients use the skills I taught them?!"

Art therapies can be an advantage here; as with psychoeducation, integrating a more hands-on teaching approach makes skill building feel more concrete, activates more emotional connections to skills, and emphasizes creative problem-solving capacities. Additionally, art experience is inherently grounding due to the action-based and sensory elements in creative expression. Being more grounded and mindful during skills training may yield a more alert and focused client who can absorb new knowledge and retain it.

Below I will describe a few ways in which creative arts therapies can easily enhance traditional approaches to skills training. Keep in mind that the integration of creative approaches has endless variations, and the collaborative and spontaneous creative process is part of the task.

DEVELOPING A CALM STATE FOR EMOTIONAL REGULATION

Calming skills are critical to the processing of trauma and regulation of the nervous system. Without calming skills, the client is not safe to move toward processing traumatic material, as their compacity to shift back to a regulated state is not yet strong enough (Martin, 2016). Without the capacity to use calming skills, clients tend to spiral downward when triggered or when thinking about their trauma and can become destabilized if trauma is activated, resulting in increased dissociation and the use of defenses and quick relief behaviors.

Evidence continues to mount in support of art making for lowering cortisol levels (Kaimal et al., 2016) and helping regulate stress. The claim may feel like common sense to many people who use creative and artistic media such as music, painting, knitting, and crafts of all kinds as a relaxing and stress-relieving past times. Because engagement in creative activities appears to have this potential, it makes sense to utilize creative therapies to help clients build a stronger connection to calm and relaxed feeling states.

Below I describe one such approach, mandala making, to increase a connection to a feeling of calm. However, there are endless applications of art experience to help evoke a calm state. Keep in mind that the activity should be about evoking a relaxed emotional state, not eliciting unconscious emotions or accessing memories. Structured craft approaches such as knitting, beadwork, coloring, glass painting, wood working, and weaving can be very good choices here to help the client utilize art to access a calm state due to the structured approach and rewarding outcome.

Mandala Exercise

"Mandala" is a Sanskrit word stemming from Tibetan Buddhist meditation but has been recognized across time and cultures as an important aspect of sacred geometry. The word "mandala" is often interpreted as circle, or wholeness. In Jungian Psychology, the mandala or magic circle is visualized in dreams symbolizing the dreamer striving for unity of self and completeness (Jung 1929). Mandala making, as an exercise in mindfulness and developing calm, has the advantage of offering sensory experience which is also grounding. Complex trauma survivors often cannot endure silent meditation or do not like breathing exercises, expressing how difficult the expectations of slowing down, focusing on breathing, and being silent is for them. Mandala making, however, steps into mindfulness gently by offering a soothing external and sensory focus.

Mandala: Facilitation Steps and Script

Below I offer a script and steps to help guide the process. The script below is a general approach for making mandalas. There are many ways to begin. Any art materials can be used including found objects, collage and natural objects like stone, shells and twigs.

> Draw a circle on a piece of paper big enough to fill most of the center of the space. Now focus on the center and make any kind of marks that feel inviting. Try to let the energy you feel guide you on an expressive journey using the art materials. You might notice what col-or/s feel right, what lines or movements of the brush/marker/pastel seem right. Anything goes so allow whatever feels right to be expressed without judgement. Remember this is an exploration where the journey is the focus, not the final product. Try not to question your

---

CASE EXAMPLE: MANDALA

Clare is a 17-year-old who has been struggling with severe depression. Some days she barely leaves her room. Her family was given home-based therapy services due to her debilitating depression that has resulted in a recent long hospitalization and home instructions for school. Over the year, since her depression became severe, Clare has only minimally engaged in therapy. She was willing, however, to engage as long as she could have a distraction. On this day, I offered some pastels and paper to play around with while we met. I then introduced Clare to the idea of doodling mindfully by creating a Mandala. We discussed just letting whatever happens happen, and not trying to make a "work of art". She expressed an openness to this. I also asked if she wanted some soft music in the background as she worked. Clare was very agreeable to this. I put on some Indian flute music and quietly observed Clare as she took her time and played with the pastels creating a mandala.

After she was finished, we discussed the process and her creation. Clare expressed finding the activity soothing and fun. She created a beautiful design and seemed surprised that she liked her art. We were able to also engage in processing her self-observations. Claire reported that during the activity, she was able to mindfully notice a critical part of herself, and, as in the directive, let it float by. She also became aware of a part of herself that loved the colors of the pastels and felt energized and enlivened, as well as another part that enjoyed being creative. We discussed how she was able to observe her inner world in a witnessing way, which helped Claire recognize the depression as another part of herself, but not the whole of herself.

intentions. Observe yourself in the act of creation. If you sense a judgment arising, observe this as well. Notice any intrusive or judgmental thoughts and let them simply pass by. You may choose to replace judgment with thoughts of love and kindness toward yourself and the world. Continue with the image till you feel a sense of completeness.

[After complete], Observe your creation trying to let judgments pass by and be replaced by kindness and nurturing thoughts. What stands out? What feelings and thoughts arise? What different feelings, thoughts or parts of yourself did you notice during this process?

CREATIVE SKILLS CONTAINMENT FOR RESOURCE DEVELOPMENT

When working with CPTSD, clients often present as either too good at containment and subsequently unable to access their memories around the trauma, or chronically and compulsively looking at the trauma and unable to look away for very long. Either situation is a barrier to effective processing, where *mindful* containment of trauma material is needed to manage EMDR processing. Often in EMDR training programs, the clinician only learns basic strategies for helping the client use containment. Trainees are typically taught to help their clients imagine a container, describe it, and then imagine putting the disturbing contents of the memory into the container. This works if clients can already do containment well and can remember to use the skill enough that the contents stay mindfully contained. However, with CPTSD, the client often struggles to either allow themselves to put away material in the container, or they struggle imagining this process enough for the skill to be effective.

As with the other skills and psychoeducation described above, exploring the concept of the container in a more hands-on way may feel more real and provide a deeper impact for clients who have concrete states or who struggle with imagining. The directive below is a simple script to guide the client in the creation of a container. Keep in mind containers need not be prisons for "bad stuff". The concept of containment should be framed as a place to put important information in a safe or secure place for the future.

Creative Container: Facilitation Steps and Script

Begin with psychoeducation explaining how mindfully putting away thoughts, feelings, and memories for a later time can help bring calm and focus back to the present. Then invite your client to choose a container option. The clinician might choose to collect containers so that they can offer a variety of sizes and shapes. Clients can then feel out which one seems best for them. Choosing the right container can be a mindful exercise unto itself. Any kind of container that closes can be used including plastic food containers, gum boxes, old wallets or purses, eye glass holders, envelopes, books, plastic baggies, condiment cups with lids, file folders, tins, pill boxes, clay, spice containers, old shampoo or lotion bottles, suitcases, paper towel tubes, balloons, or create one with tape and cardboard, to name only a few.

After finding the right container, explore with your client how to put distress away. The client may want to just imagine their worries going into the container or write down in words their distress, memory, or worry. Decorating the container can also feel empowering for the client, adding symbols, words, or a design to the outside or inside.

Guide your client to visualize putting worries away to enhance the depth of the exercise and usefulness when the container is not physically present. You may want to add bilateral stimulation (BLS) in this step if you use BLS for resource installation.

> Take a nice deep breath and imagine yourself with your container. Let us breathe in together and when you breathe out, imagine breathing out all those distressing thoughts into the container.

Pause and give plenty of space to this process.

> Let's do it again until the mind can rest.

Pause.

> Now check all through your body and see if there are any hurts, worries or pain left.

If client identifies more, repeat the process a few more times.

> Take another deep breath and let any bothersome thoughts or feelings go with your out-breath into your container. Just continue to breathe out the bothersome hurts, worries or pain until it all feels in the container.

Ask the client what percentage is put away.

> What percentage of your worries are now in the container?

If under one hundred percent, identify the cause.

> What keeps it from being one hundred percent?

Attempt to solve how to help your client put more away. Clients may believe that they need to keep the worry or distress in front of them all the time. They may struggle with hypervigilance that keeps them constantly on alert. If the client is struggling in this way, you can invite them to identify a helper to support the containment process.

> Would you like to imagine a guardian or guard watching over the container? This guardian/guard could be a trusted person, animal, spiritual resource, or anyone who can watch and take care of the contents.

CASE EXAMPLE: CREATIVE CONTAINER

Gillian is a 25-year-old college student with a history of being sexually assaulted in her late teens and having experienced childhood neglect and extreme parental conflict. She struggles with rumination and seemingly constant intrusions of various memories related to the sexual assault. The frequent intrusions cause acute anxiety and often lead to the quick relief behavior of using marijuana to numb out.

To address the flooding issues Gillian was experiencing, I discussed the concept of imaginal containment, and guided her through a visualization of imagining that her distressful memories were put away in a container. Gillian returned to therapy the following week and expressed her struggle using her container. She explained that the container did not seem to work well, she forgot to use it, and when she did, she felt that it only helped a little. The struggle that Gillian had was both one of feeling the container was not real enough and that she struggled to give herself permission to put her worries away.

Gillian was invited to create a "real" container that might feel more substantial and easier to imagine. Gillian expressed excitement at this idea and began thinking about what her container should look like, how big, how she might decorate it, and what to put in it. In the next session Gillian arrived looking excited with a container she had bought at a craft store that resembled a wooden treasure chest. She explained that she wanted to keep her memories and feelings in a place that felt precious and cared for but also tightly secure. She began to design the outside to reflect beauty and calm, placing sticky jewels and bee stickers on the outside, stating that the outside was a kind of camouflage to keep the contents unknown to those who might see the outside. She carefully painted the box with purple and gold paint. On the inside Gillian filled the box with sand and buried notes containing memories and thoughts that she wanted to put away. Gillian placed a cloth doll in the container that she stated was her self-abuse thoughts. We discussed how the objects and thoughts she had placed in the box reflected messages from parts of herself that caused anxiety and distress, and how these were the ways in which her system was trying to manage the stress and trauma from her past, rather than seeing them as bad or wrong. Gillian worked on the box for about three sessions straight. She expressed feeling the whole experience was rewarding and helped her make containment concrete and meaningful. This helped her feel that putting the memories and worries in the box also honored the content and helped to hold dignity for her process of healing (Figures 1.10 and 1.11).

Figure 1.10 Container—treasure box (outside).

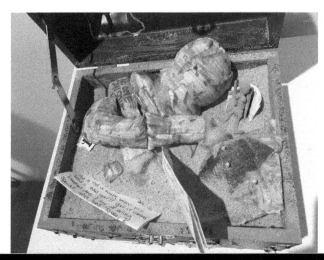

Figure 1.11 Container—treasure box (inside).

Sometimes the client feels the need or burden to keep memories out of the container, as if this is their responsibility or penance for something bad that happened. In this case clients may benefit from a trusted resource figure giving them permission to put away their worries. This may be a relative, a friend, a teacher, etc., real or imagined.

Do you know someone (animal and spiritual resources are welcome here as well) who *would tell you it's ok to put this away?*

Closing and putting away the container: When the client indicates the worries are all in, check to make sure the container feels securely closed and nothing else is needed to keep it closed. The client may want to add to the container more security around closure. Following the successful process of putting away the worries, discuss with your client the best place to put the container.

RESOURCE DEVELOPMENT AND INSTALLATION FOR EMOTIONAL REGULATION

Resource Development and Installation (RDI) is an approach developed by Deborah Korn and Andrew Leeds (2002), who advocated for the EMDR therapy community to become informed about the need for increased stabilization and skills before proceeding toward the use of the EMDR protocol in Phases Three through Six. Leeds and Korn's contribution helped to bring awareness of complex trauma to the EMDR therapy community with the RDI protocol and has helped countless clinicians prepare their complex clients for Phase Four EMDR processing.

Resource Development and Installation (RDI) is a guided set of steps to help a client identify a resource and connect with it more deeply and effectively so they can access it better when needed during future challenging situations, such as when the client may be exposed to family members that they have a traumatic history with, or when dealing with situations where they typically default into unwanted behaviors such as acting out rage, self-judgment, or withdrawal. The procedure begins with identifying a future challenge, then the proper resource needed to effectively manage the challenge. Following the identification of the resource, the client is asked to try to identify an instance of experiencing the resource directly or indirectly in the past so that the memory of having experienced the resource can be activated. The client is then asked to represent the resource with a word or metaphor to help them access it. The client is invited to resonate with the resource and vivify the connection to it. Imaginal rehearsal using the resource is then applied to the future challenging situation until the client feels confident (Korn and Leeds, 2002).

Building a Resource Reminder

Below I offer a procedure for developing a concrete resource using a creative approach inspired by Leeds and Korn's RDI protocol. Integrating the creative arts into resource development adds a concrete creative reminder that the client can use. This concrete reminder may help the client keep the resource in mind, engage in ongoing rehearsal, and connect to it more deeply, like wearing a rabbit's foot or carrying a sobriety coin. This mirrors the process of a child developing a relationship to a transitional object standing in for their caregiver.

I recommend that the client be offered a variety of creative media for making their resource like beads (including letter beads if possible), clay (palmer clay works well and can be hardened in the oven), string, fabric, stones, or any other material that appeals to the client. I have found using three-dimensional media gives the resource reminder a tactile form that can be carried or put in a place that helps the client continue to create a relationship with the resource.

Resource Reminder: Facilitation Steps and Script

When beginning the creative resource development approach, the clinician asks the client to identify a challenging situation where they may need a resource to help them effectively manage it the way they want to. The clinician may ask:

> What is a situation you are struggling with where it may be hard to manage it the way you want to?

The clinician then helps the client to identify a resource. The clinician may need to offer a list of resources such as strength, patience, hopefulness, a connection to a part of oneself, reminder of a good memory, a link to a supporter, a spiritual symbol, or something from nature. I keep a list handy if needed so the client can readily identify something useful.

> What resource might help you handle this situation successfully?

Following identifying a resource the client is asked when they experienced the resource in the past to help them connect to the resource more powerfully. This might be a challenge for some clients who may not easily be able to retrieve a memory of being hopeful or strong if they have been experiencing helplessness for a while. In such cases identifying the resource in a movie character or someone they know can be used.

> When in the past do you remember experiencing this resource? Can you take a moment and imagine the time you experienced it?

If the client can't remember a firsthand experience, you may ask,

> Can you imagine the situation where you witnessed the resource?

The next step involves helping the client identify how they may want to symbolize the resource artistically.

> How might this resource be symbolized? What color or shape would it be?

If needed, offer a menu of possibilities: symbol, shape, animal, word with colorful letters, emblem or badge, something that can be worn like a bracelet or necklace. Then invite the client to imagine the resource representation.

> Take a moment to imagine this representation of your resource. How does it feel to imagine it? Does the representation fit your resource? How would you like to refer to it, name it, or label it?

Then formally invite the client to create the representation.

> Would you like to create this representation using the art materials here today?

At this point engage with the client in the creation of the representation of the resource giving them ample time to explore and create. Offer help as needed to support the client's efforts, but otherwise stay out of the way.

Following ample time to create the resource representation, ask the client to review the creation. This step can be helpful to slow down the process in order to maintain a mindful and attuned approach. The client may at this point notice a need to add to or alter the creation.

> Now take a moment to test your resource. Imagine using it. Does your representation feel finished? Is anything else needed?

Following completion of the resource representation, invite the client to join with the resource. Clinicians who use bilateral stimulation (BLS) for installing resources may elect to add BLS here.

> Join with the resource. Imagine all the positive feelings, thoughts, and beliefs that this resource symbolizes.

One last step is to ask the client if they would like to test the resource reminder by bringing up the challenging situation mentally rehearsing accessing and applying the resource in that situation. Following rehearsal some clients may still want to add something to their reminder. At this point the client also may be invited to explore how they could carry the resource reminder with them and how they might access it on a daily basis. A concrete plan for using the resource can help the client build this object into their self-care and stabilization routines moving forward.

CASE EXAMPLE: RESOURCE REMINDER

Barbara is a 55-year-old divorced mom of three who came into therapy due to complex trauma and dissociation. She expressed having been in therapy all her adult life, including inpatient and addictions programs. Barbara struggled with what she called a scatterbrain. She expressed she must be "ADHD" as she can never seem to stay on topic or keep track of things. This scatter brain experience that Barbara described was debilitating in that she struggled at work, managing her children's needs, and with using strategies she had learned previously in therapy. She expressed feeling hopeless and trapped in her symptoms that seemed to only get worse.

I provided psychoeducation on dissociation, and how it often manifests as confusion, loosing track of things, forgetting plans, and not feeling a coherent sense of time passing, particularly when stressful events are happening. I then invited her to identify a future scenario where she anticipates struggling. She was quick to bring up her feelings of guilt over not being able to manage her teenage son's needs and how her relationship with her son has suffered as a result. She identified specifically issues related to his struggles in school and her desire to handle a meeting with his teachers without looking "scatterbrained". Barbara was invited to explore what resource she might need to keep on track in the upcoming meeting. She readily identified two resources: *courage* and *focus*.

At this point Barbara was asked when in the past she experienced *focus* and *courage*. She identified a pivotal experience with her ex-husband where she decided to leave and reach out for help in therapy. We discussed the memory to see if the experience was one where she felt comfortable (not held as an unresolved trauma). Barbara expressed feeling very proud of herself in the memory and comfortable drawing on the example of this experience.

Following this connection with a memory of feeling *focus* and *courage*, Barbara was invited to imagine how she might want to artistically symbolize these resources. Barbara took a few moments, closing her eyes, and then expressed that she wanted to create a tree with strong branches, standing firm but also reaching out. We discussed various ways of creating the tree symbol. The preferred media that Barbara chose was shrink film. (Shrink film is a clear, transparent film that shrinks in the oven at 300 degrees and is often used to make charms. It can easily be put over magazine images for tracing and when shrunk is about one third the original size with the consistency of stiff plastic.) Barbara found a tree in a magazine that expressed *courage* and *focus* for her. She put the sheet of shrink film over the tree and traced it with a permanent marker. She then colored it in, cut it out, and punched a hole in the top using a holepunch. We put the finished drawing on film in the oven. (I keep a toaster oven around for this purpose.) It quickly shrunk the tree to charm size, a process that takes only a few minutes in the oven. Barbara then turned her attention to how she wanted to hold onto the tree charm. She decided to pick out letter beads spelling out *courage* and *focus* to make a bracelet. She decided to wear it on her wrist to remind her of her resources.

After creating the bracelet with the tree charm and letter beads, Barbara was asked if anything else was needed for this bracelet to reflect the resource. Barbara expressed that she wanted to take a picture of the bracelet and put the picture on her smartphone as a background, stating that this would be another place to remind herself to focus, as her phone was at times a distraction that she struggled to manage. Barbara then took a picture of the bracelet for her phone and then began to wear the bracelet on her wrist.

Barbara was invited to resonate with the bracelet, closing her eyes and silently tapping her knees. After connecting with the bracelet, she was invited to bring up the upcoming meeting for her son and to mentally rehearse accessing it at that moment. Barbara took some time to play out the future meeting and using her bracelet until she felt confident that she could connect with the resources of *courage* and *focus* during the meeting. She imagined herself like the tree, strong and firm, but also open and willing to work with others. She expressed that this metaphor and reminder helped her embody the resources and gave her more confidence for the upcoming meeting.

ART INTERVENTIONS IN DOT FOUR: DEVELOPING MENTALIZATION SKILLS AND REFLECTIVE CAPACITIES

Mentalization is a set of skills which enable us to understand and identify our own and others' mental world in terms of desires, feelings, goals, beliefs, and intentions. Through this imaginary process, mentalization allows us to feel connection to others, empathy, similarity, difference, and share emotional intimacy; however, it begins with self-knowledge: understanding our own needs, emotions, beliefs, and intentions. When this meta-skill emerges (typically around four to five years), a child begins to feel true empathy, experience guilt, desire reciprocal interaction and play, and starts to develop values for self-actions as they relate interpersonally. This skill develops best under the conditions of a trusting attachment relationship where the child learns who they are and how to interpret their experiences and sense of self through a secure caregiver's attuned mirroring. Fonagy et al. (2002/2004) describe this secure attuned relationship between a caregiver and a child as having *epistemic trust*, which allows for a secure sharing of information interpersonally. This epistemic trust forms the foundation for the development of interpersonal skills, and ultimately emotional regulation skills.

The development of mentalization skills is disrupted when stress and trauma in childhood impacts the child's ability to form this trusting relationship with their caregiver. If the caregiver abuses or neglects the child, for instance, the child's defensive system is naturally activated, which shuts off connection in favor of self-protection and creates a rupture in the epistemic trust of the relationship. If a child is subjected to chronic abuse, betrayal, or neglect, without repair, then epistemic trust breaks down or does not take form. In its place, the child takes on a stance of *epistemic vigilance* or *mistrust* where the caregiver is seen as potentially threatening. This thwarts the development of mentalization skills in favor of a survival orientation based on ongoing feelings of threat, leaving the child siloed off from the mind of the caregiver. The child becomes psychologically isolated and confused, and without these foundational skills for objective interpersonal understanding. This isolation and confusion limits the child's ability to interact with others flexibly and effectively, benefit from the knowledge and connection from others, and feel connected to the world at large (Fonagy et al., 2004). The child is ultimately left in a state of overwhelming uncertainty and fear.

According to Fonagy et al. (2004), a child cannot maintain this unbearable state of uncertainty, fear, and isolation under the impact of childhood abuse and neglect; as a result, they are forced to "split their ego functioning to maintain dual modes of functioning" (p. 266). In a "split" self, the child finds relief from the isolation and uncertainty by either cutting off emotions unconsciously or projecting emotional experience into the external world as real. The result is experienced as either an overly personal and raw experience of the world as full of threats correlating to the emotions experienced, or a detached dissociated experience cut off from emotions, void, and emotionally colorless. Fonagy refers to these two states as *psych equivalent* and *pretend mode*. The chronic engagement of these two states represents the failure of mentalization skills and the subsequent lack of integration of interpersonal experience.

A client who remains stuck in either *psych equivalent* or *pretend mode* cannot effectively breakdown traumatic interpersonal experiences. In *psych equivalent* states emotions are made real, and they are acted out or experienced with a physicality in the external world. They are evident in the acting out of emotions behaviorally, such as when a client uses cutting as a way to externalize inner pain, giving the pain an external correlate. Very often in *psych equivalent* states the awareness of having a feeling is not yet conscious and thus the feeling is acted out or experienced as a state of threat, as mentalization skills for understanding and identifying inner feeling states are underdeveloped (or out of reach cognitively) and intense emotions ignite survival responses. The perceived threat is then treated as real even without evidence and when clearly irrational. For example, I recall a client with a history of severe childhood abuse who would crawl under my desk or sit between chairs on the floor during sessions. Under the desk, the client stated they experienced more safety. Even though a threat was not present and even though the client could acknowledge this, the threatening emotions around coming to therapy were treated as if the threat was real. The client, sitting under the desk, experienced relief from the uncertainty that the emotions elicited, as they made their emotions make sense. The process of understanding their emotion as a feeling independent of external present-day circumstances was not available.

Pretend mode states, however, are states where emotions are detached all together. These states are manifested when clients seem dissociated, alexithymic, and minimizing and dismissing of emotions as generally unimportant. In *pretend mode* clients often don't remember their trauma experiences well or minimize the impact of emotional experiences on themselves generally. Unable to feel the emotional impact, the client may make light of their trauma experiences or simply say the experiences did not affect them. The clinician may find it difficult to help the client get to their feelings and recognize them as important. The client may express a strong distaste for feelings and vulnerability in general and may therefore strive to maintain a self-reliant and detached stance while also simultaneously suffering from intense isolation, numbness, and depression. For example, I recall a client who came to therapy experiencing bouts of anxiety and depression following the sudden loss of a parent. The client expressed a lack of emotion around their parent's death and although puzzled by this, they did not believe it was useful to dwell on it. Yet they presented with intense anxiety and depression following the loss. The client could intellectually see the relationship between the anxiety and depression and their loss, but could not emotionally connect their symptoms to the loss event. Instead, they expressed feeling like they were just going through the motions and that life was meaningless.

This psychic split of *psych equivalent* or *pretend mode* is a part of all trauma experience to a degree. Under extreme stress everyone is vulnerable to a breakdown in the ability to digest difficult experience and can default into a more primitive mode of processing. However, if primitive modes of managing experience are dominant from early childhood on, the development of mentalization skills is truncated and a cascade of impacts follow. Mentalization skills form the foundation for emotional regulation as well as social skills. Without mentalizing skills, the psychological protection that comes from objective perspective-taking, and the interpersonal skills that allow for effective social functioning are greatly impacted. As a result, the client becomes increasingly vulnerable to additional traumas, which in turn results in more vigilance and less trust in others. *Epistemic vigilance* and distrust keep the individual isolated and prevent them from attaining the very skills and connection that can provide relief and healing. According to Fonagy, the lack of mentalization skill development can ultimately impact interpersonal reasoning capacity. Without having a mentalizing stance the mind of the other is misread or not accounted for all together, leaving the interpretation of actions of others to be based solely on a concrete understanding. Fonagy refers to this as a *teleological mode* of reasoning. A teleological interpretation refers to believing that the outcome is the reason for the action (Fonagy et al, 2004, p. 223). This kind of reasoning can function rationally in spheres where interpersonal knowledge is not required, but when applied to psychologically minded beings, the *teleological mode* is missing the necessary data that mentalization skills provide and that allow for interpersonal understanding to come into focus.

Clients stuck in *teleological mode* struggle with processing through their interpersonal trauma from childhood with the typical negative all or nothing child logic cognitions that seem to stay stuck even when cognitive interweaves are used. For example, I had a client who was abused by his father in childhood who took on the belief that because he was abused, he was bad. To think this way is normal for a young child who has not developed perspective-taking ability and cannot yet account for their father having a mental state independent of themselves. When processing with this client the need for a cognitive interweave to shore up perspective-taking capacity was used, "If this was your nephew being abused do you think they would be bad?". This typically works for clients who have mentalization skills but are struggling to connect with them when thinking about trauma memories. However, when mentalization skills are lacking, this interweave will fall short and the client remains self-attacking and unable to make the perspective-taking leap the interweave is intended to encourage. They may admit it does not make sense logically but yet be unable to embrace perspective-taking around their own trauma experiences. With CPTSD, clients with such deeply rooted negative self/other attacking beliefs often struggle to make the shift in perspective. Shame then becomes the primary emotion which then impacts internal organization of the self toward increased vigilance.

Art and expressive therapies hold specific qualities that are ideal for addressing mentalization skill deficits and building insight. For one, art and expression generally act as a process of assimilating the external with the internal thoughts, beliefs, emotions, and perspectives. Eric Kandel, a Nobel Laureate, psychiatrist, neuroscientist, and one of the pioneers of the relatively new field of *neuroesthetics* (which seeks to understand the importance of art for human development), asserts that art creation is an evolutionary adaptation, an instinctual response, that aids in survival, "The arts…encode information, stories, and perspectives that allow us to appraise courses of action and the feelings and motives of others in a palatable, low-risk way" (Kandel, 2012, p. 501). This evolutionary adaptive response, Kandel suggests, allows for an assimilation of information both emotional and factual in a way that increases adaptation and ultimately survival. In this way expressive arts bring together complex experiences that lead to a more resilient understanding of internal experience.

Peter Fonagy has also been a supporter of the expressive therapies specifically for the treatment of complex disorders such as borderline personality disorder. He acknowledges the work that many art therapists do in some of the most challenging settings and with the most complex treatment populations, such as those found in juvenile justice, corrections, substance abuse, and inpatient care. Fonagy (2012) writes, "Art therapy has not been well served by research but has served a complex and varied client group arguably better than any other single modality" (p. 90). His belief is that the art psychotherapies hold a possible solution, asserting that "…art therapy has the key or perhaps a key to our understanding of the mechanisms underpinning change in all kinds of psychological treatments" (p. 90). His view of expressive therapy's mechanism of healing has to do with how the creative and expressive process unites the psyche's split modes, enabling more understanding. He says that expressive therapy "allows the internal to be expressed externally so that it can be verbalized at a distance through an alternative medium and from a different perspective" (Bateman & Fonagy, 2004, p. 172). Bateman and Fonagy (2004) go on to state, "Under these circumstances mentalizing becomes conscious, verbal, deliberate, and reflective" (p. 172).

The following section will outline a few creative approaches that emphasize enhancing mentalizing and perspective-taking capacity. Many approaches taken in art and expressive therapy are naturally enhancing for mentalization skills, as the creative process allows for that which is inside to be made real externally and to be contemplated and understood. Expressive and creative approaches naturally involve this union of the external and internal and integrate a reflective process. When using art therapy to specifically enhance mentalization and reflective skills, the clinician should be mindful of the process, however, and be in a mentalizing state themselves. The intention for the therapist is to help the client build skills while maintaining contingent attunement to the client's mental state. This approach requires that the therapist take a flexible stance that defaults to the needs of the client in the moment rather than prioritizing the outcome of the activity. Additionally, the therapist supports reflection while facilitating the opportunity and conditions for the client to safely externalize their inner reality through an expressive, creative process.

EXPLORING THE SPLIT SELF IN DEVELOPING MENTALIZATION SKILLS

The gap between the *psych equivalent mode* and the *pretend mode*, which defines the experience of many clients with CPTSD, is a natural place to begin to open curiosity. Developing tolerance for inner reflection is a natural place to begin the work of developing mentalization skills. The gap between the *psych equivalent mode* and the *pretend mode* defines the experience of many clients with CPTSD, making it difficult to put their experiences into words: talking to help develop insight may be triggering for clients or may simply be ineffective. Additionally, talking can be largely unproductive due to defensive strategies that take over and prevent them from engaging feelings directly, like intellectualization, rationalizing, becoming tangential and feeling unable to stay on topic, dissociation, emotional and state change switching, somatic issue like migraines, etc. This, for some clients, is simply too much and their defensive reactions express the threat that inner noticing poses.

Offering art directives, however, can make the task of inner exploration much more manageable, productive, and even enjoyable. Art invites the sensory systems and engages the emotional parts of the brain in way that can help the client connect more productively (Steele & Raider, 2009). The invitation to make art to express internal experience is often accepted, especially as directives are linked with creativity and sensory experiences that are often seen as soothing or inviting. Additionally, the client may find the experience of inner reflection more tolerable due to the containing capacity of an art object.

Below I describe a few approaches to creatively inviting clients to engage their inner experience to gain a more mentalizing and meta-perspective. However, there are a few cautions to keep in mind when working with clients who are struggling in either *psych equivalent* or *pretend modes* and thinking in a *teleological* way. First, the power of the sensory input of art media can trigger flashbacks or flooding in clients particularly who are in *psych equivalent* or *pretend mode*. I have had clients who could not tolerate certain colors of paint, the feeling of wet clay, oil pastels, and even pencils had a bad association for one client. When *psych equivalent mode* is dominating, the experience of the media can be as if it is real, the same as the trauma experience. As one client pointed out to me, "Wet clay is yucky and scary!", not just that it feels yucky and scary. The difference is one where the client struggles to hold perspective around their triggered sensory experiences.

Second, clients may engage with the materials in a regressive way that can leave them in a dissociated state. For the clinician, it is important to keep in mind that regression happens when childhood parts are engaged. Therefore, the client may appear regressed or switch into a childlike part without perspective of their present day or adult self. For the clinician, understanding how to time orient and ground their client when they lose track of their present self is critical (Martin, 2016). If the clinician is well attuned and follows the phases of trauma treatment with mindful attention to the *window of tolerance*, they can ground and orient their client. Additionally, if the clinician has a good grasp of what media are best suited for their client, they can safely guide the client to use art materials that will help them investigate their inner experience, which will greatly enhance self-understanding as well as add a dimension of creativity and fun to this aspect of treatment.

Inside/Outside Mask: Facilitation Steps and Script

Inside/Outside Mask is a traditional art therapy directive that builds upon the idea that we all have a public and private self that is experienced as different. The use of a mask is the traditional canvas for this directive, but clients may also simply use paper and drawing materials, or a box (inside/outside box in this case similar to the container exercise above) to show the two sides of the self. The clinician may want to offer a mixture of media with mask making to enhance the activity. The use of a glue gun or glue, tape or other adhesive, and collage materials may be offered as well as paint and markers. Offering a variety of media opens creative possibilities for the client to explore.

When using a paper mâché mask form, the directive invites an exploration of the contrast between the two aspects of self in a playful way, with the face form immediately eliciting a connection to the activity. Often a client will spend more time on one part or the other, diving deeply into their public persona more than their private one, or vice versa. Following completion of the activity the therapist may invite the client to talk about their process and responses to the completed mask. When inviting a client to this directive I typically offer instructions like this:

Would you like to try a mask making activity where you can explore the aspect of yourself you show to the world and that part that is private or more hidden?

Add more psychoeducation, if needed. Additionally, normalizing that we all have a public and a private self can help some clients feel comfortable exploring.

We sometimes call this the public and the private self, which everyone has. Some aspects of ourselves we project more into the world and other aspects we may not want to show everyone or anyone. There is no right or wrong way to explore these two aspects of ourselves.

An example might be offered here to help the client understand the activity fully. Following completion of the activity, the clinician may invite the client to talk openly about their art, inquiring about what they notice and helping them to build self-reflection skills.

Did you notice anything new about yourself? How do you think others experience their public and private selves? What do you think others notice about your public self? What might others notice about your private self? What aspects if any of your private self is shared with your public self? How separate do the two parts feel?

Questions are not necessary but may invite deeper exploration of the activity.

Below are three case examples to illustrate that clients may bring a variety of responses to this directive.

CASE EXAMPLE 1: INSIDE/OUTSIDE MASK

Regina is a 60-year-old medical technician with symptoms of CPTSD and dissociation. Everyday Regina typically experiences parts of herself as very distinct about which she has expressed feeling very helpless but also desires to understand better. This is her own description of her creative process:

"I tried to make it pretty, like interesting makeup. As I was making it I still thought I was probably doing it wrong. Instead of painting with lines, I used dots of paint I thought of time passing. It got easier to make as I kept making the dots in a pattern on the mask and a pattern of time; like dot…dot…dot…dot…(like drips of water or the second hand of a clock) it made me think of the mask I put out for others to see – and the dots remind me of how slow seconds pass while I'm with people, trying to be normal; how long can I fake being a normal person. I like that the mouth is closed, this is where I get into trouble, people think I'm normal until I speak. Then I wish I never spoke, did I tell a secret? Did I offend someone? Did I tell the truth or did I tell a lie? Best to just be quiet. Smile and nod.

The inside is what I say to myself; and I had fun coming up with what I want to say to myself when I feel bad. My messages: be kind to yourself, its ok to have ups and downs, its ok to like your complex brain – time to forgive and love. I put a cross because my faith helps me and a dried flower to remember my favorite place in the park. Last and most hard to explain the chemical compound, its where my head spins when difficult things are happening now or in the past or from the past that feel like they are still happening now, and now, and now…it's a safe place, counting numbers, figuring out complex equations, math and chemistry in my head, thinking about the bonds and whether they are stable or would they rather be in another form, thinking it over, and over, and over…I think you get it" (Figures 1.12 and 1.13).

Figure 1.12 Mask #1 (outside).

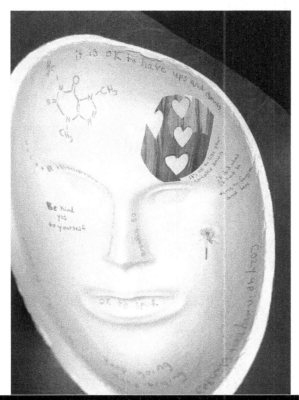

Figure 1.13 Mask #1 (inside).

CASE EXAMPLE 2: INSIDE/OUTSIDE MASK

Gina is a 30-year-old client who has a severe history of eating disorder and experienced years of childhood sexual abuse from early infancy. She often expressed feeling unsafe in her adult life and helpless at times, for example, feeling like a child in public. She took on the mask directive in a very different way, diving into it and finishing her mask in about 20 minutes using paint and her fingers. On the outside of the mask Gina smeared mostly blue paint around the eyes and lower face. She dented in the forehead with her fingers, then added black around the eyes. On the inside she drew herself in a prison cell with blue tears around her eyes and a sun on the left side of the forehead. She described her work using simple fragmented sentences, "On the outside, it's people's fingers touching me and not being able to contain sad feelings". Regarding the inside she stated, "Sad tears and water like the ocean. Mind like a prison, and the sun is out". She indicated that the sun was a little bit of hope still remaining. In this response to the directive, Gina appeared to respond in a *psych equivalent mode*, with very literal and physical responses to her felt sense of being. In her approach, she used her hands to dent in her own mask forehead as she feels happens to her when others invade her boundaries. She created an external correlate to this felt experience. We were able to discuss the mask and how the feelings on the inside and outside related naming them more over time (Figures 1.14 and 1.15).

Figure 1.14 Mask #2 (outside).

Figure 1.15 Mask #2 (inside).

CASE EXAMPLE 3: INSIDE/OUTSIDE MASK

Ellen is a 13-year-old client with a history of sexual abuse, experiencing depression, panic, and anxiety. Excited by the mask form, Ellen readily took to the directive. She decided to use color to express her feelings about her outside facing self and inside self. On the outside Ellen coated the mask with multiple layers and tones of blue paint without details of a face. On the inside Ellen depicted bright orange, red, and yellow in an explosion of disorganized chaotic color. Discussion of the two sides of the mask was explored. Initially, staying within the literal aspects of the activity was useful for Ellen as she did not want to directly engage a reference to her own experiences. The metaphor of the mask in this case provided a distance that was useful and allowed for curiosity to feel safe. Over time Ellen was able to explore the mask more directly in terms of her feelings and felt experience of inner and outer self. Ellen's response represented more of a *pretend mode* where distance was needed to engage the feelings of exploring inner experiences.

DEVELOPING PERSPECTIVE-TAKING CAPACITIES

When clients with CPTSD come to therapy one of the first aspects often observed by the clinician is the difficulty of comprehending the order of the client's story. The client may jump from one time period to another and may often also seem way out of time sequence. With CPTSD time can seem all mixed up. The use of creative timelines described above can be useful to help put order around events for clients. However, the order of events may be off due to the client's inability to hold perspective-taking within their developmental stages in life. For example, as an adult client spoke of her four-year-old sister bossing her around when she was three years old, "I hate her for being such a bitch to me then. I can't trust anyone, her and my mom were out to get me. When we are together on holidays, she acts like nothing happened". Then after a few minutes, she stated, "My kids fight constantly, but I think that is just the phase. They have to learn to work it out on their own". Here the client speaks from her three-year-old hurt child perspective without integrating an awareness of developmental stages that she and her sister occupied as young children, but then switches to her adult parenting point of view, but without a mentalizing perspective toward her own children. The lack of perspective-taking capacity, which is holding the mental states of themselves and others in mind, can keep a client stuck in their childhood trauma, often bitter, angry, afraid, and using rumination, or other avoidance behaviors.

Helping the client develop more perspective-taking capacity is one of the necessary skills for processing interpersonal trauma. With teleological thinking, clients struggle to factor in the mental states and developmental experiences in life that can help them make sense of themselves and others and ultimately process through interpersonal experiences. Creative hands-on approaches, however, can help make the learning about developmental stages more real for the client so that the knowledge can be factored in when reflecting on their traumatic early life experience. The following art therapy approach has helped many of my clients, young and old, develop this awareness in a more cellular and personal way that supports and buttresses the process stage of treatment.

Developmental Timeline

The Developmental Timeline was initially created as a psychoeducation and attachment resourcing directive to help children develop an understanding of themselves through time and connect with compassion to their child experiences. Working in foster care and with children who were adopted, this activity became a go-to for helping young clients develop an understanding of their needs, wants, and experiences over the course of growing. Later I came to discover this directive was just as useful for my adult clients with CPTSD, realizing that often their knowledge of development was poorly integrated into their thinking about themselves. The directive is simple:

> Create clay models of yourself from birth through your childhood at all the important times in your life, up to the present you. (If needed add, you may want to create a newborn you, a toddler, you, and teenager and so on.) Imagine what you needed at these various stages of your life. Create out of clay what you needed and give it to your different selves. Imagine your child selves receiving what was needed.

Tappers can be used to aid the client in imagining and taking in the good feelings of receiving what was needed. This activity can be easily paired with other resourcing attachment activities found in the work of Daniel Brown and Elliot (2016), Ricky Greenwald (2005), and Philip Manfield (2010).

In this exercise I find that polymer clay gives the most profound experience due to the three-dimensional realness for the client, as well as allowing for so many creative hands-on options. Polymer clay comes in many colors, is well tolerated by most clients, molds and tools are available to help the client create all kinds of objects, and it can be bought at most craft shops. The clay can be cooked in any oven on a low temperature so the creations can be made hard and feel permanent. The clinician should have some knowledge and experience using polymer clay so that they can effectively assist the client. As an apprentice to my client, I find this activity often very rewarding for the client who can experience my assistance and support which prevents frustration and allows for a shared and collaborative experience.

CASE EXAMPLE ONE: DEVELOPMENTAL TIMELINE

Jared is a ten-year-old youth who was adopted out of foster care at three years old into a two-parent family with three other children. He has struggled with his parents since the beginning with aggressive behaviors, conflicted relationships with peers and siblings, sleep problems, attention issues, and emotional outbursts. When he began therapy, he had already done a considerable amount of play therapy and some trauma-focused cognitive behavioral therapy. However, Jared still struggled with regression and with his relationship with his parents which at times resulted in hours of meltdowns.

On the third session with Jared, he was offered the *Developmental Timeline* directive using polymer clay, clay tools, and a clay machine (pasta machine dedicated to use with polymer clay). Assisting him was his mother and myself who acted as his apprentices. Jared seemed immediately excited to play with the clay. He enjoyed working with media that offered resistance and was tactile and polymer clay with a clay machine offered both experiences. Mom agreed to serve as Jared's main helper, and I helped coordinate the effort, offering some suggestions when needed. Jared decided he would like to create his newborn self, three-year-old (the age when he entered foster care), five-year-old, eight-year-old, and present self (a ten-year-old). As Jared began to create his newborn self, with his mom's assistance, we engaged in discussion regarding what babies need and want to feel safe and secure. Additionally, mom offered what she would have done had she been there when he was born. Jared was invited to imagine receiving his mom's love and to having her make what he needed out of clay. Mom made a baby bottle, his favorite stuffy, a turtle, and a cradle out of popsicle sticks. Jared then decided he wanted to sculpt her as well so he could imagine her standing next to him as a newborn. After the creations around the newborn self where finished, mom then invited Jared to imagine a scene where he was being rocked by her when he was a newborn. She wrapped her arms around him in his chair and tapped on his shoulders while telling the story of what she would have done had she been there and how she enjoyed the idea of caring for him (Jared's mom was instructed ahead of time on how to tap while telling the story as a part of installing the memory as a resource). Jared's face lit up, and he seemed to melt into his mom's arms. He asked for the story to be retold a few times. Jared went on to create the other self-figures with mom coming up with ideas and needs for each of the ages. These figures were later called upon when processing through the tough experiences in his young life. Each figure acted as a kind of container of what happened, as well as a way to imagine and connect with the early experiences. Older self-figures helped him hold perspective on how he had grown up and what was different now in his life. Jared and Mom reported that this exercise seemed to calm his neediness at night and their relationship improved (Figure 1.16).

Figure 1.16 Developmental clay figures (child).

CASE EXAMPLE TWO: DEVELOPMENTAL TIMELINE

Marla is a 50-year-old client who presents with dissociation, regression into childlike states, depression and anxiety, problems with focus, emotional dysregulation, conflicts in relationships, and flashbacks. Marla has a long history of trauma that began very early in her life. When she began therapy, I was very challenged due to Marla's propensity to move around in her timeline without order. Additionally, she frequently had situations in her life that were triggering for her, igniting flashbacks and regression. When Marla regressed, she would often begin swinging her legs on the chair like a young child. I worked with Marla on many grounding and orienting techniques but also elected to offer the *Developmental Timeline* directive. Being very artistically minded Marla seemed enthusiastic to use clay to create herself through time. When offering this directive to a client with considerable childhood trauma and with fragile presentation, care should be made to not revisit the past but focus on ages and what is needed at each age. Additionally, focusing on an exercise like Developing Secure Attachment (Greenwald, 2005) or Ideal Parent Figure (Brown & Elliot, 2016) can help the activity stay focused on psychoeducation and enhancing adaptive information.

Marla was engaged in the creative process of imagining her selves, electing to make a newborn self, toddler self, five-year-old self, ten-year-old self, teen self, and a present self. With each self the needs and developmental stage were discussed, and objects were made and offered over to the clay selves. Marla expressed feeling compassion and closeness to the figures which she readily expressed made her younger selves feel more real and defined. She expressed a playfulness with them and was also able to see herself orienting with the older figure more readily when she held it in her hand. We were able to use the figures to develop perspective between herself now and then when she was little so that Marla could practice noticing both at the same time. This skill helped her hold more perspective, shift into an adult self-perspective more readily, and organize how she saw her child self when thinking about trauma experiences in her youth (Figure 1.17).

Figure 1.17 Developmental clay figures (adult).

ART INTERVENTIONS IN DOT FIVE: REPROCESSING OF TRAUMATIC EXPERIENCES

After addressing the goals in the previous domains, clinical judgment can guide whether the client is ready for EMDR processing and then begin preparation for the EMDR protocol. Assuming that the client has achieved readiness (see "EMDR Phases and Complex Trauma" section), the EMDR standard protocol for clients with CPTSD is often modified to support safety of processing. *Restricted Processing* (RP) is one way of limiting the scope of the EMDR standard protocol to manage reprocessing. Restricted Processing may involve the approach of reprocessing only a small part of the trauma memory at a time, or limiting the client to the trauma memory itself not inviting associated memories to be included (Boon et al., 2017). Additionally, the client may need to begin work on a future target (instead of a past memory) or integrate resourcing strategies into processing (Shapiro, 2018). What is most important is that the client can stay in their Window of Tolerance, keeping one foot in the present while visiting the past or future (dual attention), and they should have access to the memory content, sensations, emotions, and associated beliefs (Shapiro, 2018). If the client has achieved readiness for Phase Four of EMDR then the standard or restricted protocol approach should be implemented unencumbered. However, there may be instances when supporting the client by integrating some creative approaches may be useful. Here the therapist should be careful to ask, "Can creative therapies contribute to reprocessing when using the EMDR protocol or will they get in the way and complicate this phase of treatment?" The clinician should think critically before adding an extra step to an already evidence-based approach. Conditions for including art therapies approaches as a part of Phase Four should therefore be clearly supportive and not distracting from the client's reprocessing.

I have found the use of creative arts beneficial in the conditions listed below. These approaches are added only when requested by the client as part of a more meaningful experience, and/or when the approach enhances access to the trauma material in a productive way.

DIALING UP A CONNECTION

When clients struggle to connect with their emotions, for example when they present in *pretend mode* with numb or disconnected feelings, processing may be fragile or altogether ineffective. The use of art to express an aspect of the trauma material can be effective under these circumstances for some clients, helping them to access their feelings and stay with it. Since art expression tends to access the emotional parts of the brain, an expressive art exercise designed to get to the feelings can support the process.

An example of using art to increase emotional connection can be as simple as having the client draw some aspect of the trauma material like a feeling, image, thought, and part of themself. This may be done before the processing begins to help the client connect to the target. Caution should be used when having the client expose themselves to the memory, however, outside of the use of the protocol, as a client could easily regress and become flooded without the aid of BLS and the structure the protocol provides. This approach works best in my experience when a client struggles to connect with the emotions around the memory and when the experience of distress from the memory itself was initially low.

CASE EXAMPLE: DIALING UP A CONNECTION

Peter is a 40-year-old administrator who reports struggling with work stress and connection to family at home. He expresses that his job is stressful and that he struggles keeping his cool when conflict arises. Additionally, when he gets home to his family, he often wants to numb out using alcohol and watching television. When taking a trauma and loss history, Peter reported a history of severe physical and psychological abuse by his father that went on throughout his childhood starting around seven. Peter expressed that he learned from his childhood interactions with his father to hide his emotions; showing feelings would result in his father humiliating him for crying or showing any vulnerability. Now when thinking about his past, Peter expressed not being able to connect with his feelings, mostly reporting a state of numbness and detachment when thinking about times when his father beat him and raged.

Peter was invited to bring in some photos of himself as a child to better connect with his childhood experiences. He appeared very curious about this approach and found a photo of himself at eight years old that he brought to the next session. Upon exploring the child photo initially, he expressed feeling that the boy in the picture did not seem like himself. He reported a sense of detachment from the child, even while remembering the image being taken and the place it was taken.

Peter was invited to use the photo creatively to see if he could connect more with the child in the photo. Peter was open to this expressive approach even though he readily stated he was not good at art. Peter was asked if he would like to tape the photo onto a large sheet of paper and then represent his current self somewhere else on the paper using an object (such as a sand tray figure) or drawing a figure. Peter agreed and taped the picture in the center. He then drew his current self as a stick figure holding a computer case and a cup of coffee some distance from the picture. Peter was then invited to write words, draw symbols, or use expressive lines and color to represent himself connecting to the child in the photo. Peter began by writing what he would like to say to this child in the photo, "You will survive. You will grow up and find a loving wife. You will go to college…". He then drew swatches of color with a marker around the photograph that he expressed the feelings he would have if this was his child. At this point Peter began showing emotions for the child and weeping. He was invited to reprocess a previously discussed memory from childhood that related to the child in this image. Peter agreed and was able to reprocess the memory, reporting and showing emotions.

This simple directive of using an old photo and an expressive representation of the current self in the same visual field offered a concrete approach to explore connection. This allowed for an external metaphorical and expressive representation of connection. As a concrete representation of connection, the art expression facilitated an internal felt sense that was previously out of reach. Peter used this approach repeatedly while reprocessing his childhood memories to better connect with his feelings.

DIALING DOWN DISTRESS

Creative therapy may also help when distress is extremely high. Using art to incorporate more reminders of resources can be beneficial in this circumstance. For managing distress, including resource images and objects, can help the client keep in mind their strengths, who is there for them, where they are now in their life, a goal or meaning they are connected to, a saying or prayer that holds special meaning, etc. Additionally, the externalization of parts of the trauma narrative into art form can act as a container of the emotion, allowing for distance from it.

CASE EXAMPLE: DIALING DOWN DISTRESS

Julie is a 35-year-old professional who was struggling with flashbacks and nightmares. She came to trauma therapy with a few specific memories that felt simply too large for hourly EMDR therapy to address. One memory involved a violent sexual assault as a child where she was sure she might die. Since we were working together in an *intensive format*, long sessions which are more than two hours at a time, Julie felt she might be able to finally get through the memory. However, when we began to set up the memory in Phase Three of EMDR, Julie became very anxious that she would not be able to manage the intensity of reprocessing.

Being mindful of Julie's Window of Tolerance we stopped EMDR and began to think creatively about how to help her feel safer while addressing memory reprocessing [or just] safer while memory reprocessing. Brainstorming with Julie, we arrived at a plan where Julie imagined using a metaphor for approaching the trauma memory that could help guide her and support her reprocessing. She elected to draw the metaphorical scene out on a white board to help give her a visual reminder. The metaphorical scene that Julie constructed described her journey of reprocessing like diving under water to retrieve a lost self. She expressed feeling the water was deep and she needed support from others on a boat nearby to safely dive down and make the journey to her child self. Julie took the white board and markers and began to construct the scene. She depicted her child self in a bubble deep under water. The bubble represented the boundaries of the traumatic memory. On top of the water Julie depicted a boat with both her adult self and her boyfriend, whom she identified as a resource for her in this memory. She also included reminders of her grandmother with whom she felt a positive connection. Julie expressed that her boyfriend and I would be tasked with rescuing her with a rope if needed which she drew tied around her ankle. We discussed how she might communicate that she felt the need for a rescue, and she expressed she would let me know by tugging the rope to come up. She then drew a diver's vest and tank on herself with her plunging into the water ready to retrieve her child self, which was locked in the bubble of the traumatic memory deep under the water.

At this point we began to do Phase Three, memory set-up and assessment, and then Phases Four through Six of EMDR. Julie was able to use her metaphorical scene as a resource during the memory reprocessing to support her feelings of safety and maintain dual focus. She was able to completely reprocess the memory to a SUD of 0. This strategy was used for other abuse memories thereafter.

POST-REPROCESSING INTEGRATION

For clients with CPTSD memory reprocessing may be fragile. Linking to new adaptive information often requires an integrative process when the reprocessing entails revising patterns that have been in place since early childhood and embedded in attachment beliefs and behaviors. New ways of relating take time to become habitual or even fully trusted. As outlined in Phase Three of complex trauma treatment above (see "Phase Three: Personality Re/integration and Re/habilitation" section), this phase is where the client builds a new way of being in the world interpersonally. Without this phase of therapy, new adaptive learning may not have enough repetition to become a new habit of relating. Repetition of adaptive learning therefore becomes vital to hold the full impact of the trauma reprocessing phase.

Art therapies can be very beneficial in this phase for helping clients imagine their goals in relationships, revise their identity to include healthy interpersonal boundaries, beliefs and behaviors, and strategize how to hold onto positive self-beliefs in the face of challenges. Art therapy directives that encouraged the client to imagine their revised self, a self that holds onto and enacts the new adaptive learning, can serve as a form of rehearsal of adaptive information and an anchor for the new learning. One easy approach that has mainstream popularity is vision boards. Vision boards can easily be made with any collage materials or even using digital images. Another approach is creating a slide show of pictures that describes the new vision and goals. The possibilities are endless: poetry, mantras, movement, music, etc. The emphasis however should be on helping the client find their unique voice and style of expressing themselves.

CONCLUSION

The mental health field has placed increasing emphasis on medical and evidence-based approaches, which has arguably resulted in a devaluation of the art therapies. Like the arts generally, art therapy is often viewed as an elective therapy with art therapists being seen as nonessential. As such, the mental health field has yet to fully tap into the potential of art therapy in trauma recovery. Creative arts therapies hold tremendous capacity to help clients and clinicians make their way through the treatment challenges while also offering an approach for making meaning that extends to the client's experience in society at large. Now is the time for the art therapies to come out of these marginalized roles to offer the power and meaningful approach that will help bridge the gap in treatment, making EMDR more accessible to clients with CPTSD. As the world contends with a multitude of overwhelming challenges, human expression has never been more necessary to make sense out of traumatic experiences. In the words of Camille Paglia (2012), "A society that forgets art risks losing its soul" (p. 2012). Western approaches to mental health have in many respects struggled with engaging the whole client—mind, body, and soul—in treatment. Art and expressive therapies naturally reunite all aspects of the self to facilitate an integrative and meaningful shift toward healing and recovery.

REFERENCES

Bateman, A., & Fonagy, P. (2019). *Handbook of mentalizing in mental health practice.* American Psychiatric Association Publishing.

Bateman, A., & Fonagy, P. (2013). Mentalization-based treatment. *Psychoanalytic inquiry, 33*(6), 595–613. https://doi.org/10.1080/07351690.2013.835170

Bateman, A., Fonagy P. (2004). *Psychotherapy for borderline personality disorder: Mentalization-based treatment.* Oxford University Press.

Boon, S., Steele, K., & Van Der Hart, O. (2017). *Treating trauma-related dissociation.* W.W. Norton and Company.

Brown, D. P., & Elliott, D. S. (2016). *Attachment disturbances in adults: Treatment for comprehensive repair.* W.W. Norton & Company.

Cloitre, M., Courtois, C. A., Ford, J. D., Green, B. L., Alexander, P., Briere, J., Herman, J. L., Lanius, R., Stolbach, B. C., Spinazzola, J., Van der Kolk, B. A., & van der Hart, O. (2012). The ISTSS expert consensus treatment guidelines for complex PTSD in adults. http://www.istss.org/

Courtois, C. A., Norton-Ford, J. D., & Briere, J. (2015). *Treatment of complex trauma: A sequenced, relationship-based approach.* Guilford Press.

DeYoung, P. (2015). *Understanding and treating chronic shame: A relational/neurobiological approach.* Routledge Taylor & Francis Group.

Farina, B., Liotti, M., & Imperatori, C. (2019). The Role of attachment trauma and disintegrative pathogenic processes in the traumatic-dissociative dimension. *Frontiers in psychology, 10,* 933. https://doi.org/10.3389/fpsyg.2019.00933

Fisher, J. (2017). *Healing the fragmented selves of trauma survivors: Overcoming internal self-alienation.* Routledge.

Fonagy, P. (2012). Art therapy and personality disorder. *International journal of art therapy, 17*(3), 90. https://doi.org/10.1080/17454832.2012.740866

Fonagy, P., Gergely, G. Jurist, E., Target, M., E. (2002/2004). *Affect regulation, mentalization, and the development of the self.* New York: Other Press LLC.

Fredrickson, B. L. (2001). The role of positive emotions in positive psychology. The broaden-and-build theory of positive emotions. *The American psychologist, 56*(3), 218–226. https://doi.org/10.1037//0003-066x.56.3.218

Greenwald, R. (2005). *Child trauma handbook.* Routledge.

Greenwald, R. (2013). *Progressive counting within a phase model of trauma-informed treatment.* Routledge.

Herman, J. (1992). Complex PTSD: A syndrome in survivors of prolonged and repeated trauma. *Journal of traumatic stress, 5*(3), 377–391.

Jung, C. G. (1929). *Dream analysis,* Parts II & III (Seminar Notes privately printed). Zürich.

Kaimal, G., Ray, K., & Muniz, J. (2016). Reduction of cortisol levels and participants' responses following art making. *Art therapy: Journal of the American art therapy association, 33*(2), 74–80. https://doi.org/10.1080/07421656.2016.1166832

Kandel, E. (2012). *The age of insight: The quest to understand the unconscious in art, mind, and brain.* Random House Publishing Group.

Karatzias, T., Cloitre, M., Maercker, A., Kazlauskas, E., Shevlin, M., Hyland, P., Bisson, J., Roberts, N., & Brewin, C. (2018). PTSD and complex PTSD: ICD-11 updates on concept and measurement in the UK, USA, Germany and Lithuania. *European journal of psychotraumatology, 8,* 1418103. https://doi.org/10.1080/20008198.2017.1418103

Korb, A. (2015). *The upward spiral: Using neuroscience to reverse the course of depression, one small change at a time.* New Harbinger Publications.

Korn, D., & Leeds, A. (2002). Preliminary evidence of efficacy for EMDR resource development and installation in the stabilization phase of treatment of complex posttraumatic stress disorder. *Journal of clinical psychology, 58*(12), 1465–1487. https://doi.org/10.1002/jclp.10099

Lorenzini, N., Campbell, C., & Fonagy, P. (2019). Mentalization and its role in processing trauma. In B. Huppertz (Ed.), *Approaches to psychic trauma* (pp. 403–422). Rowan & Littlefield.

Manfield, P. (2010). *Dyadic resourcing: Creating a foundation for processing trauma: 1.* Create Space Independent Publishing.

Martin, K. (2016). *EMDR & structural dissociation theory webinar series.* Webinar, January through March of 2016.

Mitchell, Stuart & Steele, Kathy. (2020). Mentalising in Complex Trauma and Dissociative Disorders. European Journal of Trauma & Dissociation. 5. 100168. 10.1016/j.ejtd.2020.100168.

Nathanson, D. (1992). *Shame and pride: Affect, sex and the birth of the self.* W.W. Norton and Company.

Paglia, C. (1992). *Sex, art, and American culture: Essays.* Vintage Books.

Seligman, P. (1985). Dream analysis: Notes of the seminar given in 1928–1930. C. G. Jung William McGuire, editor Bollingen Series, vol. 99. Princeton University Press. *Dialogue: Canadian philosophical review, 24*(1), 155–158. https://doi.org/10.1017/S0012217300046060

Siegel, D. (1999). *The developing mind: How relationships and the brain interact to shape who we are.* The Guilford Press.

Shapiro, F. (2018). *Eye Movement Desensitization and reprocessing [EMDR] Therapy* (3rd ed.). The Guildford Press.

Springham, N., & Huet, V. (2018). Art as relational encounter: An ostensive communication theory of art therapy. *Journal of the American Art Therapy Association, 35*(1), 4–10. https://doi.org/10.1080/07421656.2018.1460103

Steele, W., & Raider, M. (2009). *Structured sensory interventions for traumatized children, adolescents, and parents.* Edwin Mellen Press.

Twombly, J. (2000). Incorporating EMDR and EMDR adaptations into the treatment of clients with dissociative identity disorder. *Journal of Trauma & Dissociation,* 1(2), 61–81. https://doi.org/10.1300/J229v01n02_05

van der Hart, O., Groenendijk, M., Gonzalez, A., Mosquera, D., & Solomon, R. (2013). Dissociation of the personality and EMDR therapy in complex trauma-related disorders: Applications in the stabilization phase. *Journal of EMDR practice and research,* 7(2), 81–94. http://dx.doi.org/10.1891/1933-3196.7.2.81

van der Hart, O, Nijenhuis, E., & Steele, K. (2006). *The haunted self: Structural dissociation and the treatment of chronic traumatization.* W.W. Norton and Company.

CHAPTER 2

INVITING THE BODY, MOVEMENT, AND THE CREATIVE ARTS INTO TELEHEALTH
A Culturally Responsive Model for Online EMDR Preparation

Jennifer Marchand and Michelli Simpson

When the coronavirus disease (COVID-19) pandemic forced the mental health field to abruptly shift from in-person to online services, many trauma therapists were seeking strategies and skills to practice with clients online to increase stabilization in the face of global uncertainty and crisis. This was a distressing time for therapists as many found themselves struggling with the same issues as their clients—such as fear, loss, isolation, and powerlessness—causing them to question their capacity to effectively support their clients during these unprecedented circumstances. In addition, the COVID-19 pandemic exacerbated social injustices and racial discrimination, leading to what has been referred to as a "double pandemic" (Addo, 2020), further impacting clients and therapists that identify as Black, Indigenous, and People of Color (BIPOC). This consequently brought powerful momentum to long-standing social justice movements in North America and globally. As a mental health field, we have been asked to reflect on our role in responding to the impacts of injustice, racial inequality, and systemic oppression. There is now heightened awareness of the need for cultural humility and responsiveness in clinical practice, and the importance of viewing individual client issues within a sociopolitical, cultural, and historical context. This chapter aims to provide therapists with a model to effectively work with diverse populations, both online and in-person, using techniques that integrate the body, movement, and the creative arts into EMDR preparation and trauma reprocessing work online.

As early as 2017, the authors of this chapter were offering EMDR online to diverse populations who might otherwise not have access to specialized trauma recovery services. Providing EMDR online was not explicitly endorsed by the EMDR International Association (EMDRIA) at that time due to insufficient research to either "support or refute the efficacy of EMDR therapy through virtual means" (EMDRIA, 2020, p. 2). Both authors were, however, advocates for online EMDR and excited to share the innovative techniques they were developing to support vulnerable populations facing multiple barriers to services.

Michelli Simpson (MS), a Licensed Mental Health Professional and a Certified Telehealth Provider from Brazil, has been working over telehealth in the US, UK, and internationally since 2013 and providing EMDR online since 2017. She specializes in addressing race-based trauma and oppression, addictions, domestic violence, and sex-related trauma, working with individuals and couples. She volunteers with Brazilian community projects in Portuguese and has extensive experience working cross-culturally. As an EMDRIA Approved Consultant, she focuses on supporting consultees who are BIPOC.

Jennifer Marchand (JM), a Registered Canadian Art Therapist, Trauma Center Trauma-Sensitive Yoga Facilitator, and EMDRIA Approved Consultant, shifted her practice entirely to telehealth delivery in 2018, when she closed her private practice in Hanoi, Vietnam. She was located there for two years and at the time, there were no other EMDR therapists providing trauma services in Hanoi. Continuing to offer EMDR online to her Vietnamese and expatriate clients was an ethical decision that allowed for continuity of care. Since then, she has worked for an international women's rights organization in Germany as

DOI: 10.4324/9781003156932-3

a trauma trainer specializing in gender-based violence in conflict-affected settings, including Iraq and Afghanistan. She currently lives in Addis Ababa, Ethiopia and continues to provide online EMDR therapy to clients living in primarily non-Western settings, including humanitarian aid workers, expatriates, health professionals, and survivors of sexualized violence.

Both authors were working in different settings and cultural contexts while discovering just how effective and powerful online EMDR can be. Both had independently developed resources and training specific to delivering EMDR online and started Facebook groups to share their work with the larger EMDR community, eventually merging both groups into the EMDR Online Practitioners/Therapists Facebook group. The ethics of accessibility was a driving force in their commitment to advocating for increased acceptance of online EMDR and for greater access to effective trauma treatment for vulnerable populations both locally and globally. Many of their clients did not have the choice between in-person and online EMDR, but rather between online EMDR and no trauma treatment.

When the COVID-19 pandemic swept through Europe and North America in early 2020, there was a clear and urgent need for resources to support EMDR therapists in their transition to telehealth. It was in this context that the authors began collaborating and aligning their approaches to online EMDR. They both regarded body-based interventions as an essential component to offering EMDR over telehealth safely and effectively, especially when working in diverse cultural settings. They also recognized the need for extended preparation and resourcing when working online, to bring clients fully into the present and safely into their bodies before moving into reprocessing unresolved material from the past.

Pre-COVID-19, JM developed The COME BACK Tool as a set of stabilization practices in her work with clients to extend the EMDR preparation phase over telehealth. Each letter stands for a different stabilization strategy to help clients practice coming back to the present moment in a trauma- and culturally sensitive way. The practices are:

C—Connecting to a Comforting Presence

O—Orienting Through the Senses

M—Moving and Mobilizing Energy

E—Exploring the Breath with Movement and Sound

B—Balancing and Centering the Body

A—Anchoring and Grounding into the Earth

C—Containment and Closure

K—Kindness and Compassion

During the pandemic, she integrated these tools into her EMDR consultation work to provide consultees with simple and practical strategies to use with clients as they transitioned their work to telehealth. JM and MS have since expanded The COME BACK Tool and scripted the practices as a way to make these techniques more accessible and user-friendly for trauma therapists seeking effective online EMDR resources.

The COME BACK acronym itself is meant to offer an overarching framework for body-based skills and resources that can enhance EMDR readiness for clients with complex trauma. The individual scripts and practices for each letter can be adapted to diverse cultural and linguistic settings and individual client needs. For example, Chau Dinh, a Vietnamese psychologist and EMDRIA-Certified EMDR Therapist, has integrated The COME BACK Tool into her work with survivors of human trafficking at an NGO in Hanoi, Vietnam.

Geneviève Lepage and Fouzia Benchekri, both EMDR therapists living in Morocco, translated the activities into French and Arabic respectively and adapted them to their clinical practices and cultural contexts. MS has adapted the activities for group work in Brazil and in Portuguese.

The COME BACK practices integrate polyvagal theory and nervous system regulation, movement and Trauma Center Trauma-Sensitive Yoga (TCTSY), creative arts therapies, and mindfulness-based practice. In this chapter, the authors discuss the benefits of using body-based practices, such as trauma-sensitive yoga and creative expression, in the treatment of complex trauma and dissociation as well as their application to intercultural work. A case example using yoga to facilitate dual attention during trauma reprocessing (Phase Four of EMDR) over telehealth will be presented. Eight COME BACK Tool scripts, one practice for each letter, are provided so that readers can easily and immediately begin offering these practices to clients, and even apply them to their own self-care routine.

THE BODY AS A RESOURCE IN EMDR PREPARATION

Therapists often make the assumption that clients have access to their bodies as a resource during trauma treatment. In the assessment phase of EMDR (Phase Three) and during reprocessing and desensitization (Phase Four), therapists continually ask their clients to notice information arising from their internal world, such as thoughts, emotions, and sensations. Although this level of mindful noticing is an essential part of the EMDR process, without distress tolerance skills, many clients have difficulty being present in their bodies long enough to mindfully observe what is coming up without becoming overwhelmed (Follette et al., 2015). Clients with complex trauma and dissociation often develop a phobia of their bodies, leading to avoidance and disconnection from their internal experience (Boon et al., 2016), and a decreased capacity to tolerate an internal focus.

The concept of the *window of tolerance*, developed by Daniel Siegel (2010), is used to explain being within one's optimal level of arousal. This is a useful metaphor in understanding the aim of The COME BACK Tool in the preparation phase of EMDR: repeating and strengthening the skill of having an embodied present-moment experience slowly expands the client's window of tolerance for bodily sensations, increasing their capacity to observe and process what is arising moment to moment without getting pushed into a state of activation outside of what they can tolerate. According to Siegel's theory of Mindsight (2010), mindful awareness and tracking of internal experience builds the foundation for the successful neural integration and resolution of unresolved traumatic material. There is also increasing neurobiological evidence that mindfulness skills can increase activity in the medial prefrontal regions of the brain and decrease activity in the limbic region of the brain, leading to a reduction of hyperarousal, avoidance, intrusion, and dissociation (Boyd et al., 2018).

In EMDR, maintaining present-moment orientation while mindfully tracking internal distress associated with the past is referred to as *dual awareness* (Shapiro, 2017)—like a delicate balancing act between past and present. Dual awareness in EMDR is achieved by guiding the client to focus their attention on the distress associated with the memory (images, negative cognitions, feelings, and sensations) while adding sets of bilateral stimulation (BLS). The BLS supports trauma reprocessing by continually orienting the client to the present moment with external distraction, such as tracking the therapist's hand back and forth. According to Working Memory Theory, the continuous distraction taxes the limited capacity of the working memory, leaving less space in the client's awareness for the emotional intensity and vividness of the trauma material being recalled, which changes the way the memory is stored and ultimately reduces the distress associated with the memory (Gunter & Bodner, 2009).

Achieving dual attention that is within the client's window of tolerance is essential for safe online trauma reprocessing. Although distraction can make trauma reprocessing more tolerable for clients by pulling them out of memory and into the present moment, clients must also be able to tolerate being present in their bodies before they can safely and simultaneously track internal distress. The aim of The COME BACK Tool is to support dual attention by making the body available as a resource for self-stabilization, a way to anchor into the present, while expanding the window of tolerance wide enough to mindfully observe internal distress associated with the past. Clients with complex trauma and significant dissociative symptoms often benefit more from stabilization practices until the self-regulatory capacities needed to tolerate exposure have been increased (Spiegel, 2018).

The COME BACK Tool practices can be facilitated in session as part of EMDR preparation. Clients are encouraged to identify the strategies that are most useful and effective for them so they can practice these activities between sessions, applying them to their everyday self-care routines and to improve daily functioning. The word "practice" is used intentionally with clients to highlight that learning to come back to the present moment is like learning any new skill: it involves repetition to become like instinct or muscle memory so it can be applied even when activation levels are high. The creative arts can also promote the learning of new skills by engaging the whole body in the activity and keeping the mind in a regulated, curious, and even playful state. In addition, the imagery created by the client in the process can act as a reminder of the new skill, increasing the chances that they will apply it to their daily lives. The client's preferred body-based and creative stabilization strategies can then be woven into trauma reprocessing work whenever needed.

CULTURALLY RESPONSIVE EMDR OVER TELEHEALTH

Although advancements in the field of trauma therapy have led to a deeper understanding of complex trauma and dissociation, including the treatment guidelines developed by the International Society for Traumatic Stress Studies (ISTSS) (Cloitre et al., 2012), providing complex trauma treatment over telehealth can be daunting. Many therapists fear that they cannot effectively respond to and ground clients entering dissociative states when working through screens in separate physical spaces.

Treating complex trauma online, especially with clients who present with dissociative symptoms, can be challenging; however, contraindicating online EMDR with this population risks reinforcing barriers to treatment for clients who already face obstacles to accessing appropriate care. It would also lack the culturally sensitive acknowledgment that many BIPOC clients, and members of other marginalized groups, often use dissociative states as adaptive survival responses in the face of chronic adversity and oppressive forces, such as numbing out and conserving energy. At the same time, dissociation can impair treatment progress and be harmful to the client if therapists are not adequately prepared to assess, manage, and respond to dissociation in a telehealth context. The authors' approaches to telehealth have been shaped by work with complex trauma, dissociation, and with BIPOC clients in various cultural settings; as such, their aim has been to develop tools and strategies to make online EMDR safe and accessible for their clients while considering their cultural backgrounds and individual needs for emotional and psychological safety.

Some EMDR protocols have already been developed to titrate and restrict reprocessing work with complex trauma. Jim Knipe (2014), for example, developed the Constant Installation of Present Orientation to Safety (CIPOS) protocol, where the client is oriented to the present moment, and a state of presence is installed using bilateral stimulation. When the client is fully present, the therapist guides them to think about a specific memory for a restricted period of time (such as ten seconds), and then brings them back to present-moment orientation, again installing the state of presence through bilateral stimulation. One strategy from the CIPOS protocol is to bring the client back to the present by throwing a pillow back and forth to prompt an orienting response; another strategy is offering the client ice cubes to hold so they can focus on sensations. Such quick and effective strategies are not always possible over telehealth where the therapist and client are in separate spaces. The therapist may feel powerless and unable to offer the guidance and resources needed to support stabilization during trauma reprocessing.

Actively engaging the body through movement and the creative arts therapies can give clients the skills they need to safely engage in EMDR over telehealth, such as by increasing present-moment orientation, mindfulness skills, and self-regulation capacities. Integrating the body into the healing process can also feel familiar and resonant for many clients of diverse cultural and ethnic backgrounds (Lichtenstein et al., 2017). Ma-Kellams (2014) points out that there are cross-cultural differences in body awareness and that people from non-Western societies often have heightened connection to their body, increasing the importance of integrating somatic practices into treatment in diverse cultural contexts. The bilateral element of EMDR, such as tapping, is not a new invention: rhythm, dancing, drumming, and movement are central to rituals and traditional healing practices in many non-Western and Indigenous cultures worldwide, and have been preserved through tradition and handed down through generations upon generations. In this way, the movement and rhythm of EMDR lends itself well to cross-cultural work. Like the creative arts therapies, EMDR is also not a talk therapy, which can feel less intrusive and more appropriate for some clients depending on their cultural and linguistic backgrounds. Clients have the choice to process non-verbally, keeping material private as it comes up; they can also process verbally during sets in their native language without the therapist needing to understand. Bringing the body, movement, and creative expression into the EMDR preparation phase is not only an effective way to safely build stabilization skills with clients, but also a way to enhance culturally responsive practice.

MEETING THE CLIENT IN THEIR SPACE

Although it is easy to focus on the limitations of online EMDR, the authors recommend shifting the focus to the benefits from the client's perspective so they can be enhanced and reinforced. One example of this is taking advantage of the client being in their own space. In extended online EMDR preparation work, the therapist can guide clients to identify, gather, or create what is safe and soothing for them from their home environment, including materials from their natural environment. For example, JM's client once gathered rocks from the river by their home to hold in their hand as a way to feel grounded and connected to nature during sessions, another used rosemary from their garden as a soothing and invigorating smell to stay present. Although we may place therapeutic value on creating a space in which to meet our clients when offering in-person services, we, as the therapist, choose what is in that space, including the images, colors, smells, particular objects, art materials, and seating arrangements. Some of these materials, despite being helpful to the client within the session, may not be accessible to the client outside of session, or may not hold personal or cultural importance to the client.

In telehealth, we literally meet our clients where they are at: in their homes, their environment, and their communities. From within this context, we co-create the therapeutic space by allowing the client to identify what best supports their healing. Taking the time to invite clients to bring personally and culturally relevant objects, materials, and resources into their sessions is an empowering and culturally affirmative process that supports intercultural exchange. Working with what is available to clients also ensures that the tools and strategies practiced in session are applicable to their everyday self-care and stabilization routines between sessions. Figure 2.1 shows a basket of objects that MS's client gathered to support her therapy process in her own space.

Explicitly acknowledging that the client is in their own space, and that we are being welcomed into their world, is a way of reframing what can be seen as a limitation and turning it into a benefit of online EMDR. MS, for example, often says to clients at the beginning of a session, "Thank you for inviting me into your home today." This respectful opening can shift power dynamics in a way that helps both client and therapist feel connected and at ease. It invites a curiosity about what is happening on the other side of the screen, in the client's world, but where the therapist is a guest, rather than an expert who holds the control and power in the space.

In this way, telehealth also lends itself surprisingly well to cross-cultural exchange; this is not only because the technology allows for broader and more international reach, but also

Figure 2.1 A basket of sensory-based materials is prepared by the client to support grounding and EMDR reprocessing.

because it can provide clients with more power in the relationship, starting from the fact that they are in their own space.

THE BODY AND SOMATIC AWARENESS

The body is inherently expressive. As internal signals arise from the body—including sensations, emotions, and impulses—they are then reflected by and expressed through the body—such as posture, gesture, facial expressions, tone of voice, muscle tension, movement, and creative expression. Conscious awareness of the body provides the foundation for self-understanding; it is the pathway through which we perceive our internal states and begin to understand our needs and responses to our environment, which in turn helps build a sense of self. However, awareness of internal sensations can be overwhelming and triggering for clients, a common symptom of complex trauma (Boon et al., 2016). The creative arts therapies can make mindful noticing of the body more tolerable, such as by giving visual form to sensations through color, shape, and lines. When a client creates an external representation of their internal experience, it becomes contained by the natural boundaries of its form, and creates a psychological distance between the client and the expression. This distance allows the client to become curious, and to safely reflect on and explore their internal states, helping them to overcome the phobia of internal experience and begin to increase somatic awareness.

The inherent sensory and kinesthetic components involved in artmaking activities can also be beneficial in enhancing somatic awareness. Sensory engagement can be soothing for clients while the kinesthetic elements can provide rhythm, release, and regulation (Hinz, 2019). This can support the client in staying oriented to the present while increasing their capacity to mindfully turn their attention inward.

Combining movement and creative arts activities supports clients in effectively expressing, communicating, and taking ownership over their thoughts, feelings, sensations, and internal experiences. In EMDR trauma reprocessing, the client needs these skills in order to mindfully notice and share what is coming up for them while maintaining a state of dual attention. The COME BACK practices provide clients with these skills in the preparation phase of EMDR and therefore prepare clients for reprocessing and the adaptive resolution of traumatic material.

CO-REGULATING AND CONNECTING THROUGH MOVEMENT AND THE BODY

Many therapists wonder if they can truly offer co-regulation to their clients over telehealth. Polyvagal theory, developed by Stephen Porges (2011), highlights how offering connection, co-regulation, and safety takes place on a non-verbal level, especially through facial expression and tone of voice. We are deeply social beings, and our nervous system is highly attuned to body-based and non-verbal social cues. Our nervous system perceives and responds to these social cues below the level of conscious awareness through a process called *neuroception* (Porges, 2011). We can neurocept safety or danger from our environment, prompting our autonomic nervous system to respond accordingly. For example, we may shift into a physiological state of safety and social engagement when we neurocept cues of friendliness and warmth from others, or shift into a state of defense and survival when we neurocept cues of judgment, criticism, or danger. This shift in physiological state is involuntary and often occurs before we are even consciously aware of what our body is responding to.

Physiological states of safety are regulated by the ventral vagus nerve, which is the newest branch of the parasympathetic nervous system, in evolutionary terms, and is only found in mammals. Being in a ventral vagal state of safety regulates our whole nervous system and allows our social engagement system to come online—also referred to as the *face-heart connection* (Porges, 2021)—making it possible to tune into others and take in their eye contact, tone of voice, and facial expressions. It is through the face-heart connection that we regulate and calm physiological states in others, and are regulated and calmed by others (Porges, 2021).

Polyvagal theory offers a framework to guide therapists in effectively enhancing states of safety through co-regulation and attunement over telehealth. We actually see everything we need to see of our clients, and they see everything they need to see of us, to be able to connect and co-regulate online. Our face, eyes, voice, and heart—all the places to which our ventral vagus nerve and social engagement system is connected—are framed by the screen in telehealth. In fact, over telehealth we can often see the client's face and upper body close-up, allowing us to read the client's nuanced, non-verbal cues very clearly, such as changes in facial expressions, skin tone, muscles around the eyes and mouth, and pace of breathing—all without there being a sense of threat or violation. This makes it possible for clients to neurocept cues of safety from us as they can easily take in our nuanced, non-verbal cues of safety when our face is well-lit and framed by the screen. Therapists are also able to monitor their own facial expressions on the screen to ensure that they are not unintentionally sending cues that could be perceived as judgmental, disapproving, or threating (Lynch, 2018). A therapist's voice coming through the client's speakers or headphones in a clear, soothing way can also stimulate the vagus nerve by engaging the muscles of the middle ear, which plays an important role in picking up the frequency range of the human voice (Porges, 2021).

A telehealth setting can often enhance states of safety for clients. The client is in their own boundaried space, and we are in ours; it is clear that we cannot invade their physical space through the screen. The client can also quickly exit the session, with a click, if they feel threatened in any way. Although this can feel disempowering and even alarming for clinicians, it can feel very safe and protective for some clients, especially survivors of interpersonal and sexual violence. The authors have noted in their online EMDR practices that this unique boundaried-connection has fostered increased engagement in sessions, and that clients take novel risks that support the therapeutic process, such as making eye contact, engaging in movement activities with the therapist, and making choices about where and how to position their bodies in order to increase comfort and presence.

Movement activities can also enhance interpersonal connection and resonance between therapist and client. The client and therapist moving together, entering rhythms and mirroring states, can stimulate the ventral vagus nerve and create a sense of shared experience. In facilitating the COME BACK activities, the therapist simultaneously engages in the movement practices, connecting into their own interoceptive experience while staying attuned to the client's experience and expressions. This makes the therapist available as a real presence that can provide relational safety and resonance, fostering connection through a *shared authentic experience*, a term coined by Dave Emerson (2015), the founder of Trauma Center Trauma Sensitive Yoga (TCTSY).

YOGA IN THE TREATMENT OF COMPLEX TRAUMA

Recognizing Complex PTSD as a separate diagnostic category, as it has been in the most recent version of the World Health Organization's (2020) *International Statistical Classification of Diseases and Related Health Problems* (11th ed.; *ICD-11*), necessitates the development of approaches that safely meet the treatment needs of complex trauma survivors. Integrating trauma-sensitive yoga into treatment has been shown to effectively support the resolution of complex trauma and dissociative symptoms (Price et al., 2017) and to be an effective adjunctive treatment to clinical interventions targeting PTSD (Taylor et al., 2020).

Trauma Center Trauma Sensitive Yoga (TCTSY) is a specific model of trauma-sensitive yoga that was developed and researched at the Trauma Center in Brookline, Massachusetts beginning in 2002 and is now run through the Center for Trauma and Embodiment at the Justice Resource Institute. In collaborating and expanding The COME BACK Tool, the language and practices were influenced by trauma-sensitive yoga and especially the TCTSY model.

In TCTSY, simple yoga forms and movements provide concrete, present-oriented opportunities for clients to engage in the process of *interoception*, which can be defined as "the process of receiving, accessing and appraising internal bodily signals" (Farb et al., 2015, p. 1). By moving different parts of the body in various forms, clients practice noticing and interacting with what is happening in the body in order to rebuild neural and physiological interoceptive pathways, restoring their connection with their body. This allows survivors of complex trauma to experience having a body that is their own, which is the basis of having a tangible sense of self ("I sense, therefore I am"). Sensing into the body enhances the client's ability to interact with sensations in ways that are helpful to them, making choices that best meet their needs in the moment and increasing a sense of ownership over their body and experience (Emerson, 2015).

Interoception is a necessary skill in trauma treatment, including in EMDR, as we invite our clients to look inward to mindfully notice and report what is coming up as part of the healing process. The skill of interoception begins with the body and a focus on the felt sense; however, many trauma survivors are disconnected from their bodies. According to Emerson (2015), interoceptive pathways can be compromised by experiences of trauma. Many survivors of complex trauma are oriented toward survival and become acutely attuned to their external world, scanning for cues of threat from the environment, including the overt or subtle non-verbal communication of others. The impact of this survival strategy is an erosion of interoceptive capacity and disconnection from the body, decreasing the capacity to tolerate and integrate somatic experiences.

Disconnection from the body due to extreme and inescapable threat and harm can manifest as *somatoform dissociation*, defined as the failure to adequately process and integrate the somatic components of experience (Nijenhuis et al., 1998). According to the Nijenhuis (2009), somatoform dissociation is a trauma-related defense that can present in both negative forms (such as loss of sensory perception, feeling, and motor control) and positive forms (such as involuntary perception of pain and sensations). While dissociation can be adaptive in the sense that it helps the individual cope by avoiding the processing of unbearable and intolerable pain, based on the theory of structural dissociation (van der Hart et al., 2006), there are often other parts of self that hold the traumatic memories as well as the sensations and feelings connected to those unprocessed experiences. As these sensations and feelings are unintegrated, they are vulnerable to being triggered and intruding into the individual's awareness, causing destabilization. The triggering of implicit memories held by structurally dissociated parts can cause sensations and feelings to come flooding into the present moment without context or narrative, which can be confusing for clients as there is often no explicit indicator that these experiences are memories linked to the past (Fisher, 2017). As a result, working with the body and increasing somatic awareness in clients who present with disso-ciation is often slow and careful work, involving repetition and continuous differentiation between past and present.

The focus of TCTSY is on what is happening within the body in the present as a specific treatment for compromised interoception. Repeated experiences of noticing what is hap-pening in specific areas of the body in a contained and concrete way becomes interoceptive training for the brain, making it easier over time to stay oriented to the present moment without becoming overwhelmed or flooded by what is happening in the body.

TCTSY facilitators are also trained to remove cues of threat from the environment as much as possible so that clients can have access to enough external safety to begin to go inward. With enough external safety, clients can connect to what is happening in their bodies and practice choice-making in the moment (within each yoga form and movement). TCTSY facilitators are careful not to assume that any stimuli—such as smells, chants, props, music, lyrics, language, candles, imagery, metaphors, or ways of breathing—are relaxing or calming for a client, as any type of stimuli can be triggering based on individual experience of trauma. In telehealth, the process of creating a safe space is done collaboratively with the client. Clients are invited to identify triggering objects, images, or sensory cues in their own space, and make choices that help them to increase safety. For example, one of JM's clients identified a framed picture in her space that reminded her of a recent loss and caused her distress on a daily basis. After discussion and problem-solving, the client chose to wrap it in fabric and place it in a drawer until the therapeutic work around that loss was complete. In addition, clients are encouraged to integrate materials and objects that feel grounding or soothing into their space in a way that is useful to their therapeutic process. This is often empowering for clients and helps them restore a sense of control over their environment.

Another key element of TCTSY is the use of invitational language which emphasizes choice instead of command (Spinzolla et al., 2011). Invitational language has been par-ticularly influential in the development of The COME BACK Tool scripts and practices. Inviting choice for each movement practice, where one option is not communicated as being better than another (for example, the choice of making bigger movements is not presented as better than making smaller movements), empowers clients to make choices based on what feels most helpful for them in the moment.

Trauma-sensitive yoga as a trauma treatment modality is not about remembering, cre-ating a narrative of the trauma story, or about assigning meaning to the past (Emerson, 2015). It is an embodied practice of being fully in the present in order to restore connection between mind and body and increase capacity for self-regulation. Developing these skills in the preparation phase of EMDR is essential to working with complex trauma and dissocia-tion safely over telehealth.

CASE EXAMPLE OF YOGA AND MOVEMENT IN TRAUMA REPROCESSING

Below is a case example of how MS (referred to in the case study as "the therapist") inte-grated yoga and movement into EMDR preparation and trauma reprocessing in an online setting during the first COVID-19 lockdown in the US. Her client presented with complex trauma symptoms, including bodily complaints, frequent loss of present-moment orienta-tion, and difficulties identifying emotional states. MS and her client used yoga postures to increase grounding and stabilization during reprocessing. The names for the postures will be provided in English as well as in Sanskrit, the ancient language of India and the original language of yoga and yogic philosophy.

The therapist and her client began their work together over telehealth before the COVID-19 pandemic began. Although the client had a history of complex trauma, she only wanted to reprocess PTSD symptoms resulting from a recent car accident. The therapist respected her request to focus on the car accident to help her client reach her goal of driving again, therefore increasing her daily functioning and stabilization. The therapist conceptualized that meeting the client where she was at, without pushing beyond what she could tolerate, would provide her with experiences of success and increase trust in the therapeutic relationship. In addition, the client's cultural background ascribes a type of fortitude to women as the backbone of families and communities, making it difficult for women to express vulnerability. The therapist was attentive to this cultural factor and wanted the client to feel that their work was a safe place to be vulnerable and that boundaries would be respected.

At the beginning of their work together, the therapist helped the client prepare a space in her home for treatment and to identify and gather any resources that she would find helpful or useful to her healing process (MS refers to this step as "preparing the EMDR Workspace"). The therapist invited the client to gather materials or objects that engage the five senses. The client chose objects that connected her to her cultural background, spirituality, and homeland, including an amulet from a family member, the smell of jasmine, and particular songs. The therapist guided the client to keep those objects in a basket so they would be accessible as grounding tools in sessions. The therapist also saved the songs on her computer so they could be listened to in session together via the screenshare function.

During the process of preparing the EMDR Workspace, it was observed that the client would become restless and activated, and would sometimes enter dissociative states. As they explored this, the client identified that her bedroom, where she initially set up her therapy space, was triggering for her. Collaboratively they identified and prepared a less activating space in her home for sessions. The therapist also guided the client to problem solve around any other triggers; for example, the client closed the blinds after becoming activated by seeing movement outside. When the client had fully established and prepared her EMDR Workspace, the therapist guided her through The COME BACK Tool practices to support her in feeling resourced and grounded in her body.

The therapist and client were working through the car accident using the eight phases of the EMDR Standard Protocol online. Soon after, the COVID-19 pandemic swept across the US, which changed some elements of their reprocessing work. The client could no longer have social support available in her home during the sessions as the lockdown was in place. The client's symptoms also became more acute, and although a visit to the ER would have otherwise been advisable, they assessed that as too risky due to the infection and death rate at that time.

The client had a long history of sexual trauma, chronic suicidality, and pelvic pain that was ruled out by medical examination. The client associated her pain with the car accident, but after completely processing through the car accident, the pelvic pain remained. The therapist and client chose a new target based on triggers specific to the pandemic. It was during this work that the sexual abuse material began to emerge. The therapist helped the client recognize the connection between her present triggers, the sexual trauma, and the increase in pelvic pain, but whenever they began talking about the sexual trauma, the client would shut down as there was significant shame and stigma around the experience. The client had practiced yoga for a couple of years but had stopped due to the pelvic pain. Her motivation to feel less triggered and reduce the pelvic pain was high, and she was willing to try working through this part of her past.

In Phase Three, while asking the client to bring up the fragments of the sexual abuse memory, the client avoided verbally sharing any details of the memory. The therapist assessed how well the client could stay oriented to the present while thinking about the memory using an exercise based on the Blind to Therapist (B2T) Protocol (Blore & Holmshaw, 2009), a modification to the Standard Protocol that allows the client to keep the image of the target and associated material private due to fear, stigma, or lack of readiness to share. The client was invited to choose a nickname for the memory and was reassured that she did not need to reveal any information or details about the event during the reprocessing. Protecting the client's privacy not only increased emotional safety by decreasing shame, but was also a more culturally responsive approach than requiring her to verbalize details. As the client was guided through this assessment phase, she became overwhelmed when rating her subjective units of distress (SUD) and said it was at a 10. The therapist invited the client to move her body as a way to increase orientation to the present moment; however, the client's activation increased as they experimented with different movements. She became tearful and expressed that she could feel the "escape artist" taking over, which was a term used by the client to let the therapist know numbness was taking over her body, mainly in the pelvic and hip areas. The therapist and client then explored movements to help soothe and comfort the pain in those areas. The client moved into Extended Child's Pose (*Utthita Balasana*) by kneeling on the floor with her knees apart, folding forward to rest her forehead on the floor, and reaching her arms forward to lengthen and release pressure in her spine (see Figure 2.2). From this position, the client felt able to continue with the assessment phase.

During the assessment questions, the client spontaneously transitioned into a posture called Downward Facing Dog (*Adho Mukha Svanasana*), moving from the kneeling position

Figure 2.2 Line drawing of client in Extended Child's Pose (*Utthita Balasana*) drawn by the therapist Michelli Simson.

Figure 2.3 Line drawing of client in Downward Facing Dog (*Adho Mukha Svanasana*) drawn by the therapist Michelli Simson.

into an inverted "v" by pressing her hands and feet into the floor and lifting her tailbone and hips up and back toward the ceiling (see Figure 2.3). The client was encouraged to follow the movements that were useful to her body and helpful in staying present. The client transitioned between these two postures, back and forth, during the assessment phase and finished on Extended Child's Pose.

The therapist suggested a standing posture for the sets of bilateral stimulation. The client chose Warrior I (*Virabhadrasana I*) as this can help stretch the hip flexors, an area that would become very painful when she thought of the abuse. In Warrior I, the client could also easily and actively engage in visual BLS by following a dot on the screen for eye movements. In this standing posture, the client bent her front knee forward and extended her back leg behind her, anchoring her back foot into the floor. With her arms reaching upward, the client kept her face forward with a steady focus on the bilateral stimulation on the screen (see Figure 2.4). The client maintained dual awareness during the set and, as the BLS stopped, she moved into Child's Pose (*Baslana*), which is similar to Extended Child's Pose but more restful with the knees closer together. From there, the client verbally reported what was coming up for her. In the first two sets, the client repeated these movements, sometimes keeping material private or only reporting if there were changes in the intensity of emotions or sensations.

After a few sets, the therapist suggested that the client try Warrior II posture (*Virabhadrasana II*), a modification of Warrior I where the client extended her arms out to the sides, parallel to the floor, while bending her front knee over her front foot and straightening her back leg. The client maintained her focus on the screen in order to follow the bilateral stimulation (see Figure 2.5). The client alternated between Warrior II and Mountain Pose (*Tadasana*) between sets, where she would exhale and bring her feet together, standing tall and centered, to notice what was coming up for her. When she was ready, she would step back into Warrior II and continue with bilateral stimulation. After a few sets, the client moved into Half Spinal Twist (*Ardha Matsyendrasana*) by sitting on the floor, hugging one knee into her chest and pressing her opposite elbow against that knee to turn toward

Figure 2.4 Line drawing of client in Warrior I posture (*Virabhadrasana I*) drawn by the therapist Michelli Simson.

Figure 2.5 Line drawing of client in Warrior II posture (*Virabhadrasana II*) drawn by the therapist Michelli Simson.

Figure 2.6 Line drawing of client in Garland Pose (*Malasana*) drawn by the therapist Michelli Simson.

the back of the room. She reported that she previously used this posture to help her release tension and fatigue. The client came out of the twist and back to the center to focus on a set of bilateral stimulation before switching to the other side. She changed sides six times. In closing the session, the client reported a decrease in disturbance and pain with a SUD rating of 2. She stated that it could not decrease any further due to the COVID-19 pandemic and the stressors in her life.

As the session was incomplete, containment and closure were conducted and the client moved into Garland Pose (*Malasana*), which is like a wide squat, keeping both arms inside her thighs and pressing her hands together in front of her chest, helping her to reground and integrate the good work from the session (see Figure 2.6). In subsequent sessions, the client repeated this sequence of movements with bilateral stimulation. After seven sessions, the client reached a SUD rating of 0 on the cluster of memories related to sexual abuse and reported a significant decrease of pelvic pain.

This case study illustrates how movement and yoga helped the client maintain dual attention and tolerate the awareness and integration of bodily sensations during trauma reprocessing.

THE COME BACK TOOL: FACILITATION STEPS AND SCRIPTS

The COME BACK Tool scripts offer a combination of body-based and arts-based directives. The artmaking directives are designed to be simple, immediate, and accessible to all artistic levels and abilities with minimal set-up and clean-up. They can be done using basic art supplies, such as paper, pencils or pens, and any type of colors (crayons, color pencils, markers, oil or chalk pastels, or highlighters). These materials are inexpensive and available in many clients' home environments; however, the therapist can explore other creative materials that the client has available to them. If the client is unable to access artmaking materials for use over telehealth, a collaborative online artmaking program can be used, such as the whiteboard function on Zoom or using the drawing program available on www.aggie.io. The therapist can also mail basic art materials to the client in advance.

Therapists are encouraged to emphasize that all of the practices are invitations, and the client can choose in which way they engage in the activities. For example, some clients may be able to tolerate engaging in the activities more internally, using their imagination and connection to sensations without the use of the art materials. Other clients may be more comfortable writing instead of drawing during the art directives. Some clients may require the external focus that the art directives provide to safely identify and engage with their sensations. Therapists are encouraged to follow the process that is most beneficial for the client to connect to the resource and goal of each COME BACK practice. The authors recommend beginning and closing each COME BACK practice with the scale of presence, a psychoeducational tool and self-assessment scale to help the client identify their level of presence and how helpful the activity was in increasing present-moment awareness.

ARTS-BASED SCALE OF PRESENCE

This scale of presence is both an arts-based and telehealth adaptation of the Back of the Head Scale. The Back of the Head Scale was developed by Jim Knipe (2014) as a tool for decreasing the risk of dissociative abreaction during EMDR treatment, and is used as a resource and assessment tool within the Method of Constant Installation of Present Orientation and Safety (CIPOS). The adapted scale of presence integrates the creative arts as a way to help clients with complex trauma increase their awareness of how it feels to be fully present (such as connected and calm) on one end of the scale, and how it feels to be fully disconnected (such as highly activated or dissociated) on the other end. Inviting the client to explore and visually represent how they experience being on both ends of the spectrum makes the scale more personal and concrete, rather than an abstract concept, thereby enhancing their ability to effectively assess their level of presence.

In this arts-based adaption, the client can use their artwork to create a visual scale that can be placed in front of them for external reference. For example, JM has had clients lay their images on either side of their computer to create the scale externally, making it easier for them to assess their level of awareness before and after the COME BACK activities, and even during reprocessing.

The example artwork below was made by an adult female who identified that staying present has been a struggle for her since separating from her partner and adjusting to becoming a single mother during COVID-19. She placed disconnection and dissociation on the left of her screen, and presence on the right side of her screen (see Figure 2.7).

The benefits of using this scale before and after COME BACK activities provide comparative information to both the client and therapist on how useful and effective the activity was in bringing them into the present moment and into their body. It also strengthens self-observation skills and present-moment orientation through practice and repetition, allowing them to internalize the scale as a resource. When clients are able to observe where they are along the scale of presence, they can catch their attention shifting toward disconnection, overwhelm, or dissociation, making it easier to identify when to use a stabilization strategy to come back to the present moment. Having a concrete, visual scale in the client's own space (such as taped to their wall or on a table) also acts as a reminder between sessions to check in and notice their level of presence, and to take actions to increase presence and stabilization when necessary.

Figure 2.7 A visual scale of presence is created by placing the client's artwork on both sides of their computer.

Another benefit of the scale of presence is that it is non-verbal, which means that the client can indicate their level of presence using their hand and gesture, showing the therapist where they are at along the scale. In the original Back of the Head Scale, the client is directed to make the scale by gesturing from front to back; for example, the client indicates a state of presence by placing their hand out in front of their head, and places their hand behind their head to indicate a state of overwhelm or dissociation. Using the scale in this way over telehealth can be challenging because depth perception is skewed through the screen, making it hard to accurately gauge where the client is at along the scale. For better use over telehealth, the scale of presence runs from side –to side instead of front to back. The client creates their scale by moving their hand from left to right, with their artwork acting as a visual reference for both ends of the scale (either by placing their images to the left and right of their screen or even on the floor to the left and right of their feet). This way, when the client moves their hand from side –to side to indicate their level of presence, their hand moves across the front of the screen, making it easier for the therapist to see where the client is on their scale.

Using gesture and movement also makes this scale an effective tool for clients to communicate dissociation or overwhelm during reprocessing work, when levels of activation might make accessing speech difficult. This is especially important in trauma reprocessing over telehealth, where we want to ensure that clients have the skills to communicate if they are losing dual attention or are outside of their window of tolerance. Giving clients the skills to assess and communicate their level of presence means we can be collaborative with our clients and rely on them for information such as when to slow down or use stabilization strategies during online reprocessing.

Script for Scale of Presence

Introduction: *I would like to share a scale with you that you can use to explore and assess how present you're feeling at any given moment. Have two pieces of paper and some artmaking materials ready.*

Psychoeducation: *Sometimes we feel very alert and present, and other times our attention drifts away, like our body is here, but our mind is somewhere else: maybe in a memory somewhere in the past, or anticipating something in the future, or sometimes feeling nowhere at all, just blank or numb. Our level of presence naturally shifts along this spectrum, from being fully here* [therapist brings one hand all the way to the edge of the screen] *to being fully somewhere else* [therapist moves hand to the other edge of the screen to demonstrate the full spectrum of the scale], *and that's completely normal. Creating and using this scale will allow you to build more awareness as to where you're at on that scale at any given moment.*

Demonstrating the scale: [To adapt this activity to an in-person session, the word "screen" can be replaced with "body" to give the client the option of creating their scale from one side of their body to the other, rather than one side of the screen to the other.] *You can use your hand to show me where you are on your scale. Having your hand all the way to one side of your screen shows me that you are fully here and present in this moment. When you are over here, you are aware of the here-and-now, you can notice the things around you, how you're feeling, and can listen to cues from your body, like if you're hungry or uncomfortable. Go ahead and bring your hand all the way here, to one side of your screen. Okay, great, having your hand here shows me that you are fully here. Okay, now move that hand all the way to the other side of your screen. Having your hand there shows me that you're disconnected from the present moment—your awareness is fully somewhere else, perhaps back in a memory, so it feels like you're back in that time, or perhaps nowhere at all—like being numb or shut down. From here, it can be hard to be aware of the things and people around you and to listen to your body. Okay, now bring your hand somewhere in the middle of the screen.* [Therapist demonstrates this with their own hand.] *Having your hand here shows that you are in the middle—kind-of here, and kind-of somewhere else. From here, you may have an awareness of your body and your surroundings, but at the same time, you might feel like you're starting to get pulled into the past, maybe getting overwhelmed by thoughts or feelings from that time, or you can feel your body starting to shut down or disconnect. This is the scale of presence.*

Art directive: *It can take some time to know what it feels like to be at different points along this scale. One way to explore this is through artmaking. If you'd like, you can create your own scale to have in front of you while you practice the skill of coming back to the present moment. Begin by noticing how you experience being all the way present in your body—how do you know you are present? Can you think of an experience or an activity that makes you feel grounded, present, and connected? How do you experience that in your body? See if you can represent being fully present using color, shapes, symbols, lines, words, or, in any way you'd like, on one piece of paper. There is no right or wrong way to do this—this is just for you.* [Therapist leaves time for the client to complete their image.] *Now place your image on the side of your screen that will represent being fully present. You can place it wherever you would like on that side.* [The therapist gives the client time to place their image where they would like.] *This marks one end of the scale.*

Now we will explore the other end of the scale on a separate piece of paper. Begin by noticing how you experience being disconnected from the present moment and fully somewhere else, like back in a memory, overwhelmed or shut down? How do you know if you are all the way over here [therapist brings their hand to the side of the screen that indicates disconnection]*? See if you can represent being fully somewhere else or disconnected using color, shapes, symbols, lines, or words, on that piece of paper. Remember, there is no right or wrong way to do this.* [Therapist leaves time for the client to complete their image.] *Now place your image on the other side of your screen, the side that will represent being fully disconnected, fully somewhere else. This is the other end of the scale. Notice these two images in front of you, one on each side of your screen—this is your sale of presence.*

Gesturing the scale: *Experiment with moving your hand along your scale of presence, from being all the way present to fully somewhere else, moving your hand from side to the other. Notice where the middle of your scale is. Where are you now on your scale?* [Allow time for the client to self-assess.] *Remember that it is a scale so we naturally move along it. Sometimes you might feel* *fully here and other times you might realize, "Oh, where have I been?" as if you were somewhere else. When you catch yourself all the way over there, that's great noticing, because then you can take actions to reconnect with your body and your surroundings using the COME BACK skills that we will practice together.*

Applying the skill: *You can use this scale at the beginning and end of each activity to notice if the activity was helpful in coming back to the present moment.*

C—CONNECTING TO A COMFORTING PRESENCE

This practice offers a felt sense of being connected to a comforting presence. It is adapted from Laurel Parnell's script for resourcing and "tapping in" nurturing and protective figures using bilateral stimulation (Parnell, 2008). The authors adapted the language to place more emphasis on comfort and support rather than nurturance to move the focus away from attachment relationships. The language is also adapted to allow the client to be supported, calmed, and comforted by a presence, such as nature, rather than a person, which can be tolerated well by clients who have experienced threat or betrayal in interpersonal relationships. Artmaking is used to create an external representation of this presence. Positive or neutral sensations are then enhanced using words and bilateral stimulation so that the Comforting Presence resource is held both externally, through the artwork, and in the body, through sensations—having both an internal and external focus can help clients stay within their window of tolerance during this activity. The client's image can act as a reminder to practice connecting to this resource whenever it might be helpful for them.

The example artwork shown in Figure 2.8 was made by an adult female who identified a particular place in nature as her calming presence. She added the words "miracle" and "awe" with stamp letters as cue words to access the resource.

Figure 2.8 Example artwork of nature as a Comforting Presence.

Script for C

Introduction: *We will now explore the first letter of The COME BACK Tool, "C": Connecting to a Comforting Presence. Have some paper and art materials ready. Check in: where are you at now on your scale of presence?*

Choosing a presence: *You can begin by thinking of someone or something with a comforting, calming presence. This could be a presence in any form, perhaps the sense of something bigger and larger than you, like nature or a spiritual presence; perhaps an animal or a mythical creature; maybe someone you've known, someone from your community or family history, or even character or historical figure. Take a moment to really bring this comforting presence to mind. See if you can make this presence as vivid as possible, noticing anything about this presence that feels comforting to you, perhaps their size, energy, voice... anything that feels comforting.*

Art directive: *If you would like, you can represent this presence using color, symbols, lines, shapes, images, or words, or, in any way you would like, on a piece of paper.* [Therapist leaves time for the client to complete their image.]

Noticing sensations: *Take a look at your image. Begin to notice how your body responds to this presence, and to the sense of being comforted. If it's helpful, just breathe in that comfort, letting it move and expand in or around your body, wherever you would like it to go. If it's helpful, you may like to notice if there are any sensations in your body that feel neutral or good in this presence.*

Enhancing the resource: *Let in as much comfort as feels good for you right now. You may like to come up with a word or phrase to help you remember this comforting presence, such as "I am supported or I am cared for." Find the words that feel right to you. Feel free to add them to your image.*

Adding bilateral stimulation: *If you'd like, you can fold your arms across your chest and gently tap back and forth on your chest or arms, just a few times, as you say those words to yourself and notice any positive sensations in your body, maybe letting them deepen or expand.*

Applying the skill: *You can repeat this activity as many times as you like, using your image and those words to help your body remember this comforting presence so you can always carry it with you, wherever you go. You can also do this activity with any type of presence, such as a peaceful, grounding, ancestral, nurturing, loving, creative, or powerful presence. Choosing different resources can help you create a constellation of support to have around you, that is always present and available whenever you need it.*

Scale of presence reassessment: *Where are you at now on your scale of presence? Do you notice any shifts? What was helpful for you about this activity? Was there anything that wasn't helpful?*

O—ORIENTING TO THE PRESENT MOMENT THROUGH THE SENSES

This practice explores the benefits of mindfully orienting to neutral or pleasant stimuli in one's environment through an arts-based adaptation of an activity called 5-4-3-2-1, which promotes sensory grounding by engaging all the senses in a curious and creative way. This intentionally engages neuroception, the perception of stimuli below the level of conscious awareness (Porges, 2011), to communicate to the brain that the current environment is neutral or safe. Sight, for example, is explored using a perceptual art activity called Blind Contour Drawing, which can bring the client out of heightened affective states by objectively grounding them in their external environment (Hinz, 2019). This activity also takes advantage of

Figure 2.9 Example artwork of the arts-based 1-2-3-4-5 orienting activity.

the client being in their own space over telehealth. The client is invited to move around their space and locate objects and materials that feel supportive and grounding. This activity is often stimulating and fun for clients. It is a way to increase engagement in the therapist-client relationship as the client shares more of their space (what is beyond the frame of the screen) with the therapist. The client's artwork can also serve as a visual reminder of these new sensory-based grounding skills and the objects that they found most useful. See Figure 2.9 as an example image created by JM to share with clients when presenting this activity.

Script for O

Introduction: *We will now explore the second letter of the COME BACK Tool, "O": Orienting to the Present Moment through the Senses. Have some paper and art materials ready. Check in: where are you at now on your scale of presence?*

Psychoeducation: *In this activity, you'll explore your environment using your five senses. We are always taking in our environment through our senses, but we aren't always conscious of the things we perceive and our reactions to them. Sometimes we experience a stress or fear response, like an instinct or reflex, without knowing why. This can happen when our subconscious brain associates something in our environment with something that happened in the past. The activity we'll practice today can help you learn ways to intentionally use your senses to come back to the present moment, by bringing your attention to things that are neutral, grounding, and even interesting in your environment, so that this sensory information can tell your mind and body that you are okay, right now, here in this present moment. Your senses are one of the most powerful and quick routes back to the present moment!*

Our five senses are sight, touch, hearing, smell, and taste. Let's begin with sight.

Art activity for sight: *See if there is something you can see inside or outside of your space that you find interesting to look at in some way. Focus your attention on this object, noticing its shape, size, texture, pattern, and colors. If you would like, you can use your paper and pen/pencil to really study this object using a technique called "blind contour drawing," where you draw without looking at the paper! Of course, you can look at the paper if you want, but try not to worry about what the image looks like—just let your eyes slowly explore the details, shape, and textures of the object while your hand moves at the same time—almost as if your eye is connected to the tip of your pencil: as your eye moves, your pencil moves too. You can go really slow, exploring the details of the object. Your image does not need to look a certain way—this is a playful activity and it gets easier the more you practice!*

[Therapist leaves time for the client to complete their image.] *When you're complete, write the word "sight" on your paper.*

Art activity for touch: *Now we will explore the sense of touch. Choose something in your environment that seems interesting to explore with your sense of touch, something that you can touch or hold. Feel free to move around your space until you find it.* [Therapist allows time for the client to find and then share what their object is.] *If you'd like, you can use your art materials to trace one of your hands on a piece of paper. Write the word "touch" in the palm of your hand tracing. When you're ready, begin to explore the sensory qualities of this object:*

- *What's the texture of the surface—is it smooth, soft, rough? You may like to write or draw that into the tracing of your pinky finger.*
- *What is the object's temperature? Write or draw that into the tracing of your next finger.*
- *What is the weight of the object—is it heavy, light? Write or draw that into the tracing of your middle finger.*
- *What is the shape of the object—is it round, flat, pointy? Write or draw that into the tracing of your index finger.*
- *Lastly, what is this object called? Write or draw the object into the tracing of your thumb.*
- *You may like to add any other words or drawings to your hand tracing that describe what you notice with your sense of touch.*

Art activity for hearing, smell, and taste: *We will now explore the last three senses of hearing, smell, and taste. If you'd like, you can trace your other hand on the same piece of paper and write the words "hearing," "smell," and "taste" into the palm of this hand tracing.*

Sound: *Let's start with hearing.*

- **Something far:** *See if you can hear something outside, maybe even outside of the room you are in. What is the farthest sound that you can hear right now? Write or draw what you hear into the tracing of your pinky finger.*
- **Something close:** *Now move your attention to a sound inside the space you're in right now. You can hear my voice, but what other sounds are there in your space? Write or draw what you hear into the tracing of your next finger.*
- **Around/from the body:** *Now bring your attention to the sounds closest to you, or the sounds you are making. Maybe you can hear the sound of your body moving, or the sound of your breath as the air moves in and out. You could even make a sound with your breath, such as by humming or sighing. What is the closest sound to you? Write or draw what you hear into the tracing of your middle finger.*

Smell: *Now we'll explore the sense of smell.*

- **Soothing:** *See if you can find a smell that is soothing or interesting to you, inside or outside of your space. You may like to move around to find the right one. This could be the smell of a tea, spice, lotion, candle, the wind, a plant or flower, or anything soothing or comforting. When you find it, see if you can describe the smell. Write or draw what you smell into the tracing of your index finger.*

Taste: *Lastly, we'll explore the sense of taste.*

- **Pleasant:** *For this last one, begin by finding a flavor or sensation that is pleasant in some way. This could be gum, mints, chocolate, a cinnamon stick, or even water. It could be something cold, like an ice cube, or warm, like tea, or something crunchy and loud. Take your time. When you find it, just take a moment and slow down as you begin to explore this flavor or sensation with your sense of taste, allowing yourself to become curious about what you notice. Write or draw what you taste into the tracing of your thumb.*

Applying the skill: *You just practiced the skill of using all five senses to come back to the present moment. Perhaps there is one sense that you found particularly helpful or enjoyable to explore—what was most helpful for you? If you notice that you feel disconnected or distressed for any reason, you can use that sense to quickly ground and orient yourself to the here-and-now. You can also use your art images as a reminder that you have the skills to soothe and calm yourself using your body and your senses at any time.*

Scale of presence reassessment: *Where are you at now on your scale of presence? Do you notice any shifts? What was helpful for you about this activity? Was there anything that wasn't helpful?*

M—MOVING AND MOBILIZING ENERGY

This practice begins with psychoeducation about the role of movement in regulating our energy levels to achieve a balanced state of calm yet alert. A bilateral movement called *cross-crawl* (Dennison & Dennison, 2010) is used to bring energy into the body, followed by a progressive muscle relaxation (Ost, 1988) technique to release tension and come into a more settled and present state. The art directive invites clients to fill in a body outline by visually representing their sensations and energy levels both before and after these activities as a way to increase somatic awareness and to identify what was most helpful for them. (A body scan template is available for use in a printable format on the EMDR and Creative Therapies website, www.emdrcat.com, accessible by scanning the QR code in the introduction of this book.)

The example artwork below was made by an adult female who has experienced an increase of bodily tension, especially in her chest, and acute anxiety since the first lockdown of COVID-19. In Figure 2.10, her body scans before and after the movement activity show a reduction in bodily distress. She reported that the scattered puzzle pieces in her mind are still not solved but she has more separation from them, the activation in her chest settled slightly, and the pain in her legs is more localized rather than spread across the lower half of her body.

Script for M

Introduction: *We will now explore the third letter of the COME BACK tool, "M": Moving and Mobilizing Energy. Have a few pieces of paper and some art materials ready. Check in: where are you at now on your scale of presence?*

Psychoeducation: *Movement is an important part of coming back to the present moment. It can help us release energy and tension when our energy levels are too high, and it can increase our energy when we feel too low and tired. Movement can help bring our bodies into a balanced state somewhere in between too much and too little energy—like being calm but alert.*

Art activity (Before): *If you'd like, you can begin this activity by creating an image to represent how your body feels right now. Take a piece of paper and write the word "before" on the top, then draw a simple outline of a body, with a head, arms, legs, and a torso. Don't worry what it looks like—this is just for you.* [Therapist can also provide the client with the printed body outline when possible.] *Scan through your body, noticing where you feel energy, tension, or discomfort. Using your art materials, add color, shape, lines, or words to fill in your body outline and any areas where you notice those sensations.* [Therapist leaves time for the client to complete their image.]

Figure 2.10 Example artwork of comparative body scans before and after the Moving and Mobilizing Energy activity.

Increasing energy: Now we'll begin experimenting with energizing movements.

- **Cross-crawl:** *You can start by raising one hand, whichever hand is up to you, and bring it across your body to your opposite knee. Then try raising your other hand and bringing it to your other knee.* [Therapist demonstrates these options and continues to engage in the movement activities.] *Try making this movement back and forth, hand –o knee, hand –to knee. These movements can be as big or as little as you'd like.*

- **Fast and slow:** *You may like to try speeding up your movements. If you're standing, you could even try adding a little hop like jogging on the spot. You may also like to try slowing your movements down, noticing how slower movements can challenge your balance. How fast or how slow you move is up to you.*

- **Check-in:** *Check-in and notice your energy level now, perhaps noticing if you feel like you have more energy, less energy, or somewhere in the middle, just noticing, without needing to shift or change anything.*

Movement: *Now you can try movements that may help to release energy and tension from different muscles in your body, using a technique called progressive muscle relaxation.*

- **Feet:** *See if you can bring your awareness to the muscles in your feet. You can move your toes, maybe even looking down at them, or press your toes and heels into the floor. Now if you'd like, you could try tensing and squeezing all of those muscles in your feet as much as you can. See if you can hold it as I count to ten. When I get to ten, just let all the tension release and melt away from your muscles, down into the floor. Ready? Take a breath in and hold.* [Therapist counts to ten.] *Okay. Let it all go. Let's try that again. Tensing the muscles in your feet. Take a breath in and hold.* [Therapist counts to ten.] *Release.*

- **Legs:** *Now move your awareness to your legs. Begin by moving your legs in any way that feels comfortable, noticing your calves and upper leg muscles, and even the muscles around your knees. When you're ready, bring as much energy and tension into all of your leg muscles as you can and hold for ten seconds. Ready? Take a breath in and hold.* [Therapist counts to ten.] *Okay. Let it all go. Let's try that again. Tensing the muscles in your legs. Take a breath in and hold.* [Therapist counts to ten.] *Release.*

- **Upper body, neck, and shoulders:** *Now move your awareness to your upper body. Move around and notice all the muscles in your upper body: belly, chest, lower back, upper back, shoulders, and neck. Notice all those muscles. Now, try squeezing and tensing all those muscles in your torso, shoulders, and neck and hold for ten seconds. Ready? Take a breath in and hold.* [Therapist counts to ten.] *Okay. Let it all go. Let's try that again. Tensing the muscles in your upper body. Take a breath in and hold.* [Therapist counts to ten.] *Release.*

- **Arms and hands:** *Now move your awareness to your arms and hands. Notice all the muscles in your arms: upper and lower arms, hands, and fingers, first moving them in any way that feels comfortable to you. Now, if you'd like, you could try tensing and squeezing all of those muscles as much as you can. Ready? Take a breath in and hold.* [Therapist counts to ten.] *Okay. Let it all go. Let's try that again. Tensing the muscles in your arms and hands. Take a breath in and hold.* [Therapist counts to ten.] *Release.*

- **Head and face:** *Now move your awareness to your face and head. Notice all the muscles in your face, forehead, around your eyes, cheeks, mouth, jaw, even around the top and back of your head. Now, try squeezing and tensing all these muscles and hold for ten seconds. Ready? Take a breath in and hold.* [Therapist counts to ten.] *Okay. Let it all go. You can use some massage to help these muscles let go of any tension.* [Therapist demonstrates by massaging their own face and jaw muscles.] *Let's try that again. Tensing the muscles in your head and face. Take a breath in and hold.* [Therapist counts to ten.] *Release.*

- **Whole body:** *You may like to try that one more time with your whole body. Try to tense every small and large muscle group of your body: your feet, legs, torso, lower back, chest, shoulders, arms, hands, neck, face, head—your whole body. Move your body, bringing your awareness to all your muscles, and when you're ready, tensing and squeezing your whole body as much as you can. Ready?* [Therapist counts to ten.] *Okay. Let it all go, let it all melt away, down into the floor, into the earth. Let's try that one last time. Tensing all the muscles in your whole body. Take and breath in and hold.* [Therapist counts to ten.] *Release.*

Art activity (After): *Now, draw another simple outline of a body with a head, arms, legs, and torso—it does not need to be exact, it's just for you. Write the word "after" above it. Scan through your entire body—noticing any changes in sensations and energy levels. Use the art materials to fill in your body outline now with color, shapes, lines, or words, to show where you notice any sensations.* [Therapist leaves time for the client to complete their image.] *Take a moment to compare the two body outlines. What do you notice?*

Applying the skill: *You can try movement and progressive muscle relaxation whenever you feel it would be helpful. You may like to repeat the whole sequence we just practiced, increasing energy and* *then releasing tension, or just the parts that seem most helpful to you depending on your needs and energy levels. Another possibility is to notice where you feel tension or discomfort in your body, and then tense and release those specific areas. Use your artwork as a reminder of these strategies for releasing energy and tension.*

Scale of presence reassessment: *Where are you at now on your scale of presence? Do you notice any shifts? What was helpful for you about this activity? Was there anything that wasn't helpful?*

E—EXPLORING THE BREATH WITH MOVEMENT AND SOUND

This practice begins with trauma-sensitive ways to explore and interact with the breath. Breathing is a powerful way to regulate the nervous system through the stimulation of the vagus nerve; however, many clients find breathing techniques overwhelming or activating. Focusing awareness on the movement, sounds, and vibrations created by breath, rather than the internal sensations, can provide a grounding focus that decreases the risk of triggering. An arts-based square breathing directive also provides a way to explore the movement of the breath through lines, colors, and shape; this gives clients the opportunity to access the benefits of deep breathing while keeping their awareness externally oriented. The example art in Figure 2.11 shows an image created by an adult female during the arts-based square breathing activity.

Figure 2.11 Example artwork of externalizing the breath through the arts-based square breathing activity.

Script for E

Introduction: *We will now explore the fourth letter of the COME BACK tool, "E": Exploring the Breath through Movement and Sound. Have some paper and art materials ready. Check in: where are you at now on your scale of presence?*

Psychoeducation: *To begin, you may like to come into a position that feels neutral and settled, making any adjustments you need to feel comfortable. Gently begin to bring your awareness to your breath, noticing its natural rhythm without needing to change or modify anything. Even when we are still, our breath is always moving, always here with us in each moment. Interacting with the breath can help us focus our attention on the present moment and can even help us feel calmer and more energized.*

Movement of the breath: *From here, you can begin to explore the movement of your breath, feeling how it rises and falls by placing a hand over your chest or belly.* [Therapist demonstrates this option and continues to engage in the activity.] *As you breathe in, notice the air coming in through your mouth or nose, allowing it to move into your chest and maybe even into your belly, so your hand rises, and then feel your hand fall back down again as you breathe out. This does not have to be a big movement, just noticing any movement at all. How quickly or slowly you breathe is completely up to you.*

Arts-based square breathing: *Now you could try making a square breath, which means breathing in four steps, like the four edges of a square. They are breathing in, pausing, breathing out, and pausing. You can do this by tracing the square on your palm or lap with your finger* [therapist can demonstrate drawing the steps of the square breath on their own palm], *or, if you'd like, you could try drawing the square on a piece of paper using lines and color. If so, feel free to choose a color to begin with.* [Therapist can again demonstrate drawing the steps of the square on their palm or piece of paper.] *You can draw one side of the square as you breathe in, moving the line upward; draw the top edge of the square as you pause, moving the line across the top; draw the other side of the square as you breathe out, moving the line downward; and draw the bottom edge of the square as you pause, moving the line across the bottom, completing the square. You can try this a few times: breathing in, pausing, breathing out, pausing. You can make the squares as big or as small as you like. Feel free to change colors. You may even like to experiment with different shapes and breathing patterns as you draw. Maybe your breath looks more like a rectangle, or a circle, or different types of lines—it's completely up to you how you draw your breath.* [Therapist leaves time for the client to complete their image.]

Sound: *Now if you'd like, you could try pairing your breath with noise. Making noise when you breathe can slow your breathing down, creating a deeper sense of calm in your body.*

Humming: *You can experiment with humming sounds. When you make a humming sound with your breath, you also create vibrations that can be felt. You could try placing a hand on your chest, or wherever it feels most comfortable to you, and as you breathe out with a humming sound, see if your hand can feel the vibrations.* [Therapist demonstrates this option by humming and feeling the vibration.] *You can try experimenting with different humming sounds to create different vibrations, noticing what feels most soothing and calming to you.*

Releasing: *Now you may like to explore making a "ha" sound with your breath, like letting off steam and moving all the old air out of your lungs with energy and vitality. You can try this a few times at your own pace, noticing if there is a sense of release in the body.*

Neutral breathing: *To close this practice, you may like to bring your awareness back to the natural rhythm of your breath, just letting your breath settle without needing to change or modify anything.*

Remember that your breath is always here with you, and that noticing the movement and sound and your breath can help you connect to the present moment.

Scale of presence reassessment: *Where are you at now on your scale of presence? Do you notice any shifts? What was helpful for you about this activity? Was there anything that wasn't helpful?*

B—BALANCING AND CENTERING THE BODY

This practice begins by exploring how balance can reconnect us with the present moment, such as with movements that carefully challenge one's sense of balance, followed by a return to stability and steadiness. This activity also helps the client become aware of their center using posture and movement of the spine. The artmaking directive invites the client to represent their center as a symbol, color, image, or word so it becomes a concrete place to return to in their body. The client's visual representation of their center also acts as a reminder of this somatic resource.

The example art in Figure 2.12 was created by a female adult who has felt that her body has not stopped moving, especially since the start of the pandemic, creating the internal sense of being frantic and scattered. In this activity, she represented her center as a spin top that is able to stay balanced while being completely still, even though the world spins around it.

Script for B

Introduction: *We will now explore the fifth letter of the COME BACK tool, "B": Balancing and Centering the Body." Have some paper and art materials ready. Check in: where are you at now on your scale of presence?*

Psychoeducation: *Testing your balance can increase your awareness of your body in the present moment. When you carefully and gently challenge your balance, such as by shifting your weight onto*

Figure 2.12 Example artwork of a symbol to represent a sense of centeredness.

one leg, you naturally have to reconnect to your body in order to steady yourself so you don't topple over—this is a little brain trick to quickly bring you back into the present!

This practice can also help you begin to shift your focus from outward to inward—so you can feel your body in the here-and-now and reconnect with your center. We often focus our attention outward, scanning the environment so we know we're okay and that there are no dangers around. This is really helpful, but if all of our attention is focused on the external environment, then we can lose touch with what is happening on the inside, in our internal world.

You may like to begin this practice by sitting or standing, whichever feels most comfortable to you. You can adapt any of the movements to your body and whatever feels beneficial to you in the moment.

Shifting pressure:

- **Side to side:** *When you're ready, you may begin to shift your weight from one side to the other. If you're standing, you may like to shift your weight from one foot to the other foot, or if you're sitting, shifting your weight side to side on your sit bones. Your movements can be big or small, just moving at your own pace.* [Therapist demonstrates and participates in the movement activities throughout the script.]

- **Pressure:** *As you shift your weight, you may begin to notice a sense of pressure where your body makes contact with the surface underneath you, such as with the floor or the chair. If you'd like, you could experiment with that pressure, perhaps increasing it by pushing your weight down into the ground or onto the chair as you move from side to side, noticing any sensations in the muscles of your feet, or the muscles around your sit bones. Maybe even the sensation of being supported and held by that surface.*

- **Front to back:** *Now you could try shifting your weight forward and back, perhaps moving your weight into your toes, then back onto your heels, or if you're sitting, to the front and back of your sit bones. Just shifting forward and backward, at your own pace, noticing the sense of pressure as you move.*

- **Circles:** *Now, you may like to try combining these movements by moving back and forth, front and back, or even by making circular motions, moving in small or big circles as you shift your weight around on your feet or your sit bones. The range and pace of your movements, how big or how small, how fast or how slow, is completely up to you.*

Lifting and lowering: *You may like to try standing to challenge your balance a little more, or you can stay seated, that's up to you. When you're ready, try lifting one foot off the ground, as much or as little as you like, perhaps pausing here to challenge your balance, and then lowering it back down again. Notice yourself coming back to a place of balance and stability in your body, fully supported by the surface under you. When you're ready, try the same movement with your other foot, lifting it up off the floor, pausing for a moment to challenge your balance, and then lowering it back down again at your own pace.*

You may like to stay with this movement, or you may like to challenge your balance even more by steadying your weight on one leg, and experimenting with moving your other foot a little higher, perhaps out in front of you, out to the side, or behind you, then bringing it back down again in your own time. [Therapist demonstrates these options and continues to engage in the movement activities.] *Feel free to continue with this lifting and lowering movement on the other side, challenging your balance as much or as little as you like, always coming back to a place of balance and stability.*

Rounding the spine: *For this next activity, I recommend coming into a seated position if that's comfortable for you (you can also do this standing) and when you're ready, begin to bring your* *awareness to your spine, maybe even moving your spine forward and backward or side to side, noticing how solid yet flexible your spine is.*

You may like to experiment with rounding your spine forward and backward. Begin by brining your hands to your knees, then press into your knees to help round your spine backward. You can even tuck your chin into your chest, rounding your spine toward the back of the room. [Therapist demonstrates this option and continues to engage in the movement activities.] *At your own pace, you may like to bend your spine forward. You can pull into your knees with your hands to help uncurl and bend your spine toward the front of the room, maybe even extending your chin up toward the ceiling. Then, when you're ready, rounding your spine backward again, tucking your chin in toward your chest. You can experiment with rounding and curving your spine forward and backward, at your own pace. How big or how small your movements are is completely up to you. You may even like to pair this movement with your breath: breathing out as you round your spine backward, breathing in as you bend your spine forward, reaching your chin upward.*

You may like to stay with this forward and backward movement, or you can experiment with moving side to side, or even making circles, perhaps pressing your hands into your knees to help move your spine in whichever way feels most beneficial to you right now.

Settling in the center: *And when you're ready, see if you can make your movements smaller and smaller, and a little smaller, until the movement becomes so small it is like you are hardly moving* [therapist demonstrates this], *and you come to a place that feels settled, that feels like your center. Allow yourself to explore this settled place for a moment, noticing that this is your center. Maybe even placing a hand there, where you notice your center in your body.*

Art activity for centering: *On a piece of paper, use the art materials to represent your center in any way you like—perhaps with symbols, color, shapes, lines, or words. There is no right or wrong way. This is just for you to remember this sense of centeredness in your body.* [Therapist leaves time for the client to complete their image.]

Applying the skill: *These activities can help you find your center and your balance whenever you need to. Use your artwork as a reminder of your center, that it is always there, and you can come back to it whenever you'd like.*

Scale of presence reassessment: *Where are you at now on your scale of presence? Do you notice any shifts? What was helpful for you about this activity? Was there anything that wasn't helpful?*

A—ANCHORING AND GROUNDING INTO THE EARTH

This practice explores different ways to notice and interact with sensations of pressure, and of being supported by a surface and the earth. The client is invited to use their feet to experience being firmly anchored and planted into the earth. They are then invited to listen to their body to make a movement, or take a step, and then anchor again. Even deciding which direction to move in and how to move is an empowering way for clients to experience ownership over their bodies and choices. The client is then invited to visually represent being connected to a supportive surface using art materials, further enhancing their engagement with this activity and creating a visual image that can act as a reminder to apply this new skill to their daily life. See Figure 2.13 as an example image created by MS.

Figure 2.13 Example artwork representing being supported and held by a surface in the Anchoring activity.

Script for A

Introduction: *We will now explore the sixth letter of the COME BACK tool, "A": Anchoring and Grounding into the Earth. Have some paper and art materials ready. Check in: where are you at now on your scale of presence?*

Connecting to a surface: *You can begin this practice by sitting or standing, beginning to notice where your body makes contact with the surface underneath you—noticing the surface you're sitting on, or where your feet are connected to the floor. Maybe even noticing how underneath that surface, there is the earth, which is also supporting you here in this moment.*

You may like to begin to increase your awareness of the sense of gravity, which may feel like a gentle pull downward toward the earth. You can close your eyes if that seems helpful to you, just noticing the sense of gravity, that gentle pull. And as you notice that, bring your awareness to how the surface meets you there. You may like to explore any sensations of pressure or support by shifting your weight around on your feet or sit bones.

Anchoring through the feet: *From here, you can let your feet become your anchor, perhaps by spreading your toes and noticing all points of your feet that make contact with the floor, really planting or perhaps even pushing your feet into the ground, finding just the right amount of pressure for you.*

Lifting and grounding the feet: *If you're standing, you may like to take a step in a certain direction, any direction: forward, backward, or to the side. When you're ready, ground your feet back onto the floor, letting the earth meet you there.* [Therapist demonstrates this option and continues to engage in the movement activities.] *You could try this again, choosing which direction to step in, or what type of movement to make, and when you're ready, replanting your feet, pushing them into the ground, perhaps noticing a sense of pressure where your feet make contact with the floor. Take steps at your own pace, how big or how small your movements are is up to you. Each time, deciding what direction to move your body in and how to move. You may even experiment with making a rhythm with your movements, up and down, lifting and grounding.*

Art activity for anchoring: *If you'd like, you can use the paper and art materials to represent being supported by a surface underneath you, perhaps the sense of the ground, the earth, gravity, or something solid being present and available. What does it feel like to be supported? Use color, line, shapes, symbols, or words to represent being connected to this supportive surface in any way you would like. There is no right or wrong way to do this activity. This is just for you, to help you remember this sense of groundedness in your body.* [Therapist leaves time for the client to complete their image.]

Applying the practice: *Notice how connecting your feet to the ground can anchor you to the present moment, allowing you to be fully here instead of anywhere else, right here, where you and the ground make contact in this moment. You can try this anytime, with shoes or without shoes, on grass, sand, soil, or anywhere. The movement of pushing your feet into the ground and anchoring to the present moment can be very subtle, so you can do it without anyone noticing— even standing in a line-up somewhere! You can use your artwork as a reminder that the earth is always supporting you, in each moment and with each step, and you can connect to this support whenever it is helpful for you.*

Scale of presence reassessment: *Where are you at now on your scale of presence? Do you notice any shifts? What was helpful for you about this activity? Was there anything that wasn't helpful?*

C—CREATING CONTAINMENT AND CLOSURE

Developing a container can help increase a sense of control over mental activity and provide a secure place for any thoughts, sensations, or fragments of memories that cause distress or discomfort for clients. The skill of containment is a standard practice in Phase Two of EMDR; however, many clients struggle to engage with this activity due to the difficulties with visualization. This containment activity is body-based, using movement, gesture, and breath to increase engagement with each step of the process and to deepen the learning of this new skill. Additional containment and space from upsetting material is also provided by placing the container down in a secure place, such as in nature or with a protective figure. The client is then invited to visually represent their container and where it is securely held and protected as a reminder to apply this skill to their daily life. See Figure 2.14 as an example image created by MS.

Script for C

Introduction: *We will now explore the seventh letter of the COME BACK tool, "C": Creating Containment and Closure. Have some paper and art materials ready. Check in: where are you at now on your scale of presence?*

Figure 2.14 Example artwork of the Container activity.

Psychoeducation: *In this activity, you can create a container as a secure place to put away any uncomfortable thoughts, feelings, sensations, or memories that come up for you and pull you out of the present moment. The container provides a space for you to put these things away, so that you can return your attention to whatever it is you are doing in the present. It is important to know that putting things away does not mean that they're not important or that they need to be avoided. The container is really about keeping those things in a secure place, so that you can come back to them when you have the support and resources needed to give them your full attention.*

Creating the container: *Think of a container that can hold anything you need it to hold, and can take as much as you need it to take. It can be made of any type of material, and be any size. Let me know when something comes to mind.*

Opening and closing the container: *Think about how you open and close your container, ensuring that it opens and closes in a way that feels secure. Is there a gesture or movement that goes with that action?* [Therapist allows time for the client to experiment with gestures to open and close their container.]

Placing things in: *When you're ready, open your container—you can use your gesture if that's helpful. Now that it's open, let any images, feelings, thoughts, sensations, or memories go into it—remembering that it can take anything you need it to take. You can use movements or even your breath to help move things into your container.* [Therapist can mirror the client's movement to help put the material in.]

Closing the container: *When you are ready, you can close your container. You may like to use your movement or gesture to close the container fully. Check to make sure the container feels securely closed. You can add any layers or materials needed to make it feel as secure as possible.*

Art activity: *If you'd like, you can use your paper and art materials to draw your container. Use color, line, shapes, symbols, or words to represent anything about your container that feels important to you. There is no right or wrong way, this is just for you to remember this resource.*

Putting it down: *Think of where you would like to place your container for now. You don't have to carry it. Perhaps there is a particular spot or a place in nature where your container can be protected until you are ready to pick it back up again—or maybe there is a person or presence that could protect it for you. Go ahead and imagine yourself placing your container there, letting that place or presence hold it for you. You can use the movement or a gesture to help place it down, knowing you can pick it back up again when you are able to attend to what's inside.*

Art activity: *If you'd like, you can add this place or presence to your image in any way you would like. Use color, line, shapes, symbols, or words to represent anything about the place/presence holding your container that feels important to you. There is no right or wrong way.* [Therapist leaves time for the client to complete their image.] *Look at your image—notice how it feels to have space between you and all that you put away.*

Applying the skill: *This activity can be helpful any time you notice uncomfortable sensations, emotions, or thoughts arising from your body or mind. You can place them into the container and put it down, allowing you to refocus on the present moment, using your imagination, your movements, or even your breath—whatever is most helpful for you. You can also use your artwork as a reminder to practice this new skill of containment and closure.*

Scale of presence reassessment: *Where are you at now on your scale of presence? Do you notice any shifts? What was helpful for you about this activity? Was there anything that wasn't helpful?*

K—KINDNESS AND COMPASSION

This practice is an arts-based adaptation of Loving-Kindness meditations, which are part of Buddhist tradition and have been shown to have beneficial therapeutic effects such as the increase of positive affect and self-compassion (Hoffman et al., 2011). Self-directed compassion is an important part of trauma treatment as negative self-concept, shame, and self-criticism are core symptoms of complex trauma (Cloitre, 2020). The art directive invites clients to externally express positive thoughts and feelings toward others. They can then use the artwork as an external source of positive feelings and even physically turn the image to direct the love and kindness back toward themselves, making it more concrete and tolerable, which is especially important for clients who become dysregulated by positive affect. This activity also aims to bring attention to one's resources by honoring personal strengths and the ability to overcome challenges. See Figure 2.15 as an example image created by MS.

Script for K

Introduction: *We will now explore the eighth letter of the COME BACK tool, "K": Kindness and Compassion. Have some paper and art materials ready. Check in: where are you at now on your scale of presence?*

Psychoeducation: *This practice is about practicing kindness and compassion toward ourselves and others, which can increase a sense of peace and well-being here in the present moment.*

Settling the body: *You can begin by coming into a position that feels comfortable, making any adjustments that help you feel settled. Begin to shift your attention to the muscles of your face, and see if you can let any tension in your facial muscles go, perhaps by squeezing the muscles around your eyes and face, and perhaps even giving your face and head a little massage to help release any tension. You may like to shift your attention down to your shoulders, noticing if there is any tension you may*

Figure 2.15 Example artwork of directing love and kindness outward and inward.

like to release right now, perhaps tensing the muscles in your shoulders for a few moments and letting them drop back down again. And again, you could even give your shoulder muscles a little massage to help them let go of any tension.

Love and kindness toward others: *Now see if you can bring the image to mind of someone you care about, perhaps someone comforting and supportive, or even a loving animal. You might imagine them right here with you, by your side, noticing any feelings that come up when you think about their presence. You may notice a feeling of warmth and kindness growing and expanding inside your heart.*

Art activity: *If so, see if there is a color that goes with those feelings of warmth, love, and kindness. You can begin to direct these tender feelings in your heart outward, toward anyone who you think might need this love and kindness right now. If you'd like, you can use the art materials to direct these warm feelings in your heart outward, sending them using color and lines on your paper. You may even like to send them positive thoughts or warm wishes. If so, feel free to say them out loud or to yourself as you direct those thoughts toward them—you may even like to include these words in your image.*

Love and kindness toward oneself: *Now take a moment and see if you can direct these tender, warm feelings toward yourself. You may like to turn your image around, so that the color and lines being directed outward are now facing you. Begin to let those tender feelings and warm wishes come toward you, taking them in just a little bit at a time, with each breath. What might it feel like right now to honor yourself and your strengths, and your inner resources, by sending warmth and tenderness inward? Add any colors or lines to your image, maybe even compassionate words that you would like to send toward yourself.*

Self-compassion: *Notice how your body responds as you let this kindness and compassion in. If you notice any positive or neutral sensations, take a moment and let them expand with each breath, allowing those sensations to reach any part of you that needs kindness and compassion. When you're* *ready, bring your attention back into the room, knowing that you can practice sending and receiving kindness and compassion anytime that it may feel helpful to you.*

Applying the skill: *It is normal that we can get stuck in thinking patterns where we criticize and are unkind to ourselves. Practicing this new skill of kindness and compassion can help develop new patterns that increase a sense of ease and well-being. You can do this activity as often as you like, remembering that developing new patterns takes practice and repetition.*

Scale of presence reassessment: *Where are you at now on your scale of presence? Do you notice any shifts? What was helpful for you about this activity? Was there anything that wasn't helpful?*

CONCLUSION

The COVID-19 pandemic has necessitated a shift to online practice for many EMDR therapists in order to meet the continued and increasing need for psychological support during this global crisis. In the beginning stages of the pandemic, there was a lack of evidence to support the efficacy of online EMDR; consequently, many therapists felt anxious that shifting to online practice would compromise the quality of their work and be ineffective or unethical. Preliminary research is now emerging that shows online EMDR to be an effective and promising alternative to in-person EMDR (Mischler et al., 2021; McGowan et al., 2021).

According to Mischler et al. (2021), further research into characteristics and diagnoses that might contraindicate the use of online EMDR is the necessary next step. As the research continues to advance in this area, there is the risk that online EMDR for clients presenting with dissociation may be contraindicated, especially as commonly used grounding techniques can be triggering or inadequate for clients with dissociative symptoms, as different parts of self may respond differently to the activities (Kezelman & Stavropoulos, 2020). The authors believe that developments in the field must strive to make online trauma reprocessing safe for vulnerable clients who face barriers to accessing in-person services due to constraints in time, finances, mobility, geographical location, or other factors that reinforce vulnerabilities. Instead of contraindicating online EMDR for clients who present with dissociation, the authors believe that our understanding of Phase Two of EMDR must be expanded to increase safety and readiness for reprocessing. The COME BACK Tool provides a comprehensive framework for managing symptoms of complex trauma and building somatic skills and resources that help make reprocessing safe. By integrating movement and the creative arts therapies, the whole body is engaged for a present-moment experience and provided with a concrete, external focus so mindfully connecting to thoughts, feelings, and sensations is more tolerable and titrated. New research on EMDR over telehealth must consider new and innovative tools that make online EMDR therapy safer for clients who present with complex trauma and dissociation. This places the ethics of accessibility at the forefront of further research in order to increase access to effective trauma treatment for vulnerable populations online.

REFERENCES

Addo, I. Y. (2020). Double pandemic: Racial discrimination amid coronavirus disease 2019. *Social sciences & humanities open, 2*(1), Article 100074. https://doi.org/10.1016/j.ssaho.2020.100074

Blore, D., & Holmshaw, M. (2009). EMDR "blind to therapist protocol". In M. Luber (Ed.), *Eye movement desensitization and reprocessing (EMDR) scripted protocols: Basics and special situations* (pp. 233–240). Springer Publishing Co.

Boon, S., Hart, O. v. d., & Steele, K. (2016). *Treating trauma-related dissociation: A practical, integrative approach* (Norton Series on Interpersonal Neurobiology). W. W. Norton.

Boyd, J. E., Lanius, R. A., & McKinnon, M. C. (2018). Mindfulness-based treatments for posttraumatic stress disorder: A review of the treatment literature and neurobiological evidence. *Journal of psychiatry & neuroscience, 43*(1), 7–25. https://doi.org/10.1503/jpn.170021

Cloitre, M. (2020). ICD-11 complex post-traumatic stress disorder: Simplifying diagnosis in trauma populations. *The British journal of psychiatry, 216*(3), 129–131. https://doi.org/10.1192/bjp.2020.43

Cloitre, M., Courtois, C.A., Ford, J. D., Green, B. L., Alexander, P., Briere, J., Herman, J. L., Lanius, R., Stolbach, B. C., Spinazzola, J., Van der Kolk, B. A., & van der Hart, O. (2012). *The ISTSS expert consensus treatment guidelines for complex PTSD in adults.* https://istss.org/ISTSS_Main/media/Documents/ComplexPTSD.pdf

Dennison, P. E., & Dennison, G. (2010). *Brain gym.* Hearts at Play.

EMDRIA International Association. (2020). *Guidelines for virtual EMDR therapy.* https://www.emdria.org/wp-content/uploads/2020/04/Virtual_TG_Report_for_Member.pdf

Emerson, D. (2015). *Trauma-sensitive yoga in therapy: Bringing the body into treatment.* W. W. Norton.

Farb, N., Daubenmier, J., Price, C. J., Gard, T., Kerr, C., Dunn, B. D., Klein, A. C., Paulus, M. P., & Mehling, W. E. (2015). Interoception, contemplative practice, and health. *Frontiers in Psychology, 6,* 763. https://doi.org/10.3389/fpsyg.2015.00763

Fisher, J. (2017). *Healing the fragmented selves of trauma survivors: Overcoming internal self-alienation.* Taylor & Francis.

Follette, V. M., Briere, J., Rozelle, D., Hopper, J., & Rome, D. I. (Eds.). (2015). *Mindfulness-oriented interventions for trauma: Integrating contemplative practices.* The Guildford Press.

Gunter, R. W., & Bodner, G. E. (2009). EMDR works... but how? Recent progress in the search for treatment mechanisms. *Journal of EMDR Practice and Research, 3,* 161–168. https://doi.org/10.1891/1933-3196.3.3.161

Hinz, L. D. (2019). *Expressive therapies continuum: A framework for using art in therapy.* Taylor & Francis.

Hofmann, S. G., Grossman, P., & Hinton, D. E. (2011). Loving-kindness and compassion meditation: potential for psychological interventions. *Clinical psychology review, 31*(7), 1126–1132. https://doi.org/10.1016/j.cpr.2011.07.003

Kezelman, C. A., & Stavropoulos, P. A. (2020). *Practice guidelines for identifying and treating complex trauma-related dissociation.* https://blueknot.org.au/product/practice-guidelines-for-identifying-and-treating-complex-trauma-related-dissociation-digital-download/

Knipe, J. (2014). *EMDR toolbox: Theory and treatment of complex PTSD and dissociation.* Springer Publishing Company.

Lichtenstein, A. H., Berger, A., & Cheng, M. J. (2017). Definitions of healing and healing interventions across different cultures. *Annals of palliative medicine, 6*(3), 248–252. https://doi.org/10.21037/apm.2017.06.16

Lynch, T. R. (2018). *Radically open dialectical behavior therapy: Theory and practice for treating disorders of overcontrol.* Context Press.

Ma-Kellams C. (2014). Cross-cultural differences in somatic awareness and interoceptive accuracy: a review of the literature and directions for future research. *Frontiers in psychology, 5.* https://doi.org/10.3389/fpsyg.2014.01379

McGowan, I. W., Fisher, N., Havens, J., & Proudlock, S. (2021). An evaluation of eye movement desensitization and reprocessing therapy delivered remotely during the Covid-19 pandemic. *BMC psychiatry, 21,* Article 560. https://doi.org/10.1186/s12888-021-03571-x

Mischler, C., Hofmann, A., Behnke, A., Matits, L., Lehnung, M., Varadarajan, S., Rojas, R., Kolassa, I-T., & Tumani, V. (2021). Therapists' experiences with the effectiveness and feasibility of videoconference-based eye movement desensitization and reprocessing. *Frontiers in psychology: Psychology for clinical settings, 12.* https://doi.org/10.3389/fpsyg.2021.748712

Nijenhuis, E. R. S., Spinhoven, P., Vanderlinden, J., van Dyck, R., & van der Hart, O. (1998). Soma-toform dissociative symptoms as related to animal defensive reactions to predatory imminence and injury. *Journal of abnormal psychology*, *107*, 63–73. https://doi.org/10.1037//0021-843X.107.1.63

Nijenhuis, E. R. S. (2009). Somatoform dissociation and somatoform dissociative disorders. In P. F. Dell & J. O'Neil (Eds.), *Dissociation and dissociative disorders: DSM-IV and beyond* (pp. 259–277). Routledge.

Ost, L. G. (1988). Applied relaxation vs progressive relaxation in the treatment of panic disorder. *Behaviour Research and Therapy*, *26*(1), 13–22. https://doi.org/10.1016/0005-7967(88)90029-0

Parnell, L. (2008). *Tapping in: A STEP-by-step guide to activating your healing resources through bilateral stimulation.* Sounds True.

Porges, S. W. (2021). *Polyvagal safety: Attachment, communication, self-regulation.* W. W. Norton.

Porges, S. W. (2011). *The polyvagal theory: Neurophysiological foundations of emotions, attachment, communication, and self-regulation* (Norton Series on Interpersonal Neurobiology). W. W. Norton.

Price, M., Spinazzola, J., Musicaro, R., Turner, J., Suvak, M., Emerson, D., & van der Kolk, B. (2017). Effectiveness of an extended yoga treatment for women with chronic posttraumatic stress disorder. *Journal of Alternative and Complementary Medicine, 23*(4), 300–309. https://doi.org/10.1089/acm.2015.0266

Shapiro, F. (2017). *Eye movement desensitization and reprocessing (EMDR) therapy: Basic principles, protocols, and procedures* (3rd Ed.). Guilford Publications.

Siegel, D. J. (2010). The mindful therapist: A clinician's guide to mindsight and neural integration. W.W. Norton & Co.

Spiegel, D. (2018). Integrating dissociation. *American journal of psychiatry*, *175*(1), 4–5. https://doi.org/10.1176/appi.ajp.2017.17101176

Spinazzola, J., Rhodes, A. M., Emerson, D., Earle, E., & Monroe, K. (2011). Application of yoga in residential treatment of traumatized youth. *Journal of the American psychiatric nurses association, 17*(6), 431–444. https://doi.org/10.1177/1078390311418459

Taylor, J., McLean, L., Korner, A., Stratton, E., & Glozier, N. (2020). Mindfulness and yoga for psychological trauma: systematic review and meta-analysis. *Journal of trauma & dissociation, 25*(5), 536–573. https://doi.org/10.1080/15299732.2020.1760167

van der Hart, O., Nijenhuis, E. R. S., & Steele, K. (2006). *The haunted self: Structural dissociation and the treatment of chronic traumatization* (Norton Series on Interpersonal Neurobiology). W. W. Norton.

World Health Organization (2020). *International statistical classification of diseases and related health problems* (11th ed.). https://icd.who.int/

CHAPTER 3

FROM TRAUMA TO RECOVERY
Group Work with Refugees and Displaced Youth

Jocelyn Fitzgerald

Cultural humility strategies included a self-reflective process by examining the experience within individual and collective healing models, consultation from both Ethiopian and Eritrean mental health professionals, access to training, and culturally appropriate modes of intervention. Discussion includes critical analysis of how EMDR and art therapy might complement healing strategies in two cultures and be used efficiently within refugee communities. This chapter contributes to the dialogue around culturally humble application of Western modalities of treating trauma.

There are more displaced people now than at any other time in recorded human history. The refugee population is growing in the United States and abroad. Therapists must provide culturally sensitive services to this population and be willing to work in a group setting to provide services to all in need.

Eye Movement Desensitization and Reprocessing (EMDR) offers one of the most potent tools for treating Post-Traumatic Stress Disorder (PTSD), and art therapy offers significant value for creative expression and deeper insight (Beasley, 2018). As adolescents make the shift from parental to peer influence, group work provides a means for youths to develop and access their own wisdom. This chapter highlights cultural and clinical considerations while exploring art therapy and EMDR with refugee youth in a community group setting in the United States and Ethiopia. Cross-disciplinary approaches focused on the strengths of both individuals and the community for healing from individual and collective traumas.

The United States group—a multi-year program—followed several principles: encouraging the adolescents to lead, maintaining an open curiosity around creativity, and holding space for cultural strengths. Creative interventions were used to further interweave EMDR into the group setting.

In Ethiopia, training in Western models such as EMDR and art therapy is prohibitively expensive for most practitioners. Services are costly for clients, and access to these models in developing countries is limited. This chapter challenges elitist therapy practices in developing countries by suggesting alternative ways to incorporate EMDR and art therapy in trauma-informed community-based settings for practical change and growth.

During a two-week cultural exchange workshop in Ethiopia, local community leaders collaborated with Caucasian female therapists from the United States to incorporate art therapy and a modified EMDR protocol into the traditional ways of supporting and caring for refugee minors. The collaboration required a shift in EMDR and art therapy models from pathology-focused and individualistic practice to a positive, developmentally, and culturally appropriate collective approach. The process was researched and documented using qualitative and quantitative approaches and a self-reflective process by the therapists to embrace and consistently maintain a culturally humble stance.

DOI: 10.4324/9781003156932-4

CHAPTER PURPOSE

EMDR provides protocols for short-term interventions that focus on natural disasters and other types of intense situations. There are also EMDR protocols for ongoing groups. Both group types—short-term intensive and long-term—are addressed. The latter focused on relationship building along with using art therapy and EMDR. General guidelines are offered for conducting long-term psychotherapeutic art therapy and EMDR in a group setting. The importance of the therapeutic relationship in the emotional healing process is supported with vivid examples.

HOW ART THERAPY OPENED THE DOOR

My background as an art therapist led to the opportunity to work cross-culturally when an International Foster Care program with Catholic Community Services for adolescent boys invited me to work with their organization in the United States. The sponsors of the program recognized that art therapy provided the participants with a means to communicate while they developed emotional communication skills. Saying yes to that opportunity radically changed the trajectory of my practice and my understanding of how the combination of art therapy and EMDR can transform the lives of traumatized youth.

As a board-certified art therapist and an EMDR consultant, my early work focused primarily on emotionally disturbed adolescents struggling with self-harming behavior. Art gave them a tool to express themselves in ways that words could not. The nuanced nature of art's use of color, scale, and symbolism provided a window to assess their emotional state and developmental level. Using art therapy with complex trauma clients gave me the ability to play with metaphors that would be difficult to access with words. For example, using stained glass as a medium, the very tools of self-harm at first seemed counterintuitive, yet showed them how much I trusted them in this setting. They were able to both literally and metaphorically use the pieces of broken glass to create something whole and new. While giving teens glass to work with carried some risk, they were closely supervised in individual sessions—creating a space for them to express themselves in a novel way. All the teens reported that being trusted played a role in the result of how they felt about themselves. Their self-harming behavior stopped.

Working with refugee teens from Eritrea and Myanmar in the United States inspired me to take my experience abroad working with refugee teens for two weeks from Camp Shimelba on the Northern Ethiopia border. Like the refugee teens I worked with in the United States, the teens in Camp Shimelba also migrated from Eritrea. This chapter is based on the learning that came about from my active involvement in two group programs and the importance of applying both EMDR and art therapy together in group settings when working with refugee populations.

Grounding Framework before Diving into Casework

- Who refugees are
- Why group work is ideal for teens and refugees from collectivist cultures
- Trauma, PTSD, and the specific dynamics driving Eritrea's mental health crises

- The role of art therapy group work with teens and refugees
- A modified EMDR protocol interwoven with art therapy to address large-scale trauma
- Essential therapist prep in working with refugee populations

WHAT DOES IT MEAN TO BE A REFUGEE?

A refugee is an individual forced, for safety reasons, to leave their country due to war, violence, or persecution (UNHCR, n.d.). Refugees typically cannot return to their homes or are afraid to.

WHY GROUP WORK IS IDEAL FOR REFUGEES AND TEENS

Making the Case for Group Work with Collective Cultures

Group work provides an opportunity for people to come together, converse about their situation, and exchange ideas to help stimulate new alternative solutions to solve problems (Metcalfe, 1998). This simulating what is also experienced in the collective cultures of East Africa, where the emphasis is on the needs of the group rather than the individual, where it is common for individuals to find support within the group setting.

When refugees come to new countries, sharing space and time with others who share similar cultural backgrounds and experiences offers normalizing and healing. This helps refugees connect to cultural resources for healing and strengthens their sense of identity while they adapt to a new and different culture.

The need for social interconnectedness was readily apparent with the group of refugee boys that I worked with in the United States. Each Sunday, they would spend over an hour driving to a church or mosque where people came from their home country. The entire day would be spent speaking the same language and eating familiar foods together. When we met on Sunday evening, they brought their native food and stories to share.

Collectivist versus Individualistic Cultures

Depending on the culture, group work can provide a familiar environment. Many African cultures—including Ethiopia and Eritrea—are highly collectivist. Collectivist cultures focus on relationships, group obligations, and interpersonal harmony. The group can act as a place for individuals to express feelings, symbols, and shared experiences. In many African countries, there is a culture of singing and dancing together in a circle, and in this way, refugees can share their special cultural identity. In Ethiopia, this is reflected in the way the meals are presented—on a circular plate where everyone shares. Conversely, Western cultures—particularly in the United States—are highly individualistic. Individualistic cultures focus on self-interest, self-expression, and the uniqueness of every person. Working within this group gave me an opportunity to notice both the societal pressures of individualism and the teens' native collectivism.

The Power of Group Work with Adolescents

There are many powerful benefits to having teens participate in group therapy. I experienced firsthand the effect that group therapy can have in reducing feelings of isolation, getting wisdom from their peers, and finding inspiration to deal with internal struggles. The teen years are a time in our life when peers are one of the greatest influences, a steppingstone for relating to others whose ideas may differ from their parents or adults in their lives. In the process of pulling away or individuating from the adults they eventually determine their own thoughts and feelings. This is often the natural progress toward adulthood.

When I started as a therapist, I worked for a school with emotionally disturbed adolescents. The school had group therapy five days a week. At one point, Maria (not her actual name), a young gay Latinx teen, confronted Lucas (not his actual name), an 18-year-old neo-Nazi. Lucas just shared with the group that his father caught him smoking cigarettes. Maria boldly called Lucas out on his behavior, stating, "You're too smart to do that. Only stupid people smoke." I distinctly remember holding my breath, waiting for what could have been an angry answer, but instead of getting mad, he took in her words. Soon after that group, Lucas reported that he quit smoking. We will never know if Maria provided the inspiration for him to quit smoking, but either way, that experience created growth and change for both of them. After that interaction, Maria was more empowered to speak up in the group setting, and when she did, Lucas always listened. This exchange would not have been the same if one of the therapists had suggested Lucas quit smoking. When teens realize they are not alone in their feelings and have ideas to help others, they feel empowered. In group therapy, teens discover a sense of relief and hope while talking to peers about their experiences. Knowing that they are not battling trauma alone helps overcome struggles in a supportive environment.

THE MENTAL HEALTH OF ERITREAN REFUGEES

Eritrea: A Mental Health Crisis

Within Eritrea, many children as young as five years old make the treacherous border crossing from Eritrea into Ethiopia on their own or in small groups of children as unaccompanied minors. Given this backdrop, it is not surprising that refugees experience elevated levels of PTSD. Few receive treatment (Fazel, Reed, Panter-Brick, & Stein, 2011). In a 2021 Swiss Biomed central research study of Eritrean youth, researchers found nearly half (48.5%) of the youth met diagnostic criteria for PTSD. For many Eritrean youth, the mental health consequences of living in a refugee camp, family separation, and displacement combined to create depression and anxiety. An April 2021 *Guardian* news story reported on a group of four unaccompanied Eritrean youth all committed suicide within a 16-month period. The article speculated that a lack of mental health services, coupled with data that refugees continue to experience an elevated level of stress even after they arrive in asylum countries—primary risk factors contributing to a high suicide level.

Historical Trauma and Its Impact on Eritrean Adolescents

Historical trauma—a term that emerged from recent Indigenous culture research—is defined as

> cumulative emotional and psychological wounding over the lifespan and across generations, which emanates from massive group trauma.... Historical trauma response often includes depression, self-destructive behavior, suicidal thoughts and gestures, anxiety, low self-esteem,

anger, and difficulty recognizing and expressing emotions. It may include substance abuse, often an attempt to avoid painful feelings through self-medication.

(Wiechelt, Gryczynski, Johnson, & Caldwell, 2012)

From famine to war, in Ethiopia and Eritrea, there has been little reprieve from stress and trauma on the social system and for individuals. When Eritrean teens migrating to a new country go untreated, the cumulative trauma often carries a lasting negative effect on their mental health.

Youth and Trauma

Within the refugee population, it is not uncommon that multiple traumatic experiences occur over their lifespan, particularly for those lacking in resources, members of vulnerable populations who are susceptible to aggressions from others, and those oppressed by institutionalized systems. Children and youth often manifest amazing resilience in the aftermath of traumatic experiences, particularly when the trauma is a single incident. However, youth who have experienced multiple traumas often are plagued with a history of anxiety and are likely to be at a higher risk for showing PTSD symptoms.

The American Psychological Association determined youth dealt with trauma in three ways: first, it played out as mood problems, then negative perceptions, and finally somatoform symptoms. With the youth in the United States, we observed tempers that would easily flare up when there was a miscommunication. The boys' foster parents reported that fights would break out in the home around minor arguments. Refugee youth sometimes felt they were not a fit with their foster families due to negative perceptions because of cultural or communication misunderstandings. The boys' somatoform symptoms manifested themselves in the form of migraine headaches, stomachaches, and nightmares.

Safety and Support for Trauma Survivors

Engaging in group work was important for both the refugees living in the United States and the refugees within the Ethiopian camp. Most of the participants in both groups experienced trauma and dislocation from their culture and ethnicity. Traumatic events take up a central position in the survivor's mind. Often individuals who experience extreme trauma withdraw and create strong boundaries to protect themselves (Carswell, Blackburn, & Barker, 2011). Thus, group treatment focused on softening rigid boundaries and redefining a posttraumatic personality, a connection forged through shared experiences. Groups provide participants with the opportunity to become involved in others' lives and difficulties within a safe setting. It also invites individuals to keep their boundaries open while fostering a sense of psychological safety. In both the United States and Ethiopia, probably the most profound of the psychological challenges the refugees face is the nature and degree of losses endured and their need for real and intense mourning. Within the group setting, that grief and loss can be shared, and the isolation is lessened.

Healing from Trauma

The word "trauma" is translated from Greek to mean a metaphorical "wound." That etymology explains our concept of traumatized people's wounded psyche. The accepted idea is that what comes after the wound is healing; thus, a new concept emerged called post-traumatic growth, representing adaptive responses to trauma. Post-traumatic growth represents resilience and demonstrates a flexibility, and ability to bounce back from adversity.

The term "trauma" is also recognized as a Euro-American metaphorical idiom of distress that does not always coincide with other cultures' experiences in the aftermath of severe adversity (Marsella, 2010; Summerfield, 1999). Typically, in white middle-class Western culture communities, the process of overcoming adversity is the burden of the individual, and it usually requires personal effort with a therapist. Within non-Western groups, adversity is seen as a social problem, requiring a collective form of processing (Karasz, 2005). Often in these cultures, resilience cannot come by understanding an individual trait but rather by looking at the universal system of which the individual is a part. Within refugee camps, a noticeable emphasis is placed on promoting community resilience. Therefore, the protocol using group processing with EMDR and art therapy is culturally appropriate. Art therapy in conjunction with EMDR helps strengthen communal bonds and provides novel opportunities to build new norms around what people have experienced.

Working with PTSD

It is also critical that practitioners address their own unresolved personal issues regarding culture, privilege, and oppression (Backos, 2021). Working with refugee clients diagnosed with PTSD requires a therapist to have both personal awareness and an intellectual understanding of both trauma and cultural humility. Understanding how trauma is encoded within neuropsychological components of PTSD is essential when working with any population. When working with refugees, it is imperative that a mental health provider also understands the depth of the oppression, discrimination, and trauma of their experience of fleeing from their home country. A therapist who chooses to work with refugees and trauma must master an awareness of the triggers specific to this population and their unique avoidance strategies. With the US teen refugees I worked with, I saw this play out in the form of social withdrawal or angry outbursts because of misunderstandings or a sense of not feeling connected to their host country or family. Within the refugee camps, the avoidance showed up in the form of alcohol and illicit drug use.

Many traditional treatments for PTSD have emerged from a therapist with the empathic capacity to sit, explore the horrific trauma, the difficult reactions and sensations that this experience created [for the client]. The beauty of combining EMDR and art therapy is its ability to allow clients to process through their trauma [while] titrating their experience without becoming flooded or overwhelmed. It also shifts agency in the process from the therapist to the client who takes responsibility for decisions on the way therapy proceeds.

ART THERAPY AS A TOOL FOR REFUGEE HEALING

The Origin of Art Therapy with Refugee Groups

One of the earliest mentions of therapeutic art with a group of refugee children dates to the early 1930s when Edith Kramer and Friedl Dicker-Brandeis worked with refugee children in Austria. Dicker-Brandeis continued her work with children while imprisoned in a concentration camp in Czech Republic. A student from this early art therapy group reported that for hours every week Dicker-Brandeis managed "to create a fairy world in which the student would forget about the surroundings and hardship" (p. 43). Another youth said, "She didn't make us draw the concentration camp. Instead, she asked the students to draw or paint their inner world" (p. 53; Wix, 2009).

How Art Therapy Bridges Place and Time for Refugees

The German philosopher Martin Heidegger stated that "art is truth." He recognized that art transports us through time, allowing us to travel back in history and import past experiences into the here and now. We see this in the work of the refugees: their art is happening in the present, the images bridge us back to the past into ways of remembering, knowing, and being seen. Visual arts give them the power of a present tense from where they can name their terrible experiences and begin to heal them. Creating art can serve to find meaning. In the process of creating, memories are released. Even within the physical activity in the process of creating, as creators' hands and bodies move, those very movements enable them to reclaim lost power and become aesthetic experiences within their own bodies.

The arts provide a clinical pathway to reach individuals through their senses and promote the integration of traumatic memories, which can then lead to positive transformation. In literature on expressive arts therapy and working with refugees, there is a value in creating bridges through familiar music, imagery, dance, role-playing, and movement.

The longing for home is especially poignant when the original home is no longer accessible. Creative arts therapy can act as a temporary home for refugees who have been forced out of their home country, using their imagination to activate memories and then make a concrete reminder of their past (Callaghan, 1998). The art therapy space can help to regulate arousal and work through symbolized trauma within the art. Additionally, the creative arts not only provide a means for self-empowerment but also serve as a bridge to adjusting to and becoming part of their host country's community.

Using art aims to produce a product, which also results in the creation of symbolic reminders participants can relate to for further dialogue and exploration.

Through visual media, we repeatedly observed refugees reclaim their lives and sense of self through the stories they told in drawings of their home, their loved ones, and themselves. This act of strengthening their identities and experience creates a sense of momentary home, stability, and remembrance. Clearly defined activities kept within a specific timeframe left no room for uncertainty and strengthened the therapeutic relationship (Dieterich-Hartwell & Koch, 2017).

EMDR OVERVIEW AND INTERNATIONAL APPLICATION

Traditional EMDR

EMDR is a well-researched psychological treatment originally developed in the late 1980s by Francine Shapiro for clients struggling with PTSD. EMDR traditionally requires the individual client to recall the traumatic memory. The client is then asked a series of questions by a trained therapist. This rings the proverbial bell of the lived experience. Once the memory is activated, a series of bilateral movements are used intermittently with brief check-ins.

EMDR therapy has been recommended by the World Health Organization as a treatment of choice for PTSD (WHO, 2013). However, there is still a need for specific research regarding the use of EMDR to help the growing population of African refugees with PTSD symptoms.

EMDR Integrative Group Treatment Protocol for Ongoing Traumatic Stress (IGTP-OTS)

The EMDR-IGTP-OTS is a gentle combination of both art therapy and EMDR, using only bilateral tapping or the butterfly hug (BH). This model has been used around the world with enormous success in natural disaster settings, and substantial research supports its success (Jarero & Artigas, 2009).

The original use of the EMDR-IGTP-OTS was created in Mexico by Dr. Ignacio Jarero and Lucina Artigas, to be used with a large group of people who experienced the same natural disaster. Over time this protocol has adapted and changed in group sizes, with participants ranging from children to adults. This versatile protocol can be used with similar experiences of trauma or diverse trauma histories. For large groups within the refugee camp, this protocol combines teaching basic resources with deep breathing and safe state, processing the traumatic memories within the art, asking scaling questions with the subjective units of distress, using bilateral stimulations with butterfly hugs, and looking at a future template within the art.

Treatment resulted in improved sleep, mood stabilization, regular employment, and group participants actively helping other refugees in their community. Many mental health centers are increasing their usage of EMDR with their refugee clients (e.g., Lab, Santos, & De Zulueta, 2008; Robertson, Blumberg, Gratton, Walsh, & Kayal, 2013; Sjölund, Kastrup, Montgomery, & Persson, 2009). As the mental health field witnesses EMDR's effectiveness in the field of trauma treatment, many practitioners around the world are eager to learn more about this powerful therapeutic tool.

ESSENTIAL PREPARATION: DEVELOPING CULTURAL SENSITIVITY AND HUMILITY

"Developing *cultural competence* as a professional is a journey, not a destination" (Nickerson, 2017). Developing cultural sensitivity is essential preparation work for any clinician working cross-culturally.

Mental health professionals must be sensitive to understanding trauma through a cultural lens, especially when working outside of their own culture. This concept of cultural humility is a lifelong commitment to self-evaluation and self-critique to exploring the power and differentials while developing advocacy partnerships with vulnerable communities.

Three key pieces define cultural sensitivity:

1. To become aware of the cultural differences and similarities that exist without assigning value to them.
2. Noting that cultural differences and similarities between people exist and influence values, learning, and behavior.
3. Having a set of skills that allow you to understand and learn about people who have different cultural backgrounds than your own.

(Akiba &Miller, 2004)

To better understand and relate to my clients, I read and watched videos about their culture, learned about tools designed for working with youths for whom English was a second language, consulted with other therapists and teachers in the community who worked with refugees. Throughout my planning stage, I determined that embracing openness, curiosity, and flexibility would be essential in creating a safe group environment.

Examining and reviewing literature on art therapy, EMDR, and mental health professionals who can reflect critically on their work is strongly recommended as a core curriculum for therapists committed to working with vulnerable populations. When working with a refugee population, cross-cultural ramifications around power and privilege must be continually re-examined. This requires diligent, conscious examination of one's own underlying beliefs—around the division between us and them, awareness of power dynamics, and deliberately seeking ways to encourage those who may feel disempowered to express their own wants and needs. While art and EMDR therapists often deny their colonial logic bias, research suggests that those biases exist, but practitioners are unaware of them or how they unconsciously impact their behavior (Watson, 2013). Additionally, there is a prevalent underlying belief that Western psychology is more valid than folk or ethnic healing systems. This assumption is likely to create a barrier and undermine cross-cultural work.

EMDR has the potential to be a leader in the field of mental health services because of how culturally adaptive its model is to treatment. EMDR's success in alleviating the effects of trauma including culturally based trauma is well documented, with more than two dozen published randomized studies (Lee & Cuijpers, 2003). However, cultural competence is a perennial challenge. It is imperative that clinicians never stop objectively assessing their attitudes and beliefs, and that they strive to continuously stretch their skills and deepen their understanding of the cultures of the clients they work with.

CASEWORK: US-BASED

Goals

This section outlines the structure and interventions used within the international foster refugee program for teens in the United States group and illustrates the combined use of art therapy and EMDR in the group context. The group was composed of adolescent boys who came from Africa and Asia, where the risk of staying in their home country was more dangerous than fleeing. Ranging in age from 11 to 17, the boys came from cultures with a collectivist emphasis and where healing often occurred in a group context. Group dynamics and sharing came naturally for them. The group was a closed group with only five boys, to keep the conversations confidential and safe. There was no set end date for the program or even specific program objectives from the sponsor to know when the program would end.

Structuring the Group Work

Catholic Community Services hired me for this group work to help their clients and their foster families overcome the challenges they were experiencing in the boys' adjustment to a radically different culture from their home countries. I had the opportunity to design the program and structure the therapeutic work the way which best met these goals and the needs of the participants. As an ongoing group, I responded to unfolding themes as they emerged. My plan was to provide mental health support by incorporating art therapy and EMDR in a group context.

The meetings initially were weekly; over time the duration between sessions stretched out to twice a month. They were 90 minutes long, which allowed enough time to begin with an opening activity and to provide adequate closure at the end. It was important that each session followed a consistent opening and closing ritual to establish a strong sense of predictability. The group was important to support the boys in their transitions into a new family and culture. It also served as a place to process feelings of grief and loss. They all shared the knowledge that a return to their country of origin was associated with a deep longing, tempered with a fear that they might not ever see their home due to the hardships of war. My hope was that this new therapeutic environment offered safety and an opportunity to process what was vastly different in their new community.

Refugee or not, teens are on a roller coaster of hormones and experience a wide range of emotions. It is normal for them to have trouble grasping abstract thinking and connecting actions with consequences. "Your brains are still under construction," I would only half-teasingly remind them when the concepts of a particular group topic did not fully stick. The goals of the group were to explore identity, a sense of self, and emotion regulation skills. These were issues that I worked on with all my adolescent clients but seemed especially important when working with refugees, given their level of trauma, loss, and displacement. As the group progressed over the years, we also took on developmental transitions into adulthood.

Choosing the Setting

The setting was an important consideration. My therapy office was large enough to accommodate the small group, and created a calm and consistent place for them, with the added convenience of easy access to the art supplies already there.

Mobile Phone Use

One early decision we made as a group revolved around the use of mobile phones in our sessions. Each of the boys owned their own cell phones, and we talked about whether cell phones should be allowed in the group. The cell phone served as a translator when our language created a barrier to communication. The group also decided that it was fair for them to answer the phone if a family member called from their home country; this small gesture helped them regain a sense of control and connection. We also agreed to re-evaluate the use of phones in the group if it became too disruptive to the flow of the group and the connections, they were creating with each other.

Setting Expectations

Together we also created a list of group rules poster that I would hang during each session.

Group Rules

1. What was said in the group needed to stay in the group.

2. Passing was always an option if one did not want to answer a question or do an exercise.

3. Respect ourselves, others, and our art.

They all signed the poster and we discussed at length what each rule meant until they were understood.

Opening Rituals

Rituals were an important way to establish predictability. We opened each group with tea and hot cocoa. The drinks were a means to recognize and acknowledge that the boys came from cultures where tea and coffee ceremonies were a part of life (and none of the boys objected to substituting coffee for hot cocoa). Our opening ritual also gave the boys a moment to settle into the session. They took turns as the maker of tea or hot cocoa and enjoyed taking the drink orders and serving each other. The boys were also able to compare the ritual nature of the art therapy session with descriptions of coffee or tea making from their cultures. They linked this to the hospitality shown to guests in one's home with the preparation for the art therapy session.

Activities

After pouring the tea or hot chocolate, an art activity was introduced, and we would focus on a new theme or learning a new art skill. Themes included their experience of immigration, what their families were like, what the new host family was like, how school was going, and fun adventures that they had experienced back home and in the United States. Sometimes the group would focus on the latest news from their home countries and what was happening with their families.

For most of the session, we would tackle an art project. In the beginning, the projects provided a way for me to get to know the boys as individuals as well as get a sense of the group overall. As their skills evolved, the projects gave them an avenue to express their longing for their home country and their hopes for the future.

I came prepared with at least one idea for an activity, whether that was a new project or a continuation of one we had recently started. However, I paid close attention to what captured the boys' attention and what did not and followed that energy which sometimes spontaneously led to a new, completely unplanned activity.

This overriding theme of flexibility emerged in many contacts with these boys. They found multiple ways to simultaneously be close to their families yet independent and autonomous. They could choose different narratives from their cultural traditions to endorse and value the host society they wanted to adopt. These boys would often create new hybridized identities that combined different ethnic categories and could change according to the setting or context in which they found themselves. This corroborated with research that associated flexibility with better adjustment among youth (Berry, Phinney, Sam, & Vedder, 2006). This flexibility within the group led to more cultural sensitivity and group cohesion. Often an idea was presented and together the boys would decide whether they all wanted to follow my art directive or to create a new activity.

Closing Rituals

The closing ritual involved two steps. First, as a group, we reviewed and reflected on what we learned and what the boys got out of it. Second, the closing ritual involved putting music on and getting up and moving our bodies. Over time, these rituals evolved, while remaining consistent. They reinforced the foundation of trauma treatment: empowering the boys to create the changes they needed, yet still honoring a consistent safe environment.

As the weeks passed and the boys felt more comfortable, the closing rituals became more playful. We would create a circle in the middle of the art studio and the boys would take turns being the leader of the group. Whatever movement the leader did, everyone else would follow. They would make up elaborate dance moves, or try to have everyone do a one-handed pushup, then stand back and watch as we all tried to replicate what they did. These mirroring movements serve to strengthen the relationships through feeling seen, nonverbal connections, reciprocation, and create a deeper attachment. When we were done, they were ready to go out in the world.

The more that space was given to embracing all aspects of their huge transition, the more their collective resilience increased, along with their capacity to acculturate and integrate into their host country. This shift—a melding of cultures—also played out with the music played during sessions. Over time the music they played on the computer for our closing ritual changed from traditional music from their home countries to 2Pac rapper songs.

Field Trips

With parental permission, we also made some cultural field trips: eating out in local restaurants that served their homelands' food. This offered another way to honor and celebrate their connection to their cultural home while living in a foreign country. Together they shared stories around food and drink from their host countries over Ethiopian and Burmese cuisine. This also strengthened the therapeutic relationship and created a healthy attachment.

Additionally, this experience gave the boys a welcome respite from their now overly routine life, especially when compared to the relative freedom they enjoyed in their home country. As Westerners in a "free culture," we might not consider how rigid our lifestyles are in comparison to youths in oppressive societies that are devastated by war and cultural clashes. However, the boys reported that in the refugee camps they were sometimes free to wander at will and would often skip school to go swimming or watch a movie. In the United States, most youths find their days are rigidly directed by schedules and highly structured: woken up by an alarm clock, eating breakfast, going to school, doing homework, or other parentally approved activities, followed by a family dinner and bedtime.

Choosing Art Projects

When it comes to working with groups with little or no prior exposure to art concepts and materials, the first step is to realistically assess where the group is at in their skill level. Learning a new language is a skill that evolves with practice and experience, starting with simple concepts and words to build new learning. Learning a visual, expressive language is much the same: you begin with simple tasks and modes of expression, building the skills to communicate more complex and nuanced concepts using a broader selection of materials.

Art is a universal language that overcomes obstacles and sidesteps traditional spoken and written communication. With the complex problems refugees experience while their language skills are still limited in their host country, art offers a window to when interventions are needed and what they should focus on (Rubin, 2011). Art in its various forms can empower an individual who has experienced complex problems (Andemicael, 2013). Visual arts can contribute to the development of community and connection and help refugees reinforce their cultural identity (Kay, 2000). The use of art activities helped adolescents to cope with dilemmas, to be more creative at problem-solving with conflicts, to gain self-awareness and empathy for others (Rousseau & Guzder, 2008).

When a child experiences trauma it has a profound effect on the developing brain. This can influence the future cognitive functioning of the child. Trauma can rewrite both the body and the mind of the individual, which can result in dissociation or separation from the self (Hagood, 2000).

To bypass language issues and compensate for an initial skill level far younger than their chronological age in my group, we began by using collages. The use of collage followed the Expressive Therapies Continuum (ETC) model and is believed to contribute to the client's ability to regulate their emotions and continue to grow. The ETC offers a framework for art therapists in the selection of different art media and art directives that best relate to the client's particular needs at a developmental level (Lusebrink & Hinz, 2016). Using art therapy assessments, within Viktor Lowenfeld's stages of art the boys' skill level would be on par with a child at five or six years of age (Lowenfeld & Brittain, 1987). For example, when we first started, the boys could doodle or draw a circle with tiny stick legs for a body but drawing a face and connecting it to a proportional body was beyond their skill level.

Early on, I recognized the importance of finding art directives that were neither too easy nor too hard. I needed to be alert to multiple factors simultaneously: to the art media, to language, and to the nonverbal cues that a group member might need help with or encouragement in using the media chosen. For example, when they found images of flags from their home countries, we broke down each symbol and used the ruler to create straight lines rather than having me draw out the images for them. Simultaneously I became alert to the social interactions between the boys, the languages they were speaking, their tone of voice, speed, and cadence.

In the beginning, the communication between us consisted of art, charades, and a cell phone translation application. I asked the boys to use collage to decorate the portfolios they would use hold their future art pieces. Searching for images was a collaborative process and required patience because of the language barrier. The boys would think about image ideas they wanted to present in their art, and then pulling out their cell phones would type in the words they wanted to show me. I was reading cell phone words, nodding, reflecting, and shuffling through magazines right along with them to find images that would fit their collage. It was powerful to see the similarities within their magazine clippings: fast cars, pets, kids playing in nature. This exercise in creating together felt supportive and inclusive. I learned more about each boy, what they missed and what they hoped for in the future.

The sand tray became an exercise in storytelling, using metaphors, images in phase two of creating resources and safety. I learned many more details about what the boys had been through by looking at the figures, hearing their words, and recognizing their strengths. I discussed the skills the boys used to survive leaving their homes and families. At times, the boys would offer a suggestion of a toy that could add an added level of protection to the story.

One day a boy created a sand tray, told us a story, and then asked us to all close our eyes. We did. Then he told us to look at the sand tray and see what changed. We all took turns guessing. Finally, he held up the figure he had removed. This playful game taught us that he really wanted us to pay close attention to what he was doing within the art and with his words. After this, all the boys followed in this game of guessing what had changed and paying close attention.

As the sessions progressed, and their art skill developed, the projects evolved. The boys loved integrating their own images into their art. I would take pictures of them and print them out before the next session. Sometimes they would dress up for their photos. They also enjoyed sharing images from their home countries, photos of friends they had to leave in the camp, family photos from when they were little, and images of their new family pets. We would use their images in a variety of ways, such as tracing them with tracing paper, layered with wet paint to create peaceful places where they visualized themselves.

Pencils, paints, pastels, felt pens, crayons, clay, and other art materials we used were completely new to them. With access to a buffet of art options, time, and support in learning to use these new tools, their enthusiasm grew, and further fueled their creative growth. The more options they had to experiment with, the more innovation and resourcefulness blossomed in the art studio.

When the boys focused their artmaking on present moment experiences and on their resiliency, they became more engaged in both their artwork and the group process. This fostered a feeling of safety and cohesion within the group. It also developed their interpersonal learning and ability to work through catharsis, aligning well with some of the curative therapeutic group factors identified by Dr. Irvin Yalom, a pioneer of adolescent group work, and author of the *Theory and Practice of Group Psychotherapy* (Yalom, 1995). When a complicated issue came up in the art, we would pause and recognize the moment. I relied on the curative power of the group as we joined together using the EMDR protocol of fast bilateral movements to process the stressful memories, then as we found solutions within the art, we would install a positive reframe in the experience by doing slow bilateral movements.

Learning Together

As the boys' English improved, it only seemed fair for me to learn a new word or phrase from their culture each week. To learn:

- First, I wrote the words down on a piece of paper phonetically.
- Then I used my phone to record one of the boys saying the words slowly.
- Finally, I practiced throughout the week.

The boys appreciated my willingness to grow and learn alongside them and laugh at my mistakes. Toward the end of our work together, one of the boys told me "I really like it when you try to speak my language." Taking time to learn a few phrases in the boys' languages was an act of cultural sensitivity. It helped to balance the dynamics of the therapy relationship, learning more about their culture as part of a culturally affirming practice. Sharing this time and space with these boys became time to value and affirm their rich cultural history.

Celebrating Milestones through Art

At the beginning of the new year, we used an art directive designed to celebrate accomplishments. For this project, a cake was brought in with a container of frosting for each boy and cake-decorating materials. This project was a celebration of each of them and what they appreciated about themselves. They could create the cake to look however they wanted it to look. Again, introducing new art media brought a new level of enthusiasm and innovative art to the group.

Several of the boys traveled to a refugee camp outside of their home country without their birth certificates or information about their birthdays. As a result, like many refugees, the boys celebrated their birthday on January 1st. We discussed how birthdays were celebrated at home and how different birthdays were here in the United States.

Cultural Traditions and Missing Home

I am a firm advocate of letting my clients take an active role in the flow, determining what they want and need as it directly influences their growth. Sometimes that meant opening a session with an idea of how it would go and learning to let go and doing something completely different.

For example, one night as we enjoyed our usual opening ritual of sipping tea and cocoa, the boys started talking about the food they missed. They recognized that we ate many snacks here in the United States, something not typical back home. Then one of the Eritrean boys remembered that one of his favorite snacks was sweet popcorn with coffee. Another boy pulled out his phone and showed us a photo of him and a friend on a hill overlooking a valley in Ethiopia, drinking coffee, and eating popcorn.

Art and Play-Acting with Coffee and Popcorn

This moment inspired me to use art materials to help him express his longing for home. I grabbed some clay and started making a miniature bowl filled with white popcorn (Figure 3.1). Another boy started making a traditional Ethiopian coffee pot, and the group became an imaginary Ethiopian coffee ceremony. Deciding to invite the imaginary play to go further, I pretended to eat the popcorn. It was heartwarming to witness the group expressing homesickness while connecting. By engaging in each other's cultural traditions

Figure 3.1 Ethiopian coffee and popcorn ceremony made out of clay.

through the art materials and imaginative play therapy, there was a shared understanding of the effects of homesickness that helped to soothe this longing, bringing the memories into the present brought a deeper level of connection to the group dynamic. Playfully, I exclaimed, "This is the best popcorn I've ever eaten!"

There was a feeling of pride and nostalgia in bringing a piece of their culture into the room. While we passed the pretend popcorn around the table, another boy who had been creating his clay coffee pot asked, "Does anyone want coffee?" Half the boys in the group were from Eritrea and half were from Myanmar. The boys from Myanmar were excited and curious about the coffee traditions from Ethiopia. After the Ethiopian boys shared their coffee traditions the Myanmar boys talked about the tea traditions in their culture and how tea is used both as a hot drink and pickled for a food delicacy.

The Symbolism of Flags

When I asked the boys to tell me about both their foster and their home country families, I brought in images of families worldwide and then pointed to the flags from their countries of origin, and the countries they traveled to (Ethiopia and Thailand) before coming to the United States. They wanted to represent several different flags in their artwork to show the places they had lived.

The boys' desire to create images of their families quickly shifted to excitement about creating flags (Figure 3.2). How important a flag would be to the boys surprised me.

Figure 3.2 Flag made from popsicle sticks, paper, and makers. These flags were used in the model homes they made later.

Recognizing that, we quickly pivoted to several sessions centered around creating the flag of their choice. During the flag project, the art continued to grow in detail. By the end, each boy created several different-sized flags, painted and ready to hang in their new homes. The flags brought back memories of their journey, what was left behind, and their hope for a future where they could return home.

As the boys continued to develop skills in creating art with symbols and metaphors, they also became more confident in their use of language and communication. The boys were progressing up the developmental hierarchy of information processing and image formation. Using the ETC framework, it became clear that the boys were heading into the perceptual/affective level, which represents the interaction between awareness and the use of formal art elements. The perceptual side of experience shows the emotions, and the affective side shows the media with bright or intense colors that evoke affective awareness (Ichiki & Hinz, 2015; Lusebrink, 1991). Later, the boys created masks representing their internal feelings on the inside and how the boys believed the outside world viewed them. The masks, like the flags, used imagery that underscored how their internal world was intrinsically tied to their memories of home (Figure 3.3).

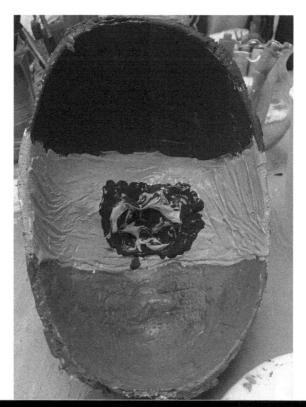

Figure 3.3 The boys chose to hand paint their country's flags on the inside of the masks they created. The inside was a representation of what they felt on the inside—a strong identification to their country of origin.

Skill Building through Art

As the sessions progressed, I demonstrated how to use paint and mix colors to create a rainbow of new colors. The boys boldly explored, laughed, and discovered the magic of mixing colors. I would demonstrate lines, shapes, and colors to create simple compositions. They grew more confident in using different media and eventually brought in art ideas to teach me. One of the boys would watch an art lesson on the computer between sessions to learn how to draw advanced animals and people. He would later come to the group and teach us how to draw his newest creation. This process clearly built a sense of proficiency and leadership, which was evident by the pride he displayed in each art lesson.

Reinventing Home

One rainy midwinter day, one of the boys started picking up popsicle sticks. Then, with the help of a hot glue gun, he began creating a shape that represented his home in the refugee camp. This led to many months of meetings when the boys worked on creating their elaborate homes. I looked forward to hearing each boy's latest ideas about what they wanted to add to their homes.

As one boy finished his home, he would start helping his friend; one would be holding the stick as the other would glue. Over time the boys painted the outside and the inside walls of their tiny homes. They added graffiti to the outside representing their love of art and friends. One boy added the words "I love art."

Linking Past and Future

Toward the project's end, an exciting moment came in the form of light and energy (Figure 1.5). When one of the boys noticed a battery-operated tea light in my office, all the boys decided they needed lights within their homes. Electricity was not something easily found in their camps. But in their imagination and this new creation, they could add electricity with these battery-operated tea lights. I brought in over two dozen tea lights that they could use however they wanted. The boys were thrilled to incorporate the lights into their houses (Figure 3.4). The day we turned off the lights to witness their illuminated homes was magical. I felt as if the group had created the perfect healing metaphor. The experience of seeing it come alive with twinkling lights moved us all.

Some were homes from their host country, and some were from the refugee camp where they lived together with other youth. The boys talked about home and what they missed. They all talked about missing friends in camp and how hard it was to say goodbye. We talked about the concept of home and how they could bring parts of their past into their current home. As their homes glowed with light and warmth, they too felt a connection to each other and their shared experiences.

Art for Attachment and Emotional Processing

The art therapy activities helped the boys build relationships, share culture, and create a straightforward way to communicate feelings. The art was also used to facilitate the new attachment relationships between participants and their foster parents. For example, on

Figure 3.4 An art model, one of the refugee boys made of his Ethiopian home—with electrical lights—a modern addition he wished it had.

Mother's Day, they all decided to copy a piece of artwork in my office to give to their foster moms. Again, I was reminded of how the group worked together and wanted to share in the same experience. Each painting felt different, but the general composition was the same, much like the group.

When art projects brought the boys' difficulties to the forefront, we would reinforce essential information by slowing down and creating art around big emotions that had turned into stressful behaviors. In those cases, the boys would create two pieces of art: one on what had happened and the other on what could have been an alternative solution. The act of artmaking can encourage authenticity, a space where the client can integrate different pieces of their identity through self-expression and can also begin to build a link to a new environment.

Integrating EMDR into Sessions

EMDR was integrated with the group experience during moments of installing positive resources with bilateral stimulation. The boys learned that doing these types of exercises was one way to "glue in" new information into our brains that felt soothing or positive. At the end of the meeting, we would go around and check in with what each boy would take from the group experience that would help him in the upcoming week. They might say, "I'm going to slow down. I am going to take three deep breaths before I react. I am going to take a nap if I am tired after school. I am going to draw if I feel upset." The boys discovered that they could self-soothe throughout the week by using bilateral stimulation and thinking of their favorite place back home or in their current home. We found that tapping was easiest form of bilateral movements to use as a group.

Using the EMDR-IGTP-OTS was remarkably effective with the teens during moments of dysregulation or when stress levels were too high. This model was effective in working with teens from unfamiliar cultures because by sharing similar experiences, they felt less isolated.

During the group process they did not have to talk about their traumatic experience, and they could instead express feelings within their art. This protocol was valuable in that it helped to minimize the barriers inherent with sharing traumatic experiences that they were not yet ready to talk about.

When we found that there was a topic they all shared and struggled with, we would spend time using this protocol to process the feelings. One common shared experience discussed was that all these teens missed their friends, who they had to leave behind in the refugee camp. One session was spent processing feelings around missing friends and feeling guilty that their friends could not be with them. identify the worst fragment of the event that they would like to process and draw a picture of it, then identify the subjective units of disturbance (SUDs) scale, then do the self-administered butterfly hugs. After doing four rounds of this they would turn the paper over and draw the future that served as an installation phase. This protocol provides a protective layer of privacy and protection, especially when dealing with issues that are sensitive (Jarero & Artigas, 2009).

Ending the Group

While there was no predefined ending, the group ended naturally. Some boys moved, other activities, such as taking on a job to send money home, took priority. Overall, the boys transitioned into adults and became independent. They were able to move forward successfully into new roles, responsibilities, and jobs.

As each boy left the program, we made them a goodbye celebration during the closing session. The meeting before, the boy who was leaving chose their favorite snack for us to share for the farewell celebration. We each made a piece of art for him to take as a keepsake. Some of the boys leaving also chose to create a piece of art to give to each member of the group. We went around the circle and everyone in the group each shared memories and their wishes for him.

The group achieved its ultimate objective: the boys grew up and found their place in both worlds without giving up their identity—the home they left behind and hoped to someday return to and the one where they lived now. Even though we've long since ended the program, thanks to the wonders of modern digital communication, the boys—now young men—remain in touch with each other, and I with them.

Lessons Learned

Over the course of our work together I learned many important lessons. It seemed paradoxical that joy was such a huge factor in each group session with these boys who had experienced so much significant loss. Yet the awareness of even a moment of joy seems to offer a glimpse that healing was indeed possible. I had not considered the impact of playfulness within the group setting. The playfulness and flexibility helped the boys select media and helped them regulate their emotions. "Play is a core element of attachment because it provides ample opportunities for the attunement that is necessary for developing emotional regulation and the anticipation of positive relations" (Kestly, 2014, p. 96).

Play provided an essential component of the connection and healing process. I wondered how much of these boys' childhood was bypassed because circumstances forced them to grow up and make tough decisions before their time. Some of the boys left home, traveling alone when they were only five years old.

For these teens, art and bilateral movements helped fill in some of the gaps of a missed childhood by providing a much-needed safe space to imagine and grow. Creativity and play go together with developing imagination, building dexterity, cognitive ideas, and emotional strength (Shonkoff & Phillips, 2000). With play, children engage and interact in the world around them. Play gives them a sense that they can master the world and conquer their fears while practicing different roles (Tamis-LeMonda, Shannon, Cabrera, & Lamb, 2004).

I used art and play to create attachment in which I would observe the boys' actions, joining in when asked, or holding space with gentle support. Creating a playful environment helped build a healthy foundation for the boys to explore their inner worlds, their relationships within the group, and to develop themselves as individuals. The work with art, play, and attunement filled a developmental gap that had been disrupted by their early childhood trauma. EMDR helped to deepen the new learning and integrate disruptive memories creating a new narrative and experience.

The refugee group in the United States created a safe way to keep parts of their identity alive and symbolically expand their identity by being in two places at once. Metaphorically, refugees experience encompasses having one foot in the host country and the other foot still in their home country. As they gain a sense of power and control over their situation, transformation and change can occur.

WORK IN AFRICA

Ethiopia's Mental Health Crises

My years of trauma-informed care working with Eritrean refugees in the United States inspired further research into the mental health climate in both Eritrea and Ethiopia. According to a 2015–2016 study by the National Mental Health Strategy (of Ethiopia) *for every 85 million Ethiopians, there are only three trained social workers, 40 practicing psychiatrists, and 14 psychologists* (Hanlon et al., 2019). In Ethiopia's rural areas, mental illness comprises 11% of the total burden of disease, but only 2% of the health budget is allocated to address mental health concerns (Desta, 2008).

Ethiopia: Continued Instability

Ethiopia's political climate is critically unstable. Only two months before we arrived in Ethiopia in June of 2018, the Prime Minister Abiy Ahmed was awarded the Nobel Peace Prize for ending the 20-plus year civil war. While it was a time of celebration and great hope, many Ethiopians were suspicious of Prime Minister Ahmed who they believe deliberately exacerbated hatred between different groups. Those concerns came to fruition, as the conflict in Ethiopia flared up to civil war proportions again in November 2020.

CASEWORK: ERITREAN YOUTHS IN ETHIOPIAN REFUGEE CAMP

Bringing EMDR-IGTP-OTS to Paraprofessionals in Ethiopia

EMDR-IGTP-OTS had already been used to train paraprofessionals in other parts of the world to treat trauma in a safe and straightforward way (Jarero & Artigas, 2018). To deliver training in EMDR-IGTP-OTS to the paraprofessionals living in refugee camp Shimelba, Ethiopia, I partnered with Kelly Smyth-Dent, an EMDR certified colleague with international experience. The training covered how to implement firsthand trauma-sensitive work, protocols, practice, supervision, and support. In the first part of the course, the paraprofessionals experienced the process themselves (Figure 3.5). Then, under our supervision, paraprofessionals provided EMDR-IGTP-OTS to the camp's refugee adolescents in small groups. Our objective was to validate the use of EMDR-IGTP-OTS for symptom reduction associated with PTSD, depression, and anxiety.

Paraprofessionals

Yibeyin Hagos, one of the few Ethiopia Camp Shimelba social workers, was interested in bringing trauma education and EMDR into the refugee camp where he was working with a group of paraprofessionals. These supportive adults were all refugees from Eritrea with their own stories of trauma ranging from rape, torture, and kidnappings for ransom (Figure 3.6). Each paraprofessional supported several dozen unaccompanied minors in the camp. The adults were leaders within the camp, nominated by their peers for their strong work ethic and their ability to connect with the youth in the camp.

Figure 3.5 Paraprofessionals in Ethiopia lead a group of Eritrean refugee camp girls.

Figure 3.6 A self-portrait of one of the paraprofessionals created to show what had happened to him when he was kidnapped.

Since many children in the refugee camp were unaccompanied minors, these parapro-fessionals served many roles. Their support ranged from helping a child get a toothbrush, to encouraging the child to attend school. They also offered refugee minors emotional support—assisting with everyday stressors and coping with overwhelming feelings. One of our goals was to make sure the training tools and techniques we provided the local paraprofessionals could be applied to their work and continue to be used long after we left Ethiopia. Upon leaving, a system was put in place for ongoing paraprofessional support and continued communication. Since the war in Ethiopia resumed, Camp Shimelba was decimated. However, I still hear from the paraprofessionals via email as they continue to help youth recover from PTSD in Addis Ababa the capital in Ethiopia, using and building on the knowledge they gained.

Art Material Selection Implications

Choosing which art materials to bring carried economic and environmental considerations. For example, bringing materials from the United States such as paper and crayons allowed us to implement the art protocol; these materials are available in a limited amount in the refugee camp. We discussed the implications of using art supplies not readily available and the economic privilege that was required to purchase these materials. A portion of the training was spent discussing how to use alternative tools to experience the art within the work, it was just as enriching and scientifically valid by using materials such as sticks, pencils, and rocks, to complete the art portion of the protocol (Jarero & Artigas, 2018). We discussed with the paraprofessionals that equally positive results could be achieved by using readily available materials. The success of the protocol is not dependent on expensive art supplies, the act of doing the art with any material delivers the same benefits.

Advantages of Art Therapy within a Structured EMDR Group Protocol

The art within the EMDR-IGTP-OTS gave key insights into the refugee experience and the integration of fragmented memories. This five-part drawing series was used to explore the shared experience of being a refugee. The last drawing would end with an image of how they see themselves in the future. We collected images of the artwork from both the teens we worked with for the two-day workshop and the social workers from the camp who practiced with their own experiences before working with the teens using the protocol. The ways they portrayed themselves throughout their art in self-portraits revealed the effects of forced migration and being disconnected from the trauma they had experienced within their bodies. This protocol supported the process of accessing traumatic memories and created distance where they could gain a new felt experience (Appleton & Spokane, 2001).

Accurately Applying Native Symbolism When Interpreting Artwork

While art therapists are trained to be circumspect before interpreting their clients' art, when working with refugees, it is particularly imperative that practitioners study their clients' culture beforehand and work closely with their local hosts for additional cues. After looking at many drawings practitioners may begin to understand cross-cultural symbols, associations, and discern culturally specific meanings and make a context-sensitive interpretation that maintains the host country's narratives and considers their unique social constructs. For example, in the United States, getting caught in the rain is typically associated with sadness or misfortune, but in drought-ridden Ethiopia, rain represents prosperity and growth (Figure 3.7). What looks like a dog in an image could be a friendly companion for a youth in the United States, but in Ethiopia it more likely represents a wild, dangerous hyena.

Somatic Effects of Trauma Seen in the Art

The drawings created by the paraprofessionals and the teens provided us with rich data around the somatic effects of the refugee experience. Although there were numerous recurring graphic forms, the most frequently observed were floating heads within the art. Within the four-part drawing sequence, labeled A through D, the heads would appear as in box A or B. Then, by box C or D the participants drew a whole, complete body, sometimes with greater details such as a weapon for protection (Figures 3.8 and 3.9). The work in Africa was not intended to pathologize, nor to be used as an assessment tool, yet the symbols created in the art reflected traumatic experiences of fragmented memories, sensations, affect, cognition, and finally integration of memories.

Figure 3.7 A woman is standing in rain surrounded by flowers. Getting rained on is considered is a positive cultural experience in her parched country.

Body-Based Trauma Therapy

Neuroscience research tells us the portions of the brain involved in trauma may avoid or shut down the verbalization of the traumatic events (Bremner, 2006). Specific therapies that are body-based rather than talk-based have been found to be more effective and resolving trauma experiences. For refugee's trauma survivors, this approach of using art and EMDR offers a way to reconnect to the body, experience positive emotions, and gain insight into their stories to move forward.

How the Body Deals with Trauma

The feeling of intense fear, feeling out of control, and a threat of death is a common thread running through most psychological trauma. Often within trauma, we are left without language. Our body becomes a symptom and relives the terror or the impulse to fight, freeze, flee, faint, or fawn in a way that is often impossible to understand and difficult to articulate (Bracha, 2004). The body acts as a library holding all the memories from the past. As we worked with the refugees in Ethiopia, we observed them figuratively reclaiming their bodies and sense of self as they processed their trauma within their art.

Figure 3.8 This four-part drawing series moves from floating heads to the representation of a full human. In the final drawing, a woman is standing in rain surrounded by flowers. Getting rained on is considered is a positive cultural experience in her parched country.

Figure 3.9 Here we see the top two floating heads that transform into an empowered full body.

From Floating Heads to Body Reconnection

A camp Shimelba paraprofessional created the image in Figure 1.8. We see the beginning drawing with a disembodied head, floating, then by the fourth drawing a body is formed. In the fourth image, both bodies are holding something in their hands, possibly representing empowerment. Using art and EMDR allows an internal awareness to be raised. It gives us an opportunity to achieve a successful symbolization by integrating symbolic illusion with concrete thinking. This can also serve to represent the experience of feelings. These floating heads could represent the fragmentation of memory and cognition, feelings of helplessness, and entrapment. The philosopher Jacques Maritain (1953) states that art becomes, "that inner communication between the inner being of things and the interbeing of the human self which is a kind of division" (p. 3).

PTSD Research: The Role of Physical Awareness and Acceptance for Healing

Many PTSD sufferers find themselves disconnected or disassociated from their own bodies. This is often the result of having experienced the trauma physically. Learning to have a relationship with the body is critical to recovering from the experience. Dr. Bessel van der Kolk writes in *The Body Keeps the Score*, "to change, people need to become aware of their sensations and the way that their bodies interact with the world around them. Physical self-awareness is the first step in releasing the tyranny of the past." Many trauma and PTSD specialists find that much of our work centers around helping our clients reclaiming the safety of their own bodies. As we see in Figure 3.10, the process starts with a floating head in box A, progresses to a head and torso in box B, and by the final square we see the full body along with a foundation under the individuals' feet.

Artwork and EMDR: A Bridge for Externalizing Trauma

Art therapy mixed with EMDR excels in bodywork because clients can manipulate the artwork outside of themselves. By externalizing difficult pieces of their trauma story, clients begin to safely access their physical experiences and re-learn that their bodies are safe once again. Just as art can provide a bridge for both feelings and words it can also perform as a bridge to feeling grounded and safe inside one's body.

CASE REVIEW: AN AFRICAN TEEN WITH PTSD

Backstory

Aaron (not his actual name) grew up on the border of Eritrea and Ethiopia, an area where many landmines were placed during the 1998 war. He presented with selective mutism (SM), anxiety, and depression due to witnessing many devastating moments in his young life.[1] In two separate incidents, each of Aaron's two brothers died after stepping on landmines. He witnessed one of those violent deaths firsthand. Aaron also narrowly escaped his own death twice in two car accidents in which others did not survive.

---

1   Selective mutism is a lack of speech in some social situations but not in others. Experts in the field of SM view it as social communication anxiety where mutism is only one symptom of the problem.

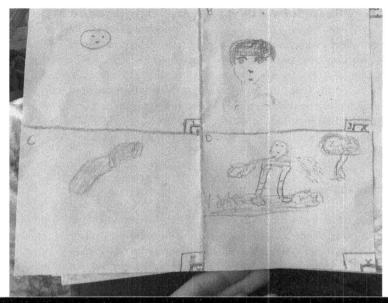

Figure 3.10 The transformation from a floating head to a head with a torso to a full body standing firmly on the ground.

His 40-mile escape on foot from Eritrea to Ethiopia—like that of many other young refugees—nearly cost him his life. Chased by soldiers with guns, hunted by hyenas, and nearly drowned while crossing a river trying to get to safety, Aaron and his peers' survival demonstrated a near-miraculous testament of their determination to live (Smyth Dent, Fitzgerald, & Hagos, 2019).

Despite Aaron's ability to use and comprehend language, he often chose to remain silent, a form of selective mutism (SM). Selective mutism is a lack of speech in some social situations but not in others. Experts in the field of SM view it as social communication anxiety where mutism is only one symptom of the problem (Gosney, 2020).

Initial Engagement

Aaron lived in the Ethiopian refugee camp with his uncle. After much encouragement from both his social worker and his uncle, Aaron came to the two-day treatment. The one rule Aaron insisted upon was that he must be allowed to sit at the physical margins of the space next to his social worker, and away from the group. Aaron often slouched looking down at the ground. Despite his dark skin, I could see even darker circles around his eyes, which made me wonder if he was sleeping at night. Hagos, the camp's social worker, told me beforehand about the devastating trauma this young boy had experienced. I remember feeling inspired that Aaron showed up for this event, yet sad that he did not feel safe enough in the group to sit with his peers.

How Aaron Transformed through Art Therapy and EMDR

Aaron's art offers compelling insight into the refugee experience, his memories of distress, and his hopes for the future. His art allowed us to see his nonverbal experience within the imagery. His formerly fragmented memories slowly consolidated into images to make sense of his traumatic experiences. As the process continued over two days, and new information emerged within his art, Aaron began to metabolize and integrate his past experiences, leading to a transformation. The adaptive information became increasingly clear as Aaron expressed himself in his art, while tapping into EMDR further activated his whole brain.

Physical Observations

Over the two days we observed not only a drastic change in Aaron's physical distance from his group of peers, slowly his willingness to communicate began to emerge. During the first round of EMDR-IGTP-OTS Aaron sat away from the group, by the second set he moved his chair to the edge of the table. For the last set he placed his chair directly in the middle of the group. As we arrived for the second day of treatment, Aaron was the first teen waiting outside for group to begin. By the end of the day, we asked all the teens if anyone would like to share their art individually with one of us. To our surprise, Aaron *spoke* and shared his refugee experience with Smyth Dent, using his art as a guide.

Memory Integration within the Art

Aaron's art tracks the fragmented memories of his trauma experiences. Within this drawing series we see how the gestalt of his body changes, both in detail and developmental age. I hypothesize that it shows reduced emotional numbing and dissociation within the details as the drawings and EMDR progress. The images within the art shift to somatic memories and body sensations. By focusing on a single image of each experience of his journey from Eritrea to Ethiopia, Aaron was able to break down each moment into manageable memories to avoid flooding and overwhelm.

In Aaron's art, we see a significant shift in his self-portraits. This change reflects the reality of what is happening in his progress within the group setting. We see him in the first image being encapsulated in a box, with sketchy line quality, possibly representing anxiety, avoidance, and regression. The snake is coming toward him and without legs to run he is stuck (Figure 3.11). In the next series of drawings, the snake reappears but this time there is a house, possibly representing containment using rectangular shapes to encapsulate sensitive material or provide compartmentalization for overwhelming emotions (Figure 3.12).

As the EMDR-IGTP-OTS continues he jumps to another memory. We see him standing with a man holding a gun to his back. At the time he fled, Eritrean soldiers were trained to kill anyone who was trying to escape to Ethiopia (Figure 3.13).

Then again in square C we see a jump to another traumatic memory from Aaron's journey. The drawing is representative of a car accident he was in. At this point in the sequence his body has left the car and is seen lying on the ground (Figure 3.14). In the final drawing of the series, we see him alone walking with longer hair (Figure 3.15). This could represent the passing of time as he moved toward his freedom in Ethiopia.

Figure 3.11 A boy inside a box with a snake coming to attack him.

Figure 3.12 A house with a snake quickly approaching.

Figure 3.13 Boy being held at gunpoint by Eritrean solder.

Figure 3.14 The boy and a man outside of a car, after a car accident. You can see the swirling effects of the car accident with the man's arm movement.

Figure 3.15 The boy walking toward something. His longer hair shows the passing time and bent body parts show the movement toward his future.

Figure 3.16 A simple floating head without hair.

Research shows that when a child experiences trauma there is often arrested development within the art they create. The children will draw art developmentally appropriate to the age that the trauma occurred (Figure 3.16). Notice the bodies and how they lack a bottom line indicating a torso, as if they are hollow (Figure 3.17). This could potentially represent a disassociation from the body. In the last drawing on this page, we see Aaron's arms are bent, potentially moving toward something. In square B we see the head and a floating torso. Aaron's hands have disappeared, but his torso is defined. There is more detail given to the head and upper torso than in previous images. There is also a change in the developmental

Figure 3.17 The same artist moves from a floating head (in Figure 3.16) to a more complete yet hollow body, capable of holding an object, in this case, a bowl.

Figure 3.18 This is the final drawing in a set that shows a fully formed boy, reading an open book on a desk.

stage of the drawing, correlated with his actual age. The final drawing of the sequence is profound (Figure 3.18). There is depth to Aaron's body. He is fully clothed with his hands behind his back, a three-dimensional book opened on a table. The drawing is centered on the page. He has a smile on his face and his hair is cut short.

The artwork that Aaron made throughout this two-day intervention shows a tangible progress from disassociation to integration. By the end of the drawing series Aaron has become more empowered within his artwork with an emphasis placed on the realism and composition of a three-dimensional table and book.

CONCLUSION

The EMDR-IGTP-OTS creates a space in processing and regulating the sensory information associated with the trauma, giving the client time to process through the fragments of the memories. Even without research to back up this protocol seeing Aaron's transformation would have been an indication of the success this two-day workshop had on individuals with trauma. But luckily with the help of paraprofessionals in camp Shimelba we were able to track the effects of the work, our pre- and post-research, culturally sensitive training and support was indeed beneficial to the mental health needs of the community (Smyth Dent et al., 2019).

In treating trauma, it is not the verbal account of the events that is important, but the nonverbal memories, the emotions, and sensations of the experience (van der Kolk, 2003). Combining EMDR and art lights up both right and left hemispheres of the brain, promoting sensory awareness, which increases affect and emotional regulation. The simple act of deciding what colors to use signifies sequential decision and analytical thinking.

Mental health needs continue to increase while the resources for assistance have dwindled.

During the writing of this chapter, we are amid a global pandemic with COVID raging. It has been said that the next pandemic will be that of mental health (Dong & Bouey, 2020). As economic resources constrict and long-term affordability for mental health care shifts, group work is becoming increasingly more relevant and important.

"Trauma is a very complex phenomenon... trauma can weaken individuals and communities, but it can also lead to a stronger sense of identity and a renewed social cohesion" (Visser, 2015). As professionals we need to find ways to cross-culturally enhance communication and understanding within the therapeutic field. I believe that in a global world, using art and EMDR as therapeutic tools in cross-cultural therapy is still in its infancy.

In closing, I would like to leave you with a story.

We had just completed the first round of our trauma protocol with a group of 20 girls. The paraprofessional stepped aside, and I stepped in to ask a question. "Does anyone want to share with me how this experience was for you?" They all looked at me with blank expressions. No one raised their hand or volunteered in any other way. I changed my question to, "Does anyone want to share their artwork with me?" Promptly all 20 girls raised their hands and lined up to share the art that they had just created.

Just as these girls eagerly lined up to share their art, imagine all the people who could find healing by telling their stories through their art and the power of using the proven strategy of EMDR.

REFERENCES

Akiba, D., & Miller, F. (2004). The expression of cultural sensitivity in the presence of African Americans. Small-Group Research. *Sage journals, 35*(6), 623–642. https://doi.org/10.1177/1046496404265902

Andemicael, A. (2013). The arts in refugee camps: Ten good reasons. *Forced migration review, 43*, 69–71. Retrieved from https://www.fmreview.org/fragilestates/andemicael

Backos, A. (2021). *Post-traumatic stress disorder and art therapy*. London and Philadelphia: Whurr Publishers.

Beasley, J. (2018). Art therapy with refugee youth: "My soul was dancing." (Doctoral dissertation). Mount Mary University, Milwaukee, WI. Retrieved from https://my.mtmary.edu/ICS/icsfs/Beasley%2c_Jennifer__1260634681.pdf?target=109a62dd-b9fe-452b-b693-62f994308206

Berry, J., Phinney, J., Sam, D., & Vedder, P. (2006). *Immigrant Youth in Cultural Transition: Acculturation, Identity, and Adaptation across National Contexts*. Lawrence Erlbaum Associates Publisher.

Bracha, H. S. (2004). Freeze, flight, fight, fright, faint: Adaptationist perspectives on the acute stress response spectrum. *CNS spectrums, 9*(9), 679–685. https://doi.org/10.1017/s1092852900001954

Bremner, J. D. (2006). Traumatic stress: effects on the brain. *Dialogues in clinical neuroscience, 8*(4), 445–461. https://doi.org/10.31887/DCNS.2006.8.4/jbremner

Callaghan, K. (1998). In limbo: Movement psychotherapy with refugees and asylum seekers. In D. Dokter (Ed.), *Arts therapists, refugees, and migrants: Reaching across borders* (pp. 25–40). London: Jessica Kingsley Publishers.

Carswell, K., Blackburn, P., & Barker, C. (2011). The relationship between trauma, post-migration problems and the psychological well-being of refugees and asylum seekers. *The International journal of social psychiatry, 57*(2), 107–119. https://doi.org/10.1177/0020764009105699

Desta, M. (2008). *Epidemiology of child psychiatric disorder in Addis Ababa, Ethiopia*. Umeå: Division of Child and Adolescent Psychiatry, Department of Clinical Science, Umea University.

Dieterich-Hartwell, R., & Koch, S. (2017). Creative arts therapies as temporary home for refugees: Insights from Literature and practice. *Behavioral sciences, 7*, 69. https://doi.org/10.3390/bs7040069. Retrieved from https://www.researchgate.net/publication/320460076_Creative_Arts_Therapies_as_Temporary_Home_for_Refugees_Insights_from_Literature_and_Practice

Dieterich-Hartwell, R., & Koch, S. C. (2017). Creative arts therapies as temporary home for refugees: Insights from literature and practice. *Behavioral sciences (Basel, Switzerland), 7*(4), 69. https://doi.org/10.3390/bs7040069

Dong, L., & Bouey, J. (2020). Public mental health crisis during COVID-19 pandemic, China. *Emerging infectious diseases, 26*(7), 1616–1618.

Fazel, M., Reed, R.V., Panter-Brick, C., & Stein, A. (2012). Mental health of displaced and refugee children resettled in high-income countries: risk and protective factors. Lancet (London, England), 379 (9812), 266-282. https://doi.org/10.1016/S0140-6736(11)60051-2

Figures at a Glance. (2020). Retrieved from https://www.unhcr.org/en-us/figures-at-a-glance.html

Franklin, M. (2010). Affect regulation, mirror neurons, and the third hand: Forming mindfulness empathic art interventions. *Journal of the American art therapy association, 27*(4), 160–167. https://doi.org/10.1080/07421656.2010.10129385

Gosney, C. J. (2020, March 6). Selective mutism in teens and adults. *Anxiety.org*. www.anxiety.org/selective-mutism-in-teens-and-adults-treatment-and-accommodation

Hagood, M. M. (2000). *The use of art in counseling child and adult survivors of sexual abuse:* London & Philadelphia: Jessica Kingsley Publishers.

Hohenshil, T. H., Amundson, N. E., & Niles, S. G. (Eds.). (2013). *Counseling around the world: An international handbook*. Hoboken, NJ: American Counseling Association.

Ichiki, Y., & Hinz, L. D. (2015). *Exploring media properties and expressive therapies continuum: Survey of art therapist*. [Paper Presentation]. American Art Therapy Association Conference, Minneapolis, MN.

Jackson, L. (2020). *Cultural humility in art therapy*. London & Philadelphia: Jessica Kingsley Publishers.

Jarero, I. N., & Artigas, L. (2020). The EMDR integrative group treatment protocol for early intervention and the EMDR integrative group treatment protocol adapted for ongoing traumatic stress©. (EMDR-IGTP-OTS)©. https://doi.org/10.13140/RG.2.2.18347.59685.

Jarero, I., & Artigas, L. (2009). EMDR Integrative group treatment protocol. *Journal of EMDR practice and research, 3*(4), 287–288. https://doi.org/10.1891/1933-3196.3.4.279

Jarero, I., & Artigas, L. (2018). AIP model-based acute trauma and ongoing traumatic stress theoretical conceptualization (Second Edition). *Iberoamerican journal of psycho traumatology and dissociation, 10*(1), 1–7.

Kay, A. (2000). Art and community development: The role the arts have in regenerating communities. *Community development journal, 35*(4), 414–424. https://doi.org/10.1093/cdj/35.4.414

Kestly, T. A. (2014). *The interpersonal neurobiology of play: Brain-building interventions for emotional well-being.* New York: W.W. Norton.

King, J. (Ed.). (2016). *Art therapy, trauma and neuroscience: Theoretical and practical perspectives.* New York & London: Routledge/Taylor & Francis Group.

Lee, C. W., & Cuijpers, P. (2013). A meta-analysis of the contribution of eye movements in processing emotional memories. *Journal of behavior therapy & experimental psychiatry, 44,* 231–239.

Lowenfeld, V., & Brittain, W. L. (1987). *Creative and mental growth.* New York: Macmillan Publishing Company.

Lusebrink, V. B. (1991). A systems-oriented approach to the expressive therapies continuum. *The arts in psychotherapy, 18* (5), 395–403.

Lusebrink, V. B., & Hinz, L. D. (2016). The expressive therapies continuum as a framework in the treatment of trauma. In J. L. King (Ed.), *Art therapy, trauma, and neuroscience: Theoretical and practical perspectives* (pp. 42–66). New York & London: Routledge/Taylor & Francis Group.

Metcalfe, J. (1998). Cognitive optimism: Self-deception or memory-based processing heuristics? *Personality and social psychology review, 2*(2), 100–110. https://doi.org/10.1207/s15327957pspr0202_3

Nickerson, M. (2017). *Cultural competence and healing culturally based trauma with EMDR therapy.* New York: Springer Publishing.

Rousseau, C., & Guzder, J. (2008). School-based prevention programs for refugee children. *Child and adolescent psychiatric clinics of North America, 17*(3), 533–549. https://doi.org/10.1016/j.chc.2008.02.002

Rubin, J. A. (2011). *The art of art therapy: What every art therapist needs to know.* London: Routledge.

Shonkoff, J. P., & Phillips D. A. (2000). *From neurons to neighborhoods: The science of early childhood development.* Washington, DC: National Academy Press.

Smyth-Dent, K., Fitzgerald, J., & Hagos, Y. (2019). A field study on the EMDR integrative group treatment protocol for ongoing traumatic stress provided to adolescent Eritrean refugees living in Ethiopia. *Journal of psychology & the behavioral sciences, 12*(4), 1–12. https://doi.org/10.19080/PBSIJ.2019.12.555842.

Tamis-LeMonda, C. S., Shannon, J. D., Cabrera, N. J., & Lamb, M. E. (2004). Fathers and mothers at play with their 2- and 3-year-olds: Contributions to language and cognitive development. *Child development, 75*(6), 1806–1820. https://doi.org/10.1111/j.1467-8624.2004.00818.x

UNHCR. (n.d.). What is a refugee? Retrieved from https://www.unrefugees.org/refugee-facts/what-is-a-refugee/

van der Kolk, B. A. (2003). Frontiers in trauma treatment. Presented at the R. Cassidy Seminars, St. Louis, MO.

Visser, I. (2015). Decolonizing trauma theory: Retrospect and prospects. *Humanities, 4*(2), 250–265.

Watson, M. D. (2013). The colonial gesture of development: The interpersonal as a promising site for rethinking aid to Africa. *Africa today, 59*(3), 2–28. https://doi.org/10.2979/africatoday.59.3.3

Wertheim-Cahen, T. (1998). *Arts therapists, refugees, and migrants: Reaching across borders* (pp. 41–61). London, England: Jessica Kingsley Publishers.

Wiechelt, S., Gryczynski, J., Johnson, J., & Caldwell, D. (2012). Historical trauma among urban American Indian: Impact on substance use and family cohesion. *Journal of loss trauma, 17*(4), 319–336. https://doi.org/10.1080/15325024.2011.616837

Wix, L. (2009). Aesthetic empathy in teaching art to children: The work of Friedl Dicker- Brandeis in Terezin. *Art therapy: Journal of the American art therapy association, 26*(4), 152–158. https://doi.org/10.1080/07421656.2009.10129612

Yalom, I. D. (1995). *The theory and practice of group psychotherapy* (4th ed.). New York: Basic Books.

CHAPTER 4

GEN Z IN CRISIS
Blending EMDR and Art Therapy for a More Robust Therapeutic Experience

Sherri Jacobs

The challenges facing young people in the United States have led to an unfolding crisis, well documented by staggering statistics of increased depression, anxiety, and suicide rates over the past decade (Haidt & Twenge, 2021). These trends have been exacerbated by the COVD-19 pandemic, as teens and young adults navigate through uncertainty and change (Magson et al., 2021). Innovative models for therapy are essential to meet the needs of this young generation of people born and raised in the 21st century. This chapter offers techniques for enhancing the eight phases of EMDR through a variety of art therapy directives identified in multiple case studies. Creative interventions demonstrate the effectiveness of incorporating visual art to complement the Adaptive Information Processing (AIP) framework of EMDR.

Recent research in neurodevelopment validates the unique conditions of the adolescent brain as it radically reorganizes itself (Jenson & Nutt, 2015). This robust time is a crucial stage for lifelong emotional and physical health. The plasticity of the human brain is most active in infancy and again in the adolescent period (Siegel & Bryson, 2012). Healthy brain development is enhanced by effective therapeutic intervention to address stressors and traumatic experiences that occurred in younger stages or during this adolescent time of rapid change (Siegel, 2015).

EMDR and art therapy both serve as effective therapeutic modalities for people to confront emotional issues that have resulted in unresolved trauma and *DSM-5* diagnoses common in this young population. EMDR has been well researched as a model for treating trauma, anxiety, reducing depression, and processing difficult memories (Shapiro, 2018; Cuijpers et al, 2020). Similarly, art therapy is a discipline in the mental health field that incorporates art making and creativity in the therapeutic experience to access implicit memories (King, 2016). When EMDR and art therapy are combined, these two disciplines can be incredibly effective and transformative, serving as a new avenue to meet the specific needs of young people. Art directives listed in this chapter are designed to be replicated by clinicians using EMDR or used independently as stand-alone techniques.

FACTORS CONTRIBUTING TO THE GENERATION Z CRISIS

Young people born between 1997 and 2010 in the United States have been referred to colloquially as Gen Z (Lutrell & McGrath, 2021; Dimock, 2019). Many elements have contributed to a challenging time period over the 21st century, including 9/11, the United States engaging in its longest war in its history (in Afghanistan and Iraq), the economic crash of 2008, the introduction of smartphone technology, an expansion of single-parent homes, expanded gender choices, increased loneliness, the ubiquitous use of social media, and a sense of hopelessness due to climate change (Twenge, 2017; Damour, 2017, 2019). The residual effects of the COVID-19 pandemic add another layer of complexity to this young generation (Leeb, 2020; U.S. Department of Health & Human Services, 2021). These

DOI: 10.4324/9781003156932-5

collective experiences have ushered in an era of extreme distress for young people as they acclimate to these new collective experiences (Rousseau et al., 2020).

The data of this young generation is sobering; suicide ranks as the second leading cause of death in this generation, increasing 60% from 2008 to 2018 in ages 10–24 (Curtain, 2020). US Hospitals report female teen suicide attempts increased 50% from 2019 to 2021 and rates of depression and anxiety doubled in all genders (U.S. Department of Health & Human Services, 2021). Communities across the United States are dealing with a new era brought on by COVID-19 long-term shutdowns that severely impacted the mental health of this young and struggling generation. And yet, specialized and focused interventions for this generation are lacking, therefore enhancing the need for contemporary models for Gen Z.

ENHANCED MODELS OF THERAPY FOR THE 21ST CENTURY

While mental health needs of young people across the socioeconomic spectrum have expanded precipitously, resources for assistance have decreased (The White House, 2021). Contemporary models for Gen Z are essential for shorter term interventions due to economic constraints, busy schedules, and a need for a faster resolution of symptomatology. Among the G7 countries, the United States is currently ranked as having the largest socioeconomic gap between rich and poor people (Horowitz et al, 2020). This cultural shift severely impacts the American family system, as many people of this young generation have watched their parents struggle financially to stay afloat (Schaeffer, 2020). Domestic violence, substance abuse, housing insecurity, and lack of basic resources often increase within families strained by economic hardship. Longitudinal tracking through ACES scores correlates this pairing, and as many American families struggle, the result for this young population is higher acuity rates in mental illness (McLaughlin, 2017; Herzog, & Schmahl, 2018).

Many therapeutic models developed in the 20th century are simply obsolete as they address the issues of a different generation. The COVID-19 era has illuminated a neccessity for updated interventions for a generation with acute needs (U.S. Department of Health & Human Services, 2021). Families seeking therapy often shop for the most rapid and effective route to accommodate their limited budget or their kids' busy schedules. Additionally, insurance mandated shorter psychiatric hospital stays have forced therapists to alter how they operate to meet the needs of an acute population and families desperate for assistance to keep their teens and young adults safe from self-harm (Thielking, 2020). The COVID-19 pandemic exacerbated adolescent distress, including increased rates of loneliness, lack of motivation, depression, hopelessness, social anxiety, and academic disruptions (Magson, et al., 2021). Insurance companies are often unwilling to cover the costs of longer-term models of intervention (Lake and Turner, 2017). This generation needs faster, more efficient forms of therapy. As a post COVID-19 era emerges, there is speculation that recovery from the challenging era will define this young generation, as their lives were significantly disrupted (Parker & Igielnik, 2020). Although the economic realities of the American family are rarely a topic cited as a benefit for EMDR therapy, a recent European study ranked EMDR as the most economical therapeutic modality (Mavranezouli et al, 2020). Cognitive behavioral therapy was the previously favored therapy covered by insurance companies, but it takes longer to successfully implement. As this population searches for more efficient and rapid results, CBT's higher dropout rates make it a less favored intervention (Fernandez et al., 2015).

NEUROSEQUENTIAL DEVELOPMENT, ATTACHMENT, MEMORY, AND COMPLEX TRAUMA—UPDATING 20TH CENTURY DEVELOPMENTAL THEORIES

Developmental theorists of the 20th century identified several stages of human development, based on observation and speculation on how the brain and body develop. Erik Erikson conceptualized developmental stages across the entire life span and identified ages 12–19 as a time of struggling through identity vs. role confusion, followed by the next stage from 19 to 40 dealing with intimacy vs. isolation. Erikson's model proposed that success or failure in mastering the overall goals of each developmental stage built a foundation for the next stage, and negative patterns in one stage would lead to a more challenging time in the subsequent stage (Erikson, 1994).

Erikson's theories were influential in identifying healthy human development and emphasized the role trauma and other adverse events can have on early development, as well as challenges in subsequent life stages. Huge strides in memory, attachment, and trauma research have catapulted the mental health field to generate a neurobiological paradigm, offering a concrete, biological understanding of how traumatic experiences can become encoded in maladaptive ways onto lower levels of neuro development (with an understanding that the brain develops from the actual bottom up from the brainstem to cortex) (Perry, 2009). Hebbian theory proposes a simple motto, "What fires together, wires together," to identify the complex mechanism of an exquisitely tuned neural network's response to experiences that pair with sensory input as memories are made (Keysers & Gazzola, 2014). This pairing literally designs a homo Sapien infant's underdeveloped brain and nervous system for life. Poorly encoded information results in a faulty neuroendocrinology of an individual, where the messaging of perpetual danger can remain ever present, even when the danger from an initial early traumatic experience has long passed (Siegel & Bryson, 2012).

The great news is that a young person's brain and body are quite resilient, and mental health intervention at this crucial time of adolescent brain development can literally rewire the brain for a more regulated nervous system. Rehabilitation and post-traumatic growth are possible when people can access interventions that provide the opportunity to heal from adverse events previously encoded in maladaptive ways (Perry, 2009). Research in the fields of neurobiology, memory, trauma, and attachment over the past 20 years collectively has contributed to an updated understanding of human development (Hass-Cohen & Findley, 2015). Francine Shapiro's Adaptive Information Processing (AIP) model serves as a map for EMDR and describes how to process unprocessed memories and literally quiet down an activated nervous system (Shapiro, 2018).

Whereas 20th century therapeutic models favored cognitive interventions by accessing "top down" brain processing through explicit memory retrieval via talk therapy to access unconscious material, new models have emerged to replace the slow and often fruitless avenues of traditional talk therapy. Effectively accessing and reprocessing implicit memory or "bottom-up" brain processing has become the favored avenue for therapeutic intervention of many mental and physical maladies (Bergman, 2020). Art therapy and EMDR are both effective therapies to quickly access implicit memories, and both modalities can rapidly and effectively reorganize thoughts, memories, somatic responses, and negative beliefs. When combined, they offer a unique roadmap for the development of contemporary models for Gen Z, as they provide the opportunity to quickly and effectively resolve traumatic or bothersome memories and address current stressors in young people.

BENEFITS OF COMBINING EMDR AND ART THERAPY FOR YOUNG PEOPLE

EMDR is a sensory-based therapy designed to process emotions, memories, and negative beliefs into neutral events, rather than intrusive, active thoughts, sensations, and fragments of memory. EMDR therapy enlists the inner visual experience, as clients are asked to imagine many things such as a safe place and a container, yet the protocol traditionally only encourages clients to use their imaginations, without actual art making incorporated into sessions (Shapiro, 2018). Enhancing EMDR sessions with art making or externalization can add a robust element to each stage of the eight-phase protocol. This simple pairing of two successful disciplines translates into effective therapy sessions with young people.

Creative interventions in therapy sessions offer multilayered forms of communication beyond traditional talk therapy, and this is essential for adolescents in any era, but especially Gen Z, for whom an hour-long traditional talk therapy session might feel very foreign to their digital, screen-laden lives. The creative element increases engagement, making the therapeutic process more appealing, pulling teens from their screens and into a body-based, sensory experience where real shifts in cognition can happen.

The goals of art therapy have remained consistent since the discipline's inception: to incorporate creativity to access implicit memory, and create new narratives and meaning around particular memories, thus reducing distress from bothersome issues, experiences, and beliefs (Gussak & Blackwell, 2015). This pattern is very similar to EMDR's AIP model, as both modalities enlist creativity and active participation of clientele, and both can bypass verbal centers of the brain to quickly access implicit memories to process unconscious and conscious memories (Greenwald, 2007).

EMDR and art therapy both offer a dignified approach to explore clients' trauma. While traditional talk therapy relies on verbal communication to process traumatic memories, potentially leading to secondary trauma in the therapy room as shame and guilt often accompany the memories, EMDR offers a different approach. Research on the B2T or blind to therapist protocol in EMDR offers a level of control for clients by allowing them to merely think about a memory without articulating it during an EMDR reprocessing session to arrive at the same positive results of reduced distress levels as clients who verbally disclose their memories (Blore et al., 2013). Additionally, art therapy offers a platform for traumatic memories to be identified symbolically through art without the need to verbally share them. Both modalities offer avenues to make subconscious experiences conscious in non-traumatizing ways. The similarities between art therapy and EMDR offer dynamic sessions where a young person can feel empowered, engaged, and like an active participant in their healing process.

THE EIGHT PHASES OF EMDR THERAPY AND CREATIVE INTERVENTIONS

EMDR, or Eye Movement Desensitization and Reprocessing, was created in 1987 by Francine Shapiro. A rhythmic, dual attention stimulus (tactile, visual, or auditory) accompanying the recall of an event or negative belief serves as the foundation of this experiential therapy (Shapiro, 2018). To certify its effectiveness and ensure people seeking EMDR are receiving thorough therapeutic care, Shapiro designed eight specific phases of therapy in this discipline for a full therapeutic experience. To conduct EMDR in the United States, a person must hold a state mental health license and complete an official EMDR training. Shapiro insisted that early practitioners remained true to the original model to maintain continuity across various disciplines of the mental health field. This adherence to the eight-phase model allowed for consistency over time, congruent research, and a modality with a universal common structure. As it gains popularity across the world, the EMDR model continues to remain true to its original form.

The eight phases of EMDR might appear rigid, but within the structure of these phased parameters, experienced practitioners cultivate new and unique treatment ideas. Much like a chess game, which offers millions of options within an 8×8 square, the opportunity to enhance the eight phases of EMDR is not only possible, but necessary to keep the field evolving to meet the ever-changing needs of clientele and when working with specific populations such as Gen Z.

While novice EMDR therapists might rely on actual scripts, this chapter invites readers to use their own creativity to conceptualize their cases and enhance the framework of EMDR by integrating visual art and creative engagement into the process.

The following case studies offer a variety of art therapy directives for the eight phases of the EMDR journey. Art directives introduced in each case study can be easily replicated, and therapists can cultivate their own creative journey, and essentially "think" like an art therapist as they incorporate visual tools into their own work. Many of the creative interventions are versatile for a wide range of ages and issues. The art directives listed in this chapter can also be used as stand-alone art therapy directives for readers not yet trained in EMDR.

EMDR PHASE ONE: HISTORY AND TREATMENT PLANNING

Similar to all modalities of mental health treatment, the first phase of EMDR includes learning the history of the client and creating a treatment plan. This approach is essential for EMDR therapy, as the target memories associated with the clients' presenting problems are often minimized or not recognized as relevant by the client. As clients connect their current distress to past experiences to identify associated material for reprocessing, the time spent exploring a client's experience can make the reprocessing phase more beneficial for connecting various memories.

Learning a client's trauma history and the current coping tools they employ is essential to determine if and when they are ready to engage in the reprocessing phases of EMDR therapy. Using information of a client's life history and resources, a map for Phase Two of psychoeducation and the building of coping skills can be determined. If a client has few effective coping tools, this phase can be extended to ensure readiness for reprocessing. Many young people come to therapy requesting coping skills and recognizing their own limitations to navigate difficult emotions. The treatment plan with young people should include extended preparation to increase coping skills and emotional regulation.

An effective way to engage this population in the preparation phase is by offering creative interventions in this stage of therapy to allow for expansive forms of self-expression and to empower the client to identify issues without having to address them immediately. The concrete visual documentation of sessions via artmaking offers an opportunity for a client to coherently revisit topics covered in sessions. Young people are often invited to photograph their artwork on their phones so they can refer to it between sessions, especially during the reevaluation work done in Phase Eight.

ESTABLISHING RAPPORT

Working with teens and young adults can be challenging as many clients in this age group are being coerced into a therapeutic setting by their parents, have had negative therapy experiences, and often have difficulty expressing themselves. Trust is essential in this therapeutic realm, and for EMDR therapy to be successful, this initial compatibility is integral to the therapy outcome.

Creative interventions in this early stage of therapy can be impactful for enhancing the therapist-client rapport. Art making offers a non-verbal avenue for communicating difficult events and gently accessing implicit memories and creating a foundation for the EMDR work in future sessions. For example, younger clients often come to therapy following a discovery by a parent of a negative coping tool (including cutting, self-harm, poor emotional insight, poor communication, a suicide attempt, excessive drug and alcohol use), or self-report to a parent or caregiver of overwhelming emotions. There is often shame related to these discoveries, and the idea of revealing information to an outsider can generate a deep resistance to the therapy process. Young adults who are over the age of 18 often find therapy on their own when they recognize their poor coping skills, or when traumatic incidents from their childhood impact their jobs, school, or relationships.

Art making, even for non-artistic clients, can offer an added layer of comfort in the first session. Sitting at a table rather than a couch, not using eye contact with the therapist while focusing on the art making, and, most importantly, offering an expanded opportunity for communication can reduce the stigma of sitting and staring/conversing with a new person. Dual neuroimaging research by Dr. Allen Schore (2021) reveals that a therapeutic alliance results in a right brain/right brain connection between the therapist and the client. Creative art interventions can quickly establish this dynamic and create a sense of comfort and compatibility if the therapist is also engaged in a similar activity. When this rapport is developed in the first session, it sets the tone for establishing a positive therapeutic experience, and a safe place to explore difficult memories or ineffective coping skills.

The Importance of Explaining EMDR

EMDR looks and feels quite different from traditional talk therapy. Even clients who are familiar with the modality need an adequate explanation of how it might help them and how it is implemented into treatment plans. When young people are empowered with the knowledge of how this modality works, it allows them an opportunity to become a partner in their treatment. The positional nature of the therapist-client relationship can shift from the therapist as an expert on the client and their diagnosis to the therapist as an expert on how to successfully utilize EMDR so the client can activate their own healing capacities. In this new dynamic, the therapist becomes akin to a supportive coach who holds a safe space while the client works through difficult memories. For people who have experienced trauma, the need for control and having clear expectations is critical (Greenwald, 2007). Creative explanations for EMDR using concrete metaphors can be helpful when introducing the modality to young people who might feel more empowered by information that connects to their worldview and acknowledges that they are the experts on themselves, not the therapist in the room. This key shift in the therapeutic relationship is crucial to meeting the needs of young clients/people (Lutrell & McGrath, 2021).

Script for Explaining EMDR as a Stage with a Spotlight. *Imagine a dark stage in a theater with a spotlight on one part of the stage. Even though there might be more things on the stage, it is* *difficult to see anything outside of the spotlight. Our memories and beliefs are a lot like this spotlight; we get stuck and only see what is illuminated by the spotlight in the form of a negative memory and/or a negative belief about ourselves attached to a memory or event from the past. EMDR is a type of therapy that can help quickly shift our perception from seeing only what is in the spotlight to a view of the entire stage. In EMDR therapy, we can help you see/remember and understand more things that are connected to the topic of focus. We are not really adding anything new from the outer world; we are simply helping you expand the spotlight so you can see and add more to your current memory or to the belief you hold about a particular event. As you expand the spotlight, you might be able to see the outside helpers, your own resilience, and strengths to help you add more information to the memory.*

Script for Explaining EMDR as a Dot-to-Dot Game. *When we make a dot-to-dot picture, it can be confusing at the beginning as we connect the dots together to form an image. However, as we get to the end, the picture becomes more clear and complete. EMDR can sort-of feel like a dot-to-dot except with our memories. When we do EMDR around a specific incident, we can take random memories, ideas, thoughts, emotions, body feelings, and negative beliefs, and consolidate them into a coherent narrative. Before tackling these memories, they might feel like random bits and pieces floating around, almost like the points on a dot-to-dot page. Each memory, thought, emotion, or body sensation that arises during an EMDR round is another "dot" getting connected to a whole picture. One session can connect many random things to create a sense of neutrality around that memory. Your mind knows exactly where it needs to go to help complete your whole dot-to-dot story, and if we can get comfortable trusting the process, you will feel better. You are the expert on this* [this idea is empowering to young people]. *There is no right or wrong place that your mind will go in this process. Your mind knows the next "dot" it needs in order to complete the picture. You are really the expert here.*

ART THERAPY DIRECTIVES FOR EMDR PHASE ONE— HISTORY TAKING AND TREATMENT PLANNING

Creative Timeline

A timeline is an excellent tool for a first session of therapy, as it offers the client freedom to decide how much to reveal to the therapist and to themselves (Figure 4.1). A timeline can also assess a client's concept of their future self for young people experiencing a sense of hopelessness or an inability to determine short-term goals. The use of metaphor in a timeline can be a powerful avenue to distance a person from their story while still communicating their difficult experience to map out the target sequencing. This also offers both a concrete and abstract way of thinking. One idea is to offer the metaphor of a garden or something in nature to depict a timeline.

A creative timeline can offer an initial glimpse into areas for exploration in EMDR therapy, and other crucial factors such as the developmental stage when traumatic incidents took

Figure 4.1 One hundred six-year timeline depicted by 106 colorful vertical lines.

place, coping skills at the time, and attachment figures who were present or absent. Helping a client identify specific stressors in the present is essential, and some of the topics depicted on the timeline might be informing current behavior or triggers. This gentle approach can serve as a guide to show the client how their past is impacting their current distress levels.

Script for a Creative Timeline. *Please create a timeline of your life, and feel free to go a few years beyond your current time period, by drawing an actual timeline at the bottom of the page. Please use the metaphor of flowers or a garden to represent different time periods of your life. If you had a challenging time at a specific age, your flowers might be wilted. If you had a positive stage of life, this might be represented through blossoming flowers. Maybe there is a type of plant, animal, or object in your garden that could represent a positive period in your life. You could use a different type of flower, plant, or animal to represent more challenging times. Can you imagine what the garden of your whole life looks like? See if you can include your near future too. Can you imagine what your creative timeline might look like in the near future? If you don't like the garden theme, you could also use weather patterns, random shapes, vertical lines in various colors and widths, or even magazine pictures.*

The creative process allows for traumatic experiences to be depicted in metaphor symbolically without having to reveal actual events especially if the client is not ready to discuss them. Additionally, the physical depiction of this timeline can be used as a reference later in therapy as the client becomes more comfortable with exploring traumatic incidents.

Symbolic Family Portrait

We can only truly comprehend a person's current situation by bringing more awareness to the system in which their situation was created, so systems thinking is essential for the therapist to understand a client's experience (Gerhart, 2017). Learning a person's family history can be easily enhanced with creative interventions. A symbolic family portrait can give clients of all ages a unique perspective, distance, and objectivity on their situation as they reflect on their own figures or drawn images that depict their family system, even if drawing is rendered in simple stick figures (Rubin, 2005).

Young clients often blame themselves for their symptoms, and this directive can help create a new narrative of understanding of how each family member contributed to the family dynamic. When this art directive is used as a preparation for EMDR reprocessing, a symbolic family portrait can create a foundation for the EMDR work as target memories not conveyed in verbal reporting often emerge. The chosen symbols in a family portrait often represent many layers of meaning, and this creative intervention can truly expedite this stage of therapy, as many things can be expressed in the artwork rather than with verbal reports of the family dynamics. Recognition of negative cognitions developed within the family system can be addressed in a gentle way and can be explored in later EMDR sessions. Negative cognitions are often the element needing attention in the EMDR work with young people, and a symbolic family portrait is an excellent tool to incorporate into initial sessions to uncover the experiences many people identify as their truth.

Script for Symbolic Family Portrait. *Please spend a few minutes drawing a symbolic family portrait of your family of origin, or caregivers who you live/lived with in your life. Each person present should draw their own image. Everyone can share them with each other once we are finished. Instead of drawing actual people, please draw each person as a symbol. This might be an object, a symbol, a logo, an emoji, or even a word if you don't feel comfortable drawing. Please include yourself too because people often leave themselves out. If you want to add more detail to each person, you might want to add a word bubble of what each person might be saying to the family.*

Symbolic family portraits offer important clues for therapists to ask deeper questions a person might not recognize in their own system. Young people often don't recognize their own family system as problematic or contributing to their distress levels, and they often blame themselves for their issues. This transitional stage of adolescence is often the first time young people can have a subjective view of their family systems (Erikson, 1994). Revisiting this artwork at later phases of EMDR is an excellent way to determine if SUD levels around various topics have been sufficiently reduced.

Case Study Using Symbolic Family Portrait

Emma, an 18-year-old high school senior, came to therapy following her revelation to her mother of a sexual assault by a peer/family friend several years earlier (Figure 4.2). She reported panic attacks, increased anxiety, and socially isolating from her friend group. She hid this information from her family, fearing that she was to blame, and fearing it would disrupt the dynamic between her family and the perpetrator's family. Emma did not associate her current symptoms with the assault until a rape crisis center led an awareness campaign at her high school. As she learned more about the residual effects of traumatic experiences, she was able to connect her somatic symptoms to her trauma, and she finally decided to share her story with her mother.

The symbolic family portrait was introduced in the initial session, and Emma drew herself as a bottle of glue, a sun, and a cell phone within her family (she drew a few images to represent different stages). Emma reported her sister being diagnosed with bipolar disorder a few years earlier, causing a lot of distress with her close-knit family and forcing Emma to play the role of a helpful, older sibling, despite being five years younger than her sister. She reported her parents separating when she was a pre-teen, and after a few years of living apart, they reunited with Emma's assistance. Emma reported her role in the family as the wise, older person, and her symptoms of distress were not congruent with her narrative, causing even more distress.

Although Emma came to therapy to reduce emotional distress related to her sexual assault, this symbolic family portrait laid the foundation for the treatment plan and EMDR reprocessing work several sessions later. She revealed her fear of sharing details of her assault

Figure 4.2 Symbolic family portrait helps an adolescent recognize her role in the family.

with her father, whom she feared might not have the emotional strength to hear difficult news. Emma's narrative as a "bottle of glue" was also consistent in her friend groups, and this dynamic led to her belief system that she was responsible for fixing everything, and that she was the source of blame for anything that went wrong. This art directive was one of many that Emma created during her therapy journey.

During the reprocessing phase of EMDR, and as she confronted her negative cognitions related to her false belief system, Emma was able to shift her role in the family and identify this challenging role to her mom who attended a few therapy sessions. As her belief shifted to "it wasn't my fault" with her sexual assault, her anxiety and panic attacks began to subside. Emma also shifted her role in her friend group to have better boundaries. The future planning with EMDR involved setting good boundaries for her upcoming experience in college in order to safeguard her from repeating the pattern of caring for everyone except herself. Emma came back to therapy following her first semester of college and reported her ability to completely shift roles to care for herself first. The combination of EMDR with creative interventions offered a path of continuous reflection on her emotional growth. Her artwork served as markers of her process of change, and provided the clues needed about nuanced elements of her life that might have been difficult to access using only talk therapy.

EMDR PHASE TWO: PREPARATION

Phase Two of EMDR therapy is similar to traditional therapy as the focus is on important elements such as continuing to establish client/therapist rapport, psychoeducation, and planning out the therapeutic journey with target memories for reprocessing. The protocol of EMDR is often explained again during this phase. Additionally, safe state, deep breathing, and coping tools including the creation of a symbolic container to hold large memories that emerge outside of sessions are covered in these beginning sessions. It is essential that a client is skilled in using healthy coping tools before engaging in the reprocessing phases of EMDR because clients often continue processing memories in the hours and days following an EMDR session. Assessing a person's ability to self-soothe is crucial for their emotional safety following sessions.

Art directives can tremendously enhance this stage of therapy as a client can utilize physical representations to reinforce new skills and revisit topics covered during these important stages of therapy. Incorporating lessons on interpersonal neurobiology, biological mechanisms in a client's body, their rapidly changing brain, and basic ideas of neuroscience can be enhanced with artistic renderings of complex topics. Empowering young people with the knowledge of how their nervous system functions can reduce shame over anxiety and stress reactions. This primer on their mind and body can enhance self-control by pairing tools like deep breathing with an explanation of the physiology of how each technique works. Much of the art making of EMDR therapy takes place in this preparation stage.

ART THERAPY DIRECTIVES FOR EMDR PHASE TWO—PREPARATION

Safe State

Creating a safe state in one's imagination is a standard part of Phase Two of the EMDR protocol. This skill is an excellent way to enlist a client's imagination and establish healthy coping tools. Safe state thinking is used in many other modalities of therapy, and it preceded EMDR therapy as a common art therapy technique.

The visual elements of EMDR therapy offer an excellent opportunity to enhance each of these steps with actual visual art. Imagining a safe state and enhancing that thinking with an actual visual depiction can be incredibly helpful for a client. This physical rendition (even a rudimentary image) can reinforce creating a safe place in one's imagination and pair the memory of experiencing a safe place exercise in the therapist's office. It can also create a safe state within the therapy room where the art making is taking place. This process of honoring a client's creativity and lived experience while empowering them to enlist their imagination for self-healing helps guide clients in the direction of tackling their difficult emotions.

Script for Art Making with Safe State Exercises. *Please think of a place that makes you feel safe. This might be a place you have visited, a combination of places, or a place you would like to visit. Please draw, paint, or collage this safe place, and add a word to describe it, perhaps in the form of a title of your safe place. Feel free to add people, pets (even ones who have passed away). Could you draw it, paint it, or make a magazine collage of it?*

The next part of safe state thinking involves "installing" it using a bilateral stimulation for enhancing the visual experience. Testing the effectiveness of the imagery by thinking about a slightly distressing thing and then enlisting the safe state *practice* while engaging in bilateral stimulation is important (Shapiro, 2018). The visual representation of a safe place adds a sensory element that can be reinforced at home.

Containers

Creating a symbolic container is another essential tool in Phase Two of EMDR protocol. The idea is to use one's imagination to place big, traumatic memories that might arise outside of a session into the symbolic container, so it can be later explored in the therapy session. Symbolic containers are also used in other therapeutic modalities, and the therapy room itself is often offered as a symbolic container for holding big emotions for clients.

Art therapists have long incorporated the use of actual containers to serve as physical representations of safely housing memories too big or too distressing to tackle. Standard protocol in EMDR's short history asks clients to create a container only in their imagination. Art therapists often take this one step further by creating an actual container in the form of a box or jar with clients in these first sessions. Using the therapist's room to hold the container can also be important to continue to build safe thinking.

Script for Creating a Container (to hold big memories). *Please choose a box (small craft boxes, shoe boxes, wooden boxes from craft stores, and cigar boxes are all useful) and use some materials to personalize your container. This might be done with drawing, writing words on the inside and outside, adding magazine images, lining the inside with fabric or whatever works to personalize it. Please decide if you would like to store your container in the therapy room or take it home with you. If you have a very strong memory, please take time to write it down on a piece of paper and place it in your container so it can be explored in future therapy sessions.*

Create an Amygdala

Basic facts about neuroscience can empower a young person in profound ways in the therapy setting and prepare for future EMDR work. Enhancing this information through visual art offers an excellent foundation and language for a person to understand their stress response, and capacity to rewire their brain (Siegel, 2015). Clients often feel empowered when they learn the neurobiology related to their emotional experiences. This element of psychoeducation enables young people to detach from previous diagnoses they have been given and offers a space to recognize that their trauma response (fight, flight, freeze, or flop) was good, helpful, and necessary during the trauma, but it is no longer needed for the current time period (Jenson & Nutt, 2015). As clients contemplate the role their brain plays in their emotional responses, they are also preparing for EMDR reprocessing sessions.

Script to Describe the Amygdala and Triune Brain. *We have different parts of our brain that do very different things. Although people have been studying the mechanisms of the brain for a very long time, we now have the neuroimaging tools to really learn what is happening when we feel an emotion or have a thought. If you can think of your brain as being divided up into three equal sections from top to bottom, this is a great place to start learning about how our brain works. The lower third is called the brain stem, and we sometimes call this the "reptile" brain because it does things similar to a reptile's brain such as digestion, temperature control, and breathing—things that happen in our body that we don't have to pay attention to while they do their job. The middle section of our brain is called the limbic system and is the part we share with mammals. This is our danger/warning system. The top part of our brain is called the cortex and houses the prefrontal cortex (behind your forehead) and is responsible for decision-making, and "higher" thinking, like the ability to understand time, and complex ideas. It is not fully formed until about age 24 (Siegel, 2015).*

Most people "live" in their cortex, meaning the thinking part of their brain, but as soon as something big/scary/surprising/alarming happens, the limbic system (the middle part of our brain) takes over to help us stay safe. The amygdala is the very important part of the limbic system that is a real alarm system to wake the body up to prepare for surviving something big or scary. Once activated, it sends messages to our body to release chemicals to activate or quiet our body. Amygdalae are in the shape of a small bean, and you have two, one in both the left and right hemisphere of the limbic system/midbrain. The amygdala is sort of like a guard who is always on alert looking for danger. It has an excellent memory for sensory input, and it almost works like a vacuum cleaner, remembering every sensory element associated with a scary experience (Siegel, 2012).

Imagine a person is in a house fire. The amygdala will store all of the sensory input associated with that fire such as smell, sounds, sights, and feeling. Sadly, the amygdala does not have a clock, so it can't differentiate between past, present, and future. Sometimes after an impactful or life-threatening experience like a fire, those sensory memories (like the smell of smoke) will wake the amygdala up and make us feel like we are in the same big danger (even if it is something small like a birthday candle being blown out). Our job is to retrain our amygdala to let it know we are safe. Sometimes we don't know what triggers our amygdala to wake up, and this danger sends us into high alert, even if we are in a safe place. Teaching the body how to calm itself down is important to retrain our amygdalae if they are overactive. EMDR can really help this process.

The amygdala is the signaling part of our brain that tells our body to release chemicals (such as cortisol and epinephrine) to prepare us for fight, flight, freeze, or flop reactions. Some of these body reactions include dilated pupils, increased heart rate, not being able to think straight, and stomach aches. The amygdala is profoundly important, but sometimes it gets overactive by telling our body we are in danger, even if we are not. One thing we can do in therapy is to teach our amygdala to quiet itself down. How? Processing the unprocessed memories is hugely helpful. EMDR is an excellent tool to quiet down our overactive alarm system. When the amygdala threatens to take over, we can override the system with deep breathing (fun fact—the heart is one of the only organs we actually can control). As we slow down our heart rate, we can send a signal back to our brain to let the amygdala know we are not in danger.

Script for Creating an Amygdala and Bed. *Please use a small candy tin with a lid or an empty cell phone box. Modeling clay can be used to create an amygdala. Soft fabric can be used for bedding to turn the interior of the box or candy tin into a cozy bed. Describe the amygdala and then offer a box/tin*

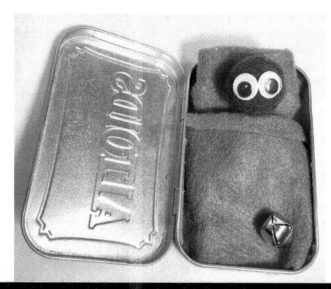

Figure 4.3 Amygdala character and bed made from a candy tin box.

that can serve as the "bed" for the amygdala's resting place. For clients willing to try this art directive, added elements such as felt for bedding are helpful for reinforcing the idea of making the amygdala feel comfortable while at rest. Feel free to include a small bell that gets to be the amygdala's alarm system. If your client doesn't want to design or shape the amygdala out of clay, a LEGO person can be used to anthropomorphize it. This same directive could be done as a simple drawing as well.

Script for EMDR Reprocessing (save for Phase Four). *Before we begin the bilateral stimulation part of EMDR, please place your amygdala character at a distance from its bed that represents your level of distress. The higher the distress level, the further away it will be. As we go through the bilateral stimulation rounds, please move your amygdala closer to the bed after each round, and as the distress level begins to go down. Our goal is to get the amygdala all the way back into its bed when the distress levels have completely dissipated. Really, we are training the amygdala that you are no longer in danger when this memory is activated.* [The clinician can then engage in rounds of BLS. At the end of each round, they can ask the client to move their amygdala closer to the bed to represent how much their SUD went down. Continue until the amygdala character is back in the bed.] See Figure 4.3.

Case Study for Creating an Amygdala

Tom, age 14, came to therapy three weeks after a terrifying incident of being caught in a tornado. Although he was not injured in the tornado, he was exhibiting symptoms of acute stress disorder and became obsessed with checking the weather forecast, refusing to go outside of his home if it was cloudy or if there was a tiny amount of wind. The initial trauma involved his father driving him home to be safely sheltered in place from a nearby approaching tornado. In the height of the moment, Tom reports that he was screaming at his father to drive in one direction, yet his father chose to drive in another direction, causing them to inadvertently drive directly toward the tornado which was a few blocks away. They arrived home safely despite being in such close proximity to the tornado. Their home was fine, but the neighborhood experienced significant damage. Unlike other natural disasters that allow for preparation/safety, tornadoes develop very fast, and can decimate entire towns in a matter of minutes.

Tom was reluctant to come to therapy, and the first sessions covered steps one to three of treatment planning, creating rapport and establishing the treatment goal of reducing the residual symptoms of the tornado experience. Tom was introduced to the role of the amygdala in his brain and the importance it played in helping him attempt to flee from danger. He learned that the residual, activated state was due to his activated amygdala.

The second session involved creating a small puff ball character representing Tom's amygdala, complete with googly eyes. He then created a comfortable bed for the amygdala using a small, empty candy tin box. The bed included a bell (to represent the amygdala's alarm system) and a small felt blanket and pillow. Tom was then given handheld EMDR tappers and asked to place the activated amygdala far from the bed to represent how much distress he felt regarding the tornado experience. He was asked to move the amygdala character closer and closer to its "bed" with each round of EMDR as the SUD related to the memory lowered in intensity.

As he recounted the experience, Tom shared the terror of the noise (tornados often sound like loud trains), the lack of control as a passenger in his father's car, and the crucial negative cognition of not feeling heard by his father. He reported the pattern of his father never listening to him, and that even in a crisis, his father chose not to listen to him by choosing to turn the opposite way which inadvertently placed them in danger. He identified anger, frustration, and the fear of death in coming so close to a destructive tornado. As he processed each element of this experience, he was able to place the amygdala character closer and closer to the bed, and after several rounds during the same session, he was able to place it back into the bed. His mother reported several days later that all of his symptoms related to this incident had completely disappeared and he comfortably stood on his porch photographing images of an approaching storm.

Boundaries

Boundary work with people in their adolescent and young adult years can be profoundly important. Although this topic is useful with adults as well, a young person's growing independence frequently serves as a time of boundary exploration. Areas of importance include their online personas, relationships, emerging sexuality, work, gender choices, substance use, and school (Pipher, 2019). This topic allows for a concrete understanding of mind and body work as clients are often introduced to the "gut" feeling that accompanies a boundary violation. Guilt and shame are often felt with boundary violations, and the therapeutic work includes processing these emotions and cognitions and offering tools for creating healthy boundaries (Siegel, 2015).

EMDR is an excellent modality for exploring boundaries, as the memory reprocessing can quickly alter a person's perception of their experience and reduce their negative cognition around boundary violations that are often internalized. Offering the language related to the concept of a boundary is one that many young people have never considered, so the linguistics of naming something, enhancing it with artwork, and then using both to reduce negative beliefs can be a powerful experience, covering many areas of need including psychoeducation, trauma work, future thinking, and an enhanced sense of self-worth (Greenwald, 2015). Describing the establishment of boundaries as a lifelong process can reduce the shame of past boundary violations, and lower unreasonable expectations for a young person's current need to create healthy boundaries in their various relationships.

The other extreme of unhealthy boundaries includes social isolation. The trend of many Gen Z teens to isolate at home has increased over the past several years and was further exacerbated as a result of the COVID-19 pandemic (Twenge et al., 2021). Helping young people adjust their boundaries to reestablish social ties is helpful and necessary in the COVID-19 pandemic time period. Experiential therapy is considered essential to trauma treatment, and actively engaging a teen or young person into exploring boundaries in the therapy room rather than just talking about it can be useful to allow for a deeper working model of how to identify healthy boundaries.

Script for Boundary Exploration (in person session). [The materials needed for this activity are string/yarn, small pieces of paper, a pen or pencil, and paper]. *Please stand up and create a space around yourself* [with the therapist standing several feet away]. *Please take the first piece of yarn* [approx. four feet long] *and place it on the ground around you so it can represent your inner boundary. Is it loose, tight, open, closed? Please take the next piece of yarn and create the next concentric boundary on the ground. Is it further away from the first one? Feel free to make a few more boundaries around the first circle using more yarn. How does it feel to be in your boundary? Who gets to be in that inner circle with you?* [The therapist can write names on the paper and place people in their inner realm.]

I am going to now briefly step into your inner boundary with you. [The therapist should determine before doing this activity how well the client can handle this level of close proximity, as it can often cause a visceral sensation to have a clinician stepping into their space. Please only stay in this space for a few seconds. It is important to not touch the client.] *Did you feel uncomfortable when I stepped into this space? In what part of your body are you feeling this discomfort?* [Note that clients often report their gut or torso area.] *THAT is a boundary violation, and we just connected a mind and body experience. Please tell me how far back I should stand for your comfort level if I just made you feel very uncomfortable? Do you want/need to shift your boundaries that you created for yourself? Is there anyone you want to be in or out of your space? Can you think of these circles of yarn as your boundaries as you go through your week? Please be gentle with yourself as you learn to shift your boundaries and how and when you say yes or no to various things. Boundary work takes time to master.*

Script for Boundary Exploration (Telehealth Session). *Please take a pen and paper. Write your name in the middle of the paper and create concentric circles around your name. Please imagine each of these circles as a boundary that can help you determine where people in your world belong. Who gets to be in your sacred inner space/circle? Is there anyone you would like to move outward or inward? Can this model be helpful for deciding how you are "doing" your boundaries?*

Case Study of Boundary Exploration over Telehealth

Kate, age 24, came to teletherapy reporting increased anxiety and depression related to her relationship and family issues while living at home during the COVID-19 pandemic (Figure 4.4). Travel restrictions forced her to be separated from her fiancé for over a year. Kate also reported an unresolved trauma of being assaulted in college by a pizza delivery person.

Much of the therapy work with Kate was related to her boundaries with friends, family, and relationships. She reported being the "resident therapist" in her friend group, often sacrificing her own wants and needs to place her friends' needs first. She feared if she didn't play this role, she would lose her friends. She found this pattern repeated in many of her relationships.

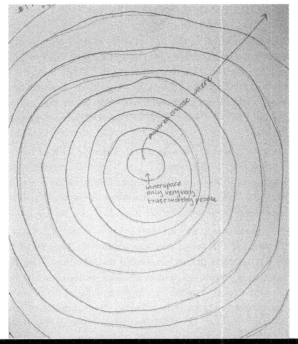

Figure 4.4 Concentric circles to identify client's personal boundaries.

Her drawings of concentric boundaries, with her in the middle, helped give her a framework to better understand her pattern of placing everyone ahead of her own wants and needs. The visual tool helped immensely, as Kate was able to decide in real time who she allowed into her inner circle, and how it made her feel.

Through EMDR reprocessing several sessions after this image was created, Kate chose to focus on a high school memory of working in a restaurant at age 14 and being groomed by an older coworker, who was eventually fired for making advances at her in the workplace. Her parents chose to avoid legal intervention, and she always felt they sided with the perpetrator instead of her. In one EMDR reprocessing session, she was able to quickly reduce her negative cognitions. She was able to remember her attempts to say no to the perpetrator's advances and misunderstanding his kindness due to her inexperience and young age. This recognition helped reduce her sense of shame she carried with her for years for allowing the experience to happen.

As Kate began to recognize her own strength through the updated cognitions related to this memory, she was able to regroup in her current life, placing her needs over others. During this time period, her fiancé broke off the engagement, but he continued to send mixed signals with requests to repair the relationship followed by long bouts of silence. Kate was able to create healthy boundaries and eventually saw his behavior as toxic. Her imagery and positive cognitions from EMDR reprocessing allowed her to see a repeated pattern of attempts to express herself (to be left alone), and not being heard (as her ex-fiancé and a male perpetrator in high school continued to bother her despite her requests to be left alone). Rather than stay stuck with the ex-fiancé, Kate broke off ties and felt a sense of relief and empowerment of caring for herself.

EMDR PHASE THREE: ASSESSMENT

Determining the topics to address in therapy can be challenging, especially with teenagers who often feel overwhelmed by the many compounding issues that brought them to therapy. Narrowing the topics down to what will be addressed in EMDR can be even more challenging, as young clients are still untangling the many issues they are working through. Enlisting the creative process can help clients safely address events, memories, and cognitions causing distress to be explored in EMDR. Phase Three involves creating a very specific road map for the EMDR work.

Listing various topics empowers the client as they decide what order to place their memories in and decide what they wish to explore first. Externalizing difficult themes or events can create some distance from the emotional pain without having to explain it to the therapist. As specific topics are chosen to explore, this phase identifies current distress levels and the negative cognitions associated with the client's experience.

In phase three of assessment, Shapiro (2018) refers to an important part of this stage as "selecting the picture" of the target memory. Although the goal of EMDR therapy is to make the negative emotional charge connected to the image disappear, creative interventions in this stage can be very helpful in articulating more nuanced elements of clients' memories. Capturing the negative cognitions in the art allows for clients to return to their art once the distress levels have been reduced to see how much they have shifted in their belief system.

Adding concrete visual imagery offers an expanded opportunity for communication and offers an easy way for a client to access their implicit memories. The artwork can be changed, altered, destroyed, and enhanced at any point during or after EMDR reprocessing to reinforce and highlight updated cognitions, and for a client to further distance themselves from their previous thought patterns. Externalizing imagery in a concrete way enhances Shapiro's original goals of "creating a picture." Multiple neurological pathways must be activated to use one's imagination to create a picture and verbally identify this to the clinician (Kandel, 2012). Artwork is the bridge to simplify this process; the external imagery offers a concrete and physical thing to name and identify with verbal processing. Based on the latest understanding/research that traumatic imagery is stored in the non-verbal hemispheres of the brain, asking a client to verbalize their experience can be challenging and simply ineffective (Kandel, 2006).

ART THERAPY DIRECTIVE FOR PHASE THREE—ASSESSMENT

Design a Record Album

This art directive is a creative approach to explore and identify specific memories in preparation for the reprocessing phases of EMDR. The creative structure of a record album allows the client to list many target memories for reprocessing, or to identify many fragments of one specific memory. Some clients might choose actual song titles that resonate with their experience, and others might use the overall structure of a record to creatively depict their experience through imagery they design themselves on the cover and song titles they *invent* (as seen below in the case study) to capture overall themes related to their memory. The use of metaphor and symbolism can serve as a protective factor in addressing traumatic memories (Gonzalez & Masquera, 2012). Materials needed are a pen and paper and prefer-ably a 12×12 inch piece of paper to mimic the size of a record album.

Script for Designing an Album Cover. Materials needed are a pen and paper and preferably a 12×12 inch piece of paper to mimic the size of a record album. *Today we are going to explore some of the topics we will work on as we engage in EMDR. We are not going to go into detail about any of them, but we will simply identify the bothersome memories we plan to tackle in future sessions. Core negative beliefs we develop in our lives often run on auto-pilot until we explore them, and recognize they are often outdated. Today we are going to make a plan for the EMDR work we will be doing together. We will not be going into any detail on anything, but just looking at it with a "birds' eye" view. Instead of just creating a traditional list of topics, we will use our creativity to create a record album. If you feel triggered as you list a topic, we can stop and regroup.*

Can you think of an image or work to be on the cover of your album that might be symbolic of how you are feeling or what brought you into therapy? Think of your favorite records or CDs and how the artist chose their cover image to represent their music. There is no need for perfection here, but this symbolism offers a way to capture some of the emotional things you are working through.

Can you list the topics we will eventually cover in the reprocessing part of EMDR? We could just make a list, but it might be easier and more interesting to create song titles on your "album" to identify the main themes we will cover. These might be real song titles that actually exist, or this might be a place to creatively express parts of your story with made up song titles. Maybe the most difficult one or the one causing the most distress will be the first song listed. Instead of just writing down the topic, the song title can be more metaphorical to hint at the topic.

To prepare for an EMDR reprocessing session (hopefully a session following this one), we will choose one of these topics and explore many elements of it including the emotions, the places in your body you might be feeling these emotions, and the negative and positive cognitions associated with this particular topic. You get to decide which "song title" or topic is the most important to do first. [The clinician can use the chosen topic to then explore the NC, PC, VOC, and SUD related to the image or song title.] See Figure 4.5.

Case Study for Design a Record Album

Amanda was introduced to the Design a Record Album EMDR directive during a teletherapy session as she navigated through the complexities of the COVID-19 pandemic. She had come to therapy in person the previous year, and she already had rapport with this author. Her isolation in a stressful home contributed to her depression, anxiety, and overall despondence. She had a history of cutting and reported having a relapse in self-harming behavior. Amanda also reported symptoms of depersonalization. Creating song titles helped her to fully express the many emotions she was experiencing but was unable to articulate in teletherapy sessions. Without having to go into detail, she was able to express herself in a short amount of time. Amanda reported feeling *heard* as she read off each title. She also felt empowered as she chose which topic to tackle first in EMDR reprocessing in the following session.

The week after Amanda drew this image, she chose her forth song on her list entitled "Wall of Shame" instead of "Hall of Fame" as a topic for reprocessing. She reported the pressure to be perfect in school due to her mom's high expectations for her to do well in her community college classes despite her young age, the pandemic, and her isolation. She ranked her level of distress at a nine and identified negative and positive cognitions related to the topic. Through EMDR reprocessing, she processed a memory of a sexual assault at

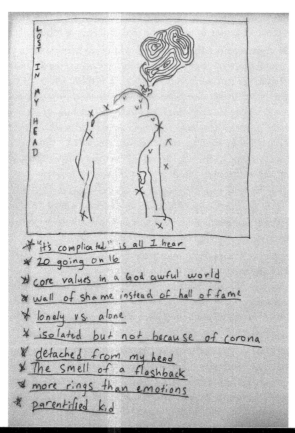

Figure 4.5 Imaginary album cover and songs to identify topics for EMDR.

age 12 that she had only recently disclosed to her family. Her perceived need to refrain from sharing this with her parents related to feelings of shame and their expectations for her to be perfect. This session provided somatic relief and eliminated the desire to cut. A follow-up mother/daughter session focused on disrupting negative patterns was very helpful in the therapy process. Amanda was able to tackle other themes from this art piece and identify reduced levels of distress in the reevaluation Phase Eight of EMDR when looking back at this piece of art. Amanda's small American town experienced an unprecedented amount of teen suicides during the pandemic, and the implementation of EMDR in her therapy helped her continue to express herself as she dealt with the grief and uncertainty within her peer group.

EMDR PHASE FOUR: DESENSITIZATION AND REPROCESSING

Phase Four of EMDR offers an opportunity for a client to experience the rapid reprocessing of memories, cognitions, and somatic sensations through the desensitization of a target memory via bilateral stimulation. Much of the creative preparation work is designed to enhance this reprocessing phase, which is the culmination and key element of EMDR (due to the rapid reduction of distress as a result of the BLS). The artwork created to identify target memories can be helpful to prepare for this crucial phase of EMDR because the client has already begun to creatively tackle the issues and name the unnamable elements of their memories and experiences. Artwork made in previous sessions can be displayed during the desensitization and installation phase to further activate the multiple layers of target memories.

EMDR is considered a three-pronged approach that addresses past memories, present levels of distress, and future templates, with the assumption that negative, present-tense thinking will lead to continued negative patterns (Shapiro, 2018). Exploring one's past, present, and future can be enhanced through creative self-expression in place of a traditional interview during the initial therapy sessions.

The goal of EMDR therapy is to reduce the current stressors allowing a person to access unresolved memories that contribute to their current distress. Sadly, earlier versions of trauma therapy explored issues that seemed distressing, even if they were not currently bothersome, often creating secondary trauma in the therapy room as non-bothersome memories were activated (Hass-Cohen & Findley, 2015).

Art making can allow a client to be simultaneously transparent and private. The client can externalize their memories by symbolically depicting their trauma into the artwork but choosing when and how to verbally articulate a difficult experience. Artwork used in the reprocessing phase can also be useful for Phase Eight as well so clients can reevaluate their previous cognitions and measure their emotional growth with a concrete piece of art that physically represents their old cognitions. Enhancing reprocessing with art can contribute to more comfortable and open communication and allows for nuanced elements to be woven into a young person's reprocessing experience.

ART THERAPY DIRECTIVE FOR PHASE FOUR OF EMDR DESENSITIZATION AND REPROCESSING

The Triptych Technique (Highlighting the Three-Pronged Approach to EMDR)

A triptych form is iconic in pre-Renaissance art and was often used to depict religious scenes in three panels of wood or other materials (Kandel, 2012). This art directive mimics the triptych by using three separate pieces of paper for past, present, and future thinking and to reflect the three-pronged approach to EMDR. Even if the client depicts their storyline in simple stick figures or words, the creative experience of assembling a triptych enhances the narrative by offering an external place to "capture" the information and elevate the idea to a concept from art history.

Although this art directive is similar to a timeline, the idea of three separate images on three separate sheets of paper offers a concrete place for a client to identify their current distress, what contributed to the current distress, and their level of hope for the near future. This artwork is useful to look at again in Phase Eight as clients can reevaluate their previous cognitions and measure their emotional growth with a concrete piece of art that physically holds their old cognitions. This art directive serves multiple goals as it helps consolidate many elements from Phases One to Three, while serving an important purpose during Phase Four of reprocessing. Placing the art in the client's line of vision to stay present in the unique three-pronged approach, and allowing them to alter their imagery in real time as their cognitions are changing can enhance the reprocessing phase.

Script for Creating a Triptych. *A triptych is a common art form found in pre-Renaissance art, often on wood panels. Although imagery was created on three different panels, the three distinct images usually had a coherent theme. We will be imitating this art form today by dividing our art into three different sections with one common theme of the memory we are reprocessing. Please use these three sheets of paper to create your own triptych. One paper will represent the past memory / experience / cognition, the second one will represent the distress levels and elements of this memory or experience that is currently troubling you, and the third one will depict something you imagine for the near future, or what you might be doing when you are no longer in distress. You might want to keep it very simple by working in stick figures, words, cartoons, magazine collage, or symbols.*

Let's start with the paper that will represent the present, then it might be easier to create the other two images. With EMDR work, we always explore what the current distress level is, and explore the old memories we are working to process. Please don't feel like you need to draw an exact image of what your stress looks like. You might want to have that image just be symbolic (a color, symbol, logo, or basic image that represents the here and now). Some people choose the same symbol for all three images, like a heart, a sun, a star, or something simple to give their images some continuity.

We will now take the second piece of paper to create the imagery related to the past. If your memory is traumatic you don't need to depict exactly what happened, but maybe you will have a symbol or a color represent this experience. As you work, you might be aware of sensations, body feelings, or emotions as you think about this. We want to use this information to reduce the distress that arises, and in the reprocessing we will be revisiting these memories, body feelings, negative beliefs, and emotions you have around this experience.

The third image will represent a time with reduced distress over your memory. We will call our new thinking a "positive cognition" as it is an updated version of your experience with more accurate information such as "I was just a kid" or "I was doing the best I could." This third image might represent what you will be doing, thinking, or feeling when you are less stuck with your current level of distress.

This directive is designed to help clients conceptualize their past, present, and future cognitions and emotions. Once the art is created, it is helpful to have them identify the negative and positive cognition, either just articulating it, or actually adding it into their artwork. It is best for clients to create this in Phase Two or Three to establish the negative/positive cognitions, current level of distress, and then is useful to use during the reprocessing phase. Placing the artwork in front of the client during reprocessing can be helpful, and they might choose to add elements to the various images as their SUD are reduced. This imagery can also be very useful for reinforcing positive cognitions in Phase Six. Having the artwork present during the reprocessing is helpful for young clients to stay focused on their particular memory.

Case Study for Creating a Triptych

David, age 17, was introduced to a triptych for the reprocessing session based on several months of work in therapy. He was entering into his second romantic relationship following a devastating breakup with his first boyfriend. He is an only child, and his mother got full custody of him following his parents' divorce when he was five, even though his father served as his primary secure attachment figure. His mother was often emotionally distant, angry, and rarely took care of his basic needs.

David recognized his pattern of looking for love, validation, and attention from peers to compensate for his attachment disruptions in childhood. He was asked to make a triptych

Figure 4.6 Image represents current level of distress.

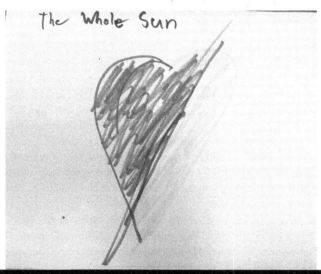

Figure 4.7 Future image represents self-love and feeling fine either in or out of a relationship.

preceding a reprocessing session. For the present tense image, he drew a heart with color starting to fill the heart, recognizing that his own wants and needs were important. Following each round with the tappers, he added more images to the present tense image. He included a dark and faded scribble to represent how his desire for deepening his relationship with his father was indicated by a deeper level of intensity in the darkened line (see Figure 4.6).

For his future image, David drew a heart divided into two, and identified this as true self love, representing his desire to be fine when he is either in or out of a romantic relationship (see Figure 4.7).

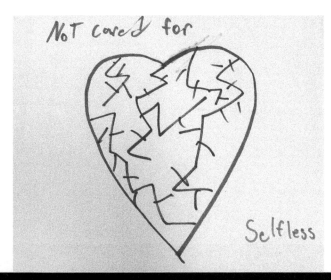

Figure 4.8 Image of past and recognition of the client's need to be selfless.

David drew the past as a broken heart to represent his first romantic breakup, his pattern of giving to others to mimic what he wanted for himself, and the misattunement from his mother (see Figure 4.8).

David was able to connect many elements of previous sessions that these topics explored. Between reprocessing rounds, he added more elements to his imagery. The physical changes to his artwork directly reflected the mental processing of his memories. The combination of the art making and reprocessing seemed to enhance his insight and ability to shift his self-blame for his mother's neglect and his need to be perfect to win her love. His positive cognition was recognizing he has wants and needs and this can happen in romantic relationships, and he can be comfortable with himself in or out of relationships.

David was often reluctant to share his art with his father at the end of sessions, but following this reprocessing, he asked this author to help him explain everything that had happened in the session to his father. He identified the experience of drawing, coloring, and using the tappers in the session as very helpful to give a voice to the information he was not previously able to express verbally.

EMDR PHASE FIVE: INSTALLATION

As SUD related to negative cognitions are reduced for people as they work through Phase Four EMDR, it can be challenging with members of this generation to quickly transition into the installation phase (Phase Five), as prescribed by the eight-phase model. Although this age group has not been widely researched or discussed in EMDR literature, contextual issues should be taken into consideration during the transition from Phase Four to Five in order to intensify the installation of positive and updated cognitions. Research on the effectiveness of a rapid shift in cognition with EMDR has been demonstrated in work with all populations (Shapiro, 2018), but Gen Z's lived experience is radically different from any previous teen/young adult generation (Lutrell & McGrath, 2021).

The clinician's expectation of this generation to quickly pivot to embrace positive cognitions about themselves and the world around them might be overly optimistic. The algorithms of social media reinforce negative cognitions, making the negativity harder to shift in young minds (Rousseau & Maconi, 2020). Therefore, Phase Five may take longer and involve more interweaves and exploration to help adolescents shift to a new belief about who they are. Art can support this shift by providing flexible perspectives and new insights.

The sophistication of complex algorithms that dictate one's digital feed through social media are so responsive that the vast majority of new information people see through their social media channels directly reflects their searches. Negativity begets more negativity (Pew Research, 2018). As adolescents and young adults turn to their devices for solace or advice, they inadvertently receive highly curated data, perpetuating and enhancing the adolescent developmental stage of extreme and siloed thinking (Riehm et al., 2019). Convincing but inaccurate information (information not verified by research, facts, or fact checking) is often reflected as the relentless and remunerative current iteration of the internet offers endless information to an age group with an underdeveloped prefrontal cortex and an inability to sift through this vast amount of data (Iqbal, 2021). This age group appears to be living a dual life consisting of their online persona and a real-world persona, which are often incongruent. Shame and guilt often accompany this dichotomy as their online selves are often unabashed in over-communicating or seeking solace from strangers or worse, engaging with some form of bot or artificial intelligence posing as a supportive human (Twenge, 2018). Tending to their real-world self is new territory for many people in this age range.

This young generation's isolation has been further escalated by living through or maturing through the COVID-19 era. Perpetuating their often-unrealistic mindset, their digital devices function as a conduit of their "truth" with relentless incoming and often inaccurate information. The therapist must recognize the potential battle of convincing a young person that there are other ways to "see" themselves and their lived experience beyond what their digital feeds might be reflecting. Algorithms might have populated their news feeds with a false reality filled with negativity and images/videos of peers engaged in the same negative behaviors they themselves are engaged in such as cutting, eating disorders, self-harm, substance abuse, and other poor coping tools. Whistleblower and former employee of Facebook, Frances Haugen, reported that the social media giant knew this negative outcome of their system, especially with teen girls and body image, but failed to intervene to protect their users' well-being (Haugen, 2021). By the time members of this age group begin working with a therapist, their skewed versions of reality have often gone unchecked for months or years, as most people in Gen Z have lived much of their teen and young adult years with a cell phone, and often without the adults in their lives truly understanding the complexity of their teenagers' digital worlds (Riehm et al, 2019). Negative cognitions magnified by complex and intensely personal algorithms require new and robust levels of attention in the therapy process before this transitional phase of EMDR can be successful.

Explaining and thus slowing down the installation phase of EMDR empowers a young client as they fully embrace the possibility that the transition from negative to positive cognitions is even possible. Using metaphor can enhance new ways of thinking and feeling, and reduce suspicion that therapists are being too optimistic with the role of EMDR therapy to address their lived experience. Lakoff (2014) identifies the important role of metaphor to enlist abstract thinking and emotional connections in the form of embodiment. In the transition from Phase Four to Five, the use of metaphor to explain this shift in cognitions can be helpful, especially with clients in the Gen Z population. As the probing for positive cognitions should be explored in Phase Three, it is helpful to transition between Phase Four and Phase Five with a simple metaphor to delineate between the phases.

Script for Explaining Phase Five of Installation. *Sometimes using a metaphor to explain what we are doing can better help to understand this EMDR experience. A great way to think about this stage of EMDR is with an image of a candy cane or a candy stick. If you can imagine a typical red and white candy cane, could you think of the memory we are exploring as the actual candy cane, and everything you thought, believed, felt (felt in your body) is the red stripe swirled around the candy cane. The work we just did of lowering your level of distress was sort of like taking the red stripe off that candy cane, leaving you with just the plain white stick or just a neutral memory. With EMDR, we don't want to leave you with just the neutral memory, we want to enhance it with new, updated thinking, feelings, and understanding. Using our candy cane metaphor, it's almost like we are taking the plain white candy cane and rewrapping it with a new color that can represent a new belief about that old memory. We can't change the past, but we can change how we think about the memory, which not only quiets the whole thing down, but can empower us to store the memory differently.*

ART THERAPY DIRECTIVE FOR PHASE FIVE OF EMDR— INSTALLATION

Identifying an Inner Spark

The sense of hopelessness in this generation is palpable, and young people coming to therapy often have a challenging time identifying positive parts of themselves if their negative life experiences and/or negative thinking dominate their worldview. Incorporating both creativity and the client's belief in acceptance of positive parts of themselves can be helpful to prepare for the installation stage of the therapy process. If a young person is currently in a state of distress and only seeing negative elements of their identity, enlisting the creative process to identify positive parts of self allows for easier access than asking a young person to simply list them. Artwork done in Phases Two and Three of preparation can enhance this transition to Phase Five, even if clients don't quite believe in their positive cognitions as they engage in the art making.

Script for Finding an Inner Spark. *We all have an inner spark. Sometimes it is large but in some stages of our life this spark can shrink down to be as tiny as a grain of sand. Even in our darkest moments, this spark is always present. It is up to us to search inside and locate it. If you could imagine your inner spark, where in your body does it live? What does it look like? Is it tiny? Is it gigantic? Could you draw or paint it, even if it is just a shape? How big is it on the page? Could it be represented by an object? A logo? A symbol? An amorphous shape? What does it need to grow? Can you draw a simple version of it? It might be a dot on the page or a tiny circle. This simple image can be helpful to conjure something in our imagination and make it easier to imagine its future growth.*

Case Study of Finding an Inner Spark

Joe's parents brought him to therapy at age 18 during his first psychotic episode which resulted from several days with no sleep after abruptly stopping excessive marijuana use. Joe had been engaged in daily drug use for three years (Figure 4.9). The family was not comfortable placing their son in an inpatient psychiatric setting, and they felt they could supervise

Figure 4.9 Flames to represent client's inner spark.

him through this episode. This pattern of psychosis continued for five years through his cycle of excessive marijuana use and abrupt periods of sobriety until he stabilized with monthly injections of antipsychotic medication.

His recovery phase from a relapse always resulted in lack of sleep, deep shame, guilt, and paranoia. Multiple hospital stays and multiple encounters with the police coming to his home, during which his parents feared for their safety due to his homicidal threats, became the norm in his cycle. Joe's parents were also dealing with their own significant health issues during this time period, including his mother receiving a heart transplant and his father's unsuccessful surgery for chronic back pain.

Joe's psychosis continued and he eventually was given a diagnosis of schizophrenia. One full year of therapy was required to convince him to take monthly injections of antipsychotic medication. Once he began this medication, it allowed him to live a stable life. Joe's emotional journey during this period was profound, as he slowly acclimated to his new life and ended his dream of joining the US Air Force (he had already received his pilot's license in high school). Joe went through several periods of intense suicidal ideation and times of hopelessness during his therapy journey. He lost a friend to suicide during this time, and he often considered copying his friend. His visits to a forest near his home (where his friend took his own life) was a place of refuge, but also a place to fantasize his own suicide which he identified would involve hanging himself from one of the trees.

It was imperative in the therapy process to create hope where he saw none, and the slow, therapeutic journey focused on quieting down the intense feelings of guilt and shame Joe felt from various stages of his life and poor choices he made in seeking drugs. Joe was asked to contemplate what his inner spark might look like, and he identified a small campfire. Using this metaphor, he was able to recognize times his campfire felt as small as hot embers, and times it felt like a roaring fire.

Joe had trouble verbally identifying positive cognitions and he found the imagery easier to discuss. He was able to use the imagery during an EMDR reprocessing session to imagine the spark growing into a small campfire in his chest. Although he wasn't necessarily feeling hopeful in his life, he found the imagery and art helpful for initial EMDR sessions. He continued to refer to his artwork and found the installation phase of EMDR as helpful for eradicating suicidal ideation and creating a narrative of a hopeful near future. He also reported this positive cognition work and positive focus as helpful, as many other mental health professionals saw him only as his diagnosis or his police record. Three years into therapy, Joe still referred back to this imagery and symbolism, and reported that the imagery and physical art made in sessions virtually eliminated suicidal ideation.

EMDR PHASE SIX: BODY SCAN

Once the desensitization and installation phases are complete, Phase Six of EMDR shifts to a focus on somatic sensations connected to the target memory as the final check to ensure that there is no residual somatic sensation or distress, and that reprocessing is complete. The psychoeducation work preceding reprocessing sessions can help clients to pair their emotions with sensations felt in their body. EMDR is quite powerful in its ability to unite fragmented body sensations, memories, and negative cognitions as a coherent memory and experience, yet fully processing a memory or experience requires attention in all of these areas (Bergman, 2020). For young people in need of tools for self-regulation, inviting them to become both aware of their body and mind by pairing/linking various physical sensations to emotions can be empowering.

Feelings vs. Emotions

Differentiating feelings from emotions can be helpful to invite clients to focus on their bodies to sense for emotional cues. Adding visual art into the conversation can be the concrete link to help young people connect their emotions with their bodies. A sample prompt to introduce feelings vs. emotions preceding this work can enhance this phase of EMDR.

Script for Differentiating Feelings and Emotions. *People often use the words "emotions" and "feelings" interchangeably. There actually is a difference between the two concepts. Feelings are things you can name such as, "I am cold, hungry, tired, grumpy, etc." Emotions are sensations we feel in our body before our conscious mind is actually aware of them (Damasio, 2000). Fear is a common one. Your body might sense danger before you are aware of it, and your nervous system will send out signals to activate your body to protect you (increased heart rate, dilated pupils, etc.). Our nervous system responds before we are consciously even aware that we are experiencing an emotion. As we get better at feeling, naming, and consciously identifying emotions, we can begin to treat emotions like messengers. We can then learn to self-regulate and decide, "Am I really in danger, or is my body just sensing this moment as a danger?" Our body sometimes misfires based on outdated information it remembers from previous experiences (smells, sounds, sights, tastes).*

The seven universal emotions are anger, disgust, fear, happiness, sadness, surprise, and contempt (Ekman, 2005). *As we get better at detecting these emotions, we also can recognize our body signals trying to cue us into these emotions.*

When we engage in EMDR reprocessing work, we often activate the emotions (and body sensations) we experienced with our memory. As we work through these memories, these emotions you experienced might get reactivated during an EMDR session exploring difficult parts of a memory. We call these "body memories." Sometimes when we revisit an old bothersome memory, these old body sensations wake up, and we feel them all over again. This stage of EMDR helps us quiet our body down with any of these activated memories, and we can override the system to let it know it is now safe.

Artwork done preceding this session or following an EMDR reprocessing session can further enhance the importance of learning to differentiate feelings from emotions and help clients recognize the neurobiology of their bodies. As young people often turn to their digital devices or drugs/alcohol for distractions and to avoid emotional pain, this new avenue of identifying emotions through body cues can be profoundly important. As many somatic sensations activate during an EMDR session, this body awareness can empower young people to self-regulate before ending a session and outside of sessions as well.

Anger is a common theme seen in the Gen Z population and is an excellent emotion to explore as it is often stuffed down, overly expressed, or mixed with shame and guilt (Siegel, 2015). Normalizing universal emotions can empower a young person, reduce shame, and offer the important understanding of feeling, naming the sensation, and learning self-regulation. This seems like a lot for a young person to conquer in a short amount of time, so enhancing this stage with creative interventions before engaging in EMDR reprocessing can further empower a young person to unite their body sensations with their lived experience.

ART THERAPY DIRECTIVE FOR PHASE SIX—BODY SCAN

Grump Meter—Anger Management and EMDR

Emotions management is often the foundation of therapy work with teenagers and young adults. Gen Z has been forced to contend with new arenas of anger expression as the creation of social media during their lives serves as a backdrop to this population of digital natives. The ubiquitous expression of hatred online through many social media platforms, combined with a new era of politicized anger expression that marked the Trump era, has created a challenging dynamic for this generation (Hoge et al., 2017). As algorithms and media consolidation reduce social media users to see the world only from their vantage point, anger at others has shifted into a cultural norm. In the United States, this young age group has also grown up with police presence in their school settings, and students' anger outbursts often lead to police intervention, rather than trips to the principal, limiting emotional expression due to fear of negative consequences (Whitaker et al., 2017). EMDR can play an important role in identifying the mind-body connections of emotions and body sensations as anger is often felt in the body before a person is consciously aware of it (Ekman, 2005). As young people make this body and mind connection, they can learn to better control their emotions.

An excellent tool for teaching families how to deal with anger is a model called the Grump Meter. This deceptively simple tool is designed to help people express anger in an effective way. At first, families often think the experience of making a Grump Meter in session is for young children, but they tend to return to follow-up sessions surprised by how effective it is for creating rapid change in the home. It simultaneously addresses members of their family who don't know how to express anger and those who have not yet learned how to control their anger.

Using a color scale, the Grump Meter offers users a measurement to reflect and identify clients' current level of anger and other emotions, and their corresponding sensory experience, while inviting them to express themselves with the simple communication of a color word. The Grump Meter offers five choices: blue, green, yellow, orange, or red. At the bottom of the Grump Meter, the blue square signifies calm; the next color up, green, is for grumpy; the third color, yellow, is for caution—paying cautious attention to one's own emotional escalation; the fourth, orange, signals the user to "stop" before escalating to the top of the emotional ladder; and the final step, red, is "explode," for escalated feelings that can lead to explosive behavior. This tool helps users validate their anger (rather than feeling shame from their anger). When families are invited to use this tool at the beginning of the therapy process, they can disrupt old patterns, getting comfortable with the often dangerous emotion of anger.

For family members who have trouble controlling their anger, this tool can reduce their out-of-control emotions into an organized form of self-expression. Additionally, the Grump Meter offers a safe way to express oneself for those unable to access their emotions or use their voice (Kaufman & Kaufman, 2011).

This simple tool also invites family members to listen to one another differently. When a person experiencing anger identifies how they are feeling in the moment, with a non-threatening color word, they are communicating safely. A listener can learn to hear and accept that communication. A non-defensive form of listening can serve as an act of compassion. The listener can, in turn, lower their defensive stance and ask the angry person what they need (distance? comfort? conversation?). By introducing a simple vocabulary for feelings and a visual image for awareness of self and other, the Grump Meter encourages new patterns for emotional self-expression. Further, expressing anger more safely, and responding to it more calmly, reduces the guilt and shame that often accompany anger. Families who incorporate this tool into their lives report extreme and rapid shifts in communication patterns. Offering the Grump Meter in Phase Two of EMDR is useful in preparation for the body scan and somatic issues that are addressed in Phase Six.

Clients can access a digital version of the Grump Meter through an app on their phones or iPad (only iOS as of this printing). Having a digital tool to offer clients, especially youth, helps reinforce material covered in therapy and allows people to access a tool in real time if they are agitated or triggered. This phone app can be useful following an EMDR reprocessing session. Clients can personalize the app and use it to recognize their triggers and somatic sensations, and focus on healthy coping skills.

Case Study Using the Grump Meter

Ann, age 18, came to therapy reporting extreme anxiety, depression, and a fear of engaging in social activity during the final semester of high school (Figure 4.10). Her mother was present in Ann's initial sessions and was actively involved in the therapy process (at Ann's request). Ann reported out-of-control rage at home yet being socially awkward at school and distant with friends. She hoped to find tools to shift this behavior. She had insight into her negative treatment of friends. Due to her lack of management of her own emotions, Ann feared she was unlikeable, and this resulted in social anxiety and a fear of near future

Figure 4.10 The Grump Meter.

planning for college. EMDR was a goal in the treatment plan, but it was essential to have coping tools in place before Ann was ready for EMDR reprocessing.

Ann and her mother both found the Grump Meter very helpful. Through conversation about the colors, they both were able to identify that much of the anger in their home was created by Ann's father who had not dealt with his own abusive childhood. He refused to participate in family therapy. Ann recognized her own patterns of fear and shutdown for much of her childhood. This initial exploration of anger in the family helped reduce herself blame, and allowed her to explore her negative cognitions, creating a foundation for work on anger in Phases Four to Seven.

Ann's adaptation of the Grump Meter also helped her recognize her fear of self-expression and fear of failure. She returned to therapy one year later to explore extreme anxiety in a public speaking class in college. Through one EMDR session, she was able to identify a time in fifth grade where she froze in a public speaking endeavor. She was able to attribute much of her shame, shutdown, and feelings of low self-worth all back to this one moment in her childhood. The Grump Meter allowed Ann to connect her somatic sensations, anxiety, and anger related to this event. As she processed the body memories that resurfaced in the reprocessing, she was able to recall a parent in the audience who laughed at her. Her SUD dropped quickly as this memory was processed and she was quickly able to self-regulate and update her negative cognition. Ann recognized how much shame and anger was stored in her body from this brief experience of giving a speech as a child. She reported success in her speech class for the remainder of the semester and resolution over much of her self-directed anger.

EMDR PHASE SEVEN: CLOSURE

Closure is a crucial part of the eight-phase EMDR process, and it is essential to reserve enough time at the end of a session to soothe and contain any sensations that were activated during a reprocessing EMDR session. Before concluding an EMDR session, it is important to quiet down any activated emotions, prepare for more emotions to arise following the session, and to encourage clients to use healthy coping tools for self-soothing to prevent any negative and old patterns to emerge such as suicidal ideation or self-harm in the day or days following an EMDR reprocessing session. Focusing on the important step for young people to continue the closure process at home can be helpful to mitigate any reactions to big emotions that arise in the day following an EMDR reprocessing session. This author has received reports of many adolescents experiencing anger and disorganized thinking in the 24 hours after an EMDR session. Preparing young clients and their family members for the possibility of erratic emotions following a session can help the client categorize any uncomfortable emotions as a common part of the EMDR process and the brain's way of consolidating memories. Offering clients permission to feel their emotions can empower them to use their skills to self soothe and classify their emotions as something connected to the EMDR experience.

A creative safety plan is an excellent tool to expand the closure process beyond the end of the therapy session. This creative work should be done well before engaging in Phases Four to Seven of EMDR, and a client can be reminded of it as they engage in the closure process. Secrecy is often what perpetuates poor coping tools and continued self-harm. When clients are comfortable sharing their poor coping tools in the therapy room, the revelation can often reduce the tool's power (such as cutting or self-harming). The clinician can remind the client to listen for cues of old patterns in the hours and days after an EMDR reprocessing session to preempt any poor coping tools from being activated as they process their memories and consolidate their rapid shifts in thinking.

ART THERAPY DIRECTIVES FOR PHASE SEVEN—CLOSURE

Traditionally, healthy coping tools for clients who are at risk of self-harm or suicidal behavior include asking them to sign a "safety contract" to assure the clinician that they will not self-harm, but this exercise can feel flimsy with Gen Z. Copycat behavior is a known phenomenon in suicide among young populations. With the proliferation of hopelessness being magnified through social media, suicide has been normalized as just another choice for this generation to deal with their emotional struggles (Haidt & Twenge, 2021). Finding more robust safety plans with creative interventions is important and essential for EMDR with this age group.

Poured Painting Safety Plan

The options for using creative imagery to create a safety plan are limitless, and this directive enlists a popular trend called "poured painting." Viral videos of people pouring paint onto canvases spurred manufacturers to make this medium available to the public and can be found in kits at craft stores and online. Poured painting involves literally pouring several colors of high viscosity paint all over a canvas or board. It can be quite messy. Art therapists take into consideration the type of medium used in a therapy session, and this type of exercise offers a client an even mix of out-of-control and in-control sensations based on the loose properties of the paint but a sense of control as they move the paint around the canvas.

Script for Art Therapy Directive for Poured Painting. [If the clinician is unfamiliar with this art medium, a poured painting kit is recommended. Materials include a canvas, "ready to pour" or high-flow acrylic paint, small clear cups, tablecloth, and plastic gloves.] *Please choose four to five colors for your painting. Please assign an emotion to each color to explore the battle between suicide ideation and things at the opposite end of the spectrum such as hope, love, family, friends, or a happier time in your life. Please assign some of the colors as a way of staying safe if you are feeling suicidal such as speaking to a loved one, using a healthy coping skill, distracting yourself, or anything else that works for you. Using a small, clear plastic cup, please pour these colors into the cup. They will look like tidy layers of color. You will then pour the paint out onto the blank canvas (this part might feel a bit out of control as you see so much liquid and color swirling around). Once these colors are on the canvas, you can lift the canvas and move it around to watch how the colors interact with one another. People often move the paint around until the entire canvas is covered. This is messy, so please drip the paint onto a newspaper or even a second canvas. This might represent the very confusing mess of emotions we often feel in our heads where negative and positive emotions are all mixed in together. Although we have some control over this, the paint will behave in interesting ways that we can't completely control.*

Once the canvas dries, it can be hung on a wall and serve as a constant reminder to stay safe by visually reinforcing the positive elements you assigned to the colors. Because it is so abstract, people in your life can admire it, and the true nature of the content can stay private. Following an EMDR reprocessing session, this painting can be very useful as a guide to stay safe should any "big" emotions or memories surface.

Case Study of Using Poured Painting and EMDR

Melanie, a 21-year-old college student, came to therapy with suicidal ideation, symptoms of depression, reports of extreme loneliness, and trichotillomania (Figure 4.11). Melanie had a multi-year history of sexual abuse by an uncle whom she reports groomed her for years as a young child. Her mental health team included her physician and psychiatrist who were all monitoring her care. A written safety plan would have been unhelpful and would only serve as a clerical element of standard procedure, as she had met with multiple therapists for many years, and she reported the safety protocol as unhelpful.

During the first several sessions, Melanie worked on grounding skills and coping tools for stabilization and was then introduced to a poured painting exercise. She found the process exciting, edgy, and slightly decadent to use paint in this free-form style. She assigned various positive emotions to her colors, and as she poured, the colors swirled around while she moved the canvas around. Throughout the therapy process she shared that the safety plan was powerful as it served as a private but public image in her home. She reported that as she reduced her negative cognitions in EMDR, the initial assignment of colors related to positive emotions became more of a possibility for her to access and experience.

EMDR reprocessing sessions allowed her to float back to a target memory of caring for her younger, disabled brother when she was a small child. She reports her parents being out of town for a weekend with her babysitter who was unable to console her younger brother,

Figure 4.11 A creative safety plan.

leaving Melanie to feel helpless, desperate, and also unable to soothe him. She was able to recognize this particular weekend as the beginning of her symptoms related to trichotillomania as she placed undue pressure upon herself to help soothe her fussy brother.

Through Phases Four and Five in EMDR, she was able to update the irrational guilt and shame she carried for many years and recognize she was just a young child without the ability to soothe a younger sibling.

Her suicidal ideation virtually disappeared following this session, and the painting became a relic of an old way of thinking. Updating Melanie's cognition to feel empathy instead of disappointment and regret for her younger self offered a shift in lowering her expectations for perfection, allowing her to complete her school assignments. The art served as a physical manifestation of this thought process and emotional growth. She was able to complete college and go on to graduate school to study early childhood education. When contacted for permission to use this information and image a few years after her time in therapy, Melanie shared, "I look at this painting every morning before I leave the house, because it reminds me of the person I want to be."

EMDR PHASE EIGHT: REEVALUATION

The reevaluation phase of EMDR processing takes place in subsequent sessions following Phases Four through Seven. Assessment to determine if a client's distress levels have stayed low and when/where they noticed a difference in the time period between sessions is standard protocol. This important part of the therapy process allows for clients to reflect on new/updated cognitions and new things learned during the therapy process.

Art Therapy Directives in Phase Eight—Reevaluation

Artwork made in earlier sessions holds the cathectic energy that the client was experiencing when it was made. It also reflects informative content related to their memory. The physical evidence of a client's emotional experience in earlier sessions serves as an accurate barometer of how radically different they feel/think about their target memory and experience post EMDR. Referencing the artwork supports the process of reevaluation and gives the client a concrete way to mark progress between then and now.

Creating Wearable Art to Represent Growth and Change

Art made for honoring successful growth in therapy can be helpful for marking a significant change in cognitions and reduction in distress. Creating a piece of jewelry, t-shirt, scarf, or something that can be worn is beneficial for reinforcing the positive cognitions in the EMDR process. Inviting clients to "upgrade" the meaning of one of their tattoos can also pair a client's emotional growth with a visual reminder on their body. Popularity in tattoos has steadily increased over the past decade, and there has been a significant growth in the tattoo industry during the COVID-19 pandemic era (Mcclusky, 2021).

People often choose tattoos that have personal meaning, and the imagery is often a direct reflection of their lived experience. Asking clients about their tattoos during a therapy session invites them to share details that are important to them that might not be identified as they verbally report their personal histories.

As clients engage in EMDR, this connection to their tattoos can be helpful in many of the phases. If a tattoo represents something traumatic that they experienced, their negative cognitions might be reinforced each time they look at their tattoo. Asking clients to contemplate a positive or updated meaning with one of their tattoos can be helpful to prepare for Phase Five. Revisiting it again in the reevaluation phase serves as a convenient physical reminder of the shift in cognition to the memory or experience explored in EMDR.

Tattoos occasionally have negative associations with them. In the sex trafficking world, bar codes, crowns, and money symbol tattoos are often used to designate victims as "property" of their traffickers (Rote, Coverdale, Nguyen, & Gordon, 2018). It is imperative to be aware of these negative associations with some tattoos before asking a client about them. Clinicians must create trust and rapport before a client could be expected to share their extreme negative association to their tattoos. Incorporating tattoos into the therapy process, especially ones with negative meaning or memories, can be powerful and transformative.

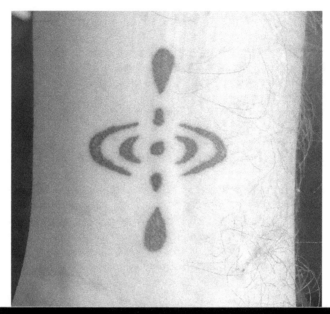

Figure 4.12 Tattoo of a ripple of water to represent the client's emotional growth.

Script for Incorporating Tattoos into the Therapy Process. [Asking about a client's tattoos can be helpful at any phase in EMDR. If brought into the therapy experience early, it can be useful as a healthy coping tool.] *I am noticing your tattoos. Can you share the symbolism behind any of them? Is there a particular one that is meaningful to your experience or anything you are working through in therapy? How did you choose the particular image or color? When did you get it? Is it connected to any other tattoos on your body? Can we use your tattoo as an image in the EMDR reprocessing? As we think of new meaning to your story and memory, can we use the image in one of your tattoos to reflect this newer thinking and updated belief about your memory and experience?*

Case Study for Incorporating Tattoo Art into Therapy

Ted came to therapy for two years, and although he tackled various personal issues related to drug addiction, anger, and emotional distress, his long-term girlfriend chose to leave him (Figure 4.12). He continued to work through grief in therapy and engage in EMDR throughout his two years of therapy. He was a musician and many of his tattoos on his forearm related to music. He was asked at the beginning of therapy to choose a few that were meaningful for him to connect to the therapy process.

Ted returned to therapy for a check in several months after concluding therapy. He had found a new girlfriend, reported feeling happy, and reported the therapy journey as integral to creating his new life. He reported getting a tattoo to remind him of the positive experience he had in therapy (see image above) and emotional growth from his EMDR experience. He shared that the new tattoo represented drops of water creating ripples of possibility and to remind him to be mindful.

CONCLUSION

The societal paradigm shift for young people in this complicated era has been so abrupt that new modes of therapy are essential to quickly meet the needs of clients who are struggling with emotional distress and unresolved trauma. Young people who fall into the Gen Z category are truly victims, pioneers, and proverbial guinea pigs of this new century (Lutrell & McGrath, 2021) Sadly, statistics related to emotional distress in this population are a true reflection of this tenuous time period. Newer research revealing the unique stage of brain development during adolescence reinforces the need to enhance EMDR protocols for adolescents and young adults with the creative interventions of art therapy. This comprehensive model includes a conceptual framework to understand this generation and to provide ideas and directives. Each creative intervention is designed to be replicated by clinicians to help young people.

REFERENCES

Bergman, U. (2020). *Neurobiological foundations for EMDR practice.* Springer Publishing Company.

Blore, D., Holmshaw, E., Swift, A., Standart, S., & Fish, D. (2013). The development and uses of the "blind to therapist" EMDR protocol. *Journal of EMDR practice and research, 7*(2), 95–105. https://doi.org/10.1891/1933-3196.7.2.95

Cuijpers, P., Veen, S., Sijbrandij, M., Yoder, W., & Cristea, I. (2020). Eye movement desensitization and reprocessing for mental health problems: A systematic review and meta-analysis. *Cognitive Behaviour Therapy,* (49) (3), 165–180. https://doi.org/10.1080/16506073.2019.1703801

Curtain, S. (2020). State suicide rates among adolescents and young adults Aged 10–24: United States, 2000–2018. *National Vital Statistics Report Volume, 69*(11). https://stacks.cdc.gov/view/cdc/93667

Damasio, A. (2000). *The feeling of what happens: Body and emotion in the making of consciousness.* Mariner Books.

Damour, L. (2020). Under Pressure: Confronting the epidemic of anxiety and stress in girls. Ballentine Books.

Damour, L. (2017). Untangled. Guiding teenage girls through the seven transitions into adulthood. Ballentine Books.

Dimock, M. (Jan 17, 2019) Defining generations: Where millennials end and generation Z begins. Pew Research Center.

Ekman, P. (2005). *Emotions revealed, (2nd Ed): Recognizing faces and feelings to improve communication and emotional life.* Holt Paperbacks.

Erikson, E. (1994). *Identity: Youth and crisis.* W.W. Norton & Company.

Fernandez, E., Salem, D., Swift, J. K., & Ramtahal, N. (2015). Meta-analysis of dropout from cognitive behavioral therapy: Magnitude, timing, and moderators. *Journal of consulting and clinical psychology, 83*(6), 1108–1122. https://doi.org/10.1037/ccp0000044

Gerhart, D. (2017). *Mastering competencies in family therapy: A practical approach to theory and clinical case documentation* (3rd Ed.). Cengage Learning.

Gonzalez, A & Masquera, D. (2012). *EMDR and Dissociation: The Progressive Approach.* A.I.

Greenwald, R. (2007). *EMDR within a phase model of trauma-informed treatment.* The Haworth Press, Inc.

Greenwald, R. (2015). *EMDR within a phase model of trauma-informed treatment.* Routledge.

Gussak, D. & Blackwell, M. (Eds.). (2015). *The Wiley handbook of art therapy.* Wiley-Blackwell.

Haidt, J. & Twenge, J. (2021). *Is there an increase in adolescent mood disorders, self-harm, and suicide since 2010 in the USA and UK?* A review. Unpublished manuscript, New York University.

Hass-Cohen, N., & Findley, J. (2015). *Art therapy and the neuroscience of relationships, creativity & resiliency.* W.W. Norton & Company.

Haugen, F. (2021). Statement of Francis Haugen. *Whistleblower Aid: United States Senate Committee on Commerce, Science and Transportation Sub-Committee on Consumer Protection, Product Safety, and Data Security.* https://www.commerce.senate.gov/services/files/FC8A558E-824E-4914-BEDB- 3A7B1190BD49.

Herzog, J. & Schmahl, C. (2018). Adverse childhood experiences and the consequences on neurobiological, psychosocial and somatic conditions across the lifespan. *Frontiers in psychiatry.* https://doi.org/10.3389/fpsyt.2018.00420

Hoge E., Bickham, D., & Cantor, J. (2017). Digital media, anxiety, and depression in children. *Pediatrics, 140*(2), 76–80. https://doi.org/10.1542/peds.2016-1758G

Horowitz, J., Igielnik, R., & Kochhar, R. (2020). Most Americans say there is too much economic inequality in the U.S., but fewer than half call it a top priority. *Pew research.* https://www.pewresearch.org/social-trends/2020/01/09/trends- in-income-and-wealth-inequality/

Iqbal, N. (2021, October 7). *The whistleblower who plunged Facebook into crisis.* [Audio podcast episode]. *The Guardian.* https://www.theguardian.com/news/audio/2021/oct/08/whistleblower-facebook-plunged-crisis-frances-haugen-podcast

Jenson, F., & Nutt, A. (2015). *The teenage brain.* Harper.

Kandel, E. (2006). *In search of memory.* W. W. Norton & Company.

Kandel, E. (2012). *The age of insight.* Random House.

Kaufman J. & Kaufman, L. (2011). *The grump meter: A family tool for anger control.* Self-Published.

Keysers, C., & Gazzola, V. (2014). Hebbian learning and predictive mirror neurons for actions, Sensations and emotions. *Philosophical transactions of the Royal Society of London. Series B, biological sciences.* https://doi.org/10.1098/rstb.2013.0175

King, J. (Ed.). (2016). *Art therapy, trauma and neuroscience.* Routledge.

Lake, J. & Turner, M. S. (2017). Urgent need for improved mental health care and a more collaborative model of care. *The Permanente journal, 21,* 17–024. https://doi.org/10.7812/TPP/17-024

Lakoff G. (2014). Mapping the brain's metaphor circuitry: metaphorical thought in everyday reason. *Frontiers in human neuroscience, 8,* 958. https://doi.org/10.3389/fnhum.2014.00958

Leeb, R., Bitsko, R., Radhakrishnan, L., Martinez, P., Njai, R., & Holland, K. (2020). Mental health–related emergency department visits among children aged <18 years during the COVID-19 pandemic. *MMWR morbidity and mortality weekly report center for disease control, 69,* 1675–1680. https://doi.org/10.15585/mmwr.mm6945a3

Lutrell, R., & McGrath, K. (2021). *Gen Z the superhero generation.* Rowman & Littlefield.

Magson, N., Freeman, J., Rapee, R., Richardson, C., Oar, E., & Fardouly, J. (2021). Risk and protective factors for prospective changes in adolescent mental health during the COVID-19 pandemic. *Journal of youth and adolescence, 50*(1), 44–57. https://doi.org/10.1007/s10964-020-01332-9

Mavranezouli, I., Megnin-Viggars, O., Grey, N., Bhutani, G., Leach, J., Daly, C., Dias, S., Welton, N., Katona, C., El-Leithy, S., Greenberg, N., Stockton, S., & Pilling, S. (2020). Cost-effectiveness of psychological treatments for post-traumatic stress disorder in adults. *PLoS One, 15*(4). https://doi.org/10.1371/journal.pone.0232245

Mcclusky, M. (2021, August 25). Pandemic woes and YOLO mentality have ignited a boom for tattoo artists. *Time.* https://time.com/6089991/tattoo-artist-boom-covid-19/

McLaughlin, K. (2017, April). The long shadow of adverse childhood experiences. *Psychological science agenda.* http://www.apa.org/science/about/psa/2017/04/adverse-childhood

Parker, K., & Igielnik, R. (2020, May 14). On the cusp of adulthood and facing an uncertain future: What we know about Gen Z so far. *Pew research.* https://www.pewresearch.org/social-trends/2020/05/14/on-the-cusp-of-adulthood-and-facing-an-uncertain-future-what-we-know-about-gen-z-so-far-2/

Perry, B. (2009). Examining child maltreatment through a neurodevelopmental lens: Clinical applications of the neurosequential model of therapeutics. *Journal of loss and trauma, 14*(4), 240–255. https://doi.org/10.1080/15325020903004350

Pew Research. (2018). Teens, social media & technology. https://www.pewresearch.org/internet/2018/05/31/teens-social-media-technology-2018/.

Pipher, M. (2019). *Reviving ophelia 25th anniversary edition: Saving the selves of adolescent girls.* Riverhead Books.

Riehm K. E, Feder, K. A., Tormohlen, K. N., Crum, R. M., Young, A. S., Green, K. M., Pacek,, L. R., La Flair, L. N., & Mojtabai, R. (2019). Associations between time spent using social media and internalizing and externalizing problems among us youth. *JAMA psychiatry*, *76*(12), 1266–1273. https://doi.org/10.1001/jamapsychiatry.2019.2325

Rote, S., Coverdale, J., Nguyen, P., & Gordon, M. (2018). Tattoo recognition in screening for victims of human trafficking. *The journal of nervous and mental disease*, *206*, 824–827. https://doi.org/10.1097/NMD.0000000000000881.

Rousseau, C., & Maconi, D. (2020). Protecting youth mental health during the COVID-19 pandemic: A challenging engagement and learning process. *Journal of the American academy of child & adolescent psychiatry*, *59*(11), 1203–1207. https://doi.org/10.1016/j.jaac.2020.08.007

Rousseau, P., Boukezzi, S., Garcia, R., Chaminade, T., & Khalfa, S. (2020). Cracking the EMDR code: Recruitment of sensory, memory and emotional networks during bilateral alternating auditory stimulation. *The Australian and New Zealand journal of psychiatry*, *54*(8), 818–831. https://doi.org/10.1177/0004867420913623

Rubin, J. (2005). *Child art therapy*. Wiley.

Schaeffer, K. (2020, February 7). 6 facts about income inequality in the United States. *Pew research center*. https://www.pewresearch.org/fact-tank/2020/02/07/6-facts-about-economic-inequality-in-the-u-s/

Schore, A. (2021). The Interpersonal neurobiology of intersubjectivity. *Frontiers in psychology*, *12*, https://doi.org/10.3389/fpsyg.2021.648616

Shapiro, F. (2018). *Eye movement desensitization and reprocessing (EMDR) therapy*. The Guilford Press.

Siegel, D. (2015). *Brainstorm: The power and purpose of the teenage brain*. TarcherPerigee.

Siegel, D., & Bryson, T. (2012). *The whole brain child: 12 revolutionary strategies to nurture your child's developing mind*. Bantam.

The White House. (2021). *FACT SHEET: Improving Access and care for youth mental health and substance use conditions*. https://www.whitehouse.gov/briefing-room/statements-releases/2021/10/19/fact-sheet-improving-access-and-care-for-youth-mental-health-and-substance-use-conditions/

Thielking, M. (2020, June 17). Facing a broken mental health system, many US teens fall off a dangerous cliff in their care. *STAT*. https://www.statnews.com/2020/06/17/cliff-teens-mental-health-transition-adulthood/

Twenge, J. (2018). *IGen: Why today's super-connected kids are growing up less rebellious, more tolerant, less happy—and completely unprepared for adulthood—and what that means for the rest of us*. Atria Books.

Twenge, J., Haidt, J., Blake, A., McAllister, C., Lemon, H., & LeRoy, A. (2021). Worldwide increase in adolescent loneliness. *Journal of adolescence*, *93*, 257–269. https://doi.org/10.1016/j.adolescence.2021.06.006

U.S. Department of Health & Human Services. (2021). Protecting youth mental health. *The U.S. Surgeon General's Advisory*. https://www.hhs.gov/sites/default/files/surgeon-general-youth-mental-health-advisory.pdf

Whitaker, A., Torres-Gullien, S., Morton, M., Jordan, H., Coyle, S., Mann, A., & Sun, W. L. (2017). *Cops & no counselors: How the lack of school mental health staff is harming students*. American Civil Liberties Union. https://digitalcommons.unf.edu/cgi/viewcontent.cgiarticle=1052&context=facultyshowcase

CHAPTER 5

ART THERAPY AND EMDR
Integrating Cognitive, Somatic, and Emotional Processing for Treating Trauma

Tally Tripp

The deleterious effects of trauma can be long lasting and life altering, negatively impacting mind, body, and spirit. While traditional talk therapy offers an important bridge to working with the explicit and cognitive elements of a traumatic event, there remains a need for treatment approaches that attend to the implicit, nonverbal, and somatically held components of the experience. Trauma-informed treatment is integrative and flexible, blending theory and clinical practices that are neurobiologically informed, relationally focused, and experientially engaging. This chapter discusses an integrative approach for working with trauma that purposefully attends to cognitions, emotions, and the body with tools and techniques informed by the creative arts therapies, the somatic and body-based therapies, and by Eye Movement Desensitization and Reprocessing (EMDR) therapy.

WHAT IS TRAUMA

Trauma can be described as an emotional response to a life-threatening situation such as war, physical assault, sexual abuse, serious illness, or natural disaster that results in the individual experiencing a feeling of being overwhelmed and helpless. Responses to trauma are subjective and not all persons confronted by such terrible events are severely traumatized. But for those who sustain enduring negative effects from traumatic stressors and events, symptoms can be pervasive and life changing. Trauma affects the mind, body, and spirit; it can disconnect one physiologically, cognitively, emotionally, spiritually, and interpersonally (Wheeler, 2007). Traumatized individuals can experience extreme mood swings and may quickly cycle out of control with unremitting feelings of sadness and despair, anger and rage, shame and guilt.

The diagnosis of Post-Traumatic Stress Disorder (PTSD) consists of several core elements: a persistent re-experiencing of traumatic memories and events, avoidance of these experiences as reminders of the trauma, fixed negative beliefs about self and the world, and heightened arousal and reactive symptoms based on the feeling that past trauma is still present as it is experienced as an ongoing threat. Some symptoms that are associated with PTSD include recurrent nightmares and flashbacks, isolation and avoidance of things that are reminiscent of the trauma, hypervigilance and increased startle response, insomnia and sleep disturbances, anxiety, detachment, difficulty concentrating, and problems with affect regulation including intense anger, depression, and self-destructive behaviors (American Psychiatric Association, 2013).

When trauma is complex, meaning there have been prolonged and repeated traumatic experiences of an interpersonal nature, the result can be even more serious and difficult to treat (Courtois & Ford, 2009; Ford & Courtois, 2020). Clients with complex PTSD may have significant challenges establishing and maintaining meaningful relationships as their early relational experiences have created a framework of distrust and suspiciousness, adversely impacting their ability to feel safe. Negative self-referencing beliefs often emerge from such

DOI: 10.4324/9781003156932-6

states including thoughts such as "I am not important" or "I can never feel safe" or "I don't deserve love." These and other similar negative beliefs can be especially problematic when attempting to establish a therapeutic relationship, as the client will bring their past perceptions, assumptions, and experiences to the therapy encounter (van Nieuwenhove & Meganck, 2019). It is not unusual that a well-intentioned therapist attempting to establish rapport will be met with a client's intense anxiety, distrust, and even hostility or avoidance. The therapist must be aware of and learn to manage significant countertransference responses including the tendency to avoid or to move too quickly through treatment, attempting to rescue or re-parent the client, and managing or containing potential feelings of resentment and rejection about the work (van Nieuwenhove & Meganck, 2019).

According to Rothschild (2017), successful resolution of trauma includes the ability to recount the traumatic memory without escalating responses of hyperarousal or dissociation, a decrease in symptoms of PTSD including lowering of avoidance behaviors, better engagement in present-day "normal" life interactions, and improvement in the nervous system's ability to recover from everyday stressors. Rothschild suggests that treatment and resolution for trauma recovery may best be obtained through working with the nervous system, noting the adverse impact that traumatic events hold in the body as well as in emotions, thoughts, and beliefs. This view recognizes the fact that we cannot change the past, but we can change the effect the past holds on the present and future.

TRAUMA AND THE BRAIN

The recent surge in literature about the neurobiology of trauma recognizes that treating trauma requires an integrative approach that assumes a fundamental connection between brain, mind, body, and interpersonal relationships (Cozolino, 2014; Siegel, 2010, 2012). Research supports the fact that trauma symptoms are emotional and neurobiological responses to negative, life-threatening events (Corrigan, 2014; Scaer, 2005; van der Kolk, 2014). Approaching trauma therapy from a neuroscience perspective helps clients recognize the silver lining that, unlike many forms of mental illness, trauma results from external events and situations, and while one cannot change the fact that the trauma has occurred, its symptoms are eminently treatable.

Survivors of trauma often hold lingering feelings of debilitating shame and guilt from their perceived lack of agency experienced during traumatic situations. Renowned trauma researcher Judith Herman (1992) asserts that our culture has historically done little to help victims overcome the denial, secrecy, and shame surrounding sexual trauma. She asserts that "traumatic reactions occur when action is of no avail" (p. 34); thus, PTSD symptoms should be viewed without judgment as they represent the nervous system's response to experiences of terror. A helpful therapeutic intervention might be to acknowledge and affirm the client's response to a traumatic experience focusing on tools for healing and recovery, making it clear that the client is not responsible for causing the trauma itself (Chu, 2011). This reframe helps reduce the denial and secrecy many clients hold about their individual trauma histories and offers the supportive suggestion that their symptoms are "normal responses to abnormal situations."

The polyvagal theory as espoused by Stephen Porges (2011) provides a neurophysiological lens describing the automatic and adaptive mechanisms of the nervous system and patterns of protection that facilitate survival in the context of trauma. Porges asserts that clients cannot make good use of therapy when feeling stressed or insecure; only in an environment that is deemed "safe" can the client "inhibit defense systems and exhibit [the] positive social engagement behavior" (p. 13) that is necessary for clinical work. He coined the term "neuroception" to describe the wordless experience whereby the nervous system constantly scans the environment for cues that identify safety vs. danger. Through an autonomic, visceral feedback system, we determine if a person or situation is deemed "safe, dangerous, or life threatening" (Porges, 2011; Dana, 2018). Deb Dana (2018), writing about the polyvagal theory in therapy, proposes four Rs of a polyvagal approach to treatment: Recognize the autonomic state, Respect the adaptive survival response, Regulate or co-regulate into a ventral vagal state, and Re-story the experience (p. 7). When therapists are actively and consistently attuned to their clients, they can help regulate and co-regulate the nervous system so that treatment can proceed through an attuned, "face- to- heart" state of social engagement.

In his comprehensive text *The Neuroscience of Human Relationships*, psychologist Louis Cozolino (2014) describes the human brain as a social organ and a "dynamic structure that undergoes modification and redevelopment across the lifespan" (p. 41). While the brain is an incredibly complex organ, it is also a malleable one and capable of change. The Hebbian axiom "Neurons that fire together, wire together" underlies this assumption where positive connection and novel experiences can facilitate new neuronal growth (neurogenesis).

According to Cozolino (2014), the repeated layering of positive experiences in treatment can revise existing neural connections (neuroplasticity). He suggests that through facial expression, physical action, and vocal tone there is an "ongoing stream of reciprocal and contingent behaviors" that "support[s] ego strength, physical health, and the ability to engage in sustained and mutually regulating social interactions" (p. 90). In this context, we can understand that weaving theories of interpersonal neuroscience in the formulation of an attuned therapeutic relationship will create the solid foundation for healing the wounds of trauma.

Certainly, neuroscience is a complex field, but it is not necessary to be a neuroscientist to understand the essential impact of trauma on the brain and its role in treatment. Even a basic knowledge of the theoretical framework about trauma and the brain can be extremely empowering for clients and can decrease the stigma that is often a huge obstacle to healing. Dan Siegel's metaphorical "hand model of the brain" (2012) has been widely viewed on YouTube and provides an easy way to talk about managing stress that even young children can appreciate. Likewise, McLean's relatively simple theory of the "triune brain" (1990) dividing the brain into three components—reptilian, mammalian, and human—provides a useful description of the essential functions of the brainstem (physical response), limbic system (emotional response), and prefrontal cortex (cognitive response). These three brain regions are interconnected and, under normal circumstances, influence one another and function as an interconnected whole with the neocortex typically dominating the lower regions in humans (Corrigan, 2014).

There is widespread interest in the topic of mind-body approaches to therapy, and it is no surprise that Bessel van der Kolk's text *The Body Keeps the Score* (2014) is a # 1 *New York Times* best seller. With his colorful and accessible writing style, van der Kolk describes the elements of the traumatized brain and nervous system through lively characterization. Citing traumatic stress as a normal (but unfortunate) part of life, he describes the thalamus as a "cook" that attempts to create an autobiographical soup from dangerous or threatening experiences. But when the processing of information breaks down due to escalating fear, the amygdala, or "smoke detector" in the brain, sounds the alarm sending messages to the hypothalamus and brain stem that signals the stress hormone system to respond. With cortisol and adrenaline pumping, the lifesaving fight flight response is initiated, effectively shutting down the frontal lobes or the brain's "watchtower" in favor of immediate survival. Within this metaphor, the "smoke detector" (amygdala) may misinterpret danger (a negative but potentially lifesaving bias to respond quickly to threat) while the "watchtower" (prefrontal cortex) takes its time and may go offline and not be able respond until after the danger has subsided. This phenomenon is also described by LeDoux (1996) as the brain's "low road" vs. the "high road," or the "quick" vs. the "dead" referring to the subcortical, fast but crude, survival-based circuitry and the slower but more accurate assessment of the world as appraised by the analytical prefrontal cortex. Likewise, Ford (2009) refers to the way a stress response can "override and reduce the functionality of the brain systems that are necessary for learning" (p. 32), thus interfering with reward-seeking activity, managing distress, making plans, and processing information. He suggests that early traumatic experiences often result in neural networks that are focused primarily on survival-based ways of thinking and feeling; and that in lieu of approach and reward-seeking and positive behavior, the trauma survivor focuses primarily on anticipating and avoiding stress (Ford, 2009). Corrigan (2014) adds that defensive avoidance responses in therapeutic encounters are common in traumatized individuals who may actively reject or unconsciously withdraw from confronting memories of painful events. These behaviors may manifest in submissive, defensive, or dissociative symptoms that are evident in the body posture and in emotions ranging from extensive self-criticism and shame to extreme avoidance, withdrawal, and physically shutting down.

TRAUMA AND THE BODY

Pat Ogden, founder of Sensorimotor Psychotherapy, describes the element of nonverbal exchange as the "heartbeat" of all interpersonal relationships (2015). Increasingly, trauma research and practice has focused on the intelligence of the body and the study of implicit, somatic sensations and physical interactions therein (Ogden et al., 2006; Ogden & Fisher, 2015; van der Kolk, 2014). Many symptoms of PTSD are directly observable in the body including the hyper- and hypo-arousal responses, the experience of being frozen with "speechless terror" and through somatoform numbing and dissociative experiences (Fisher & Ogden, 2009). As such, somatic therapies view the body "both as a source of information and an avenue for treatment intervention" (Fisher & Ogden, 2009, p. 316).

It can be said that traumatized clients present with *symptoms* rather than with a coherent narrative of their experience (Ogden et al., 2006). Somatic and psychological manifestations such as intense anxiety, flashbacks and cycles of intrusive imagery, painful bodily sensations, dissociative experiences, and heightened awareness of "triggers" associated with the fearful memories are representative of the brain and body's autonomic responses to stress. Emerging from a persistent state of terror and the feeling of being chronically under siege (van der Kolk, 2014) these symptoms attempt to manage, suppress, avoid, or even assume blame for the original traumatic events. It is not unusual for a trauma survivor to cognitively "know" they are being triggered by a trauma that is in the past, while currently experiencing the feeling that it is happening now (Duros & Crowley, 2014; van der Kolk, 2014).

The study of the body and the actions and reactions of the nervous system provide important clues about the individual that can be noted through observable elements including posture, gesture, facial expression, eye contact, prosody, and breath. Body-based models of treatment listen intently and mindfully to the nonverbal elements of the "somatic narrative" (Ogden et al., 2006; Ogden, 2015) to identify constructs that may defy verbalization and exist beyond conscious awareness. When helping the client to notice physical responses and become more mindful of the somatic experience, disturbances in sensation often spontaneously transform into something more tolerable (Levine, 1997; Ogden et al., 2006).

Traumatized clients may be unable to assimilate or narrate their life experiences and may be extremely challenged to manage the sensations, images, and other triggers reminiscent of the trauma (Ogden et al., 2006). After trauma, the emotions, thoughts, and somatosensory experiences that are normally unified may become disintegrated, fragmented, or dissociated (Ogden et al., 2006). Responses such as exaggerated reactions, intense emotions, somatic complaints, physical sensations, and faulty beliefs may be viewed as manifestations of the body's instinctual response for self-protection (Duros & Crowley, 2014).

Peter Levine (1997), founder of Somatic Experiencing, compares the human response of immobility in the face of traumatic stress with the instinctual response of animals which experience life threat in the wild. He observes that animals deal with threat by naturally discharging their somatic activation; once the animal determines it is out of danger, its body naturally begins to vibrate, twitch, and tremble to "shake it off." According to Levine (1997), animals move rhythmically between states of relaxed alertness and tense hypervigilance hundreds of times a day. In contrast, humans often find their nervous systems rigidly stuck in the "on" or "off" position in poles of autonomic dysregulation, with alternating experiences of feeling "too much" or "too little" (Ogden et al., 2006; van der Kolk, 2014). When humans are not able to discharge the physiological activation resulting from traumatic stress, that energy can become trapped in the body in a frozen state of immobilization (Duros & Crowley, 2014; Levine, 1997). Thus, the overall experience of trauma defies organization on a linguistic level but is organized on a somatosensory one through bodily sensations, intrusive thoughts, nightmares, flashbacks, and reenactments (van der Kolk & van der Hart, 1995). Effective trauma-informed interventions teach clients to "befriend the body" and to notice the physical sensations that are stored below the emotional ones, thus gaining self-awareness and flexibility, and increasing the ability to regulate stressful experiences (van der Kolk, 2014; Ogden et al., 2006; Ogden, 2021).

TRAUMA AND EMOTIONAL REGULATION

Traumatic memory may aptly be described as "unassimilated scraps of overwhelming experiences" (van der Kolk & van der Hart, 1995, p. 176). Research suggests that trauma is stored in fragmentary slices in the brain and body, often in vague, wordless, or dissociated states that lack integration or coherence (Chu, 2011; Rothschild, 2000; Scaer, 2005). Trauma is most often experienced through visual images, physical sensations, smells, tastes, thoughts, and intense emotions, and not through explicit language or verbal narrative (Levine, 2015; van der Kolk, 2014).

According to Cozolino (2014), the brain is unable to maintain neural integration when overwhelmed by traumatic experiences; "memories are stored in sensory and emotional networks [that] are dissociated from those that organize cognition, knowledge and conscious awareness" (p. 24). The goal of therapy is to reintegrate the dissociated memory networks through conscious cortical processing of the trauma.

It is evident that the emotional regulation of trauma-induced symptoms may be "job one" for the trauma therapist. However, for many clients, emotions and the body are experienced as fearful and "off limits." Trauma survivors may experience sensations and emotions emerging from stressful past experiences as both dangerous and threatening (Fisher, 2017). Trauma-informed therapists help their clients manage their responses by focusing mindfully on the present moment and the somatic experiences that are occurring in real time. Working experientially with the client's implicit memory system and defensive survival responses, trauma therapists can attend to any triggered reactions with a blend of curiosity and acceptance rather than with alarm and avoidance (Fisher, 2017). By recognizing and attending to the client's latent, nonverbal communication, and through tracking the here and now relational process of attunement and mis-attunement as it happens, the therapeutic relationship offers the possibility of creating new patterns of neural organization (Gil, 2010).

Schore and Schore (2008) describe the intersubjective dialogue between client and therapist where the "psychobiologically attuned" clinician seeks to learn from the moment-to-moment experiences with the client by "flexibly and fluidly modifying her own behavior to synchronize with that structure, thereby co-creating … a growth-facilitating context for the organization of the therapeutic alliance" (p. 16). They suggest that clinical expertise with complex clients is more reliant on the nonverbal right brain to right brain attunement (therapeutic relationship) than the left-brain cognitive focus on technical skills, analysis, and interpretation (Schore & Schore, 2008).

Furthermore, Alan Schore (2003, 2019, 2021) has extensively researched the neuropsychology of attachment, referring to the role of the therapist akin to a "psychobiological regulator" who is focused on responding to the clients' cognitive beliefs, physical sensations, and range of emotions. Schore's work on right brain-to-right brain nonverbal communication (2003, 2019) has relevance for trauma therapy as it regards the implicit attachment experiences in the earliest dyad of caretaker-child as related to the current relationship between therapist and client. He notes that emotional well-being is an interactive process with the experience *between* brains shaping the emotional circuits *within* brains (2019). In this interpersonal model of neurobiology, the therapist might take a supportive role with the client, providing a metaphorical scaffolding to the client's vulnerable state, or serve as an "auxiliary ego" providing grounding and stabilization. The therapist attunes to the client and supports co-regulation within a "window of tolerance" (Siegel, 1999, 2012) where emotional and physiological activation does not exceed a regulated autonomic arousal zone. According to Siegel (2003), interventions for trauma treatment are aimed at enhancing neural integration and collaborative interhemispheric functioning. Siegel further suggests our interpersonal emotional experiences *are* integrative (2009). As he describes it, this collaborative journey sets the stage for psychotherapy as an emotional "opportunity" where, at its heart, we "cultivate our human ability for empathy and insight" (p. 165).

TRAUMA TREATMENT: A THREE-LEGGED STOOL

Any robust treatment of trauma-related disorders demands an approach that is integrative and flexible, blending theory and clinical practices that are neurobiologically informed, interpersonally connected, and experientially engaging. Thus, the image of a three-legged stool consisting of neuroscience (the brain), somatic regulation (the body), and relational attunement (the emotions) represents aspects of a holistic trauma treatment model to help guide trauma therapists and their clients in their work. This metaphorical stool is only as sturdy as each leg; it maintains awareness of the importance of each area that holds traumatic stress and contains personal meaning. In clinical work, clinicians must constantly toggle back and forth from one leg to the other to maintain a steady equilibrium. Through engaging and supporting these three strands of connection in this metaphorical stool, treatment maintains a creative and integrative approach that offers a useful model for working with vulnerable clients who have experienced trauma.

A PHASE-ORIENTED APPROACH TO TREATMENT

Since the early writings of Pierre Janet over a hundred years ago, there has been widespread consensus recognizing the importance of a phase-oriented approach for treatment of trauma (Courtois & Ford, 2009; Gelinas, 2003; Herman, 1992). A phase-oriented approach recognizes the central dilemma of trauma treatment: "how to help individuals metabolize traumatic material without inducing greater symptomatology and destabilization" (Gelinas, 2003, p. 92). Judith Herman's seminal text *Trauma and Recovery* (1992) highlights a three-phase approach for trauma therapy: (1) establishing safety, (2) working with remembrance and mourning, and (3) reconnection with everyday life. According to Herman, recovery is an individual process that develops over time and has no unified course or sequence; it is not meant to form a linear progression. Each stage of recovery for trauma-informed therapy addresses the biological, psychological, and social components of the survivor's world (Herman, 1992).

THREE METHODS FOR PROCESSING TRAUMA: COGNITIVE, SOMATIC, AND EMOTIONAL

Cognitive or "Top-Down" Processing

Cognitive or "top-down" processing refers to the ability of the higher cortical areas of the brain to override the lower levels of emotional or sensorimotor processing (Kandel, 2012; Ogden et al., 2006). When top-down strategies are exerted, they effectively modulate emotions whereby there is increased activation in the oribitofrontal regions of the prefrontal cortex and decreased activation in the amygdala (Kandel, 2012). In practice, cognitive behavioral therapy uses a top-down approach by focusing explicitly on the individual's ability to cognitively re-appraise a situation, or re-evaluate a feeling in more realistic or neutral terms (Kandel, 2012). Cognitive processing includes executive functioning activities such as making plans, structuring time, solving problems, or setting goals. These complex abilities and related capacities for insight and self-awareness are core life skills in adulthood. For example, when we are in a resourced, grounded, and fully adult state, we can *decide* to ignore a sensation of hunger or *contain* an emotion such as anger. But when we are triggered, or in the midst of an intense trauma- related memory or flashback, the cognitive parts of the brain go typically "offline" and the ability to use top-down processing will be limited (Ogden et al., 2006; van der Kolk, 2014). Traumatized individuals may have difficulty accessing cognitive processing skills because their survival-based emotions (limbic responses) have hijacked their ability to think and plan. Bessel van der Kolk (2014) describes the resulting phenomena as "speechless terror" noting that words fail when flashbacks are triggered. He observed that when recalling traumatic memory, Broca's area, or the region in the brain that is responsible for language, tends to shut down, while Broadman's area, the area in the visual cortex that registers imagery, appears to light up (van der Kolk, 2014). Recognizing that traumatic experiences defy verbalization and focus on imagery, it follows that trauma-informed therapies might look to the creative arts (visual art, drama, dance, and music) to circumvent the wordlessness and access a strength based, expressive approach for managing traumatic stress.

SOMATIC OR "BOTTOM-UP" PROCESSING

While "top-down" processing relies on developing an explicit narrative, "bottom-up" techniques engage the lower centers in the brain by accessing somatic and emotional material that emerges in the present (Ogden et al., 2006; Schwartz & Mailburg, 2018). Because trauma overwhelmingly affects the body and nervous system, it follows that trauma treatment prioritizing "bottom-up" processing may be most effective for targeting dysregulated arousal and instinctual defensive responses (Ogden, 2021). Ogden and Fisher (2015) describe the core organizers of experience as the building blocks of therapeutically engaged practice. This refers to a recognition of the impact of multiple systems that are present in clinical encounters including emotions, thoughts, five-sense perception (sight, touch, hearing, smell, and taste), as well as physical movement and inner body sensation. Instead of urging clients to talk about their past experiences, they recommend a treatment that focuses on the present, noting in real time the habitual patterns of movement, depth of breath, and activation in the body. Furthermore, instead of analyzing or interpreting these somatic experiences, the emphasis is on inviting curiosity and mindful study of the interactions of emotions, thoughts, and embodied experiences as they unfold (Ogden et al., 2006; Ogden & Fisher, 2015). Therapists can help clients become increasingly mindful by teaching them to track bodily sensations and to identify and explore "gut feelings." The sensorimotor and emotional systems constitute important access points for "bottom-up processing" whereby somatic and affective states provide a route for deeper exploration via an experiential processing format.

Ogden et al. (2006) suggest that a singular focus on "top-down" approaches may "overmanage, ignore, suppress, or fail to support adaptive body processes" (p. 25) and may not enable full assimilation of the trauma-related sensorimotor processes. An integrative approach that systematically engages all three levels of processing (cognitive, emotional, and somatic) is therefore deemed "best practice" for treating trauma. Ogden suggests "movement and body sensation, as well as thoughts and emotions, are [all] viable targets for intervention" (Ogden et al., 2006, p. 25).

EMOTIONAL PROCESSING

Traumatic experiences, particularly when resulting from early attachment injury, can adversely impact the individual's capacity for emotional regulation (Germer & Neff, 2015; Herman, 1992; Scoglio et al., 2018). A traumatized person might experience emotions as extremely dangerous and overwhelming (e.g., uncontrolled, toxic, or "too much, too fast") or as being completely separate and detached (e.g., feeling numb, flat, or dissociated), or emotions may seem altogether wordless, unrecognizable, and empty (as in the experience of alexithymia). Trauma often results in a loss of the ability to harness emotions as a guide for action; thus, emotional responses can take control and can be experienced as destructive and overwhelming (Ogden et al., 2006). Research suggests that emotional responses related to traumatic events can be difficult to extinguish, as emotional memory can last forever (LeDoux, 1996). Past traumatic experiences are often generalized into neural networks as inflexible and maladaptive assumptions and beliefs such as "I am defective" or "I am not worthy" or "the world is unsafe." Without intervention, traumatized individuals may never learn to manage challenging emotions such as fear, grief, terror, or anger that can manifest in a range of destructive, impulsive, or irrational behaviors (Ogden et al., 2006; Scoglio et al., 2018).

Siegel (2003) proposes that emotions are "both regulated and regulatory" (p. 30) meaning that emotional processes may both regulate and be regulated by mental processes. As such, an interpersonal psychotherapeutic approach to therapy that offers attuned communication within a secure attachment frame can enable co-regulation and eventually lead to self-regulation of internal states (Siegel, 2003). Therapists may struggle with determining how to help their clients manage, regulate, soothe, contain, or express the trauma-related emotions that have emerged as lifesaving defenses in response to terror, fear, or panic (Ogden, 2021). Trauma-informed therapy may include teaching tools of mindfulness and self-compassion which can support emotional regulation, increase resilience, and lessen the deeply held negative feelings of shame, worthlessness, and self-blame (Germer & Neff, 2015; Scoglio et al., 2018). Noted as counter to the defensive survival responses to trauma (fight, flight, freeze) and the emotional constructs therein (isolation, self- criticism, and self-absorption), mindfulness and self-compassion can be cultivated in the therapeutic relationship as a "healthy alternative response to trauma" (Germer & Neff, 2015, p. 45).

ART THERAPY AND EMDR: TWO EXPERIENTIAL AND INTEGRATIVE APPROACHES FOR TREATING TRAUMA

Traditional "top-down" verbal models of psychotherapy value thinking over feeling. While such approaches may be "evidence based" (and widely empirically studied), they focus primarily on relieving symptoms through restructuring thought processes and cognitive beliefs. These tools can be quick to learn and relatively easy to teach but may not get to the underlying issues causing the distress, particularly when the trauma comes from deeper interpersonal wounds. "Bottom-up" models of treatment, however, focus primarily on the "felt sense" of the experience, noticing physiological sensations and impulses in the body that are present in the here and now. These implicit experiences are often uncomfortable for clients (and therapists) to grasp and even notice initially and may require some open curiosity and non-judgmental study.

Art Therapy and EMDR are experiential, active approaches that are posited to engage both "top-down" (cognitive) and "bottom-up" (somatic, emotional) processes. Using a bi-directional model (moving up and down the hierarchy of the brain from cognitive to emotional to somatic), experiential therapies process feedback coming from the layers of cognition, emotion, and physical sensation. In this way, we toggle between the hierarchical layers, or legs of our metaphorical stool. Ogden and Fisher (2015) describe therapy as a "dance of safety and risk" (p. 49) suggesting that therapist and client interactions are often subliminal enactments that occur beneath words and below conscious awareness. Clinicians working experientially will recognize these enactments and work to integrate the implicit (action) with explicit (insight). Treatment approaches that integrate both "top-down" and "bottom-up" processing can help clients maintain a mindful and non-judgmental stance while accessing and expressing somatic and emotional manifestations of the trauma.

Creative arts therapies employ the visual arts, drama, music, and movement as a means of self-expression to bring attention to experiential behavioral patterns while deepening self-awareness (Perryman et al., 2019). Throughout the ages, the arts have been integral to healing. Malchiodi (2020) proposes a four-part model for trauma-informed practice that integrates the creative arts within the broad categories of movement (yoga, dance, play), sound (singing, drumming, listening), storytelling (drama, visual art, journaling), and silence (mindfulness, meditation, art making). Through action and experimentation, the creative arts can offer opportunities to explore and mindfully "notice" the accompanying somatic, emotional, and cognitive experiences as they unfold. Experiential and expressive therapies conducted in this mindful state increase somatic and emotional awareness in the client and offer multiple opportunities for self-knowledge and growth.

ART THERAPY FOR THE TREATMENT OF TRAUMA

Art therapy, or the clinical use of art making and creative processes within an attuned therapeutic relationship, offers an active, engaging, and somewhat less threatening way for clients to reconnect implicit, sensory experiences with explicit, cognitive insight. Incorporating art and other creative therapies in trauma treatment is supported by extensive literature and research recommending the use of experiential and nonverbal modalities to access, process, and integrate traumatic memories (Gerge et al., 2019; Gantt & Tinnin, 2007, 2009; Perryman et al., 2019; Tripp, 2007; van der Kolk, 2014). Trauma-focused art therapy helps clients express their inner emotional state with an element of control over the intensity of the work (Naff, 2014). The focus of an art therapy session can be primarily on the creative process itself, or on attending to the symbols and metaphors contained within the product. The healing powers of the treatment exist in the context and integration of all three: the client, the therapist, and the artwork.

Art therapy engages a unique, symbolic language that may appear spontaneously through the process of creating expressive imagery that holds varied emotions, ideas, memories, and experiences (Avrahami, 2006). In bringing art media and processes into therapy, careful attention must be paid in choosing appropriate materials and techniques that prudently and systematically support the expression of a client's inner world (Avrahami, 2006; Hinz, 2009). The artwork provides a symbolic representation of the trauma; it has a unique capacity to both express and contain emotion as it can reflect, mirror, and amplify experiences (Chong, 2015; Tripp, 2007). While the multisensory focus of art therapy can provide a fertile environment for the exploration of traumatic memory (Tripp, 2016), therapists must be prepared to manage potentially dysregulated trauma responses that can ensue when implicit experiences are unearthed. As the trauma narrative may be expressed through the visual image before it is available in words, it is important for therapists to respond to clients with genuine acceptance, compassion, and care (Buk, 2009; Gantt & Tripp, 2016; Naff, 2014).

Art therapy facilitates the externalization of the inner experiences translating them into symbolic self-expression that communicate meaning. It is possible to bypass or diminish some of the relational challenges inherent in the transferential relationship when focusing primarily on the symbols and metaphors of the tangible art product. This may be especially helpful when working with traumatized clients who have come to therapy with strong distrust of interpersonal relationships and with tendencies to avoid any hint of vulnerability based on early developmental wounds (Gantt & Tripp, 2016). Because trauma is a "nonverbal problem" the proposed resolution to trauma is through treatment that does not rely on words (Gantt & Tinnin, 2009; Gantt & Tripp, 2016). The action of creating visual imagery to represent components of the traumatic memory can facilitate an imaginal reworking of the trauma and provide a format for reversal of dissociative processes (Gantt & Tinnin, 2009; Gantt & Tripp, 2016).

BENEFITS OF ART THERAPY FOR TREATING TRAUMA

There are many reasons why art therapy can be considered a treatment of choice for working with clients who have experienced trauma. Trauma's impact on memory is considerable, and the disconnect between implicit and explicit memory states can make a meaningful, verbal trauma narrative inaccessible. The creative arts offer a means to connect implicit memory with explicit memory and to bridge these experiences through a process of creative expression that creates a more coherent story (Malchiodi, 2020).

Art engages us; and the experience of creating and viewing artworks evokes a range of perceptions and responses for both artist and viewer that are based on our personal and historical associations (Kandel, 2012). Art making simultaneously activates numerous physiological and cognitive processes, enabling access to sensory memories of trauma that may have been dissociated, but now can be expressed in tangible form. Because trauma is stored primarily in visual and somatic modes, the creative arts can directly access the implicitly stored traumatic material. Furthermore, as the creative arts are experiential and active, they offer an element of structure for processing emotions, keeping the client grounded and focused in the present (Tripp, 2016).

Chapman (2014) describes a neuro-developmental model of art therapy that highlights the integrative capacity of the brain to engage the kinesthetic, right brain activities involved in art making and aligning them with the neural pathways in the left brain for processing through metaphoric self-expression and symbolic narrative. She suggests that creative art activities can simultaneously strengthen affect tolerance, help with physical control, and access information processing (2014). The sensory processes that are connected to creative art-making experiences support self-regulation and improve relational therapeutic engagement (Malchiodi, 2020). Additionally, the creative arts therapies can harness and attend to neurodevelopmental processes by helping clients express what is within that is empowering (Kolodny, 2021).

Over 40 years ago, Kagin and Lusebrink (1978) hypothesized a way of viewing the creative art therapies on a continuum, organizing responses to varied expressive media into a developmental hierarchy. Their theory, called the Expressive Therapies Continuum (ETC), provides a useful construct for understanding the creative process and for classifying interactions with art media that we may observe in treatment. The ETC theory is now widely accepted among creative arts therapists and offers practical guidelines for implementation in clinical practice (Hinz, 2009; Graves-Alcorn & Kagin, 2017; Figure 5.1).

In essence, the ETC organizes media interactions into a developmental sequence of information processing from the most basic to most complex expression (Hinz, 2009). At one end of the continuum are the bipolar elements that include the basic kinesthetic and sensory experiences (K/S), followed by the perceptual and affective level (P/A) of experience, and finally the cognitive and symbolic ones (C/S). Each component of the ETC has unique properties and functions that relate to the level of creative expression and experience. For example, the lower level (K/S) focuses on kinesthetic and sensory activity such as finger paint and scribbling. The middle level (P/A) corresponds with representational art making, highlighting the client's perceptions and the expression of emotions that are communicated via the art-making process. The most complex top level of the continuum (C/S) relates to

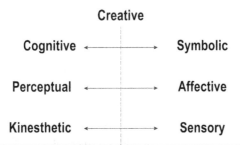

Figure 5.1 The Expressive Therapies Continuum.

the use of symbols and cognitive thought processes that connect meaning to action. There is also a creative level (C), posited to extend on a vertical axis through all previously mentioned horizontal levels, exemplifying the way creativity can be interwoven throughout each phase. Creativity opens us up to new ideas and information, accentuating the release of endorphins, reducing stress, and altering negative neural patterns (Graves-Alcorn & Kagin, 2017).

Art making provides a unique entry point into the inner world of the client and even within the first few minutes of an art therapy session, numerous inferences can be drawn regarding the client's preferred ways of expressing themselves and of processing information (Hayen et al., 2017). In practice, the therapist views and learns from artworks in conjunction with their client; interpretations are not based on static or singular images but upon a series of images that may be created across multiple levels and over time (Tripp, 2019a, 2016). When therapists ask their clients to make art in response to various themes or concerns, they invite new associative and creative answers to emerge. Working experientially, the creative arts provide a mechanism for "doing something" with the issue at hand, thus encouraging action and promoting feelings of mastery and control. The art-making process often results in uncovering unexpected insights that become evident as client and therapist review and reflect upon the experience together. An open and collaborative discussion that is imbued with non-judgmental curiosity will inevitably help the client to discover and recognize new ideas and associations, and forge new insights and mastery.

The expression that is contained within the art product can be viewed as an externalization of an aspect of the self, and while interpretation of the art is subjective, the tangible product provides client and therapist a useful and concrete starting point for dialogue. It also is worth noting that at times the artist may not be ready to view the image and all its contents; the art-making process may have brought up something that is uncomfortable, or out of conscious awareness, or it may be premature to discuss the content, or it may not seem to have any meaning at all. Regardless, the therapist can and should view the artwork with respect, taking care of it, and storing it safely in a portfolio where it can be reviewed at the appropriate time.

Looking at artwork with a process of "reflective distancing" allows client and therapist to attain a cognitive distance and perspective when reflecting upon the expressive work (Kagin & Lusebrink, 1978). An "aesthetic response" to artwork is often experienced by client and therapist alike; one is inevitably touched by the artistic expression coming from the other (Kandel, 2012; Levine, 2011). An attuned therapist might invite a "pause" during the art-making experience, for example, instructing the client to hold the piece at arm's length and examine it from a distance. In so doing, both client and therapist may gain some cognitive insight as thoughts and feelings emerge in response to the piece. This opportunity for pause and review often results in "aha" experiences where fresh perspective and meaning can be found. The experience of finding answers from within often builds a new level of confidence and provides a sense of mastery in clients who may have been previously overwhelmed by feelings of helplessness based on past traumatic experiences.

Another advantage of art making in therapy is one that is often misunderstood. While making art can be a relaxing experience that can provide some safety and distraction from confronting the trauma directly, this does not imply that art therapy is equated to working in a coloring book or other similar arts and crafts exercises. Art making can indeed promote a parasympathetic state and can lessen the intense emotionality of the work. But when incorporating art in session, we are typically doing both; we are providing a calm, soothing experience that facilitates an active but nonverbal engagement with the traumatic memory. Clients often say they prefer art therapy to the more verbally driven therapies because at least some part of them finds the experience relaxing and enjoyable. In that vein, the literature suggests that too much focus on direct exposure to the negative and fear-inducing aspects of a traumatic memory can cause a client to become overwhelmed and to terminate therapy prematurely (van der Kolk, 2014).

EMDR THERAPY FOR THE TREATMENT OF TRAUMA

Francine Shapiro's chance discovery of EMDR in 1987 came as the result of a walk in the park where she was thinking about a distressing life event and noticed her eyes moving back and forth as she moved. At the same time, she became aware of a significant decrease in the negative charge of the troubling experience and began exploring the possible mechanism that lateral eye movements might have to do with diminishing feelings of stress and anxiety. EMDR was conceived of this experience.

EMDR is a psychotherapy formulated to mitigate the symptoms of post-traumatic stress by accessing and processing negatively held traumatic memories and beliefs and finding adaptive resolution for these adverse life events (Shapiro 2001, 2002, 2018). The overarching model for EMDR exists within an Adaptive Information Processing (AIP) system of self-healing that Shapiro posits as its theoretical framework. Shapiro (2018) suggests that there is an inherent "neurological balance" in the brain that seeks to process maladaptive information and bring it to adaptive resolution. Simply put, negative experiences will naturally seek connections with new learning and positive association. The procedural elements of EMDR include accessing the unprocessed traumatic memories with associated emotions, thoughts, and beliefs and, in conjunction with alternating bilateral stimuli, accessing new memory networks where adaptive information can be activated and change the way traumatic memories are metabolized and stored in the brain (Shapiro, 2001, 2018).

While there is a wealth of research related to the proposed mechanisms of change that occur within EMDR therapy, there are numerous ingredients involved in treatment and we cannot say exactly what causes it to work (Maxfield, 2008; Oren & Solomon, 2012). It may be important to note that it is impossible to say with certainty why *any* treatment modality works, as there are unlimited variables in the therapeutic interchange (Maxfield, 2008; van der Kolk, 2014). Outcome studies suggest EMDR can achieve excellent therapeutic impact in a relatively short time, which contributes to making it a "better tolerated" therapy for many clients and therapists (Oren & Solomon, 2012). Because EMDR does not require extensive verbal discussion about the details of the trauma, clients can stay focused on the protocol with less anxiety about sharing an explicit narrative of their experience (van der

Kolk, 2014). Ultimately, the power of the therapeutic relationship may be the primary reason why therapy works and may account largely for how we heal from trauma (Cozolino, 2016; Siegel, 2003). Laliotis et al. (2021) describe the shared "moment of meeting" between therapist and client as the transformative part of the healing process, "not just because of the memory reprocessing, but also because of the relationship between the therapist and client, and the shared experience of going through it together" (p. 193).

PROPOSED MECHANISMS OF CHANGE IN EMDR

The following discussion looks at some of the specific elements of the model and proposed mechanisms of change that define EMDR's healing properties.

BILATERAL STIMULATION/DUAL ATTENTION STIMULATION

EMDR utilizes Bilateral Stimulation with Dual Attention Stimulation (BLS, DAS) that is purported to activate and engage the adaptive information processing system. In EMDR, bilateral stimulation might consist of lateral directed saccadic eye movements, or delivery of auditory tones through a headset, or tactile tapping with hands or electronic "tappers" that emit a pulsing vibration to create visual, auditory, or tactile sensations on both sides of the body, thus engaging both hemispheres of the brain. EMDR theory proposes that through the linking and assimilation of adaptive information to previously disturbing, traumatic memories, current trauma responses and symptoms can be resolved (Oren & Solomon, 2012; Solomon & Shapiro, 2008).

BLS is delivered in a series of discrete "sets" consisting of a certain number of left to right movements of the eyes or with alternating bilateral tones or taps. Short sets are typically used for resourcing (e.g., they are not associative but can be successfully used for the installation of positive resourcing or a specific affirmation) while longer sets are more appropriate for trauma processing (as they can bring up multiple new associative channels of thoughts, feelings, and sensations). In working with clients who have complex trauma, EMDR may be modified or restricted to limit the potential for accessing traumatic associations that can result in emotional flooding (Gelinas, 2003; Kiessling, 2005; van der Hart & Gelinas, 2017). Trauma-informed practice necessitates a phase-oriented approach in working with complex trauma and dissociative disorders, keeping an eye on safety and stabilization throughout treatment (Herman, 1992). In working with chronically traumatized clients, the BLS sets may be shorter and slower than when working with single incident traumas (van der Hart & Gelinas, 2017).

EMDR utilizes left to right eye movements or other bilateral stimulation (auditory, tapping) that engage directed attention to the bilateral experience while the client is simultaneously focusing on a traumatic memory. This dual attention activation focuses simultaneously on the internal distress (from the memory) while attending to the bilateral experience (from the BLS). The prevailing assumption is that BLS dislodges the traumatic material that is stored in the mind-body and accelerates processing of negative beliefs, images, and emotions along a more adaptive path, facilitating linkage to new neural networks that bring the trauma to resolution (Shapiro, 2001, 2018; Solomon & Shapiro, 2008). Dual attention is believed to promote interhemispheric integration and disrupt the traumatic memory networks (Wheeler,

2007). Dual attention focus assumes the client is oriented to the present and feels relatively "safe" in the present. Thus the client can effectively access traumatic memory without losing a mindful focus (Knipe, 2015). The integrative effect of BLS with DAS facilitates a shift in the strength of the negative, traumatic material so it can be metabolized and reprocessed in a more adaptive way (Parnell, 1997).

ORIENTING RESPONSE

Shapiro (2018) proposes that in addition to DAS, the client may experience an orienting response to the novel stimuli of BLS, and that the orienting response may also temporarily disrupt and inhibit the focus on the traumatic memory. Cozolino (2016) suggests the orienting reflex may be an evolutionarily adapted function that signals the brain to prepare for acquiring new information. Physiological and neurobiological studies have found a reduction in sympathetic arousal and limbic activation during periods of bilateral stimulation, resulting in an increase in relaxation, positive feelings, and emotional regulation (Knipe, 2015; Shapiro, 2018). With an increased relaxation response and engagement of the parasympathetic nervous system, the client may experience a state of psychophysiological dearousal and therefore may be more successful in processing traumatic memories (Schubert et al., 2011; Solomon & Shapiro, 2008).

TAXING WORKING MEMORY

During EMDR processing, the target memory is held in working memory which is posited to be overloaded by BLS/DAS. The prevailing hypothesis is that the BLS/DAS taxes the working memory and reduces the vividness and emotionality of the trauma (Maxfield et al., 2008; Schubert et al., 2011; Solomon & Shapiro, 2008). Maxfield et al. (2008) note that as targeted traumatic memories lose their vividness and emotionality, new and more adaptive associations can be evoked with improved clarity and focus. Overall, the task of dual attention focus may provide some emotional distance from the distressing traumatic memory and facilitate therapeutic action and adaptive shifts (Shapiro, 2018). Another interesting potential healing mechanism of BLS suggested by Knipe (2015) is that distinct "sets" of EMDR may help the client to separate out specific moments within the traumatic memory where they can linger; thus a "set" of BLS can slow down the thinking process and reinforce the accumulation of useful associations that shift toward positive resolution. New associated networks to the original disturbing memory can result in an increase in the recognition of the past being in the past (e.g., "I am OK now," "I survived that") to signal the trauma is over.

INTEGRATIVE ASPECTS OF ART
THERAPY AND EMDR

Schwartz and Maiberger (2018) propose seven underlying principles for trauma-informed care integrating EMDR and somatic therapies, including being phase oriented, mindfulness based, non-interpretive, experiential, relational, regulation focused, and resilience informed (Schwartz & Maiberger, 2018). These basic principles will also resonate with the practice of most experientially focused creative arts therapists. Gerge et al. (2019) suggest some interesting correlations between the creative arts therapies and EMDR. They posit that the task of art making within art therapy is akin to the BLS process in EMDR as they both tax the working memory and create some distance from potentially overwhelming emotional responses. Furthermore, they suggest that, like hypnosis, art making may happen in an "altered state of consciousness" that provides a creative means for dealing with painful emotions while also expanding the client's ability to manage stress. As such, the creative process is noted essentially as an experience of dual awareness (paying attention to more than one thing at a time) that can "create flexible pathways between the physical, emotional, and cognitive aspects of traumatic experiences" (Gerge et al., 2019, p. 9).

According to child psychiatrist Bruce Perry (2009, 2014), clinical interventions for trauma should be applied within a neurodevelopmental model that recognizes and targets the impacted regions of the brain. His neurosequential treatment approach integrates neuroscience within a multifaceted picture of the client's history and experience, targeting interventions based on developmental, not chronological, age. Perry states that through patterned, repetitive activation we can retrain and change neural networks in the brain, thus mediating dysfunction and dysregulation (2009). He suggests that patterned repetitive and rhythmic activities such as dancing, drumming, and even mindful breathing when incorporated in treatment may be useful for "short-circuiting" the traumatic memory (Perry, 2009).

BILATERAL ART THERAPY

The term "bilateral art therapy" simply refers to engagement in art processes using two hands simultaneously. Akin to EMDR, bilateral art therapy stimulates activation in both left and right hemispheres of the brain, seeking to connect the thinking parts (located primarily in the left hemisphere) to the more emotional parts (located primarily in the right hemisphere). An art therapy directive such as asking clients to purposefully use both hands in a simultaneous or alternating mark making or scribbling activity is assumed to activate neural pathways and forge connections between feeling and thinking (Elbrecht, 2018; McNamee, 2003, 2006; Tripp, 2007, 2016).

Bilateral drawing may have emerged from the teachings of pioneer art therapist Florence Cane (1951) who prescribed making scribbles to get her students to loosen up, using the whole body in a kinesthetic, creative exercise. Likewise, Elinor Ulman (1992) incorporated a scribble drawing within her assessment protocol, which she posited to release unconscious and often unbidden information stemming from the instruction to "find an image" within the intersecting lines (Tripp, 2019a). Contemporary art therapists have used rhythmic scribbling and bilateral art making in practice for a variety of reasons. Chapman (2014) uses bilateral scribbling with children to access emotional responses and prepare them for the task of developing images related to their traumatic experiences. McNamee (2006) delineates a bilateral art protocol that she developed in response to client-identified conflictual situations that engage both dominant and non-dominant hands which appear to facilitate integration between their felt and cognitive experiences. Talwar (2007) describes a bilateral approach whereby the client is directed to move back and forth between the art table with jars of paint and the wall where the paper is hung, and paint intuitively in a non-directive manner.

Cornelia Elbrecht (2018) is a sensorimotor art therapist who has developed a guided drawing approach where she encourages clients to close their eyes (or maintain a soft gaze) and use both hands to translate inner bodily sensations into sweeping "drawn movements" on the paper. In this kinesthetic process, Elbrechtt (2018) notes that the drawings may contain layers of the client's essential rhythm and repetition and she proposes that these experiences "connect with implicit memory, [focusing on] your embodied biography rather than the conscious stories of your past" (p. 4). In a similar way, Tripp (2012), Tripp & Kolodny (2016, 2017) has developed a practice of mirrored bilateral scribbling where a client and a therapist "mirror" one another's movement on a large sheet of paper that extends between them. Through mindful focus and careful attunement, one leads and the other follows, then they switch roles. The practice is at once thoughtful and enjoyable and offers an opportunity for mutually engaged clinical experience.

In their innovative Intensive Trauma Therapy approach, trauma therapists Linda Gantt and Lou Tinnin developed a bilateral writing response that invites internal "parts" of self to respond back and forth in an "external dialogue" (Gantt & Tinnin, 2009; Gantt & Tripp, 2016). In this exercise, the client may be invited to write back and forth, alternating between using dominant and non-dominant hands in a responsive journalizing task. Switching between hands appears to invite unique responses coming from left or right brain activation. The resulting dialogue can be fascinating, especially as the non-dominant hand tends to evoke responses that may have been unconscious or unexpected, but also are seen as "revelatory, supportive, wise or challenging" (Gantt & Tripp, 2016, p. 76).

EMDR DRAWING PROTOCOL: EMDR AND BEYOND

While EMDR uses imaginal, mental images and art therapy uses concrete ones, it is interesting to consider the potential of what Tobin (2006) calls "cross-pollination" between the two methodologies. And there are similarities; in art therapy we acknowledge and focus on the image, trust the process, let the creative response unfold, while in EMDR we "go with" the image, "stay with the sensation," or "just notice what happens" as if you were watching the landscape go by out of the window of a train. Both EMDR and Art Therapy use imagery and let the imagery (and adaptive information) unfold and emerge naturally, without a lot of verbal discussion or analysis. Tobin (2006) suggests we are moved by the image as experienced in our bodies as well as through our emotional connection and with our thoughts.

Tripp (2007, 2012, 2016) has integrated art making within several EMDR drawing protocols that engage BLS while creating a series of images that depict the story without reliance on words. The art-making process in this work externalizes and concretizes the traumatic image by putting it into visual form, thereby creatively transforming traumatic experiences into a series of new pictures that can be re-worked or manipulated to provide an adaptive or desired ending. Furthermore, by keeping the client in a relaxed and creatively engaged state, the trauma processing can be titrated, thus enhancing a sense of safety and control for the client, keeping them in their "window of tolerance" while dealing with the intensity of the traumatic memory.

The Butterfly Hug is another widely used EMDR-related tool that sometimes includes an element of art making in the protocol. The Butterfly Hug was developed from the work of Ignacio Jarero and Lucina Artigas who used this procedure as a self-administered form of BLS when working with groups of children who were survivors of Hurricane Pauline in Mexico (Jarero & Artigas, 2006, 2021). In this method, the client is instructed to wrap their arms around themselves with each hand touching the opposite shoulder and then tap their hands alternately in the same way that a butterfly moves its wings. When conducted in group treatment, the facilitators can ask the child to draw, rather than simply visualize the critical event, or they might invite a resource drawing (e.g., "draw a safe calm space that you can imagine") and then use the Butterfly Hug as BLS to strengthen the positive association and install that feeling in the body.

In its early form, Shapiro's approach was called EMD (not to include the R that was later added for "reprocessing" in EMDR). The early research on basic EMD found significant desensitization and symptom reduction for survivors of sexual assault and for veterans with PTSD (Laliotis et al., 2021). A restrictive protocol may be recommended for clients with more severe trauma or dissociation, to keep the focus of the work cognitive and contained. Similarly, EMDR trainer and consultant Roy Kiessling (2020) has developed a protocol called "Scribble It Out" that uses bilateral scribbling for managing stress. In this protocol, the client is invited to fold a paper into six segments of equal size and draw a series of images, starting with the traumatic issue or "target" and then developing subsequent images as they emerge from the target. The client is directed to attend to each image as it is drawn then respond to that image by scribbling over it and then to "see what you notice about the image now." Throughout this process a subjective units of distress (SUD) rating scale is taken, so that it is possible to track the overall desensitization experience. Kiessling's conjecture is that the activity of drawing and scribbling taxes the working memory with dual awareness, breaks up the fight, flight, freeze (trauma responses), and creates an opportunity for "observing" the experience from a distance (R. Kiessling, personal communication, October 11, 2021). He has found clients respond well to this simple protocol and that symptoms abate quickly.

CASE EXAMPLE

Rachel (a pseudonym) was referred to me for individual art therapy adjunctive to her ongoing twice weekly verbal psychotherapy. At the time I began working with her, Rachel had just completed an intensive outpatient treatment program (IOP) that specialized in working with trauma. She had previously spent several months on an inpatient hospital unit. In these settings, Rachel had found art therapy to be a particularly useful, if not challenging, treatment modality.

Rachel presents as a bright, highly driven young woman who lives alone, having isolated herself over the past several years, partially in response to the COVID-19 pandemic, but also because of an intense fear of vulnerability in social situations. Her small rescue dog provides some day-to-day company, but even this relationship is not ideal, as she still mourns the loss of a previous canine companion whom she considered more of a support animal.

Rachel is managing symptoms of complex PTSD; she routinely experiences heightened anxiety, major depressive symptoms, and suicidal ideation. She also exhibits significant dissociative features, and her treatment team suspects an underlying dissociative disorder. Her strengths include her intellectual acuity, which is evidenced by strong performance in a demanding, professional career. Notable is her tenacity in managing deadlines and balancing the pressures of work life with an intensive outpatient treatment regime.

Rachel is a serious athlete; she wakes at dawn and exercises every day with a combination of swimming, running, and/or biking. A competitive triathlete, she describes her compulsion for fitness as a necessary factor for keeping herself "strong." On that note, she detests any part of her body that she perceives as the least bit "weak." She frequently experiences disturbing, intrusive thoughts about causing self-harm to any soft or vulnerable body parts (for example she imagines cutting off her breasts with a knife).

Rachel is a survivor of several traumas in adulthood. These include a violent sexual assault that happened during her college years and later a serious and life-threatening injury sustained in a biking accident. Her childhood experiences are replete with interpersonal traumas as well; her mother was mentally ill, "hysterical, needy, and off and on suicidal," and her father, a "passive enabler," focused much of his attention on managing her mother and her moods while basically ignoring the needs of his two daughters. Rachel's older sister also has mental health issues, and especially in her teen years she was always in some sort of crisis, struggled with substance abuse and fought constantly with the family. Thus, sister got a lot of negative attention, while Rachel was idealized as the "good" child but was essentially ignored. She was a decent student but missed a lot of school due to nonspecific somatic complaints which no one in the family deemed problematic. The message was that there was no need to be concerned about Rachel because "she was pretty and smart, and she would be fine." Not surprisingly, Rachel developed an eating disorder during middle school, but that too was never addressed; in fact, she was continually praised for her slender, waif-like appearance. There are some vague memories of inappropriate sexual experiences that may have transpired between Rachel and the father of a close girlfriend during middle school. Rachel states that she wishes to explore these disturbing memories in therapy although she does not currently have an explicit narrative for any of them.

Rachel and I began meeting during the pandemic. We had a few "virtual" (teletherapy) sessions for history taking and to get a sense of how we might work together, but she seemed relatively disengaged on the zoom screen and it was evident that we would do much better meeting in person. Once we were both fully vaccinated, we began meeting face-to-face on a weekly basis. The following vignette describes some of our early experiential sessions, highlighting an integrative approach that blends elements of trauma-informed art therapy, EMDR therapy, and body-focused Sensorimotor Psychotherapy. Our weekly sessions were often extended to 75 or 90 minutes to allow time for the experiential work, as well as for processing complex material and providing space for adequate closure.

While Rachel had been eager to add an experiential and creative arts therapies approach to her current treatment regime, I noted some hesitation to participate actively. It became evident that our process of establishing trust, safety, and stabilization would be slow, as even inviting her to choose a chair in which to sit seemed to cause anxiety. The more I was openly engaging, inviting, or curious about Rachel and her needs, the more uncomfortable she appeared. For example, when I commented on her wide-eyed, pulled-back posture in an early session, she said my curiosity and interest brought up feelings of panic. It seemed that almost any authentic verbal or nonverbal response on my part might trigger a flight or freeze response. In Porges' language we had to work to develop an ability for ventral vagal "social engagement" or using Siegel's terminology to find a way to broaden her "window of tolerance." Thus, our work proceeded slowly and with great care, and it was over time and through repeated, attuned experience that a trusting relationship ultimately developed.

As mentioned earlier, our first obstacle was finding comfort and safety in the room. Using an embodied approach, I suggested options: perhaps she'd like me to move my chair back, or perhaps she'd like to hold on to a big pillow while she sat in hers. Because my office was set up with lots of space, art materials, couches and chairs, pillows, blankets and props, we'd spend a fair amount of time in each session negotiating space and boundaries.

In one session I invited Rachel to create a personal boundary where she could, while seated, surround herself with an assortment of objects to create a visual border that would mark a comfortable circumference around her chair. The goal was to get a sense of her personal space and determine how she felt being physically present in the room with me. This is a Sensorimotor Psychotherapy exercise I have often used to help clients learn to navigate setting personal boundaries within difficult relationships. Rachel responded well to this activity, and used a combination of pillows, books, and blankets to create a safe refuge around her chair. As she built her boundary, and eventually covered her body with a large, weighted blanket, she seemed to transform into a child peering out from a "safe place." At that point she described feeling a little better in the room and noted that she felt more comfortable taking charge of her physical environment, and that she thought she could make the space work.

Because Rachel had found art therapy useful during her previous IOP treatment, she was on board when I invited some art making in our following sessions. I offered her sheets of newsprint as an entry to art therapy and taught her a "breath tracing" technique whereby she was invited to simply make marks on the page and notice the way the breath could be translated into lines on the paper. Initially, she was quite hesitant before committing to making any marks. And while there was significant constriction noted in her initial lines, Rachel eventually was able to trace the patterns of her breath on the page and found this to be a useful exercise in both mindfulness and self-regulation.

Another tool we often used in the beginning of a session was the "body scan" where I led Rachel in a brief guided meditation focused on areas of her body and then, using a small body outline template and crayons or markers, invited her to express in line, shape, and color any sensations, stressors, or emotions that she noticed. Rachel's body scan drawings tended to reflect much tension throughout the central core of her body with discomfort noted in the chest. On one memorable occasion, Rachel became visibly frustrated during the body scanning exercise as she described feeling excessive heaviness and weight in her body. She connected this feeling to her history of the out-of-control somatic experiences when her body "didn't do what it was supposed to do." With this memory, feelings of panic with the urge for self-harm emerged. In response, I helped Rachel with somatic co-regulation through grounding exercises using the breathing and mindfulness techniques we had practiced.

Although they were not easy for her, the breath tracing and body scan exercises did seem to offer Rachel a good entry point for conversation about the body and allowed us to work toward non-judgmental self-expression. This ultimately helped her to be more aware and to notice and acknowledge her unique somatic and emotional experiences.

Along with these experiential exercises, I consistently integrated psychoeducation into our sessions. Having participated in an intensive trauma program, Rachel was familiar with the concept of the "window of tolerance" for example but had never been invited to draw hers. I introduced this directive at a moment when Rachel seemed dysregulated in the session. Drawing her "window of tolerance" helped Rachel bring cognition online and explore feelings about dysregulating states of hyper- and hypo-arousal (see Figure 5.2)

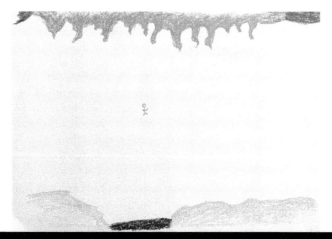

Figure 5.2 Window of tolerance.

Rachel's window of tolerance image depicts a largely blank open space where the optimal arousal zone (being regulated) should exist. This area is starkly empty. She more readily drew the experience of heightened arousal at the very top of the page (the red flames) and the cold, gray, icy area at the bottom of the page that represented dissociation and feeling numb. It was after many minutes of staring at the two distinct and well-delineated poles of heightened arousal and shutdown that Rachel finally sketched a tiny, floating stick figure in the center saying, "I guess I am here." The relative size of the figure and its lack of definition speak to Rachel's difficulty existing in a resourced, modulated state. Indeed, the feeling of being helpless, exposed, and ungrounded in the center suggests a tentative grasp on an "optimal state of arousal."

As we continued to work together, we developed a blended and integrative process that included checking in with any issues that were on her mind, focusing on attunement and somatic regulation, time for experiential work such as directed art making, and processing the experience with talking or writing to express thoughts and emotions that emerged. We started many sessions using the body scan or focusing on mindful breathing practices to help with affect regulation. I offered art materials and directives based on the issues that were elicited during the initial check-in.

Rachel was often hesitant to make art, however, and sometimes did not make art at all. She struggled to choose materials and get started; she expressed concerns about not being a "good enough" artist or not having anything meaningful to say. There were often extensive periods during the session that were spent in silence, as it was difficult for Rachel to access and verbalize her true feelings. I sometimes suggested journaling prompts that encouraged writing in a "free associative" style to explore anything that came to mind. This seemed to help Rachel communicate more openly, perhaps because she did not feel the vulnerability of having to speak the words aloud.

Overall, I offer this approach as a demonstration of the way I use my three-legged stool analogy of emotions, the body, and cognitions in the work. I am constantly moving from expression of emotion (art) to physical sensation (the body) to thoughts and insights (writing) in our sessions.

The following vignette describes an example of an integrative session:

> Rachel came into the session saying she had been struggling with feeling angry after a recent encounter with members of her family of origin where she was triggered with strong emotion yet felt shut down and unable to express herself. She said she felt her strong feelings were "unacceptable and dangerous." I was interested in this comment and wondered aloud if strong feelings might be appropriate in certain situations. I further suggested that we could find a way to try to express and understand those feelings through an art-making process, thus an interesting piece of experiential work began.

> Like the assessment phase in EMDR, we started by uncovering the negative cognitions (NC) that accompanied the experience of feeling overwhelmed by "unacceptable" feelings of anger. In relation to expressing anger, Rachel's associated negative cognitions were "my feelings are not ok, it is not safe to express my angry feelings." In contrast, her desired positive cognitions that she might prefer to believe were "my feelings are acceptable, it's OK to have and express all my feelings."

> Next, I provided Rachel a sheet of blank paper suggesting that she might try to simply express "what anger looks like" with lines, shapes, or colors. This directive came from Sandra Paulsen's (2017) EMDR protocol for early trauma where she helps clients disconnect the evocative circuits of core emotions (that they may find unacceptable) and see what they might "look like" and not what they "feel like." Paulesen's hypothesis is that when emotions are overly charged, they flood the system which interferes with the resolution of trauma. By effectively "resetting" the affective circuits and re-experiencing them as manageable constructs that can be discussed and described, Paulsen postulates that we facilitate neocortical learning and plasticity and prepare the nervous system to respond with a sense of calm, oriented to the present and prepared to engage more adaptively in the future (Paulsen, 2017).

> Rachel stared at the blank page for a long time as she considered the question: "what does anger look like?" She seemed frozen, and after a few minutes of silence pushed away the paper saying, "I really don't know."

I followed up with another suggestion that I hoped might bring some sensation back to her body and, through inviting physical movement, I hoped to connect with the "offline" emotional and cognitive parts of her brain. I retrieved a large pad of newsprint telling her that this paper is cheap and plentiful (to convey the sense that the artwork didn't have to look "good") and I'd simply like her to use it for some scribbling practice.

Rachel had done some bilateral (two-handed) scribbling with me in the past, but this exercise invited a somewhat more extensive exercise as the paper was quite large and I suggested she use oil pastels which would make a more expressive mark than her customarily preferred colored pencils on copy paper. Thus, with sheets of newsprint before her, Rachel slowly began to scribble using both hands back and forth, covering the page with sharp, horizontal lines. After a few sets of back-and-forth scribbling (perhaps 10–15 seconds duration of each set with a breath and a pause in between sets), I invited her to return to her focus on the emotion "anger."

Now she was ready to draw an image of "what anger would look like if I could express it" on a sheet of drawing paper (see Figure 5.3).

Figure 5.3 What anger would look like if I could express it. A red outline of a flame drawn with jagged lines.

The image is the outline of a flame, drawn with red colored pencil. She depicted an initial series of jagged lines to represent the flame of her anger. Then she re-traced those lines with a tight and agitated scribble that overlaid the flame adding to an overall feeling of tension and pressure. When I asked Rachel what she noticed when she looked at the image of the flame, she observed "it still looks stifled."

As I looked at this image, I too sensed the controlled quality, and I could feel the agitation of her hyperaroused state contained in the lines. I invited Rachel to engage in another set of bilateral scribbling on the large pad of newsprint. This time she began the kinesthetic process more quickly and the horizontal lines she produced were more fluid and curvy (in contrast to the first set had been much more rigid and linear). When she finished this set of scribbling (10–15 seconds) I asked her what she noticed now, and she said, "there is less tension in these lines, and I felt more comfortable with the process" (see Figure 5.4).

Figure 5.4 Bilateral scribble.

I then directed Rachel to return her attention to the picture of anger and tell me what she noticed now. Rachel said, "the fire is now moving. It spreads out… It is encroaching… and anger is dangerous. At work I can channel it [the anger] productively but here it is exhausting and all consuming."

"Notice that," I said directing her back to the newsprint and inviting another few sets of bilateral scribbling. This time the scribbling proceeded more slowly, as if she was more engaged in the present experience and staying with the process.

"Now," I asked, "what do you get when you think about the anger?"

"It seems less contained, it is more relaxed and freer" she reported.

I invited her to make another picture about anger.

The next image (see Figure 5.5) is an interesting mix of elements. She started at the bottom of the page where she depicted a large area of anger in a mix of red, orange, and yellow colors that cover the bottom quarter of the page. The colors are applied with heavy pressure, but also restrained within a clearly defined black boundary. The flames are drawn well beneath the surface landscape, which is suggested by a thin, dark, sketchy line across the middle of the page with bright green grass growing above it. There is a warning sign to the right that reads: CAUTION! HIGHLY FLAMMABLE. Rachel commented,

"I've lived all my life like this" referring to the way that anger is held down below the surface. When I asked her about the bright green grass, she said: "That's how I present myself. On the outside I look 'normal', and the feelings don't show." As she said this, I noted a sense of sadness across her face and asked her what she was feeling? She acknowledged there was sadness and voiced a feeling of frustration, saying quietly: "How am I supposed to change this?"

Figure 5.5 Caution: flammable landscape.

I then invited another set of scribbling, hoping that a new association might provide some hope about making a change and being more able to express genuine emotions. The scribbling continued for about 20 seconds this time, at which point I directed her to pause. I observed her eyes were closed during this set and I was concerned that she may have been dissociating. Inviting cognition back into the room I asked if she'd like to write about her experience.

The writing added a third element to our session, and while it invited reflection from a somewhat observing distance, it also invited dissociative parts to emerge more clearly and concretely.

The observing part, indeed, expressed feeling sad and suggested a deeply felt experience. She wrote: "I'm struck by the sadness that *I can't seem to allow myself to feel.*"

There is also evidence of another traumatized part that responded to this statement by saying "the anger has to be stifled and contained away from view… it's not safe to let any of the fire and anger out lest I/we be burned alive" (note the "we" language). Another protective part that challenges the traumatized parts declares: "She is a fraud" (because a part feels she really does not have these feelings, they are "made up"). Rachel then noted how "loud it is inside my brain…battling the intrusive thoughts…"

We spent time bringing back a sense of calm to the activated and dissociative parts. I invited Rachel to imagine a safe place where she could get some comfort, even as these dysregulating and conflictual parts were emerging. She imagined herself inside a giant cocoon, being protected on all sides. She then shared a memory from about age 11 where she recalled not being able to sleep in her own bed and falling asleep curled up next to her mother while she sat on the couch. Rachel said of the experience, "that's confusing. I know my mother was not safe. I wasn't able to express my fear with her."

As Rachel described the child asleep under the large blanket, I began to think about our relationship in therapy. I wondered if Rachel was expressing something about being able to feel a little more comfortable in my presence, letting her fears be expressed but also having some awareness that she'd be heard in this protective and safe space. We talked about how to embody the experience of comfort and safety in the here and now, and she described a positive association to the way she felt in Yoga when taking a "child's pose." We took a moment to imagine that state and engaged in some deep breathing to facilitate a parasympathetic response. Then, returning to the scribble, I wondered aloud if some part might want to explore this feeling of being comfortable.

Rachel returned to a brief set of scribbles on the newsprint (at this point we stayed with short sets 5–10 seconds) and then said, "There's fear of what's inside" and added "part of me *does* want to be seen and heard; but I think part of me wants to know and part doesn't want to know."

"I'm more comfortable being guarded and loathing myself," she continued. "But when we're vulnerable, the painful parts come out." Again, noting the use of we (not I), this statement provided a means to explore different parts of self. There was sadness evident in Rachel's description of the dialectic of being vulnerable (a part) and feeling safe vs. unsafe (another part). "Part of me wants to curl up and cry" she said. I agreed and added that I thought a part of her also wanted to be seen and heard.

I asked Rachel if she would like to draw a picture of "what does safety look like?" at this moment. Without hesitation, she began to work with the oil pastels. Her image depicts a large, gray mound that she described as herself being covered over by a big cozy blanket. The only indication there is anyone or anything underneath the blanket is several suggestions of creases where her body would be curled up beneath its folds. Notable in the right corner is the red bushy tail that peeks out of the lower right side of the blanket. "That is Chief," she said, speaking of her deceased but beloved dog whom she still considers her primary resource and whom was "always there" for her. She titled the image: "I feel contained" (see Figure 5.6).

Figure 5.6 I feel contained.

We did one more set of BLS and noticed that the "adult" part of self was "capable" of scribbling to allow the child part that is vulnerable a space to be heard.

To end the session, I invited more writing (cognition) about the experience, and she responded directly to that prompt. She wrote:

> "I can hear and feel a part of me needing to be seen and heard. Adult me wants to understand- but if I try to look at it, it just vanishes into the ether. It rears its ugly head suddenly and then just as suddenly vaporizes-disappearing as if it never exist[ed].... A[nother] part of me – scared of disrupting the status quo- worries about the consequences of knowing and understanding....and encourages parts to hide."

So, our continued work is to explore the vulnerable and traumatized parts of self that are engaged in a struggle to be seen and heard but are also fearful and avoidant, a challenging dilemma that is common in clients with early and severe interpersonal trauma. This integrative approach using art, the body, and writing seems to be helpful for Rachel as it engages three areas: the emotions that are so often quite overwhelming and uncomfortable; the physical sensations that we work to engage and regulate while in session; and the thoughts that include the pervasive negative beliefs and assumptions that we hope will shift to eventually provide some healthy, adult perspective and a more adaptive point of view.

CONCLUSION

This work highlights the importance of an integrative and flexible approach for treating trauma. My training in Art Therapy, EMDR, and Sensorimotor Psychotherapy has informed a three-legged stool construct consisting of cognitions, emotions, and somatic experiences as ever-present aspects in our clinical work. Trauma therapy is creative therapy. Experiential approaches may facilitate an engaged and embodied reworking of the impact of traumatic memory as it affects both psyche and soma. Our traumatized clients may not have easy access to words and insight; they may be riddled with extreme emotions that feel dangerous and unacceptable, and they may often be overwhelmed with physiological responses such as heightened arousal or shutdown and dissociation. Thus, our trauma-informed treatment interventions must be flexible, creative, and present focused, engaging the client in titrated experiences that toggle seamlessly between thinking, feeling, and doing. While we may begin a session by dealing with a client's pervasive negative thoughts and beliefs, we must at the same time engage with curiosity about how these beliefs affect the present set of emotions and how they are held in the body. As Ogden (2021, p. 7) states: "any of these targets would potentially have a positive therapeutic effect."

REFERENCES

American Psychiatric Association. (2013). *Diagnostic and statistical manual of mental disorders* (5th ed.). https://doi.org/10.1176/appi.books.9780890425596

Avrahami, D. (2006). Visual art therapy's unique contribution in the treatment of post-traumatic stress disorders. *Journal of Trauma and Dissociation, 6*(4), 5–38. https://doi.org/10.1300/j229v06n04_02

Buk, A. (2009). The mirror neuron system and embodied stimulation: Clinical implications for art therapists working with trauma survivors. *The Arts in Psychotherapy, 36*(2), 61–74. https://doi.org/10.1016/j.aip.2009.01.008

Cane, F. (1951). *The artist in each of us.* Pantheon Books.

Chapman, L. (2014). *Neurobiologically informed trauma therapy with children and adolescents: Understanding mechanisms of change.* W.W. Norton.

Chong, C.Y. J. (2015). Why art psychotherapy? Through the lens of interpersonal neurobiology: The distinctive role of art psychotherapy intervention for clients with early relational trauma. *International Journal of Art Therapy, 20*(3), 118–126. https://doi.org/10.1080/17454832.2015.1079727

Chu, J. A. (2011). *Rebuilding shattered lives: Treating complex PTSD and dissociative disorders* (2nd Ed.). Wiley & Sons.

Corrigan, F. M. (2014). Threat and safety: The neurobiology of active and passive defense responses. In U. Lanius, S. Paulsen & F. M. Corrigan (Eds.). *Neurobiology of treatment of traumatic dissociation: Towards an embodied self.* Springer Publishing.

Courtois, C. A., & Ford, J. D. (2009). *Treating complex traumatic stress disorders: An evidence-based guide.* Guilford Press.

Cozolino, L. (2014). *The neuroscience of human relationships* (2nd Ed.). W.W. Norton.

Cozolino, L. (2016). *Why therapy works: Using our minds to change our brains.* W.W. Norton.

Dana, D. (2018). *The polyvagal theory in therapy: Engaging the rhythm of regulation.* W.W. Norton.

Duros, P., & Crowley, D. (2014). The body comes to therapy too. *Clinical Social Work Journal, 42,* 237–246. https://doi.org/10.1007/s10615-014-0486-1

Elbright, C. (2018). *Healing trauma with guided drawing: A sensorimotor art therapy approach to bilateral body mapping.* North Atlantic Books

Fisher, J., & Ogden, P. (2009). Sensorimotor psychotherapy. In C. A. Courtois & J. D. Ford (Eds.), *Treating complex traumatic stress disorders: An evidence-based guide* (pp. 312–328). Guilford.

Fisher, J. (2017). *Healing the fragmented selves of trauma survivors: Overcoming internal self-alienation.* Routledge.

Ford, J. (2009). Neurobiological and developmental research: Clinical implications. In C.A. Courtois & J.D. Ford (Eds.). *Treating complex traumatic stress disorders: An evidence-based guide.* (pp. 31–58). Guilford.

Ford, J.D. & Courtois, C.A. (Eds.). (2020). *Treating complex stress disorders in adults: Scientific foundations and therapeutic models* (2nd Ed.). Guilford Press.

Gantt, L. & Tripp, T. (2016). The image comes first: Treating preverbal trauma with art therapy. In J. King (Ed.). *Art Therapy, Trauma and Neuroscience: Theoretical and Practical Perspectives.* Routledge.

Gantt, L. & Tinnin, L. (2007). Intensive trauma therapy of PTSD and dissociation: An outcome study. *The Arts in Psychotherapy, 34,* 69–80.

Gantt, L. & Tinnin, L. (2009). Support for a neurobiological view of trauma with implications for art therapy. *The Arts in Psychotherapy, 36,* 148–153.

Gelinas, D. (2003). Integrating EMDR into phase-oriented treatment for trauma. *Journal of Trauma & Dissociation, 4*(3), 91–135. https://doi.org/10.1300/J229v04n03_06

Gerge, A., Hawes, J., Eklof, L., & Pedersen, N. (2019). Proposed mechanisms of change in the arts-based psychotherapies. *Voices: A World Forum for Music Therapy, 19*(2), 1–27. https://doi.org/10.15845/voices.v19i2.2564

Germer, C. K., & Neff, K. D. (2015). Cultivating self-compassion in trauma survivors. In V. M. Follette, J. Briere, D. Rozelle, J. W. Hopper, & D. I. Rome (Eds.), *Mindfulness-oriented interventions for trauma: Integrating contemplative practices* (pp. 43–58). Guilford.

Gil, W. (2010). The therapist as psychobiological regulator: Dissociation, affect attunement and clinical process. *Journal of Clinical Social Work, 38,* 260–268. https://doi.org/10.1007/s10615-009-0213-5

Graves-Alcorn, S. & Kagin, C. (2017). *Implementing the expressive therapies continuum: A guide for clinical practice.* Routledge.

Haeyen, S., van Hooren, S., Dehue, F., & Hutschemaekers, G. (2017). Development of an art therapy intervention for patients with personality disorders: An intervention mapping study. *International Journal of Art Therapy, 1,* 1–11. https://doi.org/10.1080%2F17454832.2017.1403458

Herman, J. (1992). *Trauma & recovery: The aftermath of violence.* Basic Books.

Hinz, L. (2009). *Expressive therapy continuum: A framework for using art in therapy.* Routledge.

Jarero, I. N., Artigas, L. (2006). EMDR Integrative group treatment protocol: A post disaster intervention for children and adults. *Traumatology 12*(2), 121–129. https://doi.org/10.1177/1534765606294561

Jarero, I. N., & Artigas, L. (2021). The EMDR therapy butterfly hug method for self- administer bilateral stimulation. *Iberoamerican Journal of Psycotrauma and Dissociation, 2*(1).

Kagin, S. L. & Lusebrink, V. B. (1978). The expressive therapies continuum. *Art Psychotherapy, 5,* 171–180.

Kandel, E. R. (2012). *The age of insight: The quest to understand the unconscious in art, mind, and brain, from Vienna 1900 to the present.* Random House.

Kiessling, R. (2005). Integrating resource development strategies in your EMDR practice. In R. Shapiro (Ed.), *EMDR solutions: Pathways to healing* (pp. 57–87). W.W. Norton.

Kiessling, R. (2020). EMDR Consulting, Inc. "Scribble it Out Drawing Exercises" [video]. https://vimeo.com/414563291

Knipe, J. (2015). *EMDR toolbox: Theory and treatment of complex PTSD and dissociation.* Springer Publishing.

Kolodny, P. (2021). The evolution of trauma theory and its relevance to art therapy. In P. Quinn (Ed.). *Art therapy in the treatment of addiction and trauma* (pp. 89–112). Jessica Kingsley.

Laliotis, D., Luber, M., Oren, U., Shapiro, E., Ichii, M., Hase, M., La Rosa, L., Alter-Reid, K., & Jammes, J. T. (2021). What is EMDR therapy? Past, present, and future directions. *Journal of EMDR practice and research: 15*(4) 186–201. https://doi.org/10.1016/j.erap.2012.08.005

LeDoux, J. (1996). *The emotional brain: The mysterious underpinnings of emotional life.* Simon & Schuster.

Levine, P. (1997). *Waking the tiger: Healing trauma.* North Atlantic Books.

Levine, P. (2015). *Trauma and memory: Brain and body in a search for the living past.* North Atlantic Books.

Levine, S. K. (2011). Art opens to the world: Expressive arts and social action. In E.G. Levine and S. K. Levine, (Eds.). *Art in action: Expressive arts therapy and social change* (pp. 21–30). Jessica Kinsley.

MacLean, P. D. (1990). *The triune brain in evolution: Role in paleocerebral functions.* Plenum Press.

Malchiodi, C. A. (2020). *Trauma and expressive arts therapy: Brain, body & imagination in the healing process.* Guilford Press.

Maxfield, L. (2008). Considering mechanisms of action in EMDR. *Journal of EMDR Practice and Research, 2*(4), 234–238. https://doi.org/10.1891/1933-3196.2.4.234

Maxfield, L., Melmyk, W. T., & Hayman, C. A. (2008). A working memory explanation for the effects of eye movements. *EMDR: Journal of EMDR Practice and Research, 2,* 247–261.

McNamee, C. M. (2003). Bilateral art: Facilitating systemic integration and balance. *The Arts in Psychotherapy, 30*(5), 283–292. https://doi.org/10.1016/j.aip.2003.08.005

McNamee, C. M. (2006). Experiences with bilateral art: A retrospective study. *Art Therapy: Journal of the American Art Therapy Association, 23*(1). 7–13.

Naff, K. (2014). A framework for treating cumulative trauma with art therapy. *Art Therapy: Journal of the American Art Therapy Association, 31*(2), 79–86.

Ogden, P, Minton, K., & Paine, C. (2006). *Trauma and the body: A sensorimotor approach to psychotherapy.* W.W. Norton.

Ogden, P. (2015). Beyond words: A sensorimotor perspective (unpublished paper).

Ogden, P. (2021). The different impact of trauma and relational stress on physiology, posture, and movement: Implications for treatment. *European Journal of Trauma and Dissociation, 5*(4), 100172. https://doi.org/10.1016/j.ejtd.2020.100172

Ogden, P., & Fisher, J. (2015). *Sensorimotor psychotherapy: Interventions for trauma and attachment.* W.W. Norton.

Oren, E. & Solomon, R. (2012). EMDR therapy: An overview of its development and mechanisms of action. *Revue europeenne de psychologie appliquee, 62,* 197–203.

Parnell, L. (1997). *Transforming Trauma EMDR: The revolutionary new therapy for freeing the mind, clearing the body and opening the heart.* W.W. Norton.

Paulsen, S. (2017). *When there are no words: Repairing early trauma and neglect from the attachment period with EMDR therapy.* Bainbridge Institute for Integrative Psychology.

Perry, B. D. (2009). Examining child maltreatment through a neurodevelopmental lens: Clinical applications of the neurosequential model of therapeutics. *Journal of Loss and Trauma, 14,* 240–255. https://doi.org/10.1080/15325020903004350

Perry, B. D. (2014). The neurosequential model of therapeutics in young children. In K. Brandt, B. Perry, S. Seligman, & E. Tronick (Eds.). *Infant and Early Childhood Mental Health* (pp. 21–47). American Psychiatric Press.

Perryman, K, Blisard, P., & Moss, R. (2019). Using creative arts in trauma therapy: The neuroscience of healing. *Journal of Mental Health Counseling, 41*(1), 80–94.

Porges, S. W. (2011). *The polyvagal theory: Neurophysiological foundations of emotions, attachment, communication, and self-regulation.* W.W. Norton

Rothschild, B. (2000). *The body remembers: The psychophysiology of trauma and trauma treatment.* W.W. Norton

Rothschild, B. (2017). *The body remembers (volume 2): Revolutionizing trauma treatment.* W.W. Norton.

Scaer, R. (2005). *The trauma spectrum: Hidden wounds and human resiliency.* W.W. Norton.

Schore, A. N. (2003). *Affect regulation and the repair of the self.* W. W. Norton.

Schore, A. N. (2019). *Right brain psychotherapy.* W.W. Norton.

Schore, A. N. (2021). The interpersonal neurobiology of intersubjectivity. *Frontiers of Psychology, 12*. https://doi.org/10.3389/fpsyg.2021.648616

Schore, J., & Schore, A. N. (2008). Modern attachment theory: The central role of affect regulation in development and treatment. *Clinical Social Work Journal, 36*(9), 9–20. https://doi.org/10.1007/s10615-007-0111-7

Schwartz, A., & Maiberger, B. (2018). *EMDR therapy and somatic psychology: Interventions to enhance embodiment in trauma treatment.* W.W. Norton.

Schubert, S. J., Lee, C. W., & Drummond, P. D. (2011). The efficacy of psychophysiological correlates of dual-attention tasks in eye movement desensitization and reprocessing (EMDR). *Journal of Anxiety Disorders, 25*, 1–11. https://doi.org/10.1016/j.janxdis.2010.06.024

Scoglio, A. A., Rudat, D. A, Garvert, D., Jarmoloqski, M., Jackson, C., & Herman, J. L. (2018). Self-compassion and responses to trauma: The role of emotion regulation. *Journal of Interpersonal Violence, 33*(13), 2016–2036. https://doi.org/10.1177/0886260515622296

Shapiro, F. (2001). *Eye movement desensitization and reprocessing (EMDR) Therapy: Basic principles, protocols, and procedures* (2nd Ed.). Guilford.

Shapiro, F. (2018). *Eye movement desensitization and reprocessing (EMDR) therapy: Basic principles, protocols, and procedures* (3rd edition). Guilford

Siegel, D. J. (1999). *The developing mind: Toward a neurobiology of interpersonal experience.* New York: Guilford Press.

Siegel, D. (2003). An interpersonal neurobiology of psychotherapy: The developing mind and the resolution of trauma. In M. Solomon & D. Siegel (Eds.), *Healing Trauma: Attachment, mind, body, and brain* (pp. 1–56). W.W. Norton.

Siegel, D. (2012). Dr. Dan Siegel presenting a Hand Model of the Brain [Video.] You Tube. https://www.youtube.com/watch?v=gm9CIJ74Oxw

Siegel, D. J. (2009). Emotion as integration: A possible answer to the question, what is emotion? In D. Fosha, D.J. Siegel, & M. F. Solomon (Eds.), *The healing power of emotion: Affective neuroscience, development and clinical practice* (pp. 145–171). W. W. Norton.

Siegel, D. J. (2012). *The developing mind: How relationships and the brain interact to shape who we are.* Guilford Press.

Siegel, D. J. (2010) *The mindful therapist: A clinician's guide to mindsight and neural integration.* Guilford.

Solomon, R. M., & Shapiro, F. (2008). EMDR and the adaptive information processing model: Potential mechanisms of change. *Journal of EMDR Practice and Research, 2*(4), 315–325. https://doi.org/10.1891/1933-3196.2.4.315

Talwar, S. (2007). Accessing traumatic memory through art making: An art therapy trauma protocol (ATTP). *The Arts in Psychotherapy. 34*, 22–35. https://doi.org/10.1016/j.aip.2006.09.001

Tobin, B. (2006). Art therapy meets EMDR. *Canadian Art Therapy Association Journal, 19*(2), 27–38. https://doi.org/10.1080/08322473.2006.11432286

Tripp, T. (2007). A short- term approach to processing trauma: Art therapy and bilateral stimulation. *Art Therapy: Journal of the American Art Therapy Association, 24*(4), 176–183. https://doi.org/10.1080/07421656.2007.10129476

Tripp, T. (2012). *Integrating EMDR and art therapy for bilateral transformation of trauma.* Workshop presented at the Expressive Therapies Summit, New York.

Tripp, T. (2016). A body-based bilateral art protocol for reprocessing trauma. In J. King (Ed.) *Art therapy, trauma, and neuroscience: Theoretical and practical perspectives* (pp. 173–194). Routledge.

Tripp, T. (2019, May). *Bringing the body to therapy: An art therapy workshop.* Ferentz Institute.

Tripp, T. (2019a). More than an image: Revisiting the Ulman personality assessment procedure, *Art Therapy: Journal of the American Art Therapy Association, 36*(3), 133–140. https://doi.org/10.1080/07421656.2019.1649546

Tripp, T., Potash, J. S., & Brancheau, D. (2019). Safe Place collage protocol: Art making for managing traumatic stress. *Journal of Trauma & Dissociation, 20*(5), 511–525. https://doi.org/10.1080/15299732.2019.1597813

Tripp, T., & Kolodny, P. (2016, November). *Wiggle, scribble and squiggle: Bilateral approaches for transformation of trauma.* Workshop presented at Expressive Therapies Summit, New York.

Tripp, T., & Kolodny, P. (2017, October). *Bilateral techniques for brain change: Scribbling, wiggling & more.* Workshop presented at Expressive Therapies Summit, New York.

Ulman, E. (1992). A new use of art in psychiatric diagnosis. *American Journal of Art Therapy, 30*, 78–88. https://doi.org/10.1080/07421656.2019.1649546

van der Hart, O., & Gelinas, D. (2017). *Dissociation of the personality and the EMDR treatment of chronic traumatization.* PowerPoint slides. EMDR International Association Conference, Medford, MA.

van der Kolk, B. A., & van der Hart, O. (1995). The intrusive past: The flexibility of memory and the engraving of trauma. In C. Caruth (Ed.). *Trauma: Explorations in memory.* The Johns Hopkins University Press.

van der Kolk, B. A. (2014). *The body keeps the score: Brain, mind, and body in the healing of trauma.* New York: Viking Press.

van Nieuwenhove, K., & Meganck, R. (2019). Interpersonal features in complex trauma etiology, consequences, and treatment: A literature review. *Journal of Aggression, Maltreatment & Trauma, 28*(8), 903–928. https://doi.org/10.1080/10926771.2017.1405316

Wheeler, K. (2007). Psychotherapeutic strategies for healing trauma. *Perspectives in Psychiatric Care, 43*(3), 132–141.

CHAPTER 6

THE INTERWEAVE OF INTERNAL FAMILY SYSTEMS, EMDR, AND ART THERAPY

Peggy Kolodny and Salicia Mazero

Peggy Kolodny (PK) is a licensed board-certified art therapist specializing in trauma survivors across the lifespan. I took an introductory workshop in Eye Movement Desensitizing and Reprocessing (EMDR) around 1998, followed by level 1 and 2 training. I began integrating art into EMDR phasing protocol by using bilateral drawing strokes on paper with an image of the target memory during Phase 4, calling this Art Movement Desensitization and Reprocessing (ArtMDR). I then trained in level 1 and level 2 IFS in 2015–2016. Art directives used by the IFS trainers further inspired my creative brainstorming on how to integrate art interventions into the IFS model. This was further validated in my level 2 training in IFS titled "IFS, Trauma and Neuroscience" led by psychiatrist Frank Anderson and Richard Schwartz. They pointed out, similar to IFS, EMDR recognizes that the client has the resources to self-heal, the emotions and body are central to the process, the therapist stance is neutral and the relational aspect (client to parts, parts to parts, and the therapeutic alliance) at the core, weaving neuroscience in supporting the healing process (Anderson, 2013).

Salicia Mazero (SM) is an art therapist who specializes in eating disorder treatment in St. Louis, Missouri. I started my training in IFS in 2012 and then trained in EMDR two years later. I found the combination of IFS, EMDR, and art therapy to be effective with clients who have complex trauma and/or eating disorders of all ages. To continue learning, Peggy and I took several EMDR-informed IFS workshops by Bruce Hersey (2015, 2021) and began structuring my trauma-informed art therapy clinical sessions with these integrative approaches.

Kolodny et al. (2016) began presenting this art-informed IFS process in workshops internationally as their clinical experience, peer consultation, and further trainings fostered their knowledge. The American Art Therapy Association included Kolodny and Bechtel's Overview of Art Therapy and IFS workshop in The Institute for Continuing Education in Art Therapy (2016). Kolodny and Mazero have presented at the International Internal Family Systems Conference on Art-Informed IFS and Legacy Burdens (2018, 2021). This chapter is the culmination of their combined trainings and experiences and will cover how clinicians can use IFS, EMDR, and art therapy together in diverse ways to treat complex cases while maintaining their efficacy.

We respectfully offer the ethical disclaimer that this chapter's overview of art therapy, IFS, and EMDR will provide a foundational understanding; however, one is required to attain the comprehensive education in each to *ethically* practice. Art Therapy is a master's degree program; Expressive Arts Therapy, IFS, and EMDR involve post-graduate training leading to certification (or registration as in Registered Expressive Arts Therapist). If you already possess a degree or certificate in one or two of these, the chapter will support the reader in acquiring deeper skills in the interweave of the creative process, IFS and EMDR. Our main focus will be on the IFS model leading to the integration of the three disciplines. If you have no trainings in the expressive arts therapies, we invite you to begin exploring creative interventions discussed in this chapter, as we selected those with non-art therapists in mind.

DOI: 10.4324/9781003156932-7

TRAUMA PHASE/STAGE MODELS

Multiple trauma-informed models have foundations or have been influenced by Herman's (1992) Stages of Recovery: sensory somatic therapies, "embodied" models, neurobiological theories, mind-body "mindfulness" connections, and complex trauma definitions. Many trauma treatment specialists share the perspective that phase/stage trauma treatment models are the most efficient (Cloitre et al., 2012; Steele et al., 2005; Twombly, 2013; van der Kolk, 2015), supported by Herman's description of three foundational healing phases (safety and stabilization, trauma processing, remembrance and mourning, and reconnection). Fisher (2017) offers a phase-oriented integrative trauma treatment model that includes Sensorimotor Psychotherapy (Ogden & Fisher, 2015), EMDR, and IFS. She writes "the 'gold standard' of trauma therapy has been the Phase-Oriented Treatment Model" (Fisher, 2017, p. 44). Twombly's (2013) chapter "Integrating IFS with Phase-Oriented Treatment of Clients with Dissociative Disorder" specifically describes how IFS can integrate into a phase model.

Trauma-focused art therapists have utilized phase-oriented trauma approaches as well, typically grounded in Herman's stages of treatment (Gantt & Tinnin, 2009; Hass-Cohen et al., 2014; Chapman, 2014). Cohen, Barnes, and Rankin's (1995) pioneering art therapy workbook "Managing Traumatic Stress through Art" follows the multiple phases of trauma treatment from focused breathing to termination. IFS offers steps in the healing process that could be perceived as phases of healing, known as the six Fs. These six steps are a way of building safety and trust; the unburdening process allows the client to have insight into their traumatic experiences; and in the final integrative step of IFS, the client is invited to take on positive traits in transitioning back into present life. Trauma-sensitized neural responses may trigger somatic states of hyperarousal; "manager parts" in IFS may then step in to protect through the hypoarousal responses of numbing and dissociation. This is where other approaches such as EMDR, Sensorimotor, Somatic Experiencing*, and creative therapies can be integrated into IFS to help a client safely notice somatic sensation. Schwartz has mentioned in trainings that, in working with more severe dissociation found in complex trauma, time may be needed to build trust, safety, and stability before beginning IFS; and integrating other approaches to the model can be appropriate. IFS as a "stand-alone approach" can certainly achieve these goals but clinicians and clients often find utilizing other appropriate interventions can assist in shifting a client's state and attention, thus, in IFS language, help a protector part, stuck in a rigid role, experience flexibility.

We are describing ways to integrate art therapy into a phase model (EMDR) along with the guided process steps approach of IFS. Trauma approaches continue to evolve with research, clinical experiences, and academic study. We will be referring to several of these as we describe our integrative models using art therapy with IFS and EMDR. As a result, we would like to devote a brief section defining those to which we will be referencing.

Sensory Somatic Models

van der Kolk's Developmental Trauma Disorder model (2005) explores the impact of complex trauma on the developing child, supported by the influential results of the Adverse Childhood Experiences (ACE) longitudinal research study (Felitti et al., 1998). Somatic Experiencing© theory (Levine & Frederick, 1997), Ogden's Sensorimotor Psychotherapy (Ogden & Fisher, 2015), and van der Kolk (2015) all remind us that "the body keeps the score" on the sensory-somatic nature of traumas' impact. All of these models recognize the critical need to develop awareness of our "felt sense" on how we hold trauma in our bodies and its impact on the internal adaptive survival reactions of our nervous systems. Neuroception is the internal surveillance process of our neural circuits that detects if situations are safe or threatening, based on past traumatic experiences (Porges, 2004). By becoming attuned to our sensory somatic responses, our dysregulated emotional states, and our fight-fight-freeze-collapse survival reactions, we develop self-compassion that permits us to perceive our responses as survival and not as a pathology (Dana, 2018). This "felt sense" is an important component of trauma approaches, as evidenced by IFS and EMDR both utilizing a "where you feel this in your body" question in their treatment process. Felt sense is often a portal to our "parts," leading us to the "trailheads" of distressful memories.

The neurobiological effects of trauma continue to be researched and explored by multiple researchers such as Porges (2011), Siegel (2020), Perry (2006), and Perry and Winfrey (2021). Perry created the Neurosequential Model of Therapy, a "bottom-up" neurodevelopmental phase approach to trauma treatment with children. Porges developed the Polyvagal Theory, a reference to a third nervous system response that he named "the social engagement system," in which we respond to distress by disconnecting (flight/fight/freeze/fawn) or socially engaging (attunement). To offer a simplified explanation, Porges has explained that trauma compromises our ability to engage with others by "replacing patterns of connections with patterns of protections" (Porges, 2011, p. 18). Siegel developed the Window of Tolerance (WOT) in 1999 as a model based on neuroscience that dovetails with Polyvagal Theory, as well as EMDR, and IFS. WOT addresses the need for trauma survivors to identify their reactive states to triggers created by trauma with the clinical goal to increase tolerance and build resources. The "window" refers to a metaphoric space of distress tolerance where one is emotionally regulated, possessing the skills to self-soothe, maintaining a state of being calm and connected, even in disturbing situations. They may "leave" this Window of Tolerance when triggered, resulting in the Autonomic Nervous System (ANS) becoming hyperaroused (hypervigilant, rage, overwhelmed, fight or flight responses) or hypoaroused (freeze, collapse, numb, and dissociate responses). One goal of trauma-informed therapy is to widen the comfort zone (window) for increased flexibility so the person primarily functions inside their window instead of feeling hyperaroused or hypoaroused. Expanding one's WOT is useful in EMDR's Phase Four and in IFS's internal dialogues in allowing "dual attention awareness" (Shapiro, 2001; van den Hout & Engelhard, 2012), the ability to stay in the present while observing the past, which often occurs in art-making as well.

OVERVIEW OF INTERNAL FAMILY SYSTEMS (IFS)

Internal Family Systems (IFS) model is a collaborative, non-pathologizing client-centered approach to psychotherapy developed by Richard D. Schwartz (Schwartz, 1995; Schwartz & Sweezy 2020). Schwartz received his PhD in marriage and family therapy; he developed this model evolving from his clinical experience of over 30 years. Family Systems theory suggests that individuals cannot be understood in isolation from one another, but rather as a part of their family, as the family is an emotional unit (Schwartz, 1995). Schwartz took this concept, internalized it, and defined systems "as any entity whose parts relate to one another in a pattern" (Schwartz & Sweezy, 2020, p. 25). Prior to IFS, little attention was given to how these inner entities functioned in relation to each other (Schwartz, 1995). Today, IFS is listed as an effective form of treatment for one's well-being and general functioning on the

National Registry for Evidence-Based Programs and Practices (NREPP) by the Substance Abuse and Mental Health Administration (SAMSHA) (2019). It is recognized as an effective treatment approach for PTSD (Brown, 2020; Twombly, 2013; Fisher, 2017; van der Kolk, 2015). Brown (2020) offers an in-depth discussion of Complex PTSD, saying that those with this diagnosis are "…often re-experiencing aspects of their early relational trauma…" (p. 114) demonstrating why IFS is an ideal treatment fit for trauma.

The IFS model of therapy assumes that every person is born with "Self" (with a capital S). Self is defined as a whole, undamaged, healing entity (Anderson, 2021). Schwartz and Sweezy (2020) define Self as the "seat of consciousness." The model is based on the concept that everyone has multiplicity of the mind, made up of relatively discrete sub-personalities, each with their own viewpoints and qualities that can be described as "parts." Van der Kolk (2015) states "…every major school of psychology recognizes that people have subpersonalities and gives them different names…" (p. 280). Clients and therapists may prefer alternative descriptors for parts such as alters, co-consciousness, ego states, discrete states, and sub-personalities. Parts language is familiar to us; we may find ourselves commenting that a part of us wants to visit a friend, while another part wants to stay home. As Schwartz often says, we all have parts! These parts can be experienced in a number of ways through our thoughts, feelings, somatic sensations, images, words, sounds, inner voices, physical symptoms, and/or actually viewed as an internalized person. They can be relatively autonomous and have their own perspectives, life experiences, feelings, actions, and roles but their intensions are positive even though their behaviors may reflect otherwise. Neuroscience has supported this concept of multiplicity of the mind, as reported by van der Kolk in describing Michael Gazzaniga's "split-brain" research. His findings reveal that "…the mind is composed of semiautonomous functioning modules, each of which has a special role…" (van der Kolk, 2015, p. 280). This supports why IFS clinicians believe having parts is not pathological (Anderson, 2021). Schwartz (1995) conceptualizes three categories for parts: managers, firefighters, and exiles. The client who made the appointment and comes to therapy can be considered a part of the client, often the manager.

In deepening the understanding of Self, we can recognize it as a "felt" sense containing traits that Schwartz (1995) named as the eight Cs: *calm, curiosity, compassion, confidence, courage, clarity, connectedness, and creativity.* Often, the initial glimpse of one's Self emerging occurs when the client becomes *curious* about the part and *calmly* sits with the part to understand its narrative. Through this witnessing experience, Self shows *compassion* toward the part thus exhibiting traits of *clarity, connectiveness,* possessing the *confidence* and *courage* to continue building a trusting relationship with that part. When one is in Self, all parts are embodied—where the body is able to be responsive, relaxed, aligned, energized, open, calm, and centered. Schwartz and Sweezy (2020) also developed the five Ps to describe the therapist in Self: *presence, patience, perspective, persistence, and playfulness.*

Schwartz believes that parts are created over time to protect the Self (Anderson, 2021; Schwartz & Sweezy, 2020; Gomez & Krause, 2013). One of the mantras in IFS trainings is that "all parts are welcomed," as we hold the concept that each equally deserves compassion and understanding as they play integral roles in our daily functioning (Anderson et al., 2017). IFS therapists may tell clients that each part of them is equally a client of ours. Another key concept in IFS is there are "no agendas," as having an agenda may be an indication that the therapist is not in Self-energy.

In this model, dissociation and Dissociative Identity Disorder (DID) are still recognized as a system with more extreme parts resulting from complex trauma (Anderson, 2021; Schwartz &

Sweezy, 2020). Twombly (2013) and Fisher (2017) have both integrated IFS with phase-oriented dissociation treatment. In IFS, dissociation is viewed as an action of protective parts which offers the opportunity for the therapist/client to dialogue with them (Anderson, 2021). Schwartz and Sweezy state "…alters of clients with DID are parts but their inner systems are… disconnected…childhood abuse causes vigilant protectors to rely on amnesiac barriers…" (2020, p. 21) which, they explain, prevent internal relationships between these parts. They further elaborate on the prevalence of stigmatizing attitudes toward Dissociative Disorders in the United States when writing "… because our culture portrays DID as a bizarre aberration that signifies severe pathology…" clients without extreme dissociation may feel crazy when they access parts in the IFS process; and clients with complex trauma whose inner system is diagnosed as DID "…often don't realize having parts is normal…" (Schwartz & Sweezy, 2020, p. 21).

Schwartz (1995; Schwartz & Sweezy, 2020; Anderson 2021) describes the three categories of parts known as managers (preventive protectors), firefighters (reactive protectors), and exiles (wounded/protected parts). Both managers and firefighter parts serve as protectors. Managers are parts who view their role as keeping a person functional and safe by minimizing the influences of the exiles whom they fear may overwhelm the client. They represent an attempt to maintain control of every situation and relationship in an effort to protect parts from feeling hurt, rejected, overwhelmed, or humiliated. Managers are focused on external factors such as appearance or performance. Manager parts may present as a striver, perfectionist, self-criticizing, controlling, judging, care-taking, and risk avoidant. These parts typically appear in a sensory somatic manner such as rigidity in the body structure, tension or pain in the body, breath and muscle constriction, as well as cognitive thoughts (critical thoughts/voices) (Anderson, 2021; Schwartz & Sweezy, 2020). In Phase Six of EMDR, the body scan is also used to notice these somatic sensations, recognizing this is how emotions are held (Shapiro, 2001; van der Kolk, 2015). Managers would typically represent the hypo-arousal state of WOT, located below the comfort zone.

However, firefighter (FF) parts are hyper-reactive and jump into action when the system feels threatened or an exile is triggered. These parts seek to "douse the flames" of feeling as quickly as possible, thereby earning their name firefighters. They tend to be impulsive and employ tactics of overstimulation or dissociation to regain a sense of equilibrium by either soothing or distracting the exiles. Firefighter parts may present as addictions, eating disorders, dissociation, suicidality, or self-injury. These parts typically appear in a sensory somatic manner such as activation of the Autonomic Nervous System (ANS), anxiety, panic, digestive issues, cravings, and/or impulses. Working with FF is an appropriate time to introduce Siegel's concept of WOT. Firefighters would represent the hyperarousal and hypervigilant state in WOT, located above the more regulated zone.

Exiles are parts that are frozen in the past carrying painful experiences, emotions, memories, thoughts, physical sensations, and beliefs that emerged from wounding/traumatizing experiences, which Schwartz defines as burdens. Parts hold and contain these burdens, becoming increasingly extreme in their effort to be nurtured, heard, and witnessed. Exiled parts may present as fear/terror, shame, grief/loss, loneliness, dependency, abandonment, worthless, and helpless. These parts typically appear in a sensory somatic manner such as dissociation, emptiness, lethargy, hypotonicity, paralysis, catatonia, blank eyes, depression, pain, and/or illness. When exiles become triggered, a protective part also becomes activated and may take the person outside their WOT.

As parts heal, thrive, and become unburdened from their roles, they are able to take on more productive and healthy roles (Schwartz & Sweezy, 2020). Self-energy increases and can take leadership of the internal system. Self-leadership is the ultimate goal of IFS, attained through the process of unburdening exiles, restoring trust in self, and re-balancing the system. Schwartz (1995) writes, "...if I ask clients to separate from extreme and polarized parts ...most of them could shift quickly into a compassionate state of mind..." (p. 37). He explains that when the client is holding a compassionate stance, a component of Self-energy, inner wisdom will emerge and they will know how to guide their parts.

Steps of Witnessing and Unburdening Exiles: The Six Fs (Schwartz)

Listed are the IFS steps of witnessing the part's embodied and distressing experiences, leading to its healing journey of unburdening exiles. We consider these steps similar to a healthy social engagement process. We often feel cathartic relief in sharing our painful memories with a trusted friend. These six Fs allow an individual to get to know and develop relationships with their parts, with the therapeutic intention to guide parts "stuck" in roles to express then let go of painful memories they have often held on to for years. This dialoguing with parts can be client-to-part, therapist-to-part (known as direct access), part-to-part, or Self-to-part. Often when it's client-to-part or part-to-part, it can be an internal dialogue with client reporting information to therapist as desired. These steps are identified as the *six Fs.*

1. **Find**—The process of *finding* a part in and around the body (therapist asks the client focuses on body and notices any sensations; somatic awareness may be experienced as physical sensation, image, memory, thought, voice, or even perceiving a human or animal figure).

   The part may be a protector or an exile; either way we are still going through the six Fs process.

2. **Focus**—Client then *focuses* on one that captures their attention in some way. If other parts appear, they are asked to "step back"; if client is emotionally merged with the part, it's called blending and internal dialoguing will not work between the client and the part. The therapist guides the client through *unblending* from that part with separation and distancing techniques. The part may want to speak directly to the therapist, known as *direct access*. The goal is to have the client *unblend* from all parts that are trying to protect the exile.

3. **Flesh out**—Therapist guides client to ask the part permission to get to know it then asking "what do you want me to understand or know about you? What is your role?" as a way of *fleshing out* the part with dimension.

4. **Feel**—Therapist guides the client to explore their emotional response to knowing more about client's role by asking client directly "*how do you feel toward this part?*" This may be where you begin to see fears and/or critics and reactive parts known as *polarized parts*; or the beginnings of Self-energy by their nonjudgmental empathetic acceptance. This compassion is the beginning of forming a trusting relationship by befriending the part.

5. **Friend**—Also known as *facilitate relationship* or *befriend*. Therapist guides client in deepening the trust in relationship with part. Client is accessing and modeling more Self-energy.

6. **Fears**—Client explores part's *fears* by asking it questions such as, if it's a protective part, "what is it afraid would happen if...?" or if it's an exile "What story does it want you to know? What is it afraid would happen if they left where they are hiding?"

The six Fs prepare for the six steps of the *unburdening* process (Anderson, 2021). As the client builds a trusting relationship with their wounded part, known as *Self to part*, they are moving into the next step. The exile yearns to escape its pain by having its story be heard, understood, and thus *witnessed* (step 1) by the part holding Self-energy so it can be released from its painful burdens (Gomez & Krause, 2013; Anderson et al., 2017). This distressing/traumatic narrative by the client is told utilizing memories, visual images, somatic sensations, thoughts, and/or emotions (Gomez & Krause, 2013). The Self is then able to enter the scene to give the part a corrective experience, referred to as a *do-over* (step 2). If it appears that the part is "stuck" in a traumatic or distressing scene, the wounded part will be invited by the client or the therapist to leave the past where they have been "frozen in time" and enter the present in an act of *retrieval* (step 3) to a safer imaginal place of that part's choosing (Gomez & Krause, 2013). This process of *retrieval* may ease the ability of the part to unburden since the part would not actively be in distress. "Once the exile feels understood by the client's Self, it can release the burdens it acquired" starting the *unburdening* process (Gomez & Krause, 2013, p. 304). Anderson (2021) refers to this fourth step as *unloading*. The therapist may suggest to the client's part to release its burdens to one of the five elements: fire, water, earth, air, or light such as burning the memories or letting the wind carry them away. There are many opportunities here to bring art-making into the session to sculpt this release, draw an unburdening, or paint a safer imaginal place. Sometimes unburdening can happen spontaneously when a part feels that they have been witnessed and understood. Once the part has successfully let go of their burdens, they are *invited* (step 5) to internalize positive traits, strengths, and qualities such as kindness, confidence, competence, wisdom, and flexibility. The overlaps with Phases Two and Five of EMDR and resourcing are evident here. The last step in the unburdening process is *integration* (step 6) in which the part develops a new healthier role in the system and connection with those parts that possess more compassion and Self-energy (Gomez & Krause, 2013). Self then welcomes back parts that were protecting the exile and allows them to observe that the exile has been unburdened. This will allow for protectors to see that they no longer have to carry out their role of being preventive or reactive and can modify their role (Anderson, 2021). Finally, the client is invited to show appreciation for the protectors or other exiles that gave them space during the session. In Figure 6.1, we see a client's artwork after using bilateral art strokes on paper. Client, "M" diagnosed with DID, targeted a memory of being humiliated by her mother in early childhood. She drew a series of pictures following the IFS process of polarization, unblending, and finding an exile. "M" retrieved the child exile, witnessed her unburdening, then drew the child, dressed in clothes and wearing a hairstyle that were forbidden by the abusive mother, having fun at an amusement park. Certainly, this was a resourceful and reparative re-telling. Client is drawn as Self, showing compassion and nurturance in an act of integration with this child part.

Burdens can be *personal burdens* based on client's lived experiences or *legacy burdens*, defined by Schwartz and Sweezy (2020) as those absorbed from family, peers, ethnic, or culture contexts that are powerful organizers of our minds, emotions, reactions, and behaviors. They are also known as generational, historical, cultural, and racialized burdens and they can intersect (Fatter & Love, 2021; Menakem, 2017). IFS therapist Ann Sinko (2017) elaborates on legacy burdens, defining them as constraining and limiting with overt (directly from parent/child interactions) and covert (indirectly absorbed via family's emotional process) influences.

Figure 6.1 Drawing of self-energy holding the hand of younger child part.

We have used the term *legacy wisdom*, perceiving this as ancestral wisdom carried down to us by past ancestors, revealed to us as we let go of burdens and are open to Self-energy. Others have noticed this concept of intergenerational strengths; Jackson et al. (2018) call this intergenerational resilience regarding their work with chronic exposure to institutionalized racism. Anderson (2021) discusses Rachel Yehuda and Amy L. Lehrner's work on epigenetics and PTSD in explaining the legacy burdens experienced in IFS unburdenings. Sinko (2017) refers to these as positive transmissions, "…creating connections and resiliency in families…" in her IFS clinical work (p. 164). Resourcing in EMDR and the internalizing positive traits in step five of IFS emerge from our inherent wisdom and flow from the transformative lessons of our own wise elders, the epigenetics of Self. Schwartz and Sweezy (2020) mention epigenetics as a profound factor in relationship to legacy burdens. They define epigenetics as "…a process by which trauma is transferred across generations through the genes of a traumatized person…" They further note that epigenetics research indicates a link between "…environmental stressors that induce a genetic change called methylation…" (p. 57).

Studies on sleep and creativity (Marguilho et al., 2015) as well as anecdotal stories have noted that artists, including poets, musicians, and actors, have awoken with a fully written song, poem, image as if a creative gift was given to them as they slept and dreamt. It is interesting to consider if these inspirational creative bursts are legacies of wisdom from the past. This is a trailhead for future study that we are eager to pursue, especially in connection to EMDR's effectiveness being linked to replicating somatic activity present during EMDR stages in fostering memory consolidation.

OVERVIEW OF EYE MOVEMENT DESENSITIZATION AND REPROCESSING (EMDR)

As the focus of this book is on creative interventions integrated with Eye Movement Desensitization and Reprocessing (EMDR), most chapters have already offered definitions of EMDR. In the interest of those readers who may be reading individual chapters for academic purposes, the authors will briefly contribute an overview.

Francine Shapiro developed EMDR in 1987, after noticing decreased distress as her eyes paced back and forth as she walked (Shapiro, 2001). She pursued research on this phenomenon of rapidly reducing trauma symptoms in using bilateral stimulation. Shapiro developed it as a phase-oriented psychotherapy that is now considered as an essential evidenced-based, gold standard trauma treatment (Shapiro, 2001; Brown, 2020; van der Kolk, 2015; WHO, 2013). However, the effectiveness of EMDR is often challenged by complex trauma and dissociation (Brown, 2020; Forgash & Copeley, 2008). Our clinical experience, as well as the work of other art therapists, has demonstrated to the authors how art therapy has enhanced the use of EMDR with these populations (Davis, 2021; Marich, 2011; Tripp, 2016).

Specific protocols are included in the phases, incorporating diverse forms of bilateral stimulation, cognitive interweaves, adaptive information processing (AIP), and resourcing. The AIP model can be briefly defined as the client's safe or calm place that keeps them grounded in the EMDR process (Shapiro, 2001). If the processing gets blocked, the therapist might use cognitive interweaves by offering a brief statement or question to stimulate connections, and to support the client in continuing reprocessing. These interweaves include psychoeducation, established resources, and prior insights that emerged in therapy. As EMDR evolved, so did the types of bilateral movement, the emphasis now being on *bilateral stimulation*. Currently, these include tactile tappers, vibrating bands, visual light bars to track eye movement, hand-driven bilateral tapping on knees and shoulders, feet tapping, and bilateral sounds. Here is where we have found Art Therapy to be relevant; Kolodny has used bilateral scribbles during phase four Desensitization since she began using EMDR in the late 1990s, quickly developing other ways to incorporate art-making into EMDR phases (to be discussed later in this chapter). Mazero, as well, has found ways to integrate the creative process into EMDR. She has clients wear bilateral "bracelets" during art-making. The bracelets are left on for the duration of creating and processing by the client. Tappers are another option, with the advantage that the therapist has more control with intensity. Clients can place tappers in their pockets, on their knees, or in shoes. A myriad of creative techniques are explored throughout this book as other expressive arts therapists have collectively discovered the vast potential of bridging the arts with EMDR.

There are eight phases in the EMDR process. Listed below is a brief description of these phases (Shapiro, 2001):

1. **History taking and treatment planning:** Begin therapeutic alliance, assess symptoms, and identify targets for reprocessing.
2. **Preparation:** Trauma-informed psychoeducation, mindful metaphors for noticing/grounding, informed consent, Safe/Calm Place image.

3. **Assessment:** Target experience, elicit image, positive and negative cognitions, current affect, body scan, baseline for SUD (Subjective Units of Disturbance), and VoC (Validity of Cognition)

4. **Desensitization:** Use bilateral stimulation to reprocess target for adaptive resolution, assess progress, note challenges, and use "additional interventions when reprocessing is blocked" (Leeds, 2009)

5. **Installation:** BLS while client holds original target with positive cognition/belief until VoC reaches 6/7.

6. **Body scan:** Notice if any residue somatic distress remains; if so then continue with BLS.

7. **Closure:** Assess client's stability and current orientation; discuss treatment effects and possible continued internal processing.

8. **Reevaluation:** Verify if all aspects of treatment plan are being addressed and recheck targets to assess stability.

OVERLAPS OF IFS AND EMDR

Shapiro (2001) recognizes and describes innate healing as a foundational tenet of EMDR that is also found in IFS's concept of Self (Twombly & Schwartz, 2008). Multiple aspects of the EMDR protocol mirror IFS approaches. Consider that in both EMDR and IFS, the therapist guides the client in compassionate witnessing of past distressful experiences, the therapist guiding with empathetic low verbal responses while encouraging the client to engage in an internal witnessing and dialogue of their experiences. There are other very compatible concepts that bridge the two. Consider both include somatic awareness via body scans; note current affect; focus on a target, leading to "trailheads"; encourage client to notice negative thoughts; promote internal use of metaphor to create distress tolerance; create safe spaces; and elicit internal imagery. EMDR and IFS therapists have recognized the benefits of integrating these two models across the lifespan with diverse diagnosis and life challenges (Anderson, 2021; Brown, 2020; Twombly & Schwartz, 2008; Fisher, 2017; Hersey, 2015). Trauma treatment especially has been the focus of these two approaches. Many EMDR therapists become trained in IFS and vice versa. Art therapists, as well as other expressive arts therapists (Tobin, 2006; Wood, 2015) have recognized how IFS and/or EMDR have overlapped with creative approaches. IFS can be the main modality with intermittent use of EMDR, or the therapist can begin with EMDR, using IFS when needed during the phases. The authors of this chapter, as previously discussed, are among the current pioneers who integrate all three models. We hope to motivate more expressive arts therapists to train in IFS and in EMDR, an intention of this chapter.

There are compassion-driven ethics in the clinical effectiveness of such an integration of models that many therapists seek in trauma treatment. Multiple trauma experts recognize the need for these integrative trauma approaches in promoting the flexibility in meeting the client where they are, and in faster resolution of treatment goals. Brown's (2020) article "Internal Family Systems Informed Eye Movement Desensitization and Reprocessing: An Integrative Technique for Treatment of Complex Posttraumatic Stress Complex" explores the advantages and challenges of this integrative approach and states "…their integration has been found to enhance the efficacy of both modalities in the treatment of C-PSTD…" (p. 112). Twombly and Schwartz (2008) state "…IFS is an elegant, efficient and powerful ego state

treatment modality that, when used with EMDR, can increase its range of effectiveness..."
(p. 296). They go onto say that EMDR's effectiveness is occasionally limited when client's
affect is low, or when protector parts feel threatened with "... intrusions by well-meaning
therapists if their fears are not...addressed. This phenomenon is what leads EMDR processing to become blocked at times..." (p. 297). They describe other clinical scenarios that can
potentially lead to "...incomplete resolution of EMDR targets and treatment failures..." as
being caused by a therapist not recognizing "manager parts," and instead the therapist may
refer to this as resistant behaviors (p. 299). It seems that an IFS-informed EMDR therapist's
understanding of parts will lend the compassion needed to understand and thus eliminate
polarizations and power struggles that can occur in a therapeutic relationship (typically occur
between parts internally). They do offer a warning that EMDR can "override managers and
access exiles before the system is ready ..." resulting in backlash. Backlash is a term used in
IFS to describe intensely reactive behaviors by firefighters or even manager parts to punish
the client and/or sabotage the therapeutic alliance for "violating their rules..." (pp. 304–305).
An example may be self-harm behaviors immediately after a session. Twombly (2000) however, states that EMDR therapists who possess a respectful clinical understanding of "parts"
and their sensitive internal relationships will be more effective. IFS process promotes attuned
language framed by a stance of curiosity with the gentle intention of repairing internal relationships and building trust. This IFS language often leads to "softening" by manager parts,
allowing for access to Self-energy, to exiles holding painful memories, increased emotional
regulation, and stronger tolerance of stabilization all which can benefit the EMDR process
(Brown, 2020; Forgash & Snipe 2008; Twombly & Schwartz, 2008).

Conversely, EMDR can benefit the IFS trained therapist as exemplified when Phase four
BLS is used to support an exile's unburdening of distressful memories and felt experiences.
Brown (2020) considers the integration of IFS with EMDR useful for cognitive interweaves,
positive resourcing, and restoration of balance. If we return to the eight phases of EMDR,
we can see other examples of how IFS and EMDR support each other as interventions with
whichever one is primarily being utilized in a session. Twombly and Schwartz (2008), Brown
(2020), and Hersey (2015, 2021) discuss this in depth and help to inform the following. These
are examples and are not a complete list of IFS and EMDR integrated interventions, but
myriad possibilities may emerge as you read.

Overlapping IFS Concepts into Each of the EMDR Phases

> **Phase 1—History Taking:** IFS can support building therapeutic alliance when ther-
> apist accesses their own Self-energy by noticing the presence of the eight Cs such as
> calm and curious and the five Ps such as persistence and patience.

> **Phase 2—Preparation:** Introduce concept of "parts" in psychoeducation. Ask parts'
> permission to proceed with EMDR, a type of informed consent. Increasing access
> to Self-energy. Naming the negative cognitions of critical parts, helpless parts, etc.

> **Phase 3—Assessment:** Measure how much Self is present and measure the energy
> of the part. Notice and encourage curiosity in assessing a target part (trailhead) to
> soften managers from blocking access. Use IFS to find, focus, befriend, and explore
> fears of manager blocking affect or use BLS when managers block naming target in
> effort to protect fear of overwhelm from exiles.

> **Phase 4—Desensitization/Bilateral Stimulation:** Invite Self-energy in before
> beginning BLS. Asking parts to step back during BLS. Using BLS to strengthen

Self-energy. In IFS, use BLS to help identify parts. Use BLS in fostering communication between parts such as dialoguing between polarized parts and with dissociative parts (Twombly, 2013). Using BLS to soften protector parts.

Phase 5—Installation: Use IFS to work with part when SUD level seems stuck at a higher number. Use IFS to work with part holding on to a low VoC score as they are not believing a positive cognition. In IFS use BLS to assist an unburdened exile in acquiring new positive traits and install these resources.

Phase 6—Body Scan: Once you have unburdened the part, do another body scan. If somatic distress remains, use IFS somatic awareness of where sensation is and assess if this as a blended part or unfinished processing.

Phase 7—Closure Reevaluation: Use the IFS-informed questions to check in with parts to assess if closure occurred.

Phase 8—Reassessment: Assess if other parts that stepped back need attention or are trailheads for future work.

List of shared concepts between IFS and EMDR

- Both are client-guided, intuitive, strength-based, non-pathologized, and compassionate
- Encourage a mediative state to increase a mind-body connection, somatic awareness, and felt sense
- Provide emotional distancing where the client can work toward increasing their distress tolerance and affect regulation
- Transform/release distressing experiences through the use of witnessing/reprocessing
- Neurobiology:
  - Left/right brain processes
  - Dual awareness; use titration and pacing to access and process past memories
  - Both help to bridge implicit and explicit memories
- Encourage a creative process

  - What is internalized can then be externalized
  - Encourage creative thinking
  - Internal imagery can be recreated in art

ART THERAPY AND IFS

Schwartz (1995), in discussing the development of his model, considers the similarities and differences of IFS with earlier pioneering theories, such as those of Jung and Roberto Assagiola. Schwartz noted the multiplicity of the mind and exploration of the internal world of sub-personalities found in their work as well. Jung and Assagiola included a concept of Self, both defining this as a passive observer. Assagiola offered the possibility of Self becoming an active manager. Schwartz noted that his theory of IFS differed in his goal to not just dialogue with these internal individual entities but to have them communicate with each other in order to change and heal the internal system, and saw Self as an "active compassionate leader" (p. 37). What captured Schwartz's attention was Jung's concept of "Active Imagination." This concept of creativity and the use of imagination also resonate with expressive arts therapists as it is the foundation of our field. Active Imagination (Jung & Chodorow, 1997) refers to the active process of the artist dialoguing with the different elements of the art production as well as the parts within the artwork communicating with each other. As Jung himself explained (Jung & Chodorow, 1997, p. 164):

> Start with any image…observe how the picture begins to unfold. Don't try to make it into something, just do nothing but observe what its spontaneous changes are…sooner or later changes through spontaneous association…causes a slight alteration…carefully avoid impatient jumping from one subject to another. Hold fast to 1 image chosen and wait until it changes itself …note those changes and eventually step into the picture yourself… if it is a speaking figure… then say what you have to say to that figure and listen to what he or she has to say…

Jung's insistence on spontaneity is reminiscent of the "felt sense" and the tenet not to possess an "agenda" found in the IFS process. Art therapist Shaun McNiff (1998), in reviewing Jung's book *Active Imagination*, mentioned Chodorow's comment that Active Imagination was based on the normal healing function of the imagination, which is similar to IFS. McNiff noted Active Imagination as a self-healing process, describing Jung as "…opening himself to childlike states of play…" McNiff explains that Jung realized that art could give "…shape to difficult experiences…gave leadership to the unconscious… integrating conscious and unconscious into a third state of adaption…" (p. 269). In Jung and Jaffe (1961), Jung writes "…[I] translate the emotions into images—to find the images which were concealed in the emotions—I was inwardly calmed…" (p. 177). We find support in using both IFS and art to express those "images hidden in the emotions." Our parts reveal these emotion-driven burdens and art-making reveals the imagery. We like to use these quotes as a metaphor for the appropriate use of collage in art therapy, a creative way to take these torn pieces and organize the chaos of trauma, giving it meaning. Finally, Jung (1964) emphasizes the importance of art in his famous quote, "all art intuitively apprehends coming changes in the collective unconsciousness…" (pp. 34–35). It is with Active Imagination, then, that we bring art into the IFS process. There are a growing number of expressive arts therapists integrating IFS into their practice. At the time of this publication, very little has been published on the overlap of expressive arts therapy and IFS (Lavergne, 2004; Wood, 2015), but there have been workshops and papers (Kolodny & Bechtel, 2016; Kolodny et al., 2016; Bechtel, 2017; Galperin et al., 2012).

The eight Cs of Self-energy in IFS can easily be overlapped and seen in art therapy. Through the process of *creativity*, art elicits self-discovery where the client is able to express *compassion* and *curiosity* toward their creation. There is a mediative experience as one creates their art, which can lead them to feel *calm*. As they begin the process of creating, one has to show *courage* to make their first mark on the paper and start to build confidence as they share and explore the meaning, in which their insight can lead to clarity. Their art-making and processing can also form a *connectedness* to self and others.

The six Fs in IFS can be overlapped with art-making by integrating them into the creative process. The following table 6.1 shows how the authors have taken each step and apply it to the art-making process.

The Six Fs in IFS Applied to Art-Making

Find the part in and around the body → draw on body outline or create it

Focus on the part that is being visualize → add to creation

Flesh it out by asking what does it want you to know → add to creation

Feel how do you feel toward it? ➔ by visualizing, gazing at creation, add to it

Be**friend** it and facilitate relationship ➔ sit with your creation, add to it, use metaphors

Fears—what are its fear? ➔ you can create what fear looks like

If protective parts—what is it afraid will happen? ˈcreate what this would look like

If Exile—what does it want you to know? ˈ create or write what this would look like

IFS-Informed Questions to Encourage Dialoguing between Two Parts in Any Art Media

How do they feel toward each other?

How do they relate to each other?

Are any in conflict with each other? (polarization)

What is their role, their job?

How long have they been doing their job/role?

Do they like/dislike each other?

Would they be interested in doing this a different way?

What might this look like?

What are they afraid would happen if they do their job differently?

What would the part rather be doing?

What does the part need to happen today?

Would they like to live in a different environment? What might that look like?

Who is the most upset by the work we did today?

Who might be inclined to interfere with it?

Who is willing to try to help keep it going?

An important benefit of using art in the IFS process is exemplified when the imagery captures how a part appears to the client, in deepening the focus, fleshing out, and befriending the part. Often, a part may first appear internally as a "felt" sensation; by creating it in image or clay, more details regarding this part emerge. It might appear as a young child holding a burden, a wounded animal, or a raging ball of fiery anger.

Additionally, the physical distance between the client and their art literally externalizes the part, an organic process that can foster emotional distancing and unblending. To initially educate clients on unblending, I (SM) will often use both my hands to illustrate part and Self. One hand represents a wounded part from the past, while the other hand represents Self or who they are today. By moving my hands in an upright open position, I move them further part or closer together to demonstrate the blending process. If the client is blended with the part (no Self-energy present) then the hands are clasped together. This can be replicated in art by creating a Self sculpture/drawing and creating a second sculpture/drawing of a part, moving them closer or apart in a similar manner.

The Overlaps of IFS Concepts with Art Therapy

- Dialogue to enhance communication between the internal parts of self/unconscious and allows for metaphoric, symbolic, somatic, affective, and literal expression.

- Both create an avenue to explore polarities.
- Containment is used to provide less threatening expression of painful and challenging memories and emotions, allowing for pacing and boundaries.
- The internal image increases awareness and understanding of our internal images, emotions, and somatic experiences.
- Externalizing the internal process offers distance, perspective, and opportunities for unblending.
- Both view healing as inherent in the creative process and within each individual.

ART THERAPY WITH EMDR

When first using ArtMDR in the late 1990s with different child survivors who had nightmares of monsters, I (PK) invited each of them in separate sessions to draw the monster, asking them to make it as big as their fear (a modified child-friendly form of SUD). They were then invited to draw bilateral strokes next to, or on top of, the monster in sets, redrawing the monster size each time along with their verbal observations between these bilateral sets (Phase Four). It typically took less than three sets (three drawings) for the monster to be reduced to a smaller version, indicative of a lower SUD score, often resulting in spontaneous laughter and a friendly monster drawing. This was the first regulating affect displayed in therapy for several of these clients. Here is where I recognized the flexibility and efficiency of combining art with EMDR.

Art Therapy is recognized as a flexible approach that easily allows the integration of other models. As art therapists became trained in EMDR, they began to develop creative interventions within EMDR phasing; art therapists prior to the development of EMDR were utilizing bilateral movement and scribbles into art therapy, ranging from the benefits of the scribble as a warm-up movement and assessment tool in the Ulman Personality Assessment Procedure (Ulman & Dachinger, 1975; Tripp, 2019) to the benefits of scribbling developmentally (Cane, 1951; Kellogg, 1969) leading to multiple current art therapy applications. EMDR-trained art therapists continue to integrate art into this phase model and, as the focus of this book, can be explored in all the diverse ways within these chapters. We have spoken of Kolodny's unpublished early use of her ArtMDR; others, such as McNamee (2003, 2006), Tobin (2006), Tripp (2007), were early publishers of their work, either incorporating creative interventions into EMDR phasing protocol or applying bilateral principles into therapeutic art-making. McNamee (2003, 2006) developed a bilateral art protocol, using both hands to depict polarizing beliefs, cognitions, or feelings followed by VoC scale to measure the strength of the client's belief. Her research is more influenced by EMDR although she does not fully incorporate the protocol. Talwar (2007) created the Art Therapy Trauma Protocol (ATTP), a method to target specific trauma memories. It differs from EMDR in defining what constitutes as a target memory. The protocol looks at non-verbal, somatic memories emerging from a traumatic event versus a visual of a target memory. Talwar incorporated movement by having the client walk back and forth from a large piece of paper to their jars of paints to encourage dual processing, including bilateral use of hands when painting.

Multiple art therapists and expressive arts therapists continue to focus on these benefits of bilateral stimulation, developing bilateral scribble and guided bilateral art-making protocols or more improvised models. Tripp (2016) reviews how art enhances the dual awareness found in EMDR. She has developed multiple ways of including art therapy with EMDR protocol, as well as bilateral movements, drawing, and scribbling. Additionally, Tripp, certified in Sensorimotor Psychotherapy, has integrated this model in her EMDR and Art Therapy approaches. Tripp and Kolodny met at an Expressive Arts Summit in 2013, discovering that they both were art therapists trained in EMDR. They shared ideas that evolved into multiple workshops on the integration of these approaches, emphasizing bilateral body movements beyond traditional EMDR (Tripp & Kolodny 2013, 2014, 2016). "Scribble, Squiggle and Wiggle," the title of several of their trainings, encompasses that intention. Kolodny (2021) has applied bilateral focused breathing, the bilateral Kirtan Kriya "Sa-Ta-Na-Ma" hand mudra movements, and bilateral mirrored scribbling as part of her Neurosequential Art Approach process. Tripp developed the Body-Based Bilateral Art Protocol (2016). Davis (2021) has stayed within EMDR protocol but incorporated creative interventions into the phases. Others have developed bilateral art protocols outside of EMDR process (Chapman, 2014; Elbrecht, 2018). Chapman developed a bilateral scribble that focuses on "mirroring" concepts for reparative attachment work and as, what she calls, a "neuro warm-up" exercise in her neurodevelopmental approach. Kolodny refers to her BLS drawing in Phase Four as "bilateral strokes" (King, 2016, p. 181). Other expressive therapists have recognized and applied bilateral stimulation such as creative rhythmic movements, drumming, therapeutic yoga, and focused breathing into their clinical work (Marich, 2019; Wood, 2015). A few "non-art therapist" EMDR practitioners have also proposed the use of creative interventions into EMDR phasing (Schmidt, 1999; Breed, 2013). In Breed's thesis, for example, she identifies target imagery in Phase Three, Calm Place Imagery in Phase Two, drawings and photographs to measure SUD and VoC, and to illustrate positive cognitions and negative cognitions.

EMDR-trained play therapists have integrated the protocol with play therapy approaches, including creative interventions, in their work with children (McGuiness, 2001; Gomez & Krause 2013; Beckley-Forest & Monaco, 2020). I (PK), too, discovered shortly after training in EMDR how responsive children are to this model, particularly when integrated with art.

In a 2003 art therapy-informed EMDR session with a client diagnosed with DID, I (PK) developed the Art Window for Distress Tolerance, a creative intervention similar to Siegel's WOT (2020). This client drew a target trauma memory and found it too distressful to gaze at it (SUD 10), activating a hypoaroused state (manager). She was still able to access cortical function sufficiently enough to state she could not tolerate looking at the image (manager part) but was too dissociative (protector part) to continue with processing in EMDR, requesting that I cover the drawing. I then cut a small square out from a piece of drawing paper, creating a window in the paper, and asked her what it would be like to just view small sections of drawing through this "window." She responded positively, moving the window around the drawing until she found an area she could tolerate viewing without being overwhelmed (exile part), thus calming the fears of protective parts. She used this section as her target image for Phase Three and we proceeded with BLS in Phase Four. She continued to use this window to target different aspects of her trauma memory until she could observe the uncovered drawing in a calm state of "dual attention awareness" (Shapiro, 2001; van den Hout & Engelhard, 2012) with resources and insights from the EMDR process.

I have used this "Art Window" in multiple ways for clients to build distress tolerance, similarly to how the Window of Tolerance is utilized in sessions. One client, presenting with Post-Traumatic Stress Disorder and Bipolar Disorder, drew her WOT, illustrating her hyperaroused and hypoaroused behaviors, with her coping skills drawn in the center (see Figure 6.2). She used the Art Window to focus on a selected behavior to process, as viewing

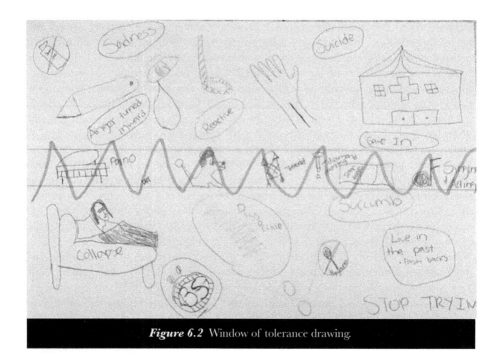

Figure 6.2 Window of tolerance drawing.

them all at once felt overwhelming. Matching this behavior with a coping strategy of her service dog, she then tapped it in as a resource (see Figure 6.3).

ART THERAPY WITH IFS AND EMDR

In this lengthy setting of the rationale of pairing these models with each other, and exploring their overlaps, we have arrived at how we use all three in a ground-breaking integrative approach. Case material, art directives, and an illustrative chart (Table 6.1) will follow a discussion of the interweaving of these three models.

Pioneer art therapists have recognized the effective use of art to externalize our internal world. Art therapist, Elinor Ulman, was often quoted as saying that art is the meeting ground for the inside world and the outside world, meaning art-making is a bridge to the subconscious/unconscious. In current trauma-informed language, we recognize that art bridges implicit and explicit memory. Recent trauma theories (Rothschild, 2000; van der Kolk, 2015; Perry and Winfrey, 2020) explain that we store sensory memories both implicitly (sensory, somatic, affective) and explicitly (conscious, declarative, organized, chronological narrative). The process of art-making can assist in re-organizing chaotic memory, foster cognitive re-structuring, and promote integration of trauma memories (Tinnin & Gantt, 2013; King, 2016). The sensorimotor quality of creative expression matches the sensory somatic "storage" of memories, allowing access to implicit memories, a recapitulation of disrupted developmental experiences, and an opportunity to grow healthier neural pathway, especially within the context of a therapeutic relationship (Kolodny, 2021; King, 2016; Malchiodi, 2020).

Leading researchers and authors in the trauma treatment field (Gaskill & Perry, 2014; Levine & Frederick, 1997; Ogden & Fisher, 2015; Siegel, 2020; van der Kolk, 2015) expound

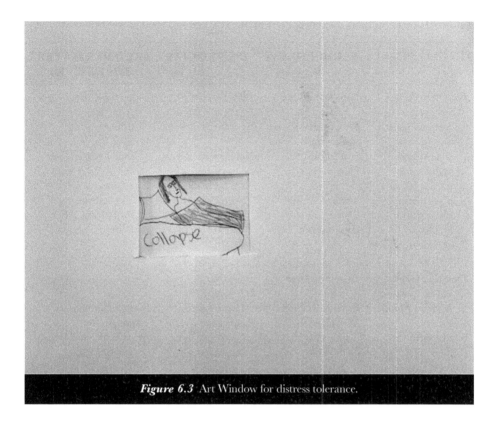

Figure 6.3 Art Window for distress tolerance.

on the importance of non-verbal interventions in trauma treatment, and refer to mindfulness, focused breathing, rhythmic activities such as drumming, and body-focused approaches as in somatic experiencing, sensorimotor approaches, and trauma-sensitive yoga, but they only briefly mention expressive arts therapies. Yet within models such as IFS and EMDR, internal imagery is promoted as a vehicle of healing; coping strategies and distress tolerance skills encourage the use of creativity and imaginal tools such as developing a mental image of a "Safe/Sanctuary Place" in EMDR (Shapiro, 2001) or the "waiting room" concept used in IFS. Internal dialoguing in both models elicits an internal image of parts or visual memories. The rhythmic movement of drawing bilateral strokes further contributes to reparative possibilities (Elbrecht, 2018; Perry & Winfrey, 2021). Art therapists recognize the need to engaging rhythm and movement in art-making to enhance and deepen trauma-informed approaches such as these.

The paucity of art-based research contributes to the tepid support of art therapy in major trauma models that seek empirical support for evidence-based status. There are pragmatic and ethical reasons for this as insurance tends to cover EB treatments; and we need evidence that treatment is effective (Breed, 2013). But there are challenges in art-based research; primarily, the subjective quality of art-making is difficult to empirically measure (King, 2016). Art therapist researchers such as Hass-Cohen (2008), Gantt and Tinnin (2009), and Lusebrink (2004) have contributed to trauma treatment by exploring the neurobiology of trauma-informed expressive arts practices. Recent developments in using brain scans as part of researching creativity will hopefully validate expressive arts therapies value in trauma-focused clinical work (Konopka, 2014; King & Kaimal, 2019; King et al., 2019;

Table 6.1 Table depicting the overlaps of EMDR, IFS, and Art Therapy

TRAUMA PHASES	EMDR PHASES	IFS PROCESS	ART THERAPY/ART DIRECTIVES
Phase One: Stabilization and Symptom Reduction Phase Gather current issues; developmental hx; trauma hx; psychosocial Create genograms; timeline Diagnostic psychometrics	*Phase One: History Taking* Psychosocial history Appropriateness for EMDR Float back technique Identify current triggers Future needs	*Phase One:* Psychosocial history Appropriateness for IFS Note potential legacy burdens Note for complex trauma and level of dissociation	Visual timeline and genogram (continue to add throughout tx) Personal flag (strengths, support, challenge, and goals) (Figure 6.8) Free drawing Art assessments (e.g., Bird's Nest, KFD DDS)
Phase One: Stabilization and Symptom Reduction Phase Goals: Build safety Decrease symptoms Increase emotional, social, and psychological competencies	*Phase Two: Preparation* Psychoeducation Metaphors for pacing and safety Neurobiology of trauma Safe/sanctuary place (BLS) Resourcing (e.g., progressive muscle relaxation)	*Phase One:* IFS perspective-paradigm shift A multiplicity model of the mind; provide psychoeducation of the model (e.g., symptoms are parts not pathology) Safe/sanctuary place Metaphor for unblending (e.g., waiting room)	Create a safe/sanctuary place Brain with resources image Art Window for Distress Tolerance Containers Body Map with resources Use toys/puppets, sandtray to introduce concept of parts
Phase Two: Working through the trauma Processing trauma memories Review and reappraisal Integrate memories into an adaptive representation of one's self.	*Phase Three: Assessment* Access target for EMDR Image of distressing memory NC, SUD, PC, VoC, somatic sensation(s)	*Phase One:* Accessing target part Getting permission to work with the part Establishing Self-energy toward the target part Find; Focus; Flesh Out; Feel Explore polarized parts; using part-to-part, Self-to-part, or direct access	Free drawing/ Spontaneous art Inside/Outside masks Body Scan→ Parts Map Parts Paper Bag Book Piecing Our Parts Collage Modeling Parts and Self (clay) Depict polarized parts

Table 6.1 (Continued)

TRAUMA PHASES	EMDR PHASES	IFS PROCESS	ART THERAPY/ART DIRECTIVES
Phase Two: Working through the trauma Processing trauma memories Review and reappraisal	*Phase Four: Desensitization* Reprocess with BLS until SUD is 0-1	*Phase Two:* Self has the capacity to heal; internal attachment Witnessing and retrieval Build trusting relationships with part and Self *Phase Three:* Attachment repair via part feeling compassion from Self; Part feels believed and understood Friend; Fear	Bilateral scribble Piecing Our Parts Collage Modeling Parts and Self Create the retrieval scene ArtMDR Art Window for Distress Tolerance
Phase Two: Working through the trauma Processing trauma memories Review and reappraisal	*Phase Five: Installation* Installing the positive cognition until VoC is 7	*Phase Four: Healing the part* Unburdening Post unburdening: new learning and integration of parts back into the system not consolidation and rehabilitation Identify/incorporate positive traits/ new role	Unburdening art Depict part's new role; new traits Piecing Our Parts Collage Modeling Parts and Self ArtMDR; tap in new traits as positive resources
Phase Two: Working through the trauma Processing trauma memories Review and reappraisal	*Phase Six: Body Scan* Check for any distressing sensations that remains If sensation is positive use BLS to strengthen	*Phase Four:* Notice any other distressing feeling Access if fully unburdened Check with other parts that appeared These may appear as body sensations (fear, shame) that may need attention	Somatic Body Mapping Modeling Parts and Self

(Continued)

Table 6.1 (Continued)

TRAUMA PHASES	EMDR PHASES	IFS PROCESS	ART THERAPY/ART DIRECTIVES
Phase Two: Working through the trauma Processing trauma memories Review and re-appraisal	*Phase Seven: Closure* Ensure clients stability to end session Use guided imagery Encourage to use coping techniques in between sessions	*Phase Five: Closing* Integration and reconfiguration Thank parts for giving space Check if other parts need attention Use resources between sessions	Graphic/sculpted/ sandtray/puppets representing Self expressing apology and compassion to part
Phase Three: Resolution/ Reintegration/ reconnection with society Consolidate Integrate Rehabilitate	*Phase Eight: Reevaluation* Evaluate treatment effects Explore anything that has come up in between sessions Future template Deepen PC, use resources	*Phase Five:* Check in with the unburdened part over the next few sessions Assess if anything else came up	Three roads

Lusebrink, 2014). Nobel Prize winner neuroscientist Eric Kandel (2012) has written several books on the topic of understanding the connections between mind, brain, and art in an understanding of bioesthetics. He writes about the current dialogues between brain scientist and other fields of knowledge including art, saying these dialogues "…explore the mechanisms in the brain that make perception and creativity possible, whether in art, the sciences, the humanities…" (p. xiv). King discusses art therapy as a "…neurotherapeutic in my research identifying neural correlates underlying creative expression…" (Personal written communication, June 25, 2019). Mobile brain scanning has allowed the expansion of this exciting research, contributing to more evidence-based approaches in the arts therapies (Kolodny, 2021; King et al., 2019). This lack of evidence-based research doesn't lessen the observable impact of art therapy in integrative trauma work and can potentially enhance the effectiveness of EMDR and IFS, both evidence-based models.

Art Therapy Techniques Interwoven into IFS and EMDR

The clinician's role is similar in art therapy, IFS, and EMDR sessions; all three use low verbal, less directive approaches. Therapists using any of these models guide with gentle process questions by recognizing that clients are the authority of themselves. Reflective listening is an observing and witnessing role; holding unconditional regard in a safe "transitional space" (Winnicott) and, perhaps most importantly, using creative thinking are all methods used in these three approaches. These commonalities allow for seamless and flexible integrations of the models.

Case Examples using Art Therapy, IFS, and EMDR

I (PK) began seeing a young teen "K" diagnosed with Pediatric Acute-Onset Neuropsychiatric Syndrome (PANS) following years of undiagnosed Lyme's disease and mold exposure that left her temporarily blind and immobilized. Once she was properly diagnosed, she slowly recovered but vestiges of her illness remained due to PTSD and chronic inflammation, resulting in dissociation, OCD, and mood dysregulation. Demonstrating great resiliency, she resumed her competitive sport, begun before her illness, and proved incredibly successful, winning national championships. K reported to me that this team sport saved her life as she felt she could begin to trust her body that had betrayed her. I surmised that creative movement (rhythm) and connecting to peers (relational) would further contribute to reparative and body-orienting experiences.

She was referred to me specifically for EMDR, IFS, and art therapy as an integrative approach. I recognized the medical trauma that contributed to her symptoms. She responded well to this integrative work and noted, along with continued holistic medical care and proper nutrition, that progress was reflected in the decrease of many of her symptoms. She had a debilitating phobia of ticks, however, that interfered with her ability to engage in any outside activities involving grass and woods. We targeted her fear of ticks for EMDR Phase Two as she (a "part") had been triggered. She was able to find and focus on this part of her that was phobic and invited the part to engage in art-making in the session. She noticed a heavy sensation in her chest and described it as "buried fear." I asked an IFS-informed question, "what is this part afraid would happen if you found a tick?" Her target image was a huge tick, her memory event was being bedridden due to a tick bite. SUD was a 10. She felt "powerless" and paralyzed with fear "all over." Her PC of "feeling empowered" had a VoC score of 2.

I had 2 1/2 feet of brown mural paper taped to a table outside and invited her to draw a tick as big as her fear, as large as she could tolerate. Drawing the image size to represent the distress, assessing how the distress feels, is a form of measuring SUD in an imaginal way (see Figure 6.4). She did so and we proceeded to Phase Four Desensitization. BLS used were bilateral strokes across the image made with black paint and colorful oil pastels (ArtMDR). Between BLS, she was offered the choice to verbally report "what came up" or draw an image of what emerged. She began drawing smaller and smaller ticks in between sets, four in all, continuing to cover each of the first three ticks drawn during BLS with bilateral strokes until there were two progressively tiny ones and began giggling with apparent relief. SUD decreased to three. I utilized IFS unburdening process here, having her ask the phobic part if there was anything else we needed to know or witness. She said she still was worried about getting bit by a tick and getting Lyme's again but she could now visualize the tick realistically; it was not a huge monster. She laughed and said that the tiny size actually contributed to its danger but recognized that was real and not overwhelming her; she would continue to be careful outside but not be as avoidant and phobic. SUD then reported at 2 and installation with more bilateral strokes across a small colorful tick image was made. She described realistic coping strategies such as checking her body after walks and wearing long pants. This part chose to release the burden of fear, visualized as a huge tick, to ocean waves and the air. She wanted to be calm at the beach, reporting a VoC of 6.5 in feeling "empowered." Body scan revealed an overall lighter feeling. BLS butterfly hug was used as resourcing. (Safe place drawing previously developed was a beach. It occurred to both of us that ticks aren't in the sand.)

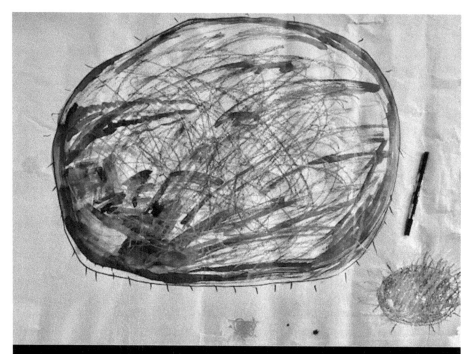

Figure 6.4 Drawing of ticks and bilateral strokes.

In a clinical case that SM worked with, Amelia, an adult woman presenting with an eating disorder, drew a picture depicting her internal somatic feelings, subsequently revealing a "part" in the center of her chest that presented a vivid image of a screaming five-year-old child. Amelia began purging in early adulthood; it took years of therapy for her to make the connection that purging was her way of getting everything out that she couldn't say as a child. I (SM) encouraged her to create a clay representation of this part (see Figure 6.5), placing the sculpture in front of her during sessions. By externalizing her child part, Amelia was able to have the child witness the work that she was doing. Initially, client reported that the part felt suffocated, unable to talk, although she expressed an urge to scream (see Figure 6.6). While holding tappers in each hand, Amelia worked on reprocessing a childhood memory. Toward the end of the session, the child part stated that she was beginning to feel more empowered and could say no if she needed. She added that if she had been able to say no as a child, she would have had better social boundaries. This part felt that she no longer had to scream to get Amelia's attention and was developing a trusting relationship with her. Client used IFS questions to dialog from part to part and part to Self.

The following is a detailed description of an IFS-informed art approach combined with EMDR BLS. This technique is done with clay but feel free to replace with any other art materials such as drawing, painting, and collage. Modeling Parts and Self in Clay: IFS often begins with guided meditation or meditative breathing. Client is then asked to notice what they are feeling in or around their body, such as body sensations, emotions, images, and or thoughts. Using the six Fs, once they *find* something, have them *focus* on it, getting to know and understand the part. Invite the client to create a sculpture of this part, literally and metaphorically *fleshing*

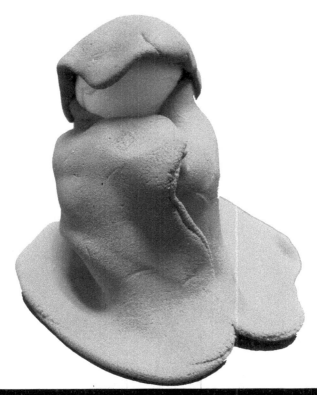

Figure 6.5 Clay figure of child part.

it out (can be done with their eyes closed, if they prefer). As the client sculpts the clay, they are encouraged to start dialoguing with the part, finding out about its role in the system. When the client feels they possess some understanding and knowledge about the part, they are invited to create another sculpture that represents how they *feel toward it*. This is a part that is reacting/ responding to the first sculpture. Polarizations or connections may be noted. If the client notices a critical part, they are asked to invite that critical part to explore its feelings. This critical part can be sculpted in clay as well. IFS processing of this polarized relationship can be explored with the two clay sculptures. Once the client notices any presence of Self such as compassion and curiosity, trust begins between part and client as they *befriend* it in sculptural form.

Client may ask what ***fears*** the parts hold in making changes to its role. If fears are blocked, EMDR Phases Three and Four may be used here to focus on a target fear, softening manager parts. BLS tapping is an appropriate choice as the client is already in tactile mode with the clay. (This may lead to an exile with an early memory of wounding, allowing the skilled IFS practitioner to invite retrieval and unburdening. Those just learning about IFS will want to proceed to unblending and noticing Self-energy. They would thank the exile and promise to return once they are in consultation/supervision.) Finally, by working with the client to *unblend* from all parts, the client is then asked to create a third sculpture to represent any Self-energy that they possess toward the first two sculptures. Because the client has externalized their parts, *unblending* becomes more accessible as it goes beyond a metaphoric state to a physical distancing between client and sculptures.

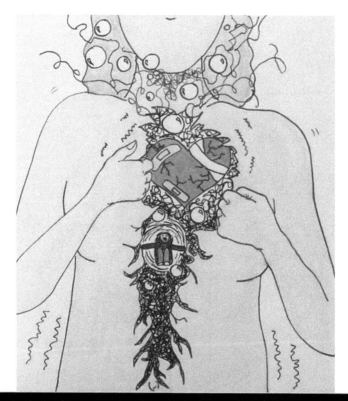

Figure 6.6 Drawing of child part inside her chest.

Client can then explore the relationship *between* each sculpture representing a part with the following process questions. These IFS questions encourage parts to dialogue with each other. Additional questions to ask the client may include: do the sculptures change the space between each of them as they befriend and understand each other? Does the client feel some "space" between them (the client) and the sculpture or do they feel as if they are *blended* with the part/sculpture?

The client can then place the sculptures in any way that they relate to each other to explore shifts in roles, decrease polarizations, and increase in connections. In using EMDR, tapping in this positive connection as a resource can happen here. The client can then move clay sculptures about to reflect self-energy's impact on the other parts.

Art directives are referenced in Table 6.1.

Art Directives Used for Phase One of EMDR and IFS

Personal Introduction Flag: Many art therapists and art teachers have a version of this art directive. We have also seen it described as a personal shield or coat of arms. Kolodny uses this as an introductory art directive with four quadrants surrounding circle. In my version, each quadrant has a theme (Strengths, Challenges, Support System, Goals or Roles) with an invitation to create a Self-symbol or portrait for the circle. Parts roles may emerge here as well.

Drawing on rectangular paper with black marker showing a circle in the middle of four squares of equal size. The circle is marked "Self Symbol"; the top left square is labeled "Strengths," the top right square is labeled "Challenges," the bottom left is labeled "Support System," and the bottom right square is labeled "Goals."

Bird's Nest Drawing (Kaiser, 1996): Single drawing art assessment focused on evaluating attachment style via drawing a Bird's Nest. Directive is to simply ask "Draw a bird's nest" using colored scented markers on 81/2″ × 11″ white paper. If the client asks if they may add anything else, the response would be a variation of "however they want to draw this." After the drawing, the client is invited to tell a story about their image. Structural elements are assessed based on research; story theme is considered for details including whimsy.

Kinetic Family Drawing (KFD) (Burns & Kaufman, 1970): Direction given is to "Draw a family doing something together" and is used to assess family dynamics and attachment style. We encourage the use of color, rather than just pencil, as required in the original protocol, as we feel it offers more affect and other relevant information such as: are two family members wearing the same colors?

Diagnostic Drawing Series (DDS) (Cohen et al., 1988): This requires a six 12-hour training and/or knowledge of the DDS Handbook. It is an art interview utilizing a series of three pastel drawings rated on structural elements rather than content. The DDS Ratings Guide is used for each drawing noting the presence of 23 criteria. Longitudinal research of the DDS with increased use with diverse global populations

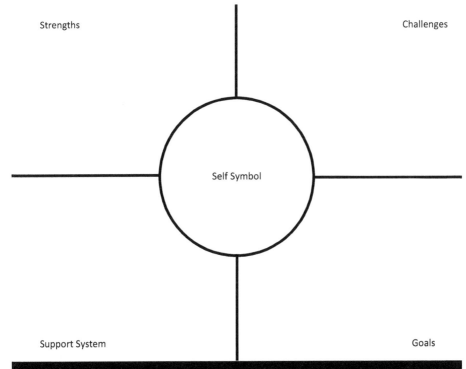

Strengths

Challenges

Self Symbol

Support System

Goals

Figure 6.7 Personal introduction flag template.

has expanded the diagnostic categories that can be measured, resulting from 30+ years of research. The DDS is particularly effective in rating where the client might fall on the dissociation spectrum and can collaborate with other evaluations.

Art Directives Used for Phase Two of EMDR and Continued Phase One of IFS

Safe/Calm/Soothing/Sanctuary Place: EMDR uses Safe/Calm Place as part of resourcing for safety in Phase Two preparation as a form of distress tolerance if triggered by exposure to disturbing memories and sensations in EMDR and in IFS. Many art therapists have developed safe place directives. Cohen et al. (1995) describe their "Establishing a Safe Place" art directive inviting the client to use their imagination to draw a safe place containing elements that are comfortable and familiar. I (PK) ask clients to create a collage or drawing with the invitation to create an image where they would like to be ("Place You'd Want to Be"), encouraging the client to place a representation of themselves within the created image. Different images can be created for different parts in IFS sessions. The authors have found that most of their trauma survivors cannot even imagine a safe place early in therapy, often considering a hiding place instead, certainly not a sanctuary but rather a place fraught with anticipatory fear. Nor can many imagine a calm or soothing place in their dysregulated trauma-sensitized emotional states. Most trauma therapists are familiar with how semantics, as in finding the appropriate word, can be triggering for clients. Finding the most neutral yet descriptive word can be challenging. Brain with Calm image can also be used for this. Using a pre-drawn outline of a head profile template, client is invited to draw/collage/write Calm Place/Sanctuary as part of EMDR Phase Two. Malchiodi (2020) suggests use as regulation resource and asks clients to imagine sending to body. Templates can be found online.

Art Window for Distress Tolerance (Kolodny): Art titration using a paper "frame" to move about in a drawing with intention to focus on one area at a time for client to build distress tolerance, reduce dissociation, or focus on one "part," as in section OR ego state, at a time (see Figures 6.2 and 6.3).

IFS-Informed Body Scan/Map: There are diverse and efficacious art approaches in using a body outline template with particular relevance to both the IFS and EMDR processes. The authors provide at least two, one to represent the front of their bodies and one to represent the back. One common direction is for client to notice what they are feeling in and around their body (or an emotion or part can be suggested), using lines, colors, shapes, images, textures, density, words, thoughts, even representation of a part. The authors have used the six Fs steps to dialogue with the resulting images.

Focus on what comes up in your body during the Phase Six: body scan. Invite the part to step forward. If other parts also appear, have them step back or give space and let them know that they will return to them later. After the client has identified a part to focus on, they are invited to draw where they notice this part in the body outline using line, shape, color, textures, collage materials, or found objects. As they *focus* on that part and ask the part what it needs you to know/understand (*fleshing* out). As the client continues to get to know the part (*befriend it*) by asking about its role, they may want to depict this in their body outline.

We may suggest having multiple body outline templates, one for each part that emerges in therapy, to track the changes in parts' roles, or in somatic awareness throughout the session. A client may see how a weighted sensation such as a racial legacy burden in the chest changes to a lighter feeling, resulting from clinical interventions such as BLS, resourcing, developing Self-energy, rhythmic and bilateral movement or using meditative breathing.

Art Directives Used for Phase Three of EMDR and Continued Phase One of IFS

Inside/Outside Mask: This is a common mask-making directive used by expressive arts therapists for decades. Using a mask template, a client is asked to draw the face they show the world on the outside and how they really feel on the inside. This art-based task is very amenable to parts work. Another IFS-informed directive the authors use invites the client to draw a protector part on the outside and an exile on the inside.

Parts Paper Bag Books: Create a journal out of several paper bags by cutting the bottoms off, folding the bags in half, and placing one inside of the fold of another to create pages with openings/pockets at the end. Book is bound with yarn, string, or ribbon strung through punched holes at the folded edge. Pages can be decorated, collaged, painted and even include writing. Pockets can hold photos, meaningful objects, secrets, creative writings, or a way to organize different "parts" of self. A page can have a drawing of a part with the pocket holding an index card with that part's role, age, traits, etc. These paper bag books are useful as containment—holding a list of triggers, photo memories, or mementoes possessing conflicted meanings. Internet search of sites such as Pinterest will reveal more visual ideas.

Piecing Our Parts Collage: This is a common therapeutic art engagement due to their amenability toward metaphor, symbol, ease, and low reliance on art skill. They are organically "trauma sensitive" in organizing chaos, offering containment and fostering "felt" sense by focusing on intuitive selection of images. The authors have developed an IFS-informed approach by having clients dialogue with each image within their collages, using the six Fs. Direct access, client-to-part, part-to-part, and Self-to-part dialogues can all be developed. Jung's "Active Imagination" can easily be witnessed in this approach.

Modeling Parts and Self in Clay (Kolodny & Mazero, 2018): As described earlier on pages 231 (Figure 6.5).

Art Directives Used for Phase Four of EMDR and Phase Two of IFS

Bilateral Scribble: There are several approaches to bilateral scribbles from guided (Chapman, 2014; Elbrecht, 2018) to EMDR-informed (Talwar, 2007; Tripp, 2007). But basically it is grasping a drawing tool in each hand and drawing guided strokes (using mirroring), intuitive movements, or random scribbling intermittently or simultaneously.

ArtMDR (Kolodny): Traditional EMDR phasing incorporating art as the BLS, and using art imagery or photograph target imagery.

SUD, VoC: Use art to illustrate these scales. For example, Kolodny has clients who select or draw 11 images to represent 0–10 units of distress. Zero may be a blue sky, 10 may be a raging tornado.

Art Directives Used for Phase Six of EMDR and Phase Four of IFS

IFS-Informed Body Scan for Installation (Kolodny & Mazero): Use IFS-informed body scan and resources for installation (EMDR) and integration (IFS). Malchiodi (2020) asks the client to depict coping skills and other resources outside the body outline that they can use to regulate and soothe, after initially drawing feelings inside the outline. Tripp in King (2016) describes her bilateral approach with body outlines.

CONCLUSION

The authors provided an overview of EMDR and IFS, laying a foundational understanding of each model to support their clinical integration into art therapy approaches. Multiple trauma models were briefly reviewed to highlight the benefits of integrative models in complex trauma treatment. Art therapy was discussed from the perspective of its overlaps with IFS and EMDR, along with its appropriate clinical use in trauma therapy. The case studies exemplified the flexibility these models allow, demonstrating diverse ways of implementing integrative use. A chart demonstrated the overlaps with suggested art directives for each stage/phase. The art directives referenced in the chart are described as well as those art directives that integrate into EMDR phases and the IFS process and can be found in the index of this book. Art is the conduit between therapist and client, allowing silent witnessing, somatic awareness, and a compassionate connection to our hearts, reminding us we aren't alone with our burdens and experiences. This alliance is also the bedrock upon which IFS and EMDR rest.

REFERENCES

Anderson, F. G. (2013). "Who's taking what?" Connecting Neuroscience, Psychopharmacology and Internal Family Systems for Trauma. In: M. Sweezy & E. L. Ziskind (Eds.), *Internal family systems therapy: New dimensions* (p. 107-126). Routledge.

Anderson, F. G., Sweezy, M., & Schwartz, R. C. (2017). *Internal family systems skills training manual: Trauma-informed treatment for anxiety, depression, PTSD & substance abuse.* PESI Publishing.

Anderson, F. G. (2021). *Transcending trauma: Healing complex PTSD with internal family systems therapy.* PESI Publishing.

Bechtel, A. (2017, June 15). *Inside out: Integrating internal family systems therapy & sandtray play therapy.* [Workshop] Chesapeake Beach Professional Seminars, LLC, Bethpage, New York, United States.

Beckley-Forest, A., & Monaco, A. (2020). *EMDR with children in the play therapy room: An integrated approach.* Springer Publishing Company.

Breed, H. E. (2013). *Integrating art therapy and eye movement desensitization and reprocessing to treat post-traumatic stress* [Unpublished thesis]. Loyola Marymount University.

Brown, G. (2020). Internal family systems informed eye movement desensitization and reprocessing: An integrative technique for treatment of complex posttraumatic stress disorder. *International Body Psychotherapy Journal, 19*(2), 112–122.

Burns, R. C., & Kaufman, S. H. (1970). *Kinetic family drawings (K-F-D): An introduction to understanding children through kinetic drawings.* Brunner/Mazel.

Cane, F. (1951). *The artist in each of us.* Pantheon Books.

Chapman, L. (2014). *Neurobiologically informed trauma therapy with children and adolescents: Understanding mechanisms of change.* W. W. Norton & Company.

Cloitre, M., Courtois, C. A., Ford, J. D., Green, B. L., Alexander, P., Briere, J., Herman, J. L., Lanius, R., Stolback, B. C., Spinazzola, J., Van der Kolk, B. A., & Van der Hart, O. (2012). *The ISTSS expert consensus treatment guidelines for complex PTSD in adults.* Retrieved from https://terrorvictimresponse.ca/wp-content/uploads/ISTSS-Expert-Concensus-Guidelines-for-Complex-PTSD-Updated-060315.pdf

Cohen, B. M., Hammer, J., & Singer, S. (1988). The diagnostic drawing series: A systematic approach to art therapy evaluation and research. *The Arts in Psychotherapy, 15*(1), 11–21. https://doi.org/10.1016/0197-4556(88)90048-2

Cohen, B., Barnes, M., & Rankin, A. (1995). *Managing traumatic stress through art: Drawing from the center.* Sidran Press.

Dana, D. (2018). *The Polyvagal theory in therapy: Engaging the rhythm of regulation.* W. W. Norton Company.

Davis, E. (2021). EMDR and creative arts therapy: How creative arts therapies can extend the reach of EMDR with complex clients. In A. Beckley-Forest & A. Monaco (Eds.), *EMDR with children in the play therapy room: An integrated approach* (pp. 183–222). Springer Publishing Company.

Elbrecht, C. (2018). *Healing trauma with guiding drawing: A sensorimotor art therapy approach to bilateral body mapping.* North Atlantic Books.

Fatter, D. M., & Love, V. E. (2021, October 15). *IFS & working with ancestral guides to repair legacy burdens related to racism, oppression, attachment, belonging and intergenerational trauma* [Conference presentation]. IFS virtual conference.

Felitti, V. J., Anda, R. F., Nordenberg D., Williamson, D. F., Spitz, A. M., Edwards, V., Koss, M. P., Marks, J. S. (1998). Relationship of childhood abuse and household dysfunction to many of the leading causes of death in adults: The adverse childhood experiences (ACE) study. *American Journal of Preventive Medicine, 14*(4), 245–258. http://doi.org/10.1016/S0749-3797(98)00017-8

Fisher, J. (2017). *Healing the fragmented selves of trauma survivors: Overcoming internal self-alienation.* Routledge.

Forgash, C., & Copeley M. (Eds.). (2008). *Healing the heart of trauma and dissociation with EMDR and ego state therapy.* Springer Publishing Company.

Galperin, L., Rechtien, M., Schwartz, M., & Wood, L. (2012, October 4). New approach to severely disturbed clients: Integrating IFS with attachment theory and in group therapy using expressive techniques. In *IFS Annual Conference,* Boston, MA, United States.

Gaskill, R., & Perry, B. D. (2014). The neurobiological power of play: using the neurosequential model of therapeutics in the healing process. In C. A. Malchiodi & D. Crenshaw (Eds.), *Creative arts and play therapy for attachment problems* (pp. 178–194). Guilford Press.

Gantt, L., & Tinnin, L. (2009). Support for a neurobiological view of trauma with implications for art therapy. *The Arts in Psychotherapy, 36*(3), 148–153. https://doi.org/10.1016/j.aip.2008.12.005

Gomez, A., & Krause, P. (2013). EMDR therapy and the use of internal family systems strategies with children. In A. Gomez (Ed.), *EMDR therapy and adjunct approaches with children* (pp. 299–318). Springer Publishing Company.

Hass-Cohen, N. (2008). CREATE: Art therapy relational neuroscience principles (ART-N). In N. Hass-Cohen & R. Carr (Eds.), *Art therapy and clinical neuroscience* (pp. 283–309). Jessica Kingsley.

Hass-Cohen, N. et al. (2014). "Check, change what you need to change and/or keep what you want": An art therapy neurobiological-based trauma protocol. *Journal of the American Art Therapy Association, 31*(2), 69-78.

Herman, J. L. (1992). *Trauma and recovery: The aftermath of violence- from domestic abuse to political terror.* Basic Books.

Hersey, B. (2015, January). *EMDR and IFS* [workshop]. Altoona, Pennsylvania, United States.

Hersey, B. (2021). *IFS-informed EMDR* [webinar]. www.emdrifs.com

Jackson, L., Jackson, Z., & Jackson, F. (2018). Intergenerational resilience in response to the stress and trauma of enslavement and chronic exposure to institutionalized racism. *Journal of Clinical Epigenetics, 4,* 15. https://doi.org/10.21767/2472-1158.1000100

Jung, C., & Jaffe, A. (1961). *Memories, dreams, reflections*. Vintage Books.

Jung, C. G., Read, H., Fordham, M., & Adler, G. (1964). Civilization in transition (*The collected works of C.G. Jung, Volume 10*). Routledge and Kegan Paul.

Jung, C. G., & Chodorow, J. (1997). *Jung on active imagination* (10th ed.). Princeton University Press.

Kaiser, D. (1996). Indicators of attachment security in a drawing task. *The Arts in Psychotherapy, 23*(4), 333–340. https://doi.org/10.1016/0197-4556(96)00003-2

Kandel, E. (2012). *The age of insight: the quest to understand the unconscious in art, mind, and brain, from Vienna 1990 to the present*. Random House Publishing Group.

Kellogg, R. (1969). *Analyzing children's art*. National Press Books.

King, J. (Ed.). (2016). *Art Therapy, trauma and neuroscience: Theoretical and practical perspectives*. Routledge.

King, J., Kaimal, G., Konopka, L., & Belkofer, C. (2019). Practical applications of neuroscience-informed art therapy. *Art Therapy, 36*(3), 149–156. https://doi.org/10.1080/07421656.2019.1649549

King, J., & Kaimal, G. (2019). Approaches to researching art therapy using imaging technologies. *Frontiers in Human Neuroscience, 13*. http://doi.org/10.3389/fnhum.2019.00159

Kolodny, P. (2013, April). *Use of art in play therapy with traumatized children: A neurosequential approach* [Workshop]. The Mid-Atlantic Play Therapy Training, Arlington, VA, United States.

Kolodny, P. (2016, July). *Trauma-focused neurosequential approach to art and play therapy* [Workshop]. The Chesapeake Beach Professional Play Therapy Institute Boot Camp, Chesapeake Beach, MD, United States.

Kolodny, P. (2017). *Integrative art therapy: Bilateral scribble, neurosequential squiggle IFS collage* [Workshop]. Expressive Therapies Summit and UCLA Arts and Healing, Los Angeles, CA.

Kolodny, P., & Bechtel, A. (2016, July 6–10). *Overview of IFS & art therapy* [Workshop]. The American Art Therapy Association Conference, Baltimore, MD.

Kolodny, P., Bechtel, A., Mazero, S. (2016, November 11). *Exploring our parts through internal family systems & art therapy: curiosity, courage, and creativity* [Workshop]. Expressive Therapies Summit, New York, NY.

Kolodny, P., & Mazero, S. (2018, November 9). *IFS & expressive art therapy: Introducing the journey through collage & clay* [Workshop]. IFS Conference, Providence, RI.

Kolodny, P., & Mazero. S. (2021, October 15). *IFS & creativity: Legacy burdens and loss in the pandemic era* [Workshop]. IFS conference, virtual.

Kolodny, P. (2021). Healing addiction and trauma with the expressive therapies continuum and a neurosequential art approach. In P. Quinn, (Ed.), *Art therapy in the treatment of addiction and trauma* (pp. 115–134). Jessica Kingsley.

Konopka, L. (2014). Where art meets neuroscience: A new horizon of art therapy. *Croatian Medical Journal, 55*(1), 73–74. http://doi.org/10.3325/cmj.2014.55.73

Lavergne, M. (2004). Art therapy and internal family systems therapy: An integrative model to treat trauma among adjudicated teenage girls. *Canadian Art Therapy Association Journal: 17*(1), 17–36. https://doi.org/10.1080/08322473.2004.11432257

Leeds, A. M. (2009). *A guide to the standard EMDR protocols for clinicians, supervisors, and consultants*. Springer Publishing Company.

Levine, P. A., & Frederick, A. (1997). *Waking the tiger: Healing trauma*. North Atlantic Books.

Lusebrink, V. B. (2004). Art therapy and the brain: An attempt to understand the underlying processes of art expression in therapy. *Art Therapy: Journal of the American Art Therapy Association, 21*(3), 125–135. https://doi.org/10.1080/07421656.2004.10129496

Malchiodi, C. (2020). *Trauma and expressive arts therapy: Brain, body, and imagination in the healing process*. Guilford Press.

Marguilho, R. et al. (2015). Sleep and creativity: A literature review. In M. Milcu, M. Gasper de Matos & I. Vasilescu (Eds.), *Advanced research in health, education and social sciences: Towards a better practice* (pp. 131–140). Editora Universitaria.

Marich, J. (2011). *EMDR made simple: 4 approaches to using EMDR with every client*. Premier Publishing & Media.

Marich, J. (2019). *Process not perfection: Expressive arts solutions for trauma recovery*. Creative Mindfulness Media.

McGuiness, V. (2001). *Integrating play therapy and EMDR with children*. 1st Book Library.

McNamee, C. M. (2003). Bilateral art: Facilitating systemic integration and balance. *The Arts in Psychotherapy, 30*(5), 283–292. http://doi.org/10.1016/j.aip.2003.08.005

McNamee, C. M. (2006). Experiences with bilateral art: A retrospective study. *Art Therapy: Journal of the American Art Therapy Association, 23*(1), 7–13. https://doi.org/10.1080/07421656.2006.10129526

McNiff, S. (1998). Jung on active imagination. *Art Therapy: Journal of the American Art Therapy Association, 15*(4), 269–272. https://doi.org/10.1080/07421656.1989.10759337

Menakem, R. (2017). *My grandmother's hands: Racialized trauma and the pathway to mending our hearts and bodies.* Central Recovery Press.

Ogden, P., Minton, K., & Pain, C. (2006). *Trauma and the body: A sensorimotor approach to psychotherapy.* W. W. Norton & Company.

Ogden, P., & Fisher, J. (2015). *Sensorimotor psychotherapy: Interventions for trauma and attachment.* W. W. Norton & Company.

Perry, B. D. (2006). Applying principles of neurodevelopment to clinical work with maltreated and traumatized children. In N. B. Webb (Ed.) *Working with traumatized youth in child welfare* (pp. 27–520). Guilford Press.

Perry, B. D., & Winfrey, O. (2021). *What happened to you? Conversations on trauma, resilience, and healing.* Flatiron Books.

Porges, S. W. (2004). Neuroception: A subconscious system for detecting threats and safety. *Zero the Three Journal, 24*(5), 19–24.

Porges, S. W. (2011). *The polyvagal theory: Neurophysiological foundations of emotions, attachment, communication self-regulation.* W. W. Norton & Co.

Rothschild, B. (2000). *The body remembers: The psychophysiology of trauma and trauma treatment.* W. W. Norton & Co.

Schmidt, S. J. (1999). Resource-focused EMDR: Integration of ego state therapy, alternating bilateral stimulation, and art therapy. *EMDRIA Newsletter, 4*(1), 8, 10–13, 25–28.

Schwartz, R. C. (1995). *Internal family systems therapy.* Guilford Press.

Schwartz, R. C., & Sweezy, M. (2020). *Internal family systems* therapy (2nd ed.). Guilford Press.

Shapiro, F. (2001). *Eye movement desensitization and reprocessing (EMDR) therapy: Basic principles, protocols, and procedures* (2nd Ed.). Guilford Press.

Siegel, D. J. (2020). *The developing mind: How relationships and the brain interact to shape who we are* (3rd Ed.). Guilford Press.

Sinko, A. (2017). Legacy burdens. In M. Sweezy & E. L. Ziskind (Eds.), *Innovation and elaborations in internal family systems therapy* (pp. 164–178). Routledge.

Steele, K., van der Hart, O., & Nijenhuis, E. (2005). Phase-oriented treatment of structural dissociation in complex traumatization: Overcoming trauma-related phobias. *Journal of Trauma Dissociation, 6*(3), 11–53. https://doi.org/10.1300/j229v06n03_02

Substance Abuse and Mental Health Services Administration (SAMHSA). (2019). *Finding evidence-based programs and practices.* America.

Talwar, S. (2007). Accessing traumatic memory through art making: An art therapy trauma protocol (ATTP). *The Arts in Psychotherapy, 34*(1), 22–35. http://doi.org/10.1016/j.aip.2006.09.001

Tinnin, L., & Gantt, L. (2013). *The instinctual trauma response and dual-brain dynamics: A guide for trauma therapy.* Gargoyle Press.

Tobin, B. (2006). Art therapy meets EMDR: Processing the paper-based image with eye movement. *Canadian Art Therapy Association Journal, 19*(2), 27–38.

Tripp, T. (2007). A short-term therapy approach to processing trauma: Art therapy and bilateral stimulation. *Art Therapy: Journal of the American Art Therapy Association, 24*(4), 176–183. https://doi.org/10.1080/07421656.2007.10129476

Tripp, T., & Kolodny, P. (2013, November 7–10). *Integrating EMDR and art therapy for bilateral transformation of trauma* [Workshop]. Expressive Therapies Summit 2013, New York, NY.

Tripp, T., & Kolodny, P. (2014, November 6–9). *Change the brain: Using bilateral methods to reduce anxiety and relieve traumatic stress.* [Workshop] Expressive Therapies Summit, New York, NY.

Tripp, T., & Kolodny, P. (2016). *Wiggle, scribble, and squiggle: Bilateral approaches in art therapy for trauma treatment* [Workshop]. American Art Therapy Association Conference, Baltimore, MD.

Tripp, T. (2016). A body-based bilateral art protocol for reprocessing trauma. In J. King (Ed.), *Art therapy, trauma and neuroscience: Theoretical and practical perspectives* (pp. 173–194). Routledge.

Tripp, T. (2019). More than an image: Revisiting the Ulman personality assessment procedure. *Journal of American Art Therapy Association, 36*(3), 133–140. https://doi.org/10.1080/07421656.2019.1649546

Twombly, J. H. (2000). Incorporating EMDR and EMDR adaptations into the treatment of clients with dissociative identity disorder. *Journal of Trauma and Dissociation, 1*(2), 61–81. https://doi.org/10.1300/j229v01n02_05

Twombly, J. H., & Schwartz, R. C. (2008). The integration of the internal family systems model and EMDR. In C. Forgash & M. Copeley (Eds.), *Healing the heart of trauma and dissociation with EMDR and ego state therapy* (pp. 295–311). Springer Publishing.

Twombly, J. H. (2013). Integrating IFS with phase-oriented treatment of clients with dissociative disorder. In M. Sweezy & E. L. Ziskind (Eds.), *Internal family systems therapy: New dimensions* (pp. 72–89). Routledge.

Ulman, E., & Dachinger, P. (1975). *Art therapy in theory and practice*. Schocken Books.

van den Hout, M. A., & Engelhard, I. M. (2012). How does EMDR work? *Journal of Experimental Psychopathology, 3*(5), 724–738. https://doi.org/10.5127/jep.028212

van der Kolk, B. (2005). Developmental trauma disorder. *Psychiatric Annals, 35*(5), 410–408. https://doi.org/10.3928/00485713-20050501-06

van der Kolk, B. (2015). *The body keeps the score: Brain, mind, and body in the healing of trauma*. Penguin Books.

Wood, L. L. (2015). Eating disorder as protector: the use of internal family systems and drama therapy to treat eating disorders. In A. Hershifelt (Ed.), *Creative Arts Therapies in Eating Disorders* (pp. 293–325). Jessica Kingsley.

World Health Organization (WHO). (2013). *Guidelines for the management of conditions that are specifically related to stress*. Geneva.

CHAPTER 7

WRITING THERAPY AND EMDR

Erin Bastow

Stephen King resolved the question, "What is writing?" with the quick answer, "Telepathy, of course." In his memoir on the craft of writing, he went on to describe the act as delivering messages from a writer in their own space and time to readers "downstream on the timeline." The famed author also dubbed books, and by extension writing, "uniquely portable magic" given their power to connect one mind to another heedless of physical reality (King, 2000, pp. 103–104).

What is writing *therapy*? King's book does not specifically cover this, or at least the message has yet to transcend to this point on the timeline. Mental health clinicians could venture their own quick answer that it is the use of writing in therapy, of course. They would be correct. The more pertinent and challenging question is, why does it work? And equally relevant for clinicians, why use it?

The American Counseling Association publication in *Counseling Today* featured an article in its June 2021 edition celebrating the 75th anniversary of Viktor Frankl's *Man's Search for Meaning* (Dieser & Wimberly, 2021). Frankl is celebrated in the piece for his many contributions to mental health counseling, particularly his development of Logotherapy. *Logos* is Greek word for "meaning." Frankl's work is based on the notion humans' main motivation is "a will to meaning." He delineated three basic principles of Logotherapy: life has meaning under all circumstances; the main motivation for living is our will to find meaning in life; people have freedom to find meaning in what they do and what they experience or at least in the stance they take when faced with a situation of unchangeable suffering (Viktor Frankl Institute of Logotherapy, 2021). He also posited how humans can discover meaning: through creativity – by creating a work or doing a deed, by experiencing something or encountering someone, by the attitude they take toward life and unavoidable suffering (Dieser & Wimberly, 2021). Clients typically seek therapy in response to or during unavoidable suffering. The term "unavoidable" indicates life events cannot be changed, but it also typically means clients can no longer return to what they knew about themselves or about life before the trauma happened. Hermann (1997) explains that traumas, "…undermine the belief systems that give meaning to human experience. They violate the victim's faith in a natural or divine order and cast the victim into a state of existential crisis" (p. 51). Clinicians often hear suffering clients ask in some form or another, "why me?" or perhaps "what does this say about me?" or "what is life supposed to mean if this bad thing is allowed to happen to me?" When answers are elusive, they remain stuck in the suffering.

What does the search for meaning have to do with writing? Elizabeth Bishop won the Pulitzer Prize for Poetry in 1956 and the National Book Award in 1970. Her poems are revered for their poignant observations of life. Bishop's biographer Megan Marshall, herself a winner of the Pulitzer, makes a clear case for the influences of the poet's early life on her craft. Bishop's father died when she was an infant. Marshall (2017) refers to this trauma as, "the first tragedy in her life, one she was too young to have words to describe" (p. 9). Also shared are Bishop's recollections of being left in a crib during a time of turmoil, crying for her mother who never came. Her poem "Sestina" is a reflection on the aftermath of her

DOI: 10.4324/9781003156932-8

mother's hospitalization for mental illness. She also endured multiple changes in caregivers and homes, many broken connections. A keen trauma therapist might hypothesize Bishop's rarely matched skill for connecting to and describing places and moments in time is an adaptation she cultivated to cope with her unavoidable suffering. Perhaps even to find meaning in it.

Elizabeth Bishop is just one example among a seemingly infinite group of poets and lyricists who use words to explore the meaning of their own life. Her friend and fellow poet Robert Lowell, for instance, wrote "Walking in Blue" to examine his time in a psychiatric hospital. Rock 'n' roll legend Jim Morrison channeled his childhood of emotional abuse into his famously dark lyrics (Riordan & Porchnicky, 2014). This chapter will review the implications of early and chronic trauma on one's ability to feel connected to others and how this affects the conception of "meaning" for life. Also explored is the potential healing power of finding freedom again through writing.

If humans are motivated by a search for meaning, if creativity is one method by which meaning can be discovered, if encountering someone else is another, and if writing is telepathy, then writing therapy seems a viable method whereby one taps into creative free expression to harvest a piece of themselves around a particular period of suffering and communicate it to another person, or part of themselves, regardless of time and space. The act of doing so alters their attitude toward the experience, and they find meaning in their life and answers to the question, "why me?" Simply put, writing is a process through which clients can find meaning in their suffering. It is not the only method. However, the distinct feature of "telepathy" and other characteristics make writing well suited for certain clients, traumas, or therapy goals. This is also not the only purpose of therapeutic writing. The discovery of "meaning," though, is one of the main reasons writing can enhance Eye Movement Desensitization and Reprocessing (EMDR) therapy.

A review of the literature shows integrations of writing therapy and EMDR are primarily done in the Preparation phase. Later in this chapter, examples are shared for such preparation exercises, and a specific intervention to be utilized in Desensitization is explained in depth.

EXPRESSIVE WRITING

Expressive writing is as it sounds. The writing is emotional, individual, and subjective. Grammar, spelling, and punctuation are of little concern. Therapists can conserve their red pens for art interventions. Expressive writing is not journalism. A specific accounting of facts on the experience is not as important as how the person *feels* about what happened. The size, brand, and color of sneakers Joe wore is of less significance than the account he wore them on the wrong feet, felt embarrassed, and now goes barefoot whenever possible. An individual's perception on what the events *mean* is also of primary importance. Only idiots wear their shoes on the wrong feet, and embarrassment must be avoided at all costs. This is not where the intervention would end, but hopefully where it would gather speed and start rattling into adaptive information knocking loose an experience or two when Joe felt proud of himself or demonstrated he was no idiot, or helped another person feel less ashamed, or he might even feel silly for attributing such significance to a childish mistake.

Writing to get in touch with inner thoughts and feelings is widely regarded for its healing ability. Writing on personal experiences in an emotional way for as little as 15 minutes in a three-day period can aid both physical and emotional health across many populations (Pennebaker & Seagal, 1999). Some studies suggest writing for even a single day can promote desirable change (Chung & Pennebaker, 2008). While these changes are noted for mood disorders such as anxiety and depression, expressive writing has also been proven to boost immune function and promote positive shifts in cortisol levels (Maroney, 2020). In addition to the evident cathartic properties of writing, it is likewise found to give voice to the inner self and allow exploration of parts of the self often not immediately accessible (Phillips & Rolfe, 2016). Also theorized is writing's ability to help individuals reorganize thoughts or construct a meaningful story around a traumatic experience (Smyth & Helm, 2003; Pennebaker & Evans, 2014). A client's search for meaning if you will.

Expressive writing works its "magic" effectively for individuals with diverse trauma histories. For instance, it can stimulate resilience in juveniles involved with systems of child welfare or juvenile justice (Greenbaum & Javdani, 2017). Expressive writing was shown to improve psychosocial functioning and openness with sexual orientation for men who reported gay-related stress (Pachankis & Goldfried, 2010). Expressive writing decreased cortisol response to trauma-related memories for individuals with post-traumatic stress disorder (PTSD) when they wrote about their trauma experiences versus a control group writing about time management (Smyth, Hockemeyer, & Tulloch, 2008). Nixon and Kling (2009) tested a future-oriented writing therapy for persons with PTSD and concluded expressive writing with a focus on future achievement to have benefit for PTSD, particularly PTSD-associated depression and unhelpful trauma-related thoughts. Expressive writing was also shown to help alleviate trauma symptoms for women with a history of childhood sexual abuse (Lorenz, Pulverman, & Meston, 2013). The study asked participants in the treatment condition to write about beliefs related to sexuality or trauma. Craft, Davis, and Paulson (2012) asked their group of breast cancer survivors to utilize expressive writing for 20 minutes per day for four consecutive days on the topics of breast cancer trauma, any self-selected trauma, and facts about breast cancer, and it was determined expressive writing significantly improved the quality-of-life outcome measure.

While there are many forms of therapeutic and/or expressive writing, this chapter focuses on those most easily integrated with EMDR.

Journaling

When asked what forms therapeutic writing takes, many clinicians might first identify journaling. It is an oft-used practice for therapists of various theoretical orientations. Journaling can facilitate emotional healing and promote learning over time (Gladding, 2021). It is typically completed on the client's personal time or as homework. Though, therapists need to provide parameters individualized to the client's needs and goals. For instance, journaling without review and reflection potentially sacrifices growth. Gladding (2021) notes it is crucial for anyone keeping a journal to review their entries regularly to promote reflection and gain insight. He suggests a schedule of every two or three days taking the time normally dedicated to writing to review the previous days' entries instead. Similarly, Pennebaker and Evans (2014) warn that "Writing in a journal every day about the same issue with the same words in the same way will probably not bring the relief you seek and may actually do more harm than good" (p. 25). They go on to recommend journal writing be done on an as-needed basis and with an expressive writing focus. Journaling on the same topics without parameters can lead to rumination or overanalyzing.

When Shapiro (2001) describes the weekly log report for EMDR, she emphasizes the importance of a client writing brief descriptions for each category, only enough to help guide a subsequent desensitization session, and then following the log work with a "self-control technique to dissipate the disturbance" (p. 429). If clients use journaling to process triggers or emotional disturbance, it is essential the journaling be followed by self-regulation strategies. Yoga, meditation, guided imagery, and safe calm place visualization are all options. Trauma survivors prone to self-destructive behaviors may require journaling to be only one stage of a multi-phased approach to guiding the body through its stress response. According to Ferentz's (2015) Communicate Alternatively, Release Endorphins, Self-Soothe (CARESS) model for self-destructive behavior, journaling would be a means of communicating a pain narrative rather than engaging in harmful behavior. It would then need to be followed by an activity that releases endorphins and one that self-soothes to complete the cycle effectively.

Prescribed Writing

It is common for clinicians to set parameters for expressive writing, and as noted in the previous section, necessary in certain situations. Some clients may be initially intimidated by the act of writing or be unsure where to start. Therapists may also gauge a client as needing to dip their toe into the writing pool to gain confidence or test survival skills before taking an emotional cannonball into the deep end of expressive writing. In each instance, prescribed writing, or writing that provides partial thoughts for each line or sentence, is a fitting approach. Writing in which a client must only provide a word or short phrase to complete a thought is also called "stem sentences" (Gladding & Wallace, 2018). Clients can be taught or reminded of metaphors and similes and then provided prompts such as "I am scared like a…" or "I am a brave…" In the case of metaphors, this descriptive device can increase access to emotions, help communicate personal experience or thoughts, and help to reframe problems or introduce new frames of reference (Gladding, 2021). Putting many prescribed sentences together can produce full prescribed poems. This technique can be particularly helpful for young children (Desmond et al., 2015). There is a high chance of success with prescribed writing. Clients who do not fancy, or even fathom, themselves writers can be sparked to develop a new healthy self-cognition – "I am a writer." Additional examples of prescribed writing are shared later in the chapter.

Letter Writing

Letter writing is a common form of writing therapy. Letters can be written to loved ones, directly to oneself, to another part of the self, or to persons playing a role in a traumatic event. White and Epston (1990) described many variations of letters written as narrative means to therapeutic ends. The act of writing a letter can be empowering, and because it is an indirect form of communication, it can also feel less intimidating than talk therapy to certain clients (Desmond et al, 2015). Lander and Graham-Pole (2008/2009) found therapeutic benefit in writing letters to deceased loved ones on healing bereavement. Adolescents whose school counselors facilitate students writing letters to themselves at the beginning, middle, and end of the school year can feel heard, learn to reflect on their experiences, and externalize negative meaning and reframe it through discussion with the school counselor (DeCino, Waalkes, & Smith, 2018).

Letter writing can also be a powerful tool for clinicians helping clients overcome childhood trauma. Prasko et al. (2009) propose clients who write letters to significant caregivers as a therapeutic intervention develop change in their beliefs about themselves and others. In addition, they describe one type of letter in particular in which clients are instructed to write from the point of view of the significant person and identify the ideal response they would have liked to receive from the caregiver. This helps clients to initiate a new narrative around the trauma experience. Similarly, having survivors of childhood sexual abuse write letters from the future can be a particularly helpful intervention. Kress, Hoffman, and Thomas (2008) suggest letters written from an older, wiser self help survivors move beyond feelings of deficiency or being overwhelmed, and they also report clients finding meaning in their suffering, or "strength through suffering" (p. 113), recognizing their trauma has helped shape them into the person they are and who they are becoming.

Clinicians might question what happens if a client does not like the person they are or is afraid of the person they might become. Since EMDR desensitization directly addresses negative self-cognitions associated with trauma, this question makes a case for integrating EMDR and letter writing. Evidence exists for both letter writing and EMDR as successful interventions for changing emotional schemas and beliefs about the self and others. Both interventions assist trauma survivors answer their "why?"

Switching Perspectives

An emerging theme in therapeutic letter writing is to write from the point of view of another person. As noted, the other person can be a caregiver, a deceased loved one, a harmful person, or another part of the self. The format for such writing does not have to be a letter. A letter is often a good vehicle for changing perspectives, but the objective can be met by free association paragraphs, journal entries, poems, etc. The important factor is the client writing in first person from the point of view of the "other." Pennebaker and Evans (2014) report, "…when individuals first write about a massive upheaval, they first describe what they saw, felt, and experienced. Recent studies indicate that people who benefit the most from writing have been able to see events through others' eyes" (p. 17). In the instance of divorce or relationship dissolution, for example, clients have been shown to find healing in a writing intervention that has them write the story of the relationship including first-person perspectives of all the characters, and in doing so, they report increased empathy (Valdez & Evans, 2005). Gomez (2012) describes the significance of parent participation in children's trauma therapy, especially if the parent was the wounding agent. However, this is not always a possibility for children and becomes rarer with adults. Yet, many adults are in therapy to address attachment wounds. Thus, in these scenarios writing from the parent's point of view may be particularly important.

Switching perspectives can help in healing disconnection with others. Though, many trauma survivors also experience disconnection from their body. Prompting a client to give voice to a body part is a frequently used interweave during EMDR desensitization. It can also be a beneficial writing prompt. The body and mind must collaborate to heal from trauma, so an intellectual understanding of the body's needs is essential. In a sense, the client begins to empathize with the body part instead of being at odds or feeling betrayed by it. Similarly, asking a client to write from the point of view of an emotion has therapeutic value as well. It is common for overwhelmed clients who are amid suffering to be avoidant toward body sensations and distressing emotions. Writing from the perspective of a dreaded entity, whether rage or ribcage, provides empowerment or a sense of control over the body part or emotion. Again, if the client can empathize with the emotion, understand its function or the needs being met by its presence, fear of the emotion may reduce. What once felt like conflict between client and emotion could turn to alliance and promote collaborative problem-solving. Specific prompts for this sort of perspective switching are provided in greater depth later in the chapter.

In television, when a cast member talks directly to the camera, it's called "breaking the fourth wall." I'm not sure what the equivalent is for professional academic publication, but I'm doing it. For anyone who prefers thoughts interrupted by parenthetical notations, I promise to resume said intrusions shortly. However, a moment is needed to explain the evolution of the forthcoming writing interventions.

For 13 years, I've worked as a clinical therapist in a psychiatric residential treatment facility for adolescent boys. Clients typically come to residential treatment because their trauma symptoms have become unmanageable or unsafe in less restrictive settings. When symptom intensity is such, it is often the result of complex, developmental, or attachment trauma. However termed, the trauma histories of children in residential treatment are usually characterized by early and chronic suffering.

EMDR therapy is effective with this population. Many of them even look forward to sessions once they recognize the benefits following initial desensitization sessions. Parents are equally pleased at the reduction in emotional reactivity and improved functioning. Nevertheless, a certain type of trauma memories proved challenging, not only with the standard protocol but also with the most commonly used variations and additions. Clients who experienced abuse and/or neglect in preverbal stages of development consistently got stuck, and the SUD did not reduce much. The sticking point was typically expressed as lingering anger, but additional examination revealed the anger to be a product of an unanswered question, "Why?" This was particularly prevalent when the harmful person was a caregiver.

I was trained in EMDR in 2014, but five years earlier I created a therapeutic writing group for the residents. After every cycle of group, I did an informal survey to identify which prompts the kids found most helpful. At the top of the list was an empathy writing exercise in which group members wrote from the point of view of a significant person from their life. Other preferred prompts were personification of emotion and writing with mantras or affirmations.

One boy who was feeling angry and stuck with "Why?" had also been in group. Go with what you know works. I proposed an option in which he could try to write from the point of view of his biological mother, who was his harmful person. After doing so, things started to move again with his memory. I also observed, as most clinicians do, that it was traumatized parts who were speaking during reprocessing. They were the ones feeling the anger and ruminating on the "Why?" For the second attempt at integrating writing into EMDR desensitization, the exercise became writing a series of letters. The first letter gave the younger part a voice and was addressed to the harmful person. Writing from the point of view of the harmful person then became the second letter. A third letter was written from the point of view of the client at his current age speaking to his younger self. SUD reduced to 0, and the positive messages his present self sent to his younger part became the cognitions he wanted to believe about himself and reached a VOC of 7 quickly.

The boys eventually started referring to the intervention as "the one with the three letters" (which sounds like an episode of Friends) or "the three letters thing." The other favored group prompts – personification and mantras/affirmations – are easily worked into the Preparation phase of EMDR, and those, along with "The Three Letters," are described in the next section of this chapter.

"The Three Letters" intervention has since proved beneficial for any scenario in which the client was harmed by another person, as well as clients grieving the death of a loved one, or in spiritual crisis. It can likely be expanded to address any trauma event in which a client is stuck searching for meaning.

We now return to our regularly scheduled professional writing.

WRITING AND EMDR

EMDR was compared to a brief cognitive-behavioral writing therapy (CBWT) intervention and deemed to be equally effective in symptom reduction for PTSD, anxiety, depression, and behavior problems but more efficient in terms of amount of therapist contact time needed for efficacy (Roos et al, 2017). In the aforementioned study, both EMDR and CBWT were found to produce symptom reduction in about half the duration of standard trauma-focused CBT protocols. However, these comparisons and conclusions were reached using participants with single-incident trauma.

EMDR therapists must be familiar with complex trauma and the unique challenges it presents for clients. According to Rosoff (2019), EMDR therapists assisting clients with complex trauma need to set the frame of therapy, help build and then utilize the capacity for adaptive information, and look for opportunities to strengthen resources and competencies. Rosoff (2019) further calls for a much more active and regulating role for the therapist when clients have complex trauma than what Francine Shapiro initially described in the standard protocol as having therapists "stay out of the way." In such cases, clients often spend more time in the preparation phase or require self-regulation during reprocessing, and therapists would be helped to have interventions that are easily paced and those which also increase the availability of adaptive information. Here is an argument in favor of the integration of therapeutic writing. Prescribed writing, letter writing, journaling with set parameters, all allow for the client to take small steps into accessing emotion or other stored material. The same interventions also enable clients to write with some sense of containment, which can decrease fear of flooding.

Complex trauma, also sometimes referred to as developmental trauma, by definition causes long-term obstacles for an individual's functioning. Heller and LaPierre (2012) identify impaired self-regulation, self-image, and capacity for relationship as primary dimensions affected by a history of early and pervasive trauma. They further posit the lack of healthy self-regulation, self-image, and capacity for relationship serve as obstacles for a person to feel connection and aliveness. This is so because if an infant's caregivers fail to meet their child's core needs, there is disconnection between infant and caregiver which compromises the core capacities of connection, aliveness, and creativity, and the child forms an adaptive survival style (Heller & LaPierre, 2012). Connection, aliveness, and creativity – each of these capacities can be examined and potentially nourished through expressive writing.

On the theme of human's search for meaning, Heller and Lapierre (2012) offer the following when describing the adaptation Connection Survival Style,

> Searching for meaning, for the *why* of existence, is one of the primary coping mechanisms that both the thinking and spiritualizing subtypes of the Connection Survival Style use to manage their sense of disconnection and the despair that disconnection brings.
>
> (p. 145)

The authors also stress this coping mechanism may fall short if the person is not in touch with bodily experience or avoids close personal relationships, common occurrences with these survival subtypes. Since EMDR facilitates client attunement to somatic experience, and EMDR therapists are trained to ensure social supports or similar resources are identified, and some of the most effective writing therapy interventions emphasize emotional self-exploration (journaling, prescribed writing) and/or target connection with others (letter writing), here again it seems the two modalities of EMDR and therapeutic writing paired together have the power to lead clients toward a fulfilling search for meaning.

EMDR and writing are both widely established as effective for addressing trauma, and they have even been compared to one another. However, this is akin to having both peanut butter and jelly on the shelf next to one another and never combining the two. The foods enhance each other's flavors. It is time now to explain how the sandwich is made.

WRITING EXERCISES IN THE PREPARATION PHASE

Prescribed Writing

If a client struggles to identify emotions, provide them a list of stems targeting various emotions. If a client cannot fathom what safety is or feels like, help them to begin exploring safety with a few short but efficient sentences. If a client is unsure of who they are, how to tell their story, needs scaffolding to learn how to express themselves, or needs containment to feel comfortable addressing what brought them to therapy, use prescribed writing interventions. Such work contributes to a person's ability to self-regulate, to explore self-image, and to build capacity for relationship. For the latter task, not only can precisely directed prompts facilitate reflection on relationships, but the written statements themselves are tools which clients can use to communicate with significant persons.

On the next pages are a few prescribed writing interventions that help clients to examine feelings and beliefs about the self and the self's experiences.

The following is a list of "stems" or sentence starters. These can be used in early stages of treatment to begin opening pieces of memories or accessing connections among images, thoughts, feelings, body sensations, etc. This is a sampling rather than an exhaustive list. Clinicians should tailor the sentence starters to the client's needs.

I feel _____.

I need _____.

I feel _____ when _____.

I am a _____ person.

I am the kind of person who _____.

I am fearful of _____.

My body betrays me when _____.

My body's strength is _____.

To feel okay, I need _____.

Anger feels like _____.

Fear feels like _____.

Calm feels like _____.

Hope feels like _____.

The future is _____.

My protector part is _____.

When I think about my childhood _____.

When I think about my parents _____.

When I think about my trauma _____.

A safe place is _____.

A safe person is someone who _____.

A child needs _____.

A parent needs _____.

Childhood is like _____.

Life is like _____.

Dying is like _____.

Saying goodbye means _____.

Love means _____.

Self-Reflection Poem

Line 1: Write your preferred name.

Line 2: Write four adjectives that describe you.

Line 3: Write "Feels" and then three things you feel.

Line 4: Write "Fears" and then three things you fear.

Line 5: Write "Needs" and then three things you need.

Line 6: Write "Has" and then three strengths you have.

Line 7: Write "Gives" and then three things you give.

Line 8: Write "Will" and then three goals you'll reach.

Line 9: Write "I am" and then a healthy belief about yourself.

Line 10: Write your preferred name again.

Alex.
Quiet, creative, alone, and invisible.
Feels scared, unsure, stuck, trapped.
Fears snakes, trust, making mistakes.
Needs help, a shoulder to cry on, confidence.
Has artistic talent, intelligence, a loyal dog.
Gives humor, respect, thought.
Will learn to trust, find hope, show in a gallery.
I am valuable.
Alex.

Finley.
Life of the party, wild like an untamed horse, beautiful, passionate.
Feels eager, anxious, fiery, stomach butterflies on speed.
Fears the woods and nature, stillness, intense conversation.
Needs iced coffee, Sundays at the gym, to keep moving.
Has energy, physical strength, an endless well of ideas.
Gives smiles, choreography suggestions, laughs to friends.
Will learn to breathe, learn to play guitar, reconnect with sister.
I am a unicorn.
Finley.

Prescribed Emotion Poem

Line 1: An emotion
Line 2: Three adjectives that describe the emotion
Line 3: Three places or situations where you feel this emotion
Line 4: Complete the line "I am _____"
Line 5: Two places where you are what you say in Line 4
Line 6: Repeat the emotion from Line 1
Line 7: Take control of the emotion with three statements beginning with "My"

Fear
Haunting, relentless, pounding
In bed, at solo entrance, kneeling before Him
I am provoked
At work, in quiet places
Fear
My fault, my motivation, my victory
Patience
Impossible, impending, illogical
When struck, when bought, at stupidity's table
I am raw
In my head, at my core
Patience
My goal, my carrot, my obligation

Personification of Emotion

The prompt for personification writing is "Write about _____ as if it was a person." When a client identifies a particular emotion that feels overwhelming or one that feels out of their control, the personification prompt becomes, "Write about (identified emotion) as if it was a person." The goals of the exercise are to help build awareness around the client's relationship with the emotion and to cultivate a sense of empowerment over the emotion. The writer makes all the choices in writing. The writer gets to decide what the emotion does, how it behaves, and its fate. A clinician could provide additional directives either before the initial writing or upon reading a first draft. For instance, a client writing about depression might only describe its menacing or voyeuristic features, i.e., "Depression lingers in the corner at parties, stares at me, and interrupts my thoughts with doubt." A clinician might then prompt the client to add, "What would you want to say to Depression?" To which a client might write, "We can learn to coexist, but you're not in charge of me. You don't make my decisions."

Mantras and Affirmations

Mantras are touted for enhancing meditation and their ability to intensify concentration. The repetition of a sound, single word, or short phrase can provide assistance in regulating emotion, intrusive thoughts, and even somatic responses to stress. Clients might have a particular word or phrase they already use for focus, calming, motivation, or other purposes. If so, they can be prompted to write either a narrative of how they use this mantra in difficult situations or a poem using the mantra as a refrain.

My wandering spirit knows no stillness.
My wandering eye no bounds; it leaps.
My wandering stirs, fires, expertly escapes.
Be still.

My spirit pursues restlessness, never too far to run.
My spirit heralds chaos, clamors for unrest.
My spirit fears the catch, the cage of calm and air.
Be still.

Take breaths. Take pause.
Be still.
Give thought. Give thanks.
Be still.

Be still.

Clients who do not already have a mantra can be helped by reviewing a menu of commonly used options. They can also be encouraged to imagine a safe, calm place and label that place with one word. Then they take that word for a mantra test run and determine if it produces the meditative or calming effect desired. Completing the mantra writing exercises can provide additional confirmation that this word is a good fit for the client.

Affirmations are positive declarative statements. In therapy, they are used to activate adaptive information at times when our brain is conditioned to access negative beliefs. If a client struggles with negative self-cognitions, and likely has a significant trauma history, affirmations can be difficult to identify without assistance. The following is a menu of common positive affirmations to be shared with clients.

I am in control of my life.
I am perfectly me.
I do my best.
I am calm and confident.
I am happy to be alive.
I am beautiful.
I am strong.
I survived or I am surviving.
I have a lot to be proud of.
I am growing every day.
I believe in myself.
I accept myself for who I am.

There are many variations of the affirmations listed above. The ones selected are mostly "I am" statements because if a client finds resonance with an "I am" statement, it can later become the positive belief in reprocessing. In effect, it embeds adaptive information into the client's toolbox, and if used throughout Preparation, it is often more easily accessed during Desensitization.

The prompts for the affirmation writing exercise are the same as for mantras. Affirmations can be written into a narrative in which the client illustrates the development and evidence of the affirmation, or affirmations can be written as a refrain in a poem or song lyrics. Clinicians can instruct a client to identify an example situation in which the affirmation felt most true and to write the story of said example. This sort of writing can augment traditional resource installation by having the written story replace the initial visualization or imaginal piece. Because writing takes a bit more time, and people are conditioned to "set a scene" when storytelling, often additional details are included in the narrative that strengthen the recollection. Clinicians should then follow their training in terms of how to install the resource once it is identified.

Parts Writing

Switching perspectives was discussed earlier in the chapter. One of the options for perspective or empathy writing is to have clients write from the point of view of their various "parts." Some clinicians' first thought here is that "parts" refers to "parts of self" or Internal Family Systems references. Other clinicians might assume "parts" refers to body parts. Both are correct.

One prompt for "parts of self" writing is to give voice to each part and see what each needs the client to know. A variation is to give voice to each part and see what each needs the therapist to know. A third modification is to give voice to each part and see what each needs the other parts to know. In each instance, writing is done from the first-person point of view. Co-consciousness is a pre-requisite for these prompts. The goal of "parts of self" writing is to generate understanding and empathy for each facet of the personality and their functions. Clinicians also gain valuable information regarding the parts' needs and what additional work may need to be accomplished prior to Desensitization.

Clients also find writing dialogue between parts beneficial. In this case, the therapist should mention scripts, screenplays, or conversations in books to ensure the client has a reference for how dialogue is written. The prompt is to first describe a situation in which parts have differing opinions, conflict, or one part that always takes charge and then write the dialogue among the parts. Optional add-ons include the following: (1) what do they say to one another? (2) Do any parts retreat or remain silent? (3) Who ends the conversation? (4) What is the result of the conversation for each part? After the initial writing, clients can be prompted to rewrite the dialogue with the healthiest possible conclusion.

A common interweave during Desensitization is to give voice to a body part, i.e., "If your stomach could talk, what would it say?" This question can also be a writing prompt. Similar to other perspective switching, one goal is to gain understanding and empathy for that body part. Another goal is to begin unlocking tension or pain stored in the body. In some cases, when this is done prior to Desensitization, reprocessing somatic trauma memories becomes more fluid. Understanding the reason for body discomfort or pain in terms of the body's efforts to survive trauma can add to the available adaptive information. It gives meaning to the pain.

I, your stomach, am alert to danger. I need you to know that I am always on the lookout for threats. I am trying to tell you something is wrong. If you tune in to me, rather than being frustrated by me, you will be safer. If you ignore me, I get angry and cause more pain. I am not a weakness. I am an asset. P.S. Stop eating jalapeños. That just confuses things.

WRITING EXERCISE FOR THE DESENSITIZATION PHASE

The Three Letters

As explained from behind the fourth wall, The Three Letters writing intervention was originally implemented with adolescent males. It has since been presented and taught in workshops to therapists who work with a variety of populations. Several of these therapists have reported effectiveness for adults with diverse presenting problems. It was designed to help clients process implicit memories or events that include a harmful person. The primary benefit has been quick acknowledgment of meaning. The intervention leads clients to answer the long lingering "why" as they tend to gain understanding of the harmful person and write what they need to hear from that person. The third letter, written from the point of view of the older self, tends to give the younger self hope and meaning for surviving such suffering.

Also significant with this intervention is the added tactile grounding during reprocessing. The client reads the letter aloud while the therapist performs bilateral tapping or a similar dual attention stimulus, but the client is usually holding the letter as well, feeling the paper in their hands. They also hear their own voice. Some clients have observed that side-to-side eye movements needed for reading remind them to some extent of the traditional eye movement stimulation of the standard EMDR therapy.

The Three Letters Facilitation Steps

This exercise is intended for individuals who experienced early life traumas and have mostly implicit memory of those traumas. It can also be utilized for individuals who have some measure of recall for traumatic events but struggle with visualization or identifying a pertinent image. It is to be used only after a thorough EMDR Preparation phase.

Clients Are Instructed to Write Three Letters:

1. **Younger Self to Other**

   Letter written from the point of view of the younger self as they speak to "other." In each case, "other" represents the harmful person who facilitated the traumatic event, i.e., a neglectful caregiver, an abusive caregiver, a perpetrator of abuse, etc. It is written in first person.

   The goal of this letter is to have the client identify thoughts and feelings at the time the traumatic event was occurring.

2. **Other to Younger Self**

   Letter written from "other" in response to the first letter. Client is asked to take on the point of view of the person to whom they addressed the first letter (the harmful person) and from that person's perspective, respond to the thoughts, feelings, and questions expressed by the younger self. It is written in first person.

   The goal of this letter is to shift from a "self" focus and gain some understanding of the traumatic event from the other person's point of view.

3. **Current Self to Younger Self**

   Letter written from client's current point of view to their younger self at the time of the trauma. It is written in first person.

The goal of this letter is reassurance and assisting shift toward positive, healthy self-cognitions and affirmations.

First letter: The first is read out loud by client and paired with bilateral stimulation. Client is prompted to take a deep breath after the first reading and then is asked to read the letter a second time, again with bilateral stimulation pairing. After second reading client is prompted to take a deep breath and asked, "What came up?"

Additional processing can be done for body sensations or other channels that do not directly pertain to "Other" person.

Second letter: The second letter is read out loud by client and paired with bilateral stimulation. Client is prompted to take a deep breath after the first reading and then is asked to read the letter a second time, again with bilateral stimulation pairing. After second reading client is prompted to take a deep breath and asked, "What came up?"

Additional processing is done to clear remaining channels. Once the client is beginning to make healthier assertions about themself, the third letter can be utilized.

Third letter: The third letter is read out loud by client and paired with bilateral stimulation. Client is prompted to take a deep breath after the first reading and then is asked to read the letter a second time, again with bilateral stimulation pairing. After second reading, client is prompted to take a deep breath and asked, "What came up?" Processing continues using EMDR standard protocol for Installation, Body Scan, and Closure.

Keep in mind:

- The Three Letters intervention is intended to be used after client has engaged in thorough preparation, i.e., affect tolerance work, soothing and grounding tools, other writing interventions, Dialectical Behavior Therapy (DBT), etc.
- Therapist should follow all standard EMDR protocols for establishing safety when utilizing The Three Letters as would be done for any other EMDR session.
- Writing is done in separate sessions from processing, and therapist explains to client that this is the case.
- Letter writing is best done in the therapy office and should be followed by grounding exercises prior to clients leaving the session. "Container" can also be used when needed. With certain clients, particularly children, the letters could be kept in an actual safe container in the therapy office.
- Letters should be kept in the therapy office.
- Length of letter is not prescribed, but therapist needs to monitor for potential "looping" and should check-in with client every few minutes during writing.
- If more than one harmful person participated in the facilitating of a trauma, the second letter (Younger Self to Other) can be done more than once – one letter from each "other" point of view. Process the letters as two separate channels. Once all "other" channels are cleared, move on to the third letter (Current Self to Younger Self) as described.
- The Three Letters intervention is to be used as a complement to the standard EMDR protocol. Therefore, the goals of the session are the same as they would be if standard processing were utilized. For instance, if forgiveness is not a goal without the letters, then it does not need to be a goal with the letters. Similarly, if

the harmful person remains in the client's life, any proactive strategies the therapist would take before a standard EMDR desensitization session would also be needed using the letters.

- The Three Letters can be used for clients who have "why" questions directed to a higher power. The letters can be written from younger self to higher power, higher power to younger self, and current self to younger self. Follow directions for reprocessing as would be done for The Three Letters with a harmful person.

The Three Letters can be used for clients with a deceased loved one. The letters are written as age of self at time of loss to loved one, loved one to that younger self, and current self to younger self. Follow directions for reprocessing as would be done for The Three Letters with a harmful person. Writing to absent, but not deceased, loved ones can also be targeted.

Example letters:

1. *Dear Bio Mom,*

   When you leave me alone, I don't have enough food, and the neighbor's dog is always barking next door, and I am scared. I don't know if you're coming back, and I can't leave to ask for help because I'm so little, and that dog is very big and loud. My tummy hurts so bad, and I've been crying so much my eyes hurt too. What did I do to make you leave? Why don't you love me? Why would you leave me all alone?

   Your Son,

   Baby Andrew

2. *Dear Andrew,*

   I am sorry for the pain you feel. It is not your fault I left. I tried my best to be your mom, but I have a hard time feeling happy. It has nothing to do with you. I had this problem before you were born. Bad people hurt me a long time ago, and it made me very sad. Sometimes to feel happy, I drink too much alcohol and lose track of time. Even though it doesn't seem like it, I love you very much. I hope you give your adoptive parents a chance. They can give you a better life than I can. You are a great baby.

   With Love,

   Mom

3. *Dear Baby Andrew,*

   I know you are feeling scared and lonely. You're hungry all the time, and you don't know what to do. But you are going to survive this. Those feelings are only going to last for a little bit, and then some nice people will come help you. You will also have adoptive parents who feed you every day, and you get to eat pizza every Friday and ice cream on Sunday after church. They also make sure you eat vegetables too because they care about you and want you to be healthy. Don't be mad at Mom. She didn't mean to hurt you. Things are going to get better, and you are going to prove how strong you are. PS…You are going to be on the football team, and you can run a 6-minute mile.

   Love,

   Teenage Andrew

CONCLUSION

Viktor Frankl listed three methods to discover meaning: through creativity – by experiencing something or encouraging someone, by the attitude one takes toward life and unavoidable suffering. The writing interventions described in this chapter provide opportunities to engage in one or multiples of these methods. The Three Letters intervention offers all three. Expressive writing, as it does not attend to specific facts, others' approval, nor grammatical parameters, also extends a freedom to wander among thoughts and feelings that may not otherwise be explored. It is a suitable and beneficial complement to EMDR, which also stimulates the brain to tap into adaptive information.

For individuals with complex trauma, the search for meaning or answers to why trauma occurred is particularly difficult due to implicit memories often formed in preverbal stages of development. Like most infants or toddlers, the "stuck" memories need a boost to see above the counter where the rest of the experience exists. Writing can be the boost as it provides safe means to utilize creativity, is in and of itself an experience that can and often does include writing encouragement to parts of the self, and promotes the formation of new attitudes toward unavoidable suffering.

Writing is magic. It can transport thoughts and feelings from a time of trauma to the present. When the time hop portal unloads directly into a safe therapy office, the trauma bits are made available for in-depth examination. With the guidance of a therapist, a client can uncover answers to enduring questions and extract meaning. Because EMDR therapy also processes thoughts and feelings from the time of trauma, blending writing and EMDR increases the potency of the magic. Writing and EMDR are perhaps soul mates that are just now finding each other but were always meant to be.

REFERENCES

Chung, C. K., & Pennebaker, J. W. (2008). Variations in spacing of expressive writing sessions. *British Journal of Health Psychology, 13*, 15–21.

Craft, M. A., Davis, G. C., & Paulson, R. M. (2012). Expressive writing in early breast cancer survivors. *Journal of Advanced Nursing, 69*(2), 305–315.

DeCino, D. A., Waalkes, P. L., & Smith, P. (2018). Letter writing: A creative tool for school counselors working with adolescents. *Journal of Creativity in Mental Health, 13*(3), 358–368.

Desmond, K. J., Kindsvatter, A., Stahl, S., & Smith, H. (2015). Creating space for connections: A column for creative practice. *Journal of Creativity in Mental Health, 10*, 439–455.

Dieser, R. B., & Wimberly, C. (2021). Celebrating man's search for meaning. *Counseling Today, 63*(12), 38–43.

Ferentz, L. (2015). *Treating self-destructive behaviors in trauma survivors: A clinician's guide* (2nd Ed.). Routledge.

Gladding, S. T. (2021). *The creative arts in counseling* (6th Ed.). American Counseling Association.

Gladding, S. T., & Wallace, M. J. D. (2018). Scriptotherapy: Eighteen writing exercises to promote insight and wellness. *Journal of Creativity in Mental Health, 13*(4), 380–391.

Gomez, A. M. (2012). Healing the caregiving system: Working with parents within a comprehensive EMDR treatment. *Journal of EMDR Practice and Research, 6*(3), 136–144.

Greenbaum, C. A., & Javdani, S. (2017). Expressive writing intervention promotes resilience among juvenile justice-involved youth. *Children & Youth Services Review, 73*, 220–229.

Heller, L., & LaPierre, A. (2012). *Healing developmental trauma: How early trauma affects self-regulation, self-image, and capacity for relationship.* North Atlantic Books.

Hermann, J. (1997). *Trauma and recovery: The aftermath of violence – from domestic abuse to political terror.* Basic Books.

King, S. (2000). *On writing: A memoir of the craft.* Scribner.

Kress, V. E., Hoffman, R., & Thomas, A. M. (2008). Letters from the future: The use of therapeutic letter writing in counseling sexual abuse survivors. *Journal of Creativity in Mental Health, 3*(2), 105–118.

Lander, D. A., & Graham-Pole, J. R. (2008/2009). Love letters to the dead: Resurrecting an epistolary art. *Omega: Journal of Death & Dying, 58*(4), 313–333.

Lorenz, T. A., Pulverman, C. S., & Meston, C. M. (2013). Sudden gains during patient-directed expressive writing treatment predicts depression reduction in women with history of childhood sexual abuse: Results from a randomized clinical trial. *Cognitive Therapy & Research, 37*, 690–696.

Maroney, D. I. (2020). The imagine project: Using expressive writing to help children overcome stress and trauma. *Pediatric Nursing, 46*(6), 300–302, 311.

Marshall, M. (2017). *Elizabeth Bishop: A miracle for breakfast.* Houghton Mifflin Harcourt.

Nixon, R. D. V., & Kling, L. W. (2009). Treatment of adult post-traumatic stress disorder using a future-oriented writing therapy approach. *The Cognitive Behaviour Therapist, 2*, 243–255.

Pachankis, J. E., & Goldfried, M. R. (2010). Expressive writing for gay-related stress: Psychosocial benefits and mechanisms underlying improvement. *Journal of Consulting and Clinical Psychology, 78*(1), 98–110.

Pennebaker, J. W., & Evans, J. F. (2014). *Expressive writing: Words that heal.* Idyll Arbor, Inc.

Pennebaker, J. W., & Seagal, J. D. (1999). Forming a story: The health benefits of narrative. *Journal of Clinical Psychology, 55*(10), 1243–1254.

Phillips, L., & Rolfe, A. (2016). Words that work? Expressive client writing in therapy. *Counseling and Psychotherapy Research, 16*(3), 193–200.

Prasko, J., Diveky, T., Mozny, P., & Sigmundova Z. (2009). Therapeutic letters – Changing the emotional schemas using writing letters to significant caregivers. *Activas Nervosa Superior Rediviva, 51*(3–4), 163–167.

Riordan, J., & Porchnicky, J. (2014). *Break on through: The life and death of Jim Morrison.* [Kindle version]. Retrieved from amazon.com.

Roos, C., Oord, S., Zijlstra, B., Lucassen, S., Perrin, S., Emmelkamp, P., & Jongh, A. (2017). Comparison of eye movement desensitization and reprocessing therapy, cognitive behavioral writing therapy, and wait-list in pediatric posttraumatic stress disorder following single-incident trauma: A multicenter randomized clinical trial. *Journal of Child Psychology & Psychiatry, 58*(11), 1219–1228.

Rosoff, A. L. (2019). How we do what we do: The therapist, EMDR, and treatment of complex trauma. *Journal of EMDR Practice and Research, 13*(1), 61–74.

Shapiro, F. (2001). *Eye movement desensitization and reprocessing: Basic principles, protocols, and procedures* (2nd Ed.). Guilford Press.

Smyth, J., & Helm, R. (2003). Focused expressive writing as self-help for stress and trauma. *Psychotherapy in Practice, 59*(2), 227–235.

Smyth, J. M., Hockemeyer, J. R., & Tulloch, H. (2008). Expressive writing and post-traumatic stress disorder: Effects on trauma symptoms, mood states, and cortisol reactivity. *British Journal of Health Psychology, 13*, 85–93.

Valdez, A. A., & Evans, M. (2005). A novel approach: Using literary writing and creative interventions for working toward forgiveness after relationship dissolution and divorce. *Journal of Creativity in Mental Health, 1*(3/4), 103–121.

Viktor Frankl Institute for Logotherapy. (2021, June 19). About logotherapy. https://www.viktorfranklinstitute.org/about-logotherapy/

White, M., & Epston, D. (1990). *Narrative means to therapeutic ends.* W.W. Norton & Company.

CHAPTER 8

THREE-DIMENSIONAL PARTS OF SELF-TOOL
(3-D POST)
An Art Therapy-Based Modality in Preparation of Clients for
EMDR Phase Four Reprocessing

Hannah Rothschild, Barbara Collins, and Isabel Beland

Survivors of trauma-related disorders typically experience a number of debilitating somatic symptoms (Levine, 2019; Ogden et al., 2006) and without resources to self-soothe and understand the negative impact of past traumas, the survivor *regulates* maladaptively through dissociation (Dana, 2018; Martin, 2018; Porges, 2017; Steele et al., 2016; van der Hart et al., 2006). They describe feeling disconnected from the environment and may even experience immobilizing fear. *Dissociation* is a coping mechanism that, at the time of the traumatic experience, is adaptive and protective. It becomes maladaptive when unresolved symptoms associated with past traumatic experiences are triggered by fear that the trauma will happen again; thus, the nervous system *sounds the alarm* and the response is to dissociate as a means of protection of the self (Dana, 2018; Porges, 2017). According to the theory of Structural Dissociation, an individual—the self—is made up of two distinct action systems: the *daily living action system* and the *defense action system* (Martin, 2020; Steele et al., 2016; van der Hart et al., 2006). Each action system is composed of parts called daily living and emotional parts respectively; they operate independently, and are typically unaware of other parts.

In our work with traumatized clients, we have noticed that inviting those prone to dissociation to hold a simple item, such as a stone or a clay sculpture, has assisted them to return focus to the present moment; additionally, asking the client a series of guided questions has enabled them to find their voice. The *3-D Parts of Self-Tool* (3-D PoST) comprises a number of clay sculptures that we have utilized to help clients realize and learn about their parts of self, their felt experiences, and emotions through projection. We have done this in conjunction with Martin's (2016) *Readiness Checklist for Complex Trauma* (see Appendix A). For example, the therapist invites the client who presents as shut-down and reports feeling helpless and hopeless to select a clay sculpture that best represents these emotions/states. They may select a curved and caved-in hollow clay sculpture. By handling and moving the sculpture in their hands, and with the assistance of the therapist and guided questions, it might come to symbolize a container for negative emotions, and potentially help to refocus the client's energy to engage more presently in session.

The aim of this chapter is to introduce and discuss the 3-D PoS Tool when it is utilized with Martin's (2016) *Readiness Checklist for Complex Trauma* with traumatized clients. We believe our tool aligns itself well with this, particularly when working with the client in preparation to engage in memory reprocessing in Phase Four of Eye Movement Desensitization and Reprocessing (EMDR) therapy. First, we review the negative, physical, and emotional impacts of complex trauma, as well as dissociation through the lens of van der Hart, Nijenhuis, and Steele's (2006) Structural Dissociation Theory. We then provide an exploration of our work using three art therapy-based interventions and the 3-D PoS Tool, coupled with Martin's checklist, using a case vignette. To protect the anonymity of clients, our subject is an amalgam of many clients we have worked with.

DOI: 10.4324/9781003156932-9

COMPLEX TRAUMA, DISSOCIATION, AND PARTS OF SELF

Judith Herman coined the term "Complex Posttraumatic Stress Disorder" (CPTSD) in her 1992 book *Trauma and Recovery* (van der Kolk, 2015). Similar in symptomatology to PTSD, clients with CPTSD also struggle with somatization, avoidance, and a sensation of imminent threat, whether real or perceived (Møller et al., 2021). Additional characteristics of CPTSD include psychological defenses, such as dissociation, problems regulating emotional affect, fragile self-concept, disturbances in relationships, and dysfunction in the storage of traumatic memories (Knipe, 2018; Møller et al., 2021). Symptoms are experienced by the client as persistent, pervasive, and occurring over innumerable and seemingly unrelated contexts.

Dissociation, a component of CPTSD (Boon et al., 2011; Steele et al., 2016), is a defense mechanism, which attempts to make the "overwhelming less overwhelming" (Martin, 2018, p. 221). Initially, it is an adaptive defense mechanism when the trauma was occurring; however, dissociation becomes a maladaptive response when it becomes overutilized by the client who is triggered by intolerable emotions, thoughts, and body sensations from traumatic memories (Boon et al., 2011; Farina & Liotti, 2013; Martin, 2018; Steele et al., 2016; van der Hart et al., 2013). This attempt at self-protection by dissociation comes at an emotional cost because as it grows, through continued experienced intrusive and dysregulating memories and symptoms, so too does the unconscious reliance on substitute maladaptive coping behavior (Martin, 2018; Boon et al., 2011). These include avoidant and/or phobic behavior such as substance misuse, self-harm, and/or eating disorders. Often the result is further fragmentation of emotional parts of the self.

The fragmentation of parts through the lens of structural dissociation theory discerns two action systems that regulate human behavior: the first is *daily life* and the second is *defense* (Steele et al., 2016; Martin, 2018). The daily life action system (DLAS) encompasses all activities involved in the survival of the species, while the defense action system (DAS) is tasked with survival of the individual, which includes responding and recuperation from threats to the self (Martin, 2018). These responses are not initially part of conscious awareness; the brain and nervous system react sympathetically and parasympathetically (via the dorsal vagal system) by enacting a fight, flight, freeze, submit, collapse, and/or attachment cry response (Dana, 2018; Porges, 2017; Martin, 2018; Farina & Liotti, 2013; Knipe, 2018; Steele et al., 2016).

When the client has experienced trauma—such as childhood sexual violence, emotional and physical abuse—maladaptively stored memories overwhelm mental health that negatively impact the intrapsychic internal communication (Boon et al., 2011; Knipe, 2018; Martin, 2018; Steele et al., 2016). For instance, defensive parts of self in a traumatized client can include a child part who experienced sexual violence in childhood and an angry adolescent part whose role is to protect and defend the younger part. A worker part attends to employment and other daily living responsibilities and may even resent the child and adolescent parts' interference in daily life. Because defensive parts are stuck in a trauma bubble, they may not be oriented to the present and may operate independently and non-contemporaneously (Frewen & Lanius, 2015). For the traumatized adult client who becomes emotionally triggered when in a large crowd, it may feel, in this particular circumstance, that the violence experienced as a child is imminently going to happen again. The dissociative defense mechanism might be for a child part to "take charge" and act in a child-like helpless manner with the intention of being heard, seen, and rescued; as the client did as a child in order to survive. Additionally, parts can present as hypo- or hyper-aroused and can be experienced directly (as internal conversations) or indirectly (as a felt sense) which is an implicit awareness of communication of the parts within the personality system (Ogden et al., 2006).

Two distinct but related processes of dissociation are *depersonalization* and *derealization* (Boon et al., 2011; Knipe, 2018; Martin, 2018; Steele et al., 2016). According to Martin (2018) and Møller et al. (2021), derealization is a downgrading process of traumatic memories and is observed when a client indicates "it could have been worse," or may be experienced as a complete amnesia of the traumatic experiences (Boon et al., 2011; Martin, 2018; Steele et al., 2016). Depersonalization is a process of fragmentation that occurs when intolerable aspects of traumatic memories are stored dysfunctionally in isolation and are unassimilated into comprehensive memory networks. A depersonalized client may experience dissociation as if they are an outside observer of their thoughts and feelings—a perception of floating in the air above themselves, watching the physical dysregulated response with a sense of emotional and physical numbness. It can be said that a type of cognitive error occurs when the self requires further fragmentation of parts in response to affective activation of intolerable traumatic material. Specifically, it becomes the client's overwhelming belief that the traumatic experiences did not happen to them (Steele, 2018; Martin, 2018).

The image of the submarine shown in Figure 8.1 is a helpful metaphor to describe the action systems and their associated parts, as well as the way they become disconnected and dissociated from other parts of self. When the submarine out at sea collides with another vessel, a hull breach results in water flooding into one compartment. The crew's task is to block and isolate the damaged compartment so the entire submarine can continue to function within *operational limits*. Similarly, traumatic experiences cause the self to fragment emotionally and remain closed off from the daily living self. This is a protectionary measure used to allow the daily self to continue functioning, split off from the traumatic event and the associated thoughts and sensations. This metaphor helps the client understand how compartmentalization works to store and hide painful memories: Parts work to isolate these memories by blocking them so that the daily living self can continue to function in the world.

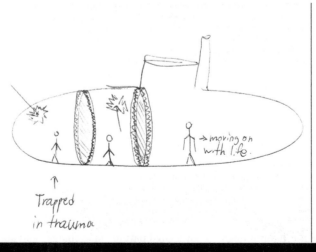

Figure 8.1 Submarine metaphor of parts of self.

The wounded or fragmented part of the self eventually becomes forgotten over time; however, when the submarine returns home to shore and is no longer in danger, wounded parts become increasingly phobic or avoidant and emerge with a fear that the traumas continue to occur. This presents a threat to the daily living action system and the entire personality system (Steele et al., 2016; van der Hart et al., 2006). It takes courage and empathy to bring that wounded part out of the flooded chamber and reintroduce it to the new, less dangerous way of experiencing the world that is experienced by other parts of the personality system.

Dissociative disorders occur on a continuum of trauma-related disorders (Steele et al., 2016). We know that clients with PTSD typically experience dissociation; however, clients with more pervasive developmental trauma are more likely to develop complex dissociation (Steele et al., 2016; Knipe, 2018). Therefore, the dissociative continuum further discerns dissociation from an ordinary experience of daydreaming to an extreme form of dissociation known as dissociative identity disorder (DID). PTSD tends to fall on the lower end of the continuum, while other specified dissociative disorders (OSDD) fall on the higher end of the continuum—clients with OSDD have similar, but milder symptomatology to DID. Our overview primarily focuses on clients who identify at the OSDD end of the continuum.

Working with clients with dissociative parts can be challenging, as they may not be aware when fragmented emotional parts are present. These clients may also experience feelings of shame and fear that they are being judged (Boon et al., 2011); as such, they may not report hearing voices or internal conversations to their therapist (Martin, 2018; Steele et al., 2016). Therapists supporting these clients must do so delicately: first, by establishing and strengthening the therapeutic alliance; second, by validating the experience in light of the complex trauma that was experienced. With client consent and collaboration, the therapeutic work can focus on furthering the understanding of the function and intent of the fragmented emotional parts of self. One helpful intervention is establishing a meeting place such as Fraser's (1991) Dissociative Table, also known as the Meeting Place (Martin, 2012), so that the fragmented parts have a space free from danger and judgment to communicate and acknowledge the work that was required to hold and protect the experienced trauma(s) from the daily living self, and to recognize them compassionately and empathically (Boon et al., 2011; Knipe, 2018; Martin, 2018; Steele, 2018).

When fragmented parts of self come together for the first time, it is tempting for the more wounded parts of self to share the traumatic memories they have been holding onto, as well as the associated emotions and body sensations; however, it is imperative the therapist first gently guide the emotional parts toward awareness, safety, and stabilization (Knipe, 2018; Martin, 2018; Steele et al., 2016). It is more important at this juncture for parts to become aware that they are, in fact, parts of the personality system and to encourage empathy with an invitation for these parts to work collaboratively. As the client becomes aware of the fragmented emotional parts, therapists can help enhance the therapeutic work with the 3-D PoST, as it facilitates a holistic approach through activation of multiple areas of the brain, such as the areas responsible for visualization and touch. The 3-D PoST, with the guidance of the therapist, assists the client to externalize traumatic experiences. We have observed that such an invitation facilitates the client's ability to speak about emotional parts with an increased sense of safety. Should the client become overwhelmed, the 3-D PoST can help to physically separate emotional parts from daily living parts through a containing intervention and the use of guided questions.

In our experience, the greater the client's ability to access physical senses, the greater the depth of their work. Other clinicians such as Gonzalez and Mosquera (2012) have evidenced similar positive results with their *thinking outside the box* interventions when help-ing clients learn to understand their fragmented emotional parts of self. They do this by incorporating tools such as drawings, puppets, and plastic block construction toys; in these interventions, clients are encouraged to create their own drawings, assign parts to puppets, and/or build representations of parts or the self. The 3-D PoST technique bears similar-ities to Gonzalez and Mosquera's work, as it also encourages the client to recruit all their senses when identifying and describing their fragmented parts as a means to give them an alternate voice that words alone cannot convey. In addition, the use of clay sculptures helps facilitate grounding of the various parts of the personality system for clients when they present as dissociative (Steele et al., 2016; Martin, 2018). We have observed that when the client holds and moves the clay sculpture in their hands, and is invited to speak to what they notice about the sculpture—such as its weight, texture, temperature, size, and shape—they are better able to reorient to the present moment. By personifying the sculpture as a trau-matized part of self, the client gives voice to the phobic or avoidant part; this process of projection allows the material internalized within the personality system to become exter-nalized and known.

Assisting clients to tolerate a shared consciousness, communication, and cooperation among parts of self helps the client move more smoothly into the fourth phase of EMDR Therapy where they can reprocess past traumatic events with a reduced risk of triggering, shut-down, and dissociation (Martin, 2020). More specifically, parts may evaluate and erro-neously perceive initial interactions as threatening. It is likely that the parts fear they will be judged, criticized, manipulated, perceived as abnormal, or fear their mental illness will require hospitalization (Boon et al., 2011; Martin, 2018; Steele et al., 2016).

Traumatized clients may present as skeptical and verbalize distrust because of a lack of positive interpersonal experiences with other clinicians or health-care providers (Steele, 2018). In our experience, it is helpful to provide clients with a sense of hope by explaining your experience in working with other trauma survivors and having witnessed the positive impact of the therapeutic process. It is the astute therapist who recognizes the symptomatol-ogy of dissociation, and validates, as well as humanizes, the experience for the client. The therapist who approaches the work in a collaborative manner with the client on the journey toward healing fortifies the dyadic therapeutic relationship (Frewen & Lanius, 2015; Knipe, 2018; Steele et al., 2016).

ART THERAPY TOOL: THE 3-D POST

The concept for the 3-D PoST was a result of Hannah's curiosity about the complexity of the psyche. Hannah, a clinical social worker with a specialty in art therapy, wondered: "What would the fragmented parts of the self look like, if they could be viewed in 3-D? And, would the parts fit neatly together, or would they appear fragmented?" Over a period of six years, Hannah created clay objects without premeditated intention. The sculptures were displayed in her therapy room and she began inviting clients to select clay sculptures that reflected their parts of self in that moment. The clay sculptures thus became the blueprint to facilitate discussion and exploration of the self and its parts through an art therapy lens. The clay sculptures, like the Rorschach inkblots, use monochromaticity and abstract shapes to elicit an organic response from within the client's own internal experience. The 3-D sculptures provide the client with both a visual and textural canvas to project emotions and to explore and learn about their fragmented parts of self.

The 3-D PoST: Enhancing Projection and Visualization

The 3-D-PoST is a therapeutic tool that combines three-dimensional sculptures with a series of guided questions to enhance the dissociative client's ability to engage with the therapist, which has been observed to help clients move toward the ability to sustain a dual awareness and to engage in the bilateral stimulation (BLS) process of EMDR therapy. Additionally, guided questions are utilized to invite projection onto the clay sculptures while enabling clients to tap into the intrapsychic and complex landscape of the fragmented emotional parts of self. The sculptures have assisted both clients and therapists to gain a deeper understanding of the origin, roles, and intentions of daily living and emotional parts.

Using the 3-D PoST in Session

We developed a 3-D PoST kit with a number of considerations, including the number of sculptures, their texture, individual weight, ability to move and to maintain containment for traumatic memories. In essence, the sculptures foster an opportunity for clients to connect with the isolated emotional parts of self. We recommend providing clients with a number of differently shaped sculptures so as to provide the client with ample choice to help identify their emotional parts. The differentiation of shapes and textures has been observed to increase understanding and collaboration of misunderstood parts of self. For example, a round sculpture could represent unity in contrast to a square sculpture with many defined sides, which could potentially represent conflicting parts within the self. Additionally, the 3-D PoST kit includes clay sculptures that are broken, cracked, irregular, rough, weathered, or deformed, which may represent more vulnerable parts of self. Alternatively, sculptures that are smooth and soft with craters or bumps may create a kinesthetic sensation of comfort or warmth, and perhaps a connection to positive memories, associated emotions, and body sensations.

In other cases, clients might select a hollow sculpture to provide containment for emotions that are overflowing and difficult to contain internally. Additionally, containment sculptures have elicited conversations of emptiness—that the containers were void from emotion and feeling. It is important to provide a variety of containment-type sculptures; the size and weight of the clay sculptures should vary from an object that fits into the palm of the hand, to one that is so small it can be held between the thumb and index finger. In our experience, a small clay sculpture typically represents a young and vulnerable part. For instance, a traumatized client who learned that they did not have a voice as a young person, and that their actions were controlled by abuse, resonated with the small sculpture when it was held between their adult index finger and thumb.

It is important to consider the abstract presentation of the clay sculptures and to avoid using symbols or concrete images such as animals or people. We have found the abstract approach elicits more organic projections and associations. The final consideration of the 3-D clay sculptures is the expression of emotions. The 3-D PoST kit of clay sculptures has the potential to reflect parts of the self that experience fear, sadness, anger, anxiety, a sense of calm, emptiness, dysregulation, intense feelings of overwhelm, or specific traumatic memories. Two recommendations for acquiring your own set of 3-D Parts of Self-Tools are given as follows: (1) obtaining a set of pre-manufactured 3-D PoST clay sculptures, or (2) creating your own set of 3-D PoST sculptures. The following images are examples of clay sculptures we have used as part of the 3-D PoS Tool in Figures 8.2 and 8.3.

Figure 8.2 Set #1 of nine 3-D PoS tool kit sculptures.

Figure 8.3 Set #2 of nine 3-D PoS tool kit sculptures.

INCORPORATING ART THERAPY INVITATIONS WITH THE 3-D POST

To deepen the conversation and invite the client to bring awareness to the role and intentions of daily living and emotional parts, we suggest using the 3-D PoS Tool collaboratively with Martin's (2016) *Readiness Checklist for Phase 4 in Complex PTSD*, and the following three art therapy invitations: (a) visual mapping of emotions and body sensations, (b) exploration and understanding the role of parts with clay sculptures, and (c) creating a visual timeline of life events. Exploring the client's daily living self and emotional parts at the client's pace is imperative so as not to overwhelm the client and risk re-traumatizing them.

Art Invitation 1: Mapping Emotions and Body Sensations

With this initiative, the client is invited to internally scan their body, to notice any internal sensations, and to name the associated emotions. They are also encouraged to create a list of emotional parts and to keep a written record. They are then invited to project the experience onto the clay sculptures. We have observed traumatized clients typically identify with emotions such as sadness, fear, anger, feeling numb, having an urge to run away, self-harm, or to hide. These have been reported to have been felt individually or collectively within the personality system.

According to van der Kolk (2015), memories are not only stored in the brain; they are also stored in the body. From a Sensorimotor Psychotherapy perspective, it is important for the client to reconnect with their body (Ogden et al., 2006). In order to elicit an organic exploration of the fragmented emotional parts using the felt sense (Levine, 2019; Ogden et al., 2006), or *gut feeling*, the invitation to handle the sculptures is approached with curiosity and distance, as if from a wide-angle lens. This distance decreases the risk of overwhelming the client to the point of emotional dysregulation. Dissociation effectively disconnects the cognitive brain from the sensory input processing system, rendering the system dysfunctional. Without the ability to access cognitive functions, the client's emotional parts are, in a sense, abandoned and unable to reconnect to the neural networks that seek and receive cues of safety (Dana, 2018; Porges, 2017). Introducing the client to this concept might look like the following:

> **Client:** This sculpture represents sadness; it looks dull. It is small, doesn't move, and is spread wide with many holes.

THERAPIST: WHERE DO YOU FEEL THIS SENSATION IN YOUR BODY?

> **Client:** I feel it in my spine and stomach. This sculpture looks like how I feel.

It may also be helpful to invite the client to reflect on what drew them to the selected sculpture, and to describe the thoughts, emotions, and body sensations they notice in that moment. Additionally, the clinician can ask questions about the sculpture's tactile stability, texture, size, and movement.

Art Invitation 2: Exploring and Understanding the Role of Parts

Here, the client is encouraged to select sculptures that personify the roles in daily living, such as parent, partner, friend, daughter, or artist. The goal is to focus on the daily living roles of the client. First, the client is invited to create a list of roles they play in their current adult life; then they are asked to select clay sculptures that are representative of these roles. With their emotions, body sensations, and thoughts, they are asked to describe the stability, texture, size, and movement of the sculpture. Clients are also invited to write about what they notice, which might include their strengths, vulnerabilities, and how adult parts regulate emotions.

Art Invitation 3: Creating a Timeline of Life Events

Clients are invited, with the aid of the clay sculptures, to explore and identify emotional parts which may have formed at various stages of development. Specifically, the work is to support the client in identifying and creating a list of significant, or traumatic, experiences in their life, and then inviting them to select sculptures that resonate with these events. For instance, the client who selects a small clay sculpture is invited to first discuss what she notices when the sculpture is in her hand. Then, she is asked to talk about what drew her to the particular sculpture and what memory might be associated with the sculpture. Inviting the client to write about and then read aloud the associated memory provides her with an alternative perspective of emotional parts—perhaps to even view emotional parts with empathy and compassion. In our experience, this initiative provides a window into a room with all the parts, their strengths, vulnerabilities, talents, tasks.

Some emotional parts are more active than others (Martin, 2020; Steele et al., 2016); while others may be avoidant or phobic, and therefore invisible or hidden from the client's awareness. When an emotional part is unreachable, connection is not possible; these elusive, often traumatized parts need more time to evaluate safety before coming forward. Our 3-D PoST offers the client and their emotional parts an olive branch to come forward, as they recruit a tactile response, as well as other senses, as a means to experience safety.

USING THE 3-D POS TOOL KIT WITH THE EMDR READINESS CHECKLIST FOR PHASE 4 IN COMPLEX PTSD

The following discussion outlines how we use our art therapy-based 3-D PoST collaboratively with Martin's (2016) *EMDR Readiness Checklist for Phase 4 in Complex PTSD*. The checklist is made up of seven items to assess client readiness for EMDR reprocessing. We also include two additional steps to prepare clients for Phase Four of EMDR memory reprocessing. They are the psychoeducation of dissociation, and the role and intentions of parts in the personality system. We do this with the aid of the three art therapy invitations discussed earlier. For further reading on the standardized EMDR protocols for preparation of Phase Four, see Shapiro (2017). At the conclusion of sessions with clients, the therapist takes photographs of the layout of parts and notes dialogue that clients identified as important. This gives the client the opportunity to review the evolution of the work completed among parts. The 3-D PoST appears to provide clients with a visual of emotional parts and an alternate way to give parts voice.

Martin (2016) refers to daily living parts as apparently normal parts (ANP) in her checklist. We have utilized the term daily living parts as it aligns with Steele's (2018) updated work. In this context ANP and daily living parts are synonymous.

Introducing Dissociation and Parts of Self with Clara

Providing psychoeducation to our clients helps humanize the feeling of constant fear and associated avoidant and phobic reactions (Fisher, 2017). For instance, Clara, a 65-year-old survivor of childhood incest, presented in therapy with symptoms of anxiety of "unknown origins." The symptoms were pervasive and impacted her ability to engage in social activities with her close friends. The therapist introduced parts of the personality system with the following dialogue:

> *Many people think that because we have one body, our self is also one. The truth is that our personality is made up of a number of parts which develop from an early age. For example, you may have a part that becomes angry when you feel someone is taking advantage of your good nature, such as a protector part, or a part that experienced trauma at a young age by a caregiver or another person of trust; this might represent a younger part of the self. All people are structured this way, and carry memories of experiences as a means to help protect the present-day adult self to cope with everyday life. People are often not aware of this because these parts are good at what they do. However, when the fragmented parts of self, the brain, and nervous system sense danger, whether it is real or perceived, it activates the defensive system in the same way it did when the trauma was actually happening to you. This can often lead to dissociation. During our work together, I am inviting you to explore these aspects of yourself and to learn more about your unique internal structure.*

As we discuss each item in Martin's (2016) checklist, we will demonstrate how Clara and her therapist incorporated 3-D PoST to prepare her for EMDR Phase Four reprocessing.

ITEM 1: DISSOCIATIVE TABLE AND THE PROCESS OF REALIZATION

The first component of Martin's (2016) checklist invites the client to realize and become aware of the role of emotional parts, as well as the daily functioning parts. Fraser's (1991) Dissociative Table Technique is a visualization intervention which invites the client to identify and access emotional parts and bring them to a room, or place where no harm can come to any of the parts, and facilitate the process of realization that they are part of one person—a person who experienced trauma(s) (Martin, 2016). This section of the checklist is outlined as follows:

Dissociative Table and the Process of Realization

_____ The parts of the personality have been accessed and identified

_____ Isolation among the parts has been reduced

_____ There is at least a growing understanding that they are all part of the same person

_____ Persecutory and Protector Parts have been treated enough to have at least a beginning sense that they are part of this one person and that the traumas happened to them too

Clara's therapist first introduced her to the psychoeducation of dissociation and emotional parts from a wide-angle lens, as to not overwhelm her with a "strange" conversation about a multi-faceted personality. Approaching the conversation this way provided Clara with time to understand the information and apply it to herself. She began learning the origins of emotional parts, the reasons they exist, and, in many cases, their intentions. Her therapist's role was to guide and help foster a greater awareness and understanding of all of Clara's daily living and emotional parts.

Using the Dissociative Table Technique (Fraser, 1991), Clara's therapist invited her to visualize a meeting room with a table and chairs to facilitate a space for parts of self to communicate. Sometimes emotional parts come into the room, and when this occurred for Clara, she was invited to simply notice the parts that show up—to be curious toward all the parts which come into the space. For some clients, the image of a table may be triggering, and therefore Martin (2020) recommends a more generic invitation for a client to visualize a meeting space. In our experience, reframing the table to a meeting space has elicited images such as a campfire with logs for chairs, or the base of a mountain under a canopy of trees. These clients have reported that such imagery feels calmer and safer.

Fraser's (1991) Dissociative Table Technique is typically only introduced once the client is able to fully engage in a visualization technique such as the Calm Place exercise using BLS (see Martin, 2012 for a complete script of the Dissociative Table Technique). In her session, Clara visualized the Calm Place, and was invited to turn her awareness to a meeting place of her choosing that included the right number of seats for the parts who showed up. Clara was asked to describe the room aloud with details using all five senses.

Martin (2012) notes that some clients experience difficulty engaging in imagery work. We postulate that in these instances, the client's difficulty may be a form of dissociation, such as depersonalization and derealization facilitated by avoidant and phobic emotional parts. Martin recommends the therapist encourage the client to access all their senses, such as olfactory, kinesthetic, auditory, and gustatory. Encouraging our client to project the emotional parts of self and the associated emotions and body sensations into a tangible object such as the 3-D PoST provides parts with a safe place to have a *voice* using projection to enrich the narrative and deepen the understanding of the burden carried by the parts. We believe that with this enriched understanding comes a greater sense of compassion, empathy, and eventually integration. When Clara's therapist incorporated the 3-D PoST with the Dissociative Table, she described her emotional parts as existing as a list on her back that was visible to the world, but not herself (Figure 8.4).

ITEM 2: CO-CONSCIOUSNESS

The second item in Martin's (2016) checklist outlined below works to address the presence of co-consciousness between daily living and emotional parts. Introducing Clara to the concept of co-consciousness was overwhelming at first, and with the guidance of her therapist, she was better able to understand the internal dynamics of her own emotional parts of self. Clara's therapist reminded her that emotional parts tend to come forward without conscious awareness of the daily living part. When this occurs, the potential for dysregulating emotional symptoms—such as increased anxiety, dissociation, and difficulty in making simple decisions—becomes more pronounced (Fisher, 2017; Steele et al., 2016).

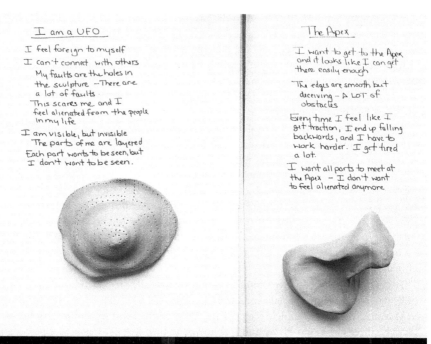

I am a UFO

I feel foreign to myself
I can't connect with others
My faults are the holes in
the sculpture —There are
a lot of faults.
This scares me and I
feel alienated from the people
in my life

I am visible, but invisible
The parts of me are layered
Each part wants to be seen, but
I don't want to be seen.

The Apex

I want to get to the Apex
and it looks like I can get
there easily enough

The edges are smooth but
deceiving – A LOT of
obstacles

Every time I feel like I
get traction, I end up falling
backwards, and I have to
work harder. I get tired
a lot.

I want all parts to meet at
the Apex – I don't want
to feel alienated anymore

Figure 8.4 Illustration of sample 3-D PoST sculptures utilized with clients.

Co-consciousness

_____ ANP knows the EPs and can stay present when EPs are activated

_____ EPs know ANP and other EPs and can stay present when another part is activated

Clara experienced a number of instances of conflicting co-consciousness in the early stages of her work. She reported feeling overwhelmed, and her therapist explained the conflict with the following analogy: *think of the emotional parts as connected by a thread, and as each part works to get away from the other, they are, in essence, simultaneously running in different directions and it results in the entire personality system to become frustrated, and eventually exhausted.* Clara's avoidant and phobic emotional parts are examples of conflicting parts that function to protect the personality system from re-experiencing the trauma. These parts were untrusting of the invitation to come together, and initially resisted the process; Clara was invited to simply notice them. She was then invited to focus on the parts that came together to the table, and to observe one another with an invitation to be curious. Conversation was not necessary; in fact, the goal, at this juncture, was to invite Clara's daily living self and emotional parts to learn how to be concurrently present—in dual awareness (Martin, 2016). As Clara progressed in her work, the daily living self and emotional parts began to communicate co-consciously, which helped her to move more cohesively toward healing.

Using the art therapy invitations described above, it is helpful to explore co-consciousness of parts by inviting the client to describe both adult present-day parts and emotional parts by selecting sculptures from the 3-D PoS Tool that represent the parts that are present in-session. The client is invited to hold or place the sculptures where they feel safe. Here, Clara selected three clay sculptures; one represented a younger Clara, the other a teenage Clara, and the third represented an adult version of Clara. She was invited to talk about what she noticed internally when all the parts were set in front of her. Clara indicated that it would feel better if the younger part of self was shielded from the teenage part, and that the teenage part wanted nothing to do with the process. In response to this, Clara built a paper wall to separate the intimidating part from the vulnerable part. The 3-D PoST was helpful for communicating what Clara could not put into words; the clay sculptures provided the parts of self an alternate way to describe roles, intentions, and needs. Clara learned that she had choice, that she could move the clay sculptures, and even create a barrier to help facilitate co-consciousness that eventually provided a space for communication, cooperation, and collaboration.

ITEM 3: COMMUNICATION, COOPERATION, AND COLLABORATION

Items 1 and 2 of the checklist help the client learn about their daily living and emotional parts as well as increasing co-consciousness. With practice and support from the therapist, the client increases the ability of the daily living part to remain present, even when emotional parts are activated (Martin, 2016). The third item supports the client by inviting increased dialogue between parts, as well as inviting parts to work together. The goal is for all the parts to eventually facilitate safety and stabilization when the client becomes emotionally activated.

Communication, Cooperation, and Collaboration

_____ There is dialogue among the parts
_____ Parts are willing to work with each other
_____ There is at least a growing sense that all parts experienced everything
_____ The ANP is not the only part that facilitates stabilization when needed

We have observed clients are more curious when invited to select a sculpture from the 3-D PoST that resonates with an emotional part. Reflecting back to our submarine metaphor, we invite clients to imagine the submarine has come to port, and the parts of self are invited to leave the submarine and to come together, first, to learn about each other, and then eventually invited to work together. This means that the part that was locked away in the damaged compartment of the submarine, who was, and continues to be, traumatized, is invited to the table and has a voice. This emotional part might become overwhelmed, and as such remains unaware that danger is no longer present. Client self-perceptions fluctuate from day to day; therefore, we recommend they be invited to practice this process at the beginning of each session to gain a better understanding of the needs of the daily living and emotional parts.

To begin this process Clara was invited to select a sculpture that resonated with an emotional part that often did not feel safe—she selected a small ball with visible cracks. She was then asked where she would like to place the sculpture on a blank piece of paper, and where the other emotional parts, represented by other sculptures from our tool, could be placed on the paper. "How do all the parts feel with where they are presently?" is a typical question that Clara was asked. She reported the younger part wanted to be shielded from the older, angrier parts. To help instill a feeling of safety, Clara and her therapist constructed a vault with construction paper. She also created a door, complete with a keyhole, and a paper key to work the lock. From this position, Clara's younger self could contribute to the conversation while feeling an increased sense of safety from intimidation and harm by the angrier parts.

Clara was able to engage in the dissociative table exercise, and hold co-consciousness with all the parts that were present in the session. She was able to identify what she and her emotional parts required to facilitate communication, cooperation, and collaboration. As she and her emotional parts became increasingly familiar with one another, Clara assigned alternate names to these parts: *Younger Clara* and *Angry Clara*. We followed her lead, as she was the expert most familiar with her daily living and emotional parts. An interesting observation was the presence of barriers to communication, cooperation, and collaboration among parts: Younger Clara needed the vault for safety before any conversation could occur. However, as Adult Clara, Younger Clara, and the other emotional parts became increasingly more familiar, the need for the vault disappeared. Without the 3-D PoST sculptures and the creation of the vault, it may have been more challenging, if not impossible, for Clara to engage and eventually collaborate with other emotional parts. Figure 8.5 is an example of communication, cooperation, and collaboration between Younger Clara, Teenage Clara, and Adult Clara.

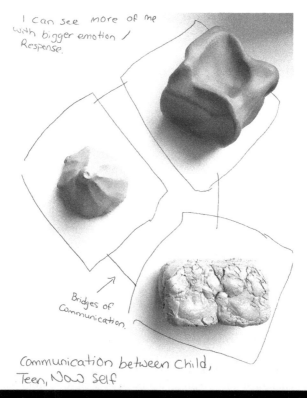

Figure 8.5 Illustration of 3-D PoST sculptures utilized with clients.

ITEM 4: COMPASSION

This item of the checklist may seem to be self-explanatory, but the process is often challenging for clients to realize (Martin, 2016). Clara reported as if a *monster* resided within her; that she was damaged and unlovable. Feeling as if what happened to her as a young person was deserved, she internalized an emotional part that reminded her of the abuser. This emotional part communicated that she too would abuse young girls herself. She reported feeling terrified and believed the intrusive memories of the abuse and the abuser were a reminder not to *lose control*. She felt as though this critical part communicated the consequences of vulnerability.

Compassion

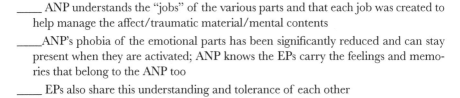

____ ANP understands the "jobs" of the various parts and that each job was created to help manage the affect/traumatic material/mental contents

____ANP's phobia of the emotional parts has been significantly reduced and can stay present when they are activated; ANP knows the EPs carry the feelings and memories that belong to the ANP too

____ EPs also share this understanding and tolerance of each other

Using the 3-D PoST sculptures, Clara was able to connect a caring part with a vulnerable teenage part, and hold both of them compassionately. She did this by selecting a clay sculpture that represented each part, and was invited to position them in a place that would feel comfortable enough to hold a conversation. In this case, Clara placed one sculpture in each hand in front of her at chest height. She was asked "how does each part feel about this placement?" She reported that the teenage part noticed it was positioned close to the heart, and knowing that Adult Clara was holding it, there was a feeling of safety and protection. The caring part noted the ease of conversation because of the felt connection among parts.

This type of connection was not always the case for Clara and the emotional parts. The conversation among parts was often angry and invalidating particularly for Adult Clara and the teenage part. This part resented the empathy that Younger Clara received from the caring part. Why were the teenage part's experiences never validated? Focusing on bringing both the parts together, Clara was invited to select representative sculptures. Each part was positioned at opposite ends of the room, and each was invited to speak about what the experience was like. The teenage part and the caring part communicated about how they felt and what they needed from the other. Over time, with increased dialogue, the sculptures representing parts and traumatic experiences started to be positioned closer together.

ITEM 5: TIME ORIENTATION

This section of Martin's (2016) checklist is the process for the client to begin to realize and construct a cohesive timeline of important life events. Correcting the distorted perception of time that the wounded emotional parts hold is delicate work. Correcting time distortions too quickly risks re-traumatization of not only the emotional parts but also the daily living part. We can do this slowly using the 3-D PoST by inviting the client to select a sculpture that resonates with the wounded part and inviting it to talk about what it understands about the personality system. Additionally, we begin to ask guiding questions about what the part notices today, and how it might know that it is no longer in danger.

Time Orientation

_____ Correct time orientation has been established with all emotional parts and they can maintain dual awareness, at least for a brief period of time while the memory is activated (clinician knows that when dual awareness is lost, reprocessing stops)

_____ EPs know that the memory that will be worked on is indeed a memory

The therapist approached time orientation with Clara by inviting her to select a sculpture that represented Younger Clara and invited this part to talk about itself. Clara selected a ball-shaped sculpture that fit between her thumb and index finger. She was asked guided questions such as: *how old are you? Now that you are aware that there are other parts in the system, what is that like for you?* Younger Clara identified as eight years old, and felt very small, scared, and unheard. She often feared that she would be *hurt*. Adult Clara, hearing Younger Clara speak, started to cry. She noted that there was a part of her that felt like a small child, and it has held a secret. *For a long time, I felt as if I was crazy.* With communication and collaboration among parts the therapist was able to begin the process of correcting the distorted time orientation; this helped Clara to understand that the trauma happened to her. Younger Clara compartmentalized the abuse so that Adult Clara could attend to the daily functioning of the self. It is in this conversation that Younger Clara asked to change sculptures to show how she was feeling; she selected a larger, square sculpture with an opening at one end, and communicated that it could hold the *secret*, and Adult Clara could *get to it whenever she wanted*.

Clients with high levels of dissociation typically experience increased phobia of emotional parts (Boon et al., 2011; Martin, 2018; Steele et al., 2016). In these cases, it is recommended that therapists guide the focus back to the first three items on the checklist. Addressing time orientation without first having "buy-in" from avoidant and phobic parts, risks re-traumatizing the client.

ITEM 6: COGNITIVE ERRORS MAINTAINING THE DISSOCIATION HAVE BEEN IDENTIFIED AND TREATED

Cognitive errors can be likened to a faulty sonar in a submarine—an echo of past experiences that continue to detect danger, even when it is no longer present. Correcting cognitive errors with Clara was complicated work, as her daily living and emotional parts were challenged to shift responses away from a familiar, but maladaptive, path. Younger Clara presented during a session and communicated finding no point in speaking about what happened because it always felt unheard. This statement is an echo of how this part recalls being treated; this response is the adoption of the cognitive error (Frewen & Lanius, 2015; Martin, 2020; Steele et al., 2016).

Cognitive Errors Maintaining the Dissociation Have Been Identified and Treated

_____Cognitive errors have been identified and repaired so reprocessing can occur.

The therapist invited Younger Clara to pick a sculpture that looked like how she felt. She once again selected the small clay ball that could be held between her thumb and index finger. The therapist invited the caring part and Adult Clara to the discussion, and to select a representative sculpture. Clara was invited to place the sculptures in a way that felt comfortable; all parts were placed on the table in front of her in the shape of a triangle, each part facing the other. The therapist talked about the importance of each part to speak and be heard by the others. Younger Clara was invited to begin by drawing or constructing a connective path between all the parts. This suggestion provided Younger Clara with a means to communicate the feeling of connection and disconnection among parts that they were unable to put into words. Adult Clara and the caring part were invited to speak to Younger Clara's needs, and to help this part to see that all parts do listen and can work collaboratively, and to help Younger Clara orient to the present when the part was dysregulated.

Using the 3-D PoST and art helped to facilitate conversations such as these among Clara's parts. It was a slow process which took place over a number of sessions. Some sessions included an angry teenage part, in which Younger Clara reported feeling as if it was doing something wrong to make it so angry. To help Younger Clara, the therapist suggested that all parts select a clay sculpture that reflected how they felt, and to position them accordingly on a table. Younger Clara, Adult Clara, and the caring part felt comfortable together and were placed on the table in front of Clara, and the angry teenage part felt more comfortable at the farthest corner of the table, away from the other parts. The therapist then supportively facilitated conversation with Clara and all the parts using guided questions. Art and expression developed cooperation among parts, and Younger Clara slowly started to realize that it was in fact no longer "stuck" in a trauma bubble; that it was the angry teenage part that needed extra support, and reacted negatively to *echoes* from its own memories of past trauma. As the parts began coming closer together in conversation, so too did the clay sculptures.

ITEM 7: DISSOCIATIVE PHOBIAS ARE REDUCED ENOUGH TO BEGIN REPROCESSING

As Clara and her therapist moved through Martin's (2016) checklist she noticed that the walls and fortresses that were once necessary to protect the vulnerable emotional parts from one another disappeared. When all parts can see and hear one another with compassion and empathy, they are better able to support and hold parts that continue to re-live the pain of associated trauma(s). It is likely at this point that emotional parts and the daily living part realize that the trauma happened to Clara—Clara as the whole self. The trauma happened to the entire personality system, despite later being isolated into a trauma bubble as a form of coping.

Dissociative Phobias Are Reduced Enough to Begin Reprocessing

____Protector and Persecutory parts have personified some of the trauma and are allowing the system to have access to this material

____ANP and EP phobias to the therapist are reduced enough

____Phobia to the traumatic material is decreased.

Clara's emotional parts coped with symptoms of CPTSD by building fortified walls around those parts that were holding the trauma, careful to protect the daily living Adult Clara. Her therapist's ability to meet Clara where she and her emotional parts were, with compassion and empathy, she could begin to feel comfortable and even safe. This helped strengthen the therapeutic alliance, and carved a path toward readiness for Phase Four of EMDR memory reprocessing with little, to no interference by emotional parts.

The 3-D PoST was helpful for Clara as she learned to reduce dissociative phobias through communication with the protector and persecutory parts and bring them out of the shadows of their trauma bubbles and orient them to the present. Here, the clay sculptures helped Clara externalize and personify these parts that she feared and learned about the cost of protection for the entire personality system. What was once secret is out in the open for all parts to begin the work of processing. Relying on conversation alone is not enough in trauma work. The 3-D PoST can metaphorically communicate what Clara and Younger Clara could not put into words. As in the other items of Martin's (2016) checklist, Clara positioned the clay sculptures in a configuration that felt safe and comfortable—as parts continued to communicate and collaborate, Adult Clara noted a sense of connectedness with the emotional parts, which was even made more evident as the clay sculptures from the 3-D PoST were positioned close together in a circle all facing one another. With this, the therapist asked the parts if they were prepared to reprocess the traumatic memories that for so long dominated Clara's narrative.

SUMMARY OF CLARA'S WORK

Clara was typically fearful of the content of her traumatic memories and experiences. She believed they defined her and that she would one day too abuse others, as she was abused. Her work utilized our 3-D PoST with each section of Martin's (2016) checklist to facilitate a realization, a co-consciousness, communication, and collaboration. Giving her emotional parts a physical shape, she noticed feeling comfortable and eventually safe. Safe that she could project her emotional parts and compartmentalize them with the clay sculptures, while providing these parts the space to communicate. Eventually, the compartments and the walls came down, and Clara was able to have open and honest communication with all parts, all while holding the thoughts, emotions, memories, and body sensations of past traumas.

Clara's daily living and emotional parts agreed that she could begin reprocessing the traumatic events of her life. Clara and the therapist could now move to Phase Four of EMDR therapy. We invited parts that wanted to be present co-consciously when Adult Clara reprocessed traumatic memories. It was important to support Clara's emotional parts in this way to ensure that healing and eventually integration could occur in a compassionate and caring way.

DISCUSSION

In this chapter we collaborated on our joint knowledge and experience in working with survivors of trauma who are on the OSSD continuum of dissociation. The clients we worked with were our teachers in developing our 3-D PoS Tool, which is currently in preliminary development. By inviting clients to explore their internal experiences of daily living and emotional parts by first being curious, they eventually learned the role of their emotional parts, which was to protect the self through a fragmentation of parts when faced with trauma (Martin, 2018; Knipe, 2018; Steele et al., 2016). These emotional parts exist in a trauma bubble, unaware that the trauma is no longer occurring. Utilizing Martin's (2016) *EMDR Readiness Checklist for Phase 4 in Complex PTSD* with our 3-D PoS Tool, we were able to introduce a three-dimensional reflection of the self in a more concrete way.

As discussed, the tool provided another avenue for clients to communicate what might have previously been uncommunicable. Using our 3-D PoS Tool as we moved through the checklist, we invited clients to physically position their daily living and emotional parts together, and to invite them to talk about the experience by asking guiding questions. In some instances, clients constructed or covered parts of the self that were frightened or felt unsafe. Gradually, as parts were able to hold co-consciousness, they began communicating, cooperating, and collaborating. This led to conversations about lived experiences through the lens of compassion. Moving through the checklist, the 3-D PoS Tool demonstrated its versatility in helping emotional parts become aware of time orientation so that the client could begin noticing and correcting cognitive errors that were formed as a result of years of dissociative responses. We noticed that by understanding the intentions and roles of emotional parts, clients dissociated less, and felt less avoidant and phobic both in-session and between sessions. By placing all the parts of the self together in a physical meeting place, clients appeared to engage more readily than by visualizing alone. When daily living and emotional parts responded cohesively and with shared awareness, clients appeared to be able to engage in Phase Four of EMDR therapy, and reprocess traumatic memories on a deeper level—in many cases with little resistance from the emotional parts of self.

Our hope is that this tool will assist therapists in supporting their clients who struggle with the debilitating symptoms of CPTSD. Humans are complex and unique structures which make up the self and are in a constant flux of change. As Martin (2018) and Steele et al. (2016) have outlined, individuals who experience complex, developmental trauma have a defense action system that is overly activated. As a result, these clients develop emotional parts that are not oriented to time. Much like the submarine metaphor, the traumatized compartment is closed off and inaccessible from the remainder of the ship and its crew. Closing off that compartment in this way means there is no access to real-time information. When the submarine lands at its port of destination, opening that compartment too quickly risks damaging the rest of the ship. It is for this reason the crew attempts to open the sealed compartment slowly while simultaneously assessing the damage. Once the compartment has been opened and explored, the entire crew can then be updated on the functionality of the ship. While humans are not submarines, the reaction to compartmentalize is similar, regardless of the vessel. It is important to remember that closing off compartments is in fact temporary, and our role as supportive and empathetic therapists is to show clients the possibilities that await them.

APPENDIX A

Readiness Checklist for Phase Four in Complex PTSD (© Kathleen M. Martin 2016)

The typical Readiness Checklist applies along with the dissociation and dissociative phobias which have been treated "enough" so the following conditions exist:

Dissociative Table and the Process of Realization

____ The parts of the personality have been accessed and identified
____ Isolation among the parts has been reduced
____ There is at least a growing understanding that they are all part of the same person
____ Persecutory and Protector Parts have been treated enough to have at least a beginning sense that they are part of this one person and the traumas happened to them too

Co-consciousness

____ ANP knows the EPs and can stay present when EPs are activated
____ EPs know ANP and other EPs and can stay present when another part is activated

Communication, Cooperation, and Collaboration

____ There is dialogue among the parts
____ Parts are willing to work with each other
____ There is at least a growing sense that all parts experienced everything
____ The ANP is not the only part that facilitates stabilization when needed

Compassion

____ ANP understands the "jobs' of the various parts and that each job was created to help manage the affect/traumatic material/mental contents
____ANP's phobia to the emotional parts has been significantly reduced and can stay present when they are activated; ANP knows the EPs carry the feelings and memories that belong to the ANP too
____ EPs also share in this understanding and tolerance of each other

Time Orientation

____ Correct time orientation has been established with all emotional parts and they can maintain dual awareness at least for a brief period of time while the memory is activated (clinician knows that when dual awareness is lost, reprocessing stops)
____ EPs know that the memory that will be worked on is indeed a memory

Cognitive Errors Maintaining the Dissociation Have Been Identified and Treated

_____Cognitive errors have been identified and repaired so reprocessing can occur

Dissociative Phobias Are Reduced Enough to Begin Reprocessing

_____Protector and Persecutory parts have personified some of the trauma and are allowing the system to have access to this material
_____ANP and EP phobias to the therapist are reduced enough
_____Phobia to the traumatic material is decreased

REFERENCES

Boon, S., Steele, K., & van Der Hart, O. (2011). *Coping with trauma-related dissociation: Skills training for patients and therapists* (Norton series on interpersonal neurobiology). W.W. Norton & Company.

Dana, D. (2018). *The Polyvagal theory in therapy: engaging the rhythm of regulation* (Norton series on interpersonal neurobiology). W.W. Norton & Company.

Farina, B., & Liotti, G. (2013). Does a traumatic-dissociative dimension exist? A review of dissociative processes and symptoms in developmental trauma spectrum disorders. *Clinical Neuropsychiatry*, *10*(1), 11–18. Retrieved from https://www.associazionearpas.it/wp-content/uploads/2021/09/Farina_Liotti_2013.pdf

Fisher, J. (2017). *Healing the fragmented selves of trauma survivors: Overcoming internal self-alienation*. Taylor & Francis.

Fraser, G. A. (1991). The dissociative table technique: A strategy for working with ego states in dissociative disorders and ego-state therapy. *Dissociation: Progress in the Dissociative Disorders*, *4*(4), 205–213.

Frewen, P., & Lanius, R. (2015). *Healing the traumatized self: consciousness, neuroscience, treatment (Norton series on interpersonal neurobiology)*. W.W. Norton & Company.

Gonzalez, A., & Mosquera, D. (2012). *EMDR and dissociation: The progressive approach*. AI.

Knipe, J. (2018). *EMDR toolbox: Theory and treatment of complex PTSD and dissociation*. Springer Publishing Company.

Levine, P. [Somatic Experiencing International]. (2019, August 16). *What is felt sense?* [Video]. You Tube. https://www.youtube.com/watch?v=ZBLe84U7AaM

Martin, K. M. (2012). How to use Fraser's dissociative table technique to access and work with emotional parts of the personality. *Journal of EMDR Practice and Research*, *6*(4), 179–186. https://doi.org/10.1891/1933-3196.6.4.179

Martin, K. (2016). *Readiness checklist for phase 4 in complex PTSD* [Measurement instrument]. Retrieved from https://warrentechnologiesgroup.com/index.php/ct-menu-item-24/downloads/category/6-edmr-week-01?download=77:edmr-week-01

Martin, K. (2018). Structural dissociation in the treatment of trauma and eating disorders. In A. Seubert, P. Virdi (Eds.), *Trauma-informed approaches to eating disorders* (pp. 221–233). Springer Publishing Company.

Martin, K. (2020, January 18). *Treating complex trauma with EMDR therapy and structural dissociation theory: Effectively treating "parts": Module 2: Fraser's dissociative table technique: When and how to use it to identify and heal emotional parts of the personality*. [Webinar]. Retrieved from http://kmccs.com/webinar.maml?page=webinar_winter_2022

Møller, L., Bach, B., Augsburger, M., Elklit, A., Søgaard, U., & Simonsen, E. (2021). Structure of ICD-11 complex PTSD and relationship with psychoform and somatoform dissociation. *European Journal of Trauma & Dissociation*, 100233. https://doi.org/10.1016/j.ejtd.2021.100233

Ogden, P., Pain, C., & Fisher, J. (2006). A sensorimotor approach to the treatment of trauma and dissociation. *Psychiatric Clinics*, *29*(1), 263–279. Retrieved from https://citeseerx.ist.psu.edu/viewdoc/download?doi=10.1.1.596.861&rep=rep1&type=pdf

Porges, S. W. (2017). *The pocket guide to the polyvagal theory: The transformative power of feeling safe*. W.W. Norton & Co.

Shapiro, F. (2017). *Eye movement desensitization and reprocessing (EMDR) therapy: Basic principles, protocols, and procedures*. Guilford Publications.

Steele, K., Boon, S., & van der Hart, O. (2016). *Treating trauma-related dissociation: A practical, integrative approach (Norton series on interpersonal neurobiology)*. W.W. Norton & Company.

Steele, K. (2018, February 9). *Organizing disorganization: Case conceptualization for structural dissociation*. [Webinar]. ISSTD. Retrieved from https://www.ce-credit.com/courses/102274/organizing-disorganization-case-conceptualization-for-structural-dissociation

van der Hart, O., Nijenhuis, E., & Steele, K. (2006). *The haunted self: Structural dissociation and the treatment of chronic traumatization* (Norton Series on Interpersonal Neurobiology). W.W. Norton & Company.

van der Hart, O., Groenendijk, M., Gonzalez, A., Mosquera, D., & Solomon, R. (2013). Dissociation of the personality and EMDR therapy in complex trauma-related disorders: Applications in the stabilization phase. *Journal of EMDR Practice and research*, *7*(2), 81–94. Retrieved from http://www.onnovdhart.nl/articles/EMDR_7-2_R1_A3_001-013.pdf

van der Kolk, B. A. (2015). *The body keeps the score: Brain, mind, and body in the healing of trauma*. Penguin Books.

CHAPTER 9

DANCING MINDFULNESS: FLOWING SYNCHRONICITIES WITH EMDR THERAPY

Jamie Marich

As a child, I regularly retreated to the basement in my parents' house, put some music on my Mickey Mouse record player, and danced for myself. Sometimes I would dance right there in my bedroom, even though I didn't have much space. While my bedroom is also where I took refuge in my imagination, especially with dolls and other toys, that form of play was more about escape—dance was always about being present with whatever I was feeling. By the time I was a pre-teen, I was using the cassette tape deck, and I cued up music to which I channeled the spirit of figure skating, the sport I loved so much. I expressed the feeling of the music on my face and with my body. Whenever I moved like that, everything felt okay in my body, even though schoolyard bullies, spiritually abusive systems, and family discord filled the world around me. In my own dance—not the dance that my teacher or figure skating coaches gave me—I felt safe and free.

When people ask me how I discovered the practice of Dancing Mindfulness, I share this reflection. The practice is so organic, it found me…reaching out its hand of healing when my child-self had few places to express emotion appropriately and healthfully. Even though Dancing Mindfulness is now a phrase I am known, as the creator of the Dancing Mindfulness approach to expressive arts therapy and author of a 2015 book called *Dancing Mindfulness: A Creative Path to Healing and Transformation*, in no way is Dancing Mindfulness mine. Dance and mindfulness are two of the oldest and most innate healing practices on our planet and have been accessed by a wide variety of people and cultures since the dawn of time, in a variety of forms. In creating a community around the practice, which led to facilitator training programs for therapists and educators, and the book that works with people on how to develop a personal Dancing Mindfulness practice in their daily life, I've simply presented a way to make these practices more accessible to modern audiences.

This chapter on Dancing Mindfulness appears in a book on EMDR therapy and the creative arts because the practices of Dancing Mindfulness can be useful adjuncts for EMDR therapists, in their clinical practices or as part of their personal plans for wellness. Indeed, the manner in which I developed Dancing Mindfulness as a formal practice that can be taught in a class, integrated into individual psychotherapy, or adopted as a manner of informal mindfulness practice in one's daily life directly flowed from my work as an EMDR therapist. Learning what it means to "go with that" is one of the greatest personal fruits in receiving EMDR therapy as a client and then going on to share it as a therapist, author, and trainer. I now live my life in a constant spirit of "go with that." My personal Dancing Mindfulness practice allows for that, and in Dancing Mindfulness experiences that we facilitate for others, it's very common to hear us use the phrase "go with that." As you will discover in this chapter, EMDR led the way for me to create the system of Dancing Mindfulness. For me, mindfulness practice can never be separated from EMDR therapy. As EMDR therapist, I hope that my sharing of this fusion will open up new possibilities for you.

DOI: 10.4324/9781003156932-10

THE MINDFUL ROOTS OF EMDR THERAPY

Prior to presenting for my first round of EMDR therapy in 2004, I had no exposure to Eastern meditation. Having grown up in an ultra-conservative Christian household, anything that was "from the East" was considered to be dangerous, and this programming kept me away from the gifts of mindfulness and yoga practice for a long time. I worked for the Catholic Church in post-war Bosnia-Hercegovina from 2000 to 2003, and there I was exposed to several forms of contemplative Christian meditation. Yet the EMDR emphasis on *go with that* and *noticing without judgment*, combined with my first EMDR therapist's passion for the holistic healing arts, prompted me to give mindfulness meditation and yoga a try for themselves. Of course, EMDR's role in helping to deprogram so many of the unhealthy and exclusionary messages from the fundamentalism in which I was raised and it certainly helped me to be more open.

When I began reading and practicing mindfulness in a secular context, largely through the work of Jon Kabat-Zinn, I started to realize just how much *mindfulness* really was at the heart of EMDR therapy. I made the same connection with yoga practice. The first time I took a yoga class and especially savored the ending meditation period, I thought to myself, "Every EMDR therapist should do this. If not for their own mental health, it will also teach them how to do resourcing and visualizations better." As I began re-reading Shapiro's books in preparation to do an EMDR-related doctoral dissertation and then later go on to teach EMDR, I recognized that there was more to the story than her mythic *walk in the park* that led to the discovery of EMDR therapy. Indeed, Shapiro was an avid practitioner of mind-body practices, including mindfulness meditation, an interest that seemed to result from using all available forms of healing to address her cancer diagnosis. She identifies one such teacher as Stephen Levine, a well-known Buddhist teacher on the West Coast and pioneer in the field of death and dying. From Levine, who passed away in 2016, Shapiro would have learned practices like classic mindfulness meditation and the particular form of it called *Vipassana*, which translates from Sanskrit as "clear seeing" or "before the eyes." Such clear seeing, or insight, results from not engaging in excessive analysis of what emerges in the present moment, rather following the flow of whatever emerged.

In essence, *go with that…*

There are many definitions in the modern era for mindfulness. Although considered to be the heart of Buddhist meditation practices and a component of yoga, another conscious practice that also originated in ancient India, there is nothing uniquely Buddhist about mindfulness. Many global traditions, even Christianity, have some type of teaching or specific teachers have shared practices with their communities that speak to the importance of being in the moment, being with the breath, or simply being with what *is*. Scholars who approach mindfulness from more of a classic Buddhist place may differ in how they define it from those whose practice may be defined as more secular. A task force composing both styles of practitioners developed this consensus definition of mindfulness: the self-regulation of attention to the conscious awareness of one's immediate experiences while adopting an attitude of curiosity, openness, and acceptance (Bishop et al., 2004).

Although the modern marketing around the secularization of mindfulness likes to emphasize its qualities as a relaxation technique, mindfulness is not just about relaxation. In fact, some people may never be able to use mindfulness as a vehicle for relaxation. We can, however, use this practice to help us be in or return to whatever is present right now. And as it relates to trauma therapy, that may include cultivating the skill of being present with difficult emotions or sensations instead of constantly shutting them down, pushing them away, or dissociating from them. In his landmark work on trauma, van der Kolk (2014) defines mindfulness as "being able to hover calmly and objectively over our thoughts, feelings, and emotions, and then take our time to respond." Both Porges (2011) and van der Kolk note that mindfulness can help to sufficiently calm or regulate a client's inner experience so that they can engage in necessary introspection and emotional work in order to bring about meaningful healing. As we will cover throughout this chapter, proper safety and adaptation measures need to be respected in sharing mindfulness practices with people who are used to the *here and now* and the *present moment* as being anything but safe.

One of the natural adaptations of mindfulness practice is recognizing that one can practice mindfulness without having to sit in silence for long periods of time. Although certain traditional practitioners may only see mindfulness as sitting still in silence and training your mind to stay present NO MATTER WHAT, this position is flawed, even from a Buddhist perspective. After interviewing many Asian women (both secular and religious Buddhist nuns), well-known meditation teacher Martine Batchelor (2013) concluded that the specific techniques of meditation do not seem to matter as much as a person's sincerity in practicing the Dharma, or "the body of principles and practices that sustain human beings in their quest for happiness and spiritual freedom." One of Jon Kabat-Zinn's (2011, p. 94) most used examples is from a 98-year-old Chan (Zen) master who stated, "There are an infinite number of ways in which people suffer. Therefore, there must be an infinite number of ways in which Dharma is available to people."

The key to trauma-informing *any* type of practice or skill is to recognize that there is always a modification and that numerous adaptations can be available. An understanding exists among most mindfulness practitioners that any human activity can be practiced mindfully, whether that be washing the dishes, walking to the bathroom, or folding the laundry. Garland and Howard (2018), in their meta-analytic work on the positive impact of mindfulness practices in addiction treatment, refer to this idea as *informal mindfulness*. Dance, and the numerous ways in which people can even interpret what it means to dance, is more than able to be engaged in and practiced mindfully. You can simplify it this way—instead of using dance as a mechanism to escape, what if you could learn to use it to be present with whatever is there for you emotionally or somatically?

EMDR THERAPY AND MINDFULNESS: A NATURAL INTEGRATION

Teaching clients to be with *what is* absent any comment or judgment is imperative to EMDR therapy's success. Together with the other mechanisms of action, this inherent mindfulness in the EMDR therapy protocol plays a role in helping countless people to heal from the impact of traumatic experiences without going into too much narrative detail (Logie, 2014; Marich & Dansiger, 2018). Mindfulness practice and EMDR therapy are so inextricably linked, and this connection can be more fully explored and leveraged by EMDR therapists in working with their clients. I believe so strongly in this idea, based on my own experiences with flowing from an EMDR client to building mindfulness practice that enhanced my daily life and knowing Shapiro's own history with mindfulness, that I co-authored a book (with EMDR therapist, trainer, and long-time Zen practitioner Dr. Stephen Dansiger) called *EMDR Therapy and Mindfulness for Trauma-Focused Care*. Moreover, my entire EMDR therapy training model is based on the idea that mindfulness is inherent to the EMDR protocol. The more I learned about and cultivated my own mindfulness practice, I was able to answer for myself tricky questions that used to stump me. For instance, why do we ask for a positive cognition in Phase Three when we ought to be focused on activating a client's neural networks for processing? In sum, we ask for a positive cognition because it invites the client to set an intention, to plant a seed of what they want to see realized. The concept of intention is powerful in both mindfulness and yoga practice, and dance-movement therapists have long observed that even when you begin to verbalize a new intention, you are already starting to reorganize your body's own neuromuscular system (Bartenieff, 1980).

Having a full mindfulness practice ourselves can help us to navigate situations in EMDR that may prove difficult, like managing abreactions or working with dissociation. Your ability to keep the calming presence, what polyvagal theory would refer to as facilitating co-regulation, is imperative when EMDR therapy sessions may get difficult or the client might be dysregulated to the point where outside intervention is needed by you. Staying out of the way and trusting both the process and the resources that the client has built can be even more important. In sum, having a mindfulness practice for myself allows me to keep a clear mind in these situations and know how to respond.

Perhaps most importantly, mindfulness skills of all kinds—from traditional grounding and breathing practices to informal mindfulness practices like dance and the expressive arts—must be taught in Phase Two Preparation. In *The Body Keeps the Score*, van der Kolk (2014) notes three specific benefits of regular mindfulness practice that directly apply to what ideally must happen in EMDR Preparation:

- Traumatized people are often afraid of feeling—mindfulness practices can help orient them to and ease them into this process by widening sensory experience
- Practicing mindfulness is calming to the sympathetic nervous system, lessening the destruction of fight/flight responses
- The practices help to promote distress tolerance as awareness develops that emotional states constantly shift

Before I move into Phases Three to Six reprocessing with clients, I want to ensure that a client at least has an ability to ground and to be able to engage in three to five practices mindfully. Not only can such practices yield the above-mentioned benefits, but skillful teaching of them can also help orient clients to what it means to *just notice* or to answer questions like *what are you noticing now* or *what's coming up in the body?*

Through the remaining sections of the chapter, I will teach you how to use skills from the Dancing Mindfulness practice with clients, ideally to be first introduced in Preparation. Then, they will be available to you if needed through the remaining phases of EMDR therapy. Some of you may love to dance and may already be on board with this—"Let's go!" you may be saying. "This is my kind of mindfulness!" Yet more often than not, people are more likely to resist dance, especially a practice such as Dancing Mindfulness that allows for a great deal of freedom in personal expression. Consider that *Dance* may not mean what you've been programmed to think it means. You will learn by the end of this chapter that you can be sitting in your chair, fully grounded and breathing, and that is a form of dance. True, many folks can get squeamish around the word "dance" (after all, the English language word *avoidance* includes the word *dance*) because they don't think that they are a good dancer by social standards, or dance can bring up many trepidations around being fully present in the body. I encourage you, as I would encourage my clients and students, to please keep as open of a mind as possible while we explore the possibilities of how simple *Dancing Mindfulness* practices can enhance the practice of EMDR therapy.

FUNDAMENTALS OF DANCING MINDFULNESS

Our breath is our life force dancing through us (Marich, 2015). When people tell me that they can dance, I challenge them to first be with their breath and notice what they notice. Any flutter that you feel in your body from tuning into this natural process of energy moving through the dynamic system that is the human body is a form of dance. The dance is already within you.

Embracing the idea that *the dance is already in you* can feel unattainable. At first, it may feel inaccessible as a statement like *you are already born whole* (common in yoga philosophy and largely accepted in Internal Family Systems Therapy). Yet through getting in touch with some simple moving mindfulness practices, which can start with simple breath awareness, it is always my hope that people will connect with their inner dance and let that move them into the life that they deserve. The powerful acceleration that EMDR therapy can provide can make this process even more potent, yet in this section, we will focus specifically on what *Dancing Mindfulness* practice is designed to do.

GUIDING ASSUMPTIONS

Dancing Mindfulness is a trauma-informed approach to expressive arts therapy and education that uses dance and other art forms as the primary vehicle for teaching mindful awareness and cultivating its healing properties (Marich, 2015). Remember, the approach assumes that any human activity can be an avenue for mindfulness practice and that every human activity can be practiced mindfully. *Dancing Mindfulness* encourages practitioners to explore the seven primary attitudes of mindfulness, identified by Kabat-Zinn (2011) as non-judging, non-striving, beginner's mind, patient, trust, letting go, and acceptance. These are not the only attitudes that one can develop from mindful practice, yet they form a solid vocabulary base that aligns well with many clinical constructs from a variety of therapeutic traditions. A clinical facilitator might offer the invitation: "How can you move your body at this moment with a sense of radical acceptance for who you are?" Another invitation might be: "How can you express *letting go* with a movement or a gesture?" A hint for EMDR therapists: both of these statements can work well as interweaves to assist with blocked processing.

The practices of *Dancing Mindfulness* can be modified however an individual practitioner requires. *Dancing Mindfulness* facilitators (either clinical or non-clinical) recognize that an individual may be bound to a hospital bed and they can still practice dance by moving what is available to be moved in their physical bodies. All of the attitudes of mindfulness are active when we facilitate in this way, especially patience and non-judging (Marich, in press).

Dancing Mindfulness, although initially developed for the group context, can also be utilized in individual counseling, coaching, or educational settings. Many practitioners use the book *Dancing Mindfulness: A Creative Path to Healing and Transformation* (Marich, 2015) to develop their own personal dancing mindfulness practice and weave it into their lives. In a preliminary, exploratory study about the impact of *Dancing Mindfulness* practice, a group of ten female-identified participants who took classes in a community setting described a positive impact on their emotional and spiritual health because of the practice. They found that dance, in addition to music and yoga elements, facilitated this impact. The participants, half of whom identified as being in recovery from addiction, noticed changes to the self primarily in the attitudes of acceptance and non-judgment. Their participation in *Dancing Mindfulness* helped them to more fully practice these attitudes in daily life (Marich & Howell, 2015).

THE SEVEN ELEMENTS OF DANCING MINDFULNESS

While the attitudes of mindfulness are drawn from the work of Kabat-Zinn, I named and codified what we call the seven core elements of *Dancing Mindfulness* practice. These are activities and experiences that human beings can access, separately or in fusion, in order to practice mindful dance. The core *Dancing Mindfulness* book (Marich, 2015) and our formal facilitator trainings are organized along with these elements. The seven main elements of the approach are breath, sound, body, mind, story, spirit, and fusion (of all the elements)— *Dancing Mindfulness* recognizes that we can dance and express using all seven of these experiential forms. We've already established that you can be attuned to the life force of your own breath moving through you and that is dance. So what happens when we can combine this awareness of dancing breath with some of the other elements? Let's explore further by establishing a working definition for each element.

Even as I give you my definitions from our training materials here in this list, I encourage you to ask, "What does breath mean to me?" "What does sound mean to me?" and so on.

- **Breath:** The basic essence of animal life. Being attuned to the power of breath is a vital doorway to mindful awareness. Checking in with your breath is critical in the *Dancing Mindfulness* practice, and mindful attunement to the breath gives the practitioner excellent information about how much further he or she is willing to delve into the practice.
- **Sound:** The vibration of life that is most often associated with the sense of hearing, but can also be channeled in a tactile manner. Sound can refer to the music that guides one's practice, but it may also refer to the tones generated by breath, heartbeat, and motions like stomping feet on the floor, clapping hands, or chanting.
- **Body:** The container of our physical experience. Honoring the body and the information that it gives you about emotional content is vital to practicing mindful awareness, especially when engaging in a process as physically engaging as dance.
- **Mind:** The information processing system in human beings, the outlet through which we take in and send out information; the mechanism of humanity that makes mindful awareness possible. When stress or holding on to negativity grips a person, it is typically what the mind does with that received information that causes the problems. Faulty negative beliefs and old patterns, engrained in the mind, fuel the fire of stressors. However, just as the mind can hold on to negativity, it can also be recalibrated to focus on more positive, adaptive material.
- **Spirit:** The realm of experience that cannot be explained by the scientific laws of nature, that which is greater than you or I. For some people, accessing the spiritual world may be done through religion, for others, it is about tapping in to the cosmic flow of the universe, and for others still, it is about a relationship with their chosen Higher Power(s). In *Dancing Mindfulness*, we honor all paths.

- **Story:** The narrative of experience, which can be manifested and expressed in a variety of ways. Stories can be told in the first, second, or third person. Stories can be the true experience of the mindful dancer or a character that emerges during a given dance. Most important within the *Dancing Mindfulness* practice is that genuineness guides the telling of the story, and that it be told in a spirit of non-judgment.
- **Fusion:** The coming together of all of these elements. There are several places within the *Dancing Mindfulness* practice where this fusion, or integration, can occur. However, a period of reflection and rest at the end of the practice to really allow the elements, and the experience of them in the practice, to settle in and crystallize is a beautiful exercise.

In your examination and reflections on these elements, what have you learned about yourself and the process? Can you see that you may be dancing more than you originally thought you were through this mindful dance that is life?

DANCING MINDFULNESS AS AN EXPRESSIVE ARTS PRACTICE

Because of the imperative of adaptation and *go with that* in Dancing Mindfulness practice, the work naturally evolved into more of an expressive arts therapy form and much more appropriately fits this description, compared to pure dance-movement therapy. Expressive arts therapy takes a multi-modal and inter-modal approach to healing, recognizing that all of the creative arts forms are valid and belong together. In my own work, I explain expressive arts therapy existing like a buffet of creative practices. As human beings, we may have that natural tendency to go for the practices that appeal to us first, yet ultimately trying out the practices that we resist indeed have the most to teach us (Marich, 2019).

Our identity as an expressive arts form shows up in many ways. First, we realize that life is a dance, and all life experiences and the opportunities for expression that we are invited to give us an opportunity to dance—metaphorically or literally. *Dancing Mindfulness* is never just about practicing with a group of people or even having a dance party one-on-one with your therapist. One of my most memorable stories from the evolution of the *Dancing Mindfulness* practice is when a fellow EMDR therapist, who said he previously wasn't much of a dancer, was inspired into daily dance parties in his kitchen just from seeing me post about *Dancing Mindfulness* and the idea of "dancing in everything" on social media. When he makes his coffee and his breakfast, he puts on some of his favorite tunes now and just moves. He declared to me, "Dancing is always a good idea." Consider how, as a busy therapist trying to manage everything you have to do, committing to dance through at least part of your morning routine may help you to be more receptive throughout the day, helping you to *dance* with whatever comes.

On our group *Dancing Mindfulness* retreats and now even in our facilitator trainings, we make visual art and writing materials available and encourage people to weave these into their physical dance practices. Most will choose to physically dance a bit and then write and/or make visual art. Some will elect to take refuge in these other expressive forms as a form of containment, or will use them to keep their processing work active even when physical dance becomes too overwhelming or physically unavailable. Not uncommon in our open spaces on retreats is the sight of people dancing *as* they paint, draw, or drum. Speaking purely for myself, most of the painting that I do in my studio space happens when the music is on and I'm dancing around my canvas or art journal.

The other aspect of expressive arts practice that aligns ideally with my intentions for creating the *Dancing Mindfulness* program and approach is the idea of process over product. Expressing one's self is not about the outcome—what you make never has to end up in a museum or on stage. Sometimes, you learn the most about yourself and the process of life by giving yourself permission to make mistakes and then *go with it* no matter what. Or better yet, not judging yourself in the first place and seeing what is revealed. In expressive arts group sharing, feedback is never about analysis or judgment based on external metrics. Rather, the sharing that we might engage in with each other, or the sharing that a client may engage in with their individual therapist, is about noticing and eliciting further conversations and explorations. Once more, these processes can be valuable to EMDR therapists as interweaves, or to assist in closure procedures. In the section that follows, I will give you some ideas on specific practices and practice combinations that you can try—all of these are "field tested" with my EMDR therapy clients over the years. I thank them publicly for the feedback that they've given me that has allowed me to better adapt the practices to them, to other clients I've served, and to students with whom I have shared practice over the years.

PRACTICAL *DANCING MINDFULNESS* SKILLS AND APPLICATIONS FOR EMDR THERAPIST

When *Dancing Mindfulness* is operating most organically, it is pure *go with that*. No facilitation is needed, no music may even be needed. A person can just drop into what their body and breath are experiencing at any given time and just *go with* whatever is coming up, moving in whatever way feels natural and then eventually settling into a renewed place of stillness. Some clients over the years have spontaneously told me that they need to get up and dance, or as part of EMDR therapy closure procedures, it would feel good to turn on a song from their playlist and just go. While these expressions of *Dancing Mindfulness* are options for certain people, most will need a little more guidance, or in some cases a great deal of guidance, to feel safe enough to explore moving their bodies in the first place.

In this section, I present four specific skills that directly emerged from *Dancing Mindfulness* work and the sources of inspiration from which we draw. All of these have applicability for the clinical setting, specifically in EMDR sessions. I will break down each skill with directions and suggestions for modifications. Please do these yourselves and experiment with some modifications in your own body before you attempt trying any of these with clients.

SKILL 1: PAINTING LIGHT

EMDR therapists are familiar with the visualization of Light Stream. One of Dr. Shapiro's favorite, Light Stream, is taught in most basic EMDR trainings as an option for closure. Like many of her recommended resources, there can be a visual bias in Light Stream. Although you can have a person sense into different qualities of the light like texture or even a sound that might accompany the light, this (and many other) Shapiro visualizations may be difficult to do for clients who struggle with visualizing. There is a simple solution here using movement to make this core skill more somatic, and thus perhaps more engaging for people who are more tactile than visual. Even for people who are able to visualize a Light Steam, adding this movement component into it can begin to facilitate a stronger sense of connection to the physical body that is required for deeper work in Phases Three to Six.

This practice begins as a simple movement form from the *Tai Chi Chuan* tradition. Then, you can invite people into more organic, *go with that* movements once they feel sufficiently comfortable with the original form.

- Come into a strong standing base position about hip-width apart. This exercise can also be done sitting as a variation. Most important is establishing a connection to the ground, which can include connecting to the touch points where you are sitting.
- On an inhale, draw both arms out in front of you about shoulder height, palms facing down. On the next natural inhale, draw the arms overhead as much as possible.
- On the next natural exhale, draw the hands and arms down synchronized with the breath, palms facing away from the body. Bring them down at least to the waist although you can go as low as the knees.
- On the next natural inhale, draw the hands and arms back up overhead connected with breath.
- Continue with this natural movement for as long as you intend, bringing to mind the phrase "Painting Light." Are there any colors or colors you wish to visualize along with your movements?
- Like with all *Dancing Mindfulness* or trauma-informed mindfulness practices, the amount of time one spends in the exercise is variable. Perhaps try this basic form for 30 seconds to start with, then check in and notice whatever you notice. If one is too activated and needs to ground or move to another exercise, honor that. If one is able to identify what they are noticing and has a willingness to try a few more sets, or add in some creative variations as described below, go with those…
- As a variation, you can add music and/or let the arms flow freely out to the sides or in different directions, coming back to the "Painting Light" form as you wrap up. Once more, the time that you spend in this exercise is variable.
- Take at least 30 seconds, preferably longer to stand (or sit) in silence and notice what you notice in the stillness after taking the movement.

With *Painting Light*, all of the moving mindfulness skills described in this section, and indeed with any mindfulness practice that you weave into your EMDR therapy practice, please take the time to check in after each practice with the phrase, "What are you noticing now?" This helps the client to build the vocabulary of awareness and work with attuning to body sensation that can make them better processors of information as the phases of EMDR therapy progress. Many therapists also ask me if they should be doing these skills along with their clients. In short, it depends and must be felt out case to case. Do not hesitate to get feedback from your clients. With a skill like *Painting Light*, I often demonstrate it first, and then I ask my clients if they'd like me to do the exercise along with them, or simply hold space and observe. Another option can be allowing the client, especially if they are self-conscious about moving in front of others, to turn away from you. I've done this skill along with clients while we've both been facing away from each other, using the voice and vocal check-ins as the primary anchor.

Specific to EMDR therapy, *Painting Light* is an excellent skill to teach as part of Phase Two Preparation and to have on-hand for Phase Seven closure. Many clients will also elect to use this exercise on their own in between sessions. Like with any skill that one might teach in Phase Two and use if needed in Phase Seven, these skills can also be used to take pause if a client elects to pause or stop processing. Moreover, such skills can also be used as assists or interweaves, especially if they are used with the intent of bringing in a resource that will help them continue to process instead of shut down the session. With *Painting Light*, clients may be guided to use it as a proactive measure. For instance, some folks who work with *Painting Light* see it as a powerful force field or shield. In these cases, it may be organic to sense into the experience of this shield with a few movements before entering into a tricky area of their own reprocessing, knowing that the shield is there to protect them. As with all resources used in EMDR therapy, the intention of it is key and knowing how and when it can be used. *Painting Light* clearly has applicability in a variety of places.

SKILL 2: NOODLING

I owe complete and total credit to this basic practice that we use to get folks into a *Dancing Mindfulness* flow to one of my former speech and debate students, Cornelius Hubbard. A brilliant dancer and organic mover, Cornelius often encourages people to find their inner *noodle*. You may have heard musicians use the phrase *noodling* to describe that organic process of just playing around, listening for whatever may come up without attachment to the product. In introducing the meaning of *Dancing Mindfulness* practice to students or to clients, the same spirit of *noodling* can be embraced.

Haven't you ever envied a cooked noodle? The way that a noodle slithers freely and easily, without stress, is an admirable quality that can teach us how to practice the attitude of letting go.

- Come to your feet (although you can also do this exercise sitting or lying down as a variation).
- With your next breath, think of taking on the role of a noodle. You can even imagine that you are moving through a magical pot of water that will soften you without burning you.
- As a suggestion, begin with your shoulders and then let the softening or "noodling" move through the rest of your body.
- Keep noodling, in a mindful way, practicing beginner's mind, non-judgment, and non-striving for 30 seconds at first, pausing to check in if you need too.
- To connect with these mindful attitudes, these questions might be helpful: "What would it feel like if you could move without censoring yourself?" or "How might it feel to move like you were a kid again, not concerned with what people think?"
- When you've completed one round, allow yourself to be still for a few moments longer (standing, sitting, or lying down). Check in and notice whatever you are noticing.
- Repeat as many times as necessary, adding in any additional variations that may feel appropriate.
- Although you can do this in silence, it is lots of fun if you put on some music that can bring out your inner noodle! Adding in the music may help anchor in the present if one tends to dissociate.
- You can also feel free to bring in props, scarves, other play elements, or even bubbles to further engage with the idea of moving freely.
- To further orient to the bilateral stimulation or dual attention stimulus idea, noodle on the right side, then the left, and keep alternating. What do you notice about moving side to side?

One of my fondest memories of leading this exercise at a professional conference caused one gentleman, a veteran, to say: "That was good. But all this Marine can manage for today is *al dente*." I smiled with delight, applauding his willingness to even identify that. Such a report is why we use these practices to orient people to the question of *what are you noticing now?* And how wonderful that he was able to at least get to a place of *al dente* after his body being locked in a frozen position for so long.

As you may already be connecting, these moving mindfulness practices can be excellent for children—or for adults with younger parts that have a great deal to express in that special way that words cannot. Use what I am sharing here in concert about what you may already know about adapting interventions to young folks. Like with *Painting Light*, teaching *Noodling* in Phase Two so that you can have it ready for use in Phase Seven or so that clients can use in between sessions is ideal. However, *Noodling* can also be elicited as a powerful interweave if a client's processing is not moving, especially if they are frozen or otherwise shut down. Sometimes the best interweave you can bring in is, "How about a *Noodling* break?" Engage it for as long as it feels appropriate to the client. They will either *keep going with that* organically, or after the *Noodling* break is over, you can always check back in with the target and keep going from there.

SKILL 3: THE WONDERFUL WORLD OF PLAYLISTS

So, I came of age in the 1980s when we made *playlists* by listening to the radio and clicking PLAY + RECORD on our tape recorders to assemble a collection of music that most spoke to us. With modern technology, making playlists can be even easier, using music service or even YouTube to assemble a collection of music that fits our personality or our mood at any given time. In the *Dancing Mindfulness* community, making playlists is an important part of group classes and can be a very important aspect of personal practice. We train facilitators to keep qualities like theme, intention, and length of a class or experience in mind when gathering the music that they will use. Personal practice can open one up to even more avenues for personal expression; and such a practice can be a vital safety companion in EMDR therapy.

One of my most memorable exchanges with an EMDR therapy client, who ended up responding beautifully to expressive arts therapy and embracing it as a vital component of her overall healing, happened over a playlist. In our initial history taking and getting to know each other period that blended into Phase Two preparation, the client revealed a tendency to dissociate when overwhelmed with too much emotional or otherwise triggering content. She expressed a willingness to work with it using skills. Somewhere in this initial Phase Two work I expressed my concern about her driving home, especially since she traveled about an hour to my physical office.

"Don't worry about me, Jamie," she said, "I got my music."

She went on to explain that playing just the right music when she drove her car was the perfect way to stay present when she operated her vehicle. I asked if she'd be willing to make a special *Driving Home from Therapy* playlist for the purposes of staying grounded and lightening her mood, and she gladly obliged. I recommend this practice to all of my EMDR clients as a base practice for grounding and staying as grounded and as safe as possible in between sessions, and I have my consultees and students do the same with their clients. In the spirit of options and variations, there is no set length for how long a playlist needs to be—it can be three songs or it can be 50 songs. This idea embraces a *Dancing Mindfulness* teaching that classes and practices experiences can happen at a variety of lengths, depending on the intention of the group and the practice.

If a client responds well to the initial playlist for grounding, safety, and containment, you may consider using variations in concert with other phases of EMDR therapy. People may elect to make playlists to correspond with different moods that they need to express, or may build a collection of music along a critical theme in their life such as hopelessness, frustration, or on the positive end, empowerment. You can explore these playlists as a form of client history, learning about the themes and cognitions that underlay their presentation. From here, target selection could become more organic. Having an awareness of a client's music choices through their playlists can also be leveraged as an interweave if needed. For instance, let's say that a client continues to be blocked emotionally when a certain memory or idea loops in Phase Four. How might inviting them to listen to a related song (and even move to or make other art to it if they are willing) clear the blocked channel? I've witnessed this phenomenon of using expression to unblock numerous times in my EMDR practice over the years, and seeing its power give me chills every time.

Another former client was stuck around expressing or even identifying her anger in a healthy way. She knew that anger existed underneath the surface as we worked through several EMDR targets, yet she articulated a fear about expressing it, concerned that her anger may cause her to lose control in the way her violent father would. An avid listener (and occasional dancer) of music, I asked her if she'd be willing to listen to some songs that other people wrote or sang to express their anger. Most of the music services now have an option where you can search a genre or a "mood" like *angry music*, and see other people's playlists or collections pop up. She listened through several of these, aware that she could skip a track if at any time she started to feel unsafe or activated. This skill is exactly what she needed to feel comfortable enough with expressing her anger in a healthy way, thus opening up the EMDR reprocessing.

Some clients will elect to simply listen to the music (which is still *Dancing Mindfulness* to me, as sound is an element of practice). Others will feel naturally led to blending music, art-making, or even writing into the process. With EMDR resourcing, consider embracing an attitude that everything from that expressive arts buffet is open to be brought in. Once you have a sense of this in Phase Two Preparation and resourcing, together with client feedback and some clinical intuition, your options for assisting people through their blocks are endless.

FURTHER TRAINING AND DEVELOPMENT FOR EMDR THERAPISTS IN MOVEMENT AND MINDFULNESS

"I could never imagine myself dancing with my clients!"

I've heard so many people I've trained declare this over the years and I first want to remind you that not all *dancing* is necessarily about getting up and having a dance party. I hope I've made that idea abundantly clear in this chapter—dance and mindful movement can take on various forms and be adapted in a variety of ways. If you cannot imagine yourself dancing with your clients, can you at least see a reality where you may be comfortable introducing movement to them?

If the answer is still no, perhaps begin by attempting to integrate the practices from *Dancing Mindfulness* into your own life and plan for wellness first. I think you will find that the more you are able to work through potential resistance and try out these skills in your own life, the more open you may become to sharing them with others. In all of my movement work, both *Dancing Mindfulness* and another program I teach called *Yoga for Clinicians*, I emphasize that the best clinical facilitators of these practices are people who are willing to share from their own practice. If you do not have a practice from which to share, you might be stuck with facilitating any of these skills to others. You can share them as worksheets or words on a page and they may have some impact, yet they really come alive when you have something to share. And if you can draw from the lived experience of having worked with resistances yourself, you'll be in a better position to assist clients in navigating theirs.

EXPANDING YOUR PRACTICE AND SKILL SET

If the content of this chapter interested you and you want to learn more, there is certainly more education out there in the field of expressive arts therapy, dance-movement therapy, trauma-informed yoga, somatics, and many other movement arts. Our *Dancing Mindfulness* facilitator training (which you can learn more about at www.dancingmindfulness.com) is part of my group's larger expressive arts therapy training program yet the Dancing Mindfulness component can also be taken on its own. We offer the program in both a group setting and an individual mentorship format. Although the training might help you develop more language that you can weave in professional and be an experience of personal development for you, please know that you do not have to be a formal "Dancing Mindfulness facilitator" to share *Dancing Mindfulness* practice. You can begin with some of the suggestions that I offer here in this chapter or in my other writing. I wouldn't put it out there publicly if I didn't want to encourage its use!

I maintain that, even with an abundance of training, clinicians are in the best position to share dance, movement, mindfulness, and other expressive practices with clients when they have experience on which to draw themselves. So, in looking at your options for training in any of these forms that bring in movement, find a training that excites you and will inspire you to deepen your own practice. The added bonus of this focus is that you will have an enhanced ability to keep a calming presence and co-regulate with your clients when sessions can get intense, either due to abreaction/intense affect or dissociation and shutdown. I am able to navigate these situations as effectively as possible as an EMDR therapist because my mindfulness practices help me to do so.

FUTURE DIRECTIONS AND CONCLUSION

The very existence of the book in which this chapter appears gives me hope that EMDR therapists and the EMDR community at large will be increasingly open to practices like *Dancing Mindfulness* and other expressive and creative arts. There is a joke that as artists we are notoriously bad at empirical research, so what is happening in practice among innovative and creative EMDR therapists may lag behind in what is seen in the research. Yet when Dr. Shapiro used the phrase "proactive measures" so frequently in the 2018 update of her classic textbook, identifying many expressive and movement-based practices as such proactive measures that can assist block processing, I smiled. I felt validated and seen, along with other creative souls in the EMDR community, knowing that we are moving in the right direction.

My mindfulness practice came to me through my engagement as an EMDR client. I've worked with and have connected with so many individuals over the years who credit EMDR therapy as opening up a greater creative potential within them. To use a term that reflects an element of *Dancing Mindfulness*, the *fusion* excites me. Fusion, cooperation, and integration are all words synonymously with healing and adaptive resolution. Let's keep *going with that...*

REFERENCES

Bartenieff, I. (1980). *Body movement: Coping with environment.* Routledge.

Batchelor, M. (2013). Meditation and mindfulness. In J. M. G. Williams & J. Kabat-Zinn (Eds.), *Mindfulness: Diverse perspectives on its meaning, origins, and applications* (pp. 157–164). Routledge/Taylor Francis.

Bishop, S. R., Lau, M., Shapiro, S., Carlson, L., Anderson, N. D., Carmody, J., & Devins, G. (2004). Mindfulness: a proposed operational definition. *Clinical Psychology: Science and Practice, 11,* 230–241.

Garland, E., & Howard, O. (2018). Mindfulness-based treatment of addiction: Current state of the field and envisioning the next wave of research. *Addiction Science & Clinical Practice, 13,* 14.

Kabat-Zinn, J, (2011). Some reflections on the origins of MBSR, skillful means, and the trouble with maps. *Contemporary Buddhism,* 12, 281–306.

Logie, R. (2014). EMDR - more than just a therapy for PTSD? *The Psychologist, 27*(7), 512–516.

Marich, J. (2015). *Dancing Mindfulness: A creative path to healing and transformation.* SkylightPaths Publishing.

Marich, J. (in press). The dancing mindfulness approach to expressive arts therapy: trauma-focused solutions for group and individual settings. In Malcholdi, C. (Ed.) *Handbook of expressive arts therapy.* Guilford Press.

Marich, J., & Dansinger, S. (2018). *Healing addiction with EMDR therapy: A trauma-focused guide, first edition.* Springer.

Marich, J. (2019). *Process not perfection: Expressive arts solutions in trauma recovery.* Creative Mindfulness Media.

Marich, J., & Howell, T. (2015). Dancing mindfulness: A phenomenological investigation of the emerging practice. *Explore: The Journal of Science and Healing, 11*(5), 346–356.

Porges, S. (2011). *The polyvagal theory: Neurobiological foundations of emotions, attachment, communication, and self-regulation.* W.W. Norton & Co.

van Der Kolk, B. (2014). *The body keeps the score: Brain, mind, and body in the healing of trauma.* Viking.

CHAPTER 10

FUTURE SELF
Developing a Felt Sense for the Future as a Resource in EMDR Preparation

Annie Monaco

One of the characteristics of profound childhood trauma is the change in perception and negative beliefs toward the self, life and the future (Terr, 2003). Childhood traumatic wounds play a crucial role in the development of a number of serious disorders and significant cognitive distortions in childhood and adulthood (Schore, 2012). As a result, clients with attachment and complex trauma often struggle with irrational beliefs that they are "not good enough", "not smart enough" and "not worthy" which were messages repetitively programmed by caregivers in their early developmental years. As children grow into adults, their experiences continue to build on and reinforce these cognitions, leading to a deep sense of powerlessness around their life, their choices and the changes they'd like to make to reach their desired future.

Without a clear sense of the steps and skills needed to work toward a future goal, the client can stay stuck in their trauma-related avoidance of hope that they are capable of attaining a different reality. Trauma robs the client of a sense of power and control over their life (Herman, 1998) and traumatic events can diminish the client's expectation for a positive future (Fletcher, 1996; Terr, 1991). Clients often do not have the confidence or belief that a realistic healthy future exists and that there is an alternative to living with their present distress and problematic behaviors. Without shifts in thinking, the client's personality and behavioral patterns can organize around these negative core beliefs and keep both the client and the therapist stuck in the present symptoms with little movement toward emotional well-being and change (Terr, 1991; van der Kolk et al., 1996).

Therapists treating significant trauma histories must work with clients to shift their core beliefs by developing a felt sense and internal reference point for their future self, which is a fundamental step to helping the client make progress toward their goals. The guiding principle of recovery is "to restore power and control to the survivor" (Herman, 2002). In the 1800s, Pierre Janet formulated that recovery from post-traumatic stress reactions occurs in three phases: the first phase is establishing safety; the second phase is treatment of the trauma memories; and the third and final stage of complex trauma treatment is reconnection and integration, where the client strengthens their new sense of self and is empowered to reemerge into their life with a desire to take care of their needs including in relationships with others (Herman, 1998). As with the three-pronged approach to EMDR, Janet's three-phase approach to complex trauma treatment integrates the future as an essential part of recovery and the successful consolidation of treatment gains. When it comes to applying EMDR to complex trauma treatment, it is recommended that the focus on the future starts in the first phase of EMDR: History and Treatment Planning.

Helping a client find what they passionately care about or want to work toward is often a difficult and omitted part in treatment. Therapists often find themselves in long-term supportive roles with clients and have a misguided belief that when a client feels supported enough, they will find the motivation to change rigid negative beliefs and defenses in their behaviors. This is often not the case. As part of Phase One of EMDR, history and treatment planning, it is recommended that the therapist introduce and assist the client in forming a detailed future goal intervention to interrupt and shift habitual patterns of hopelessness about the future.

DOI: 10.4324/9781003156932-11

The Future Self intervention presented in this chapter is a creative adaptation of Dr. Greenwald's Future Movies intervention (2015). Future Self is a Resource Development and Installation (RDI) intervention designed to provide a creative format for teens and adults to generate hope, a vision and a step-by-step plan to achieve their future self. The concepts can be utilized with younger tweens with modification and simplified language.

FUTURE SELF IN PHASE ONE OF EMDR: HISTORY AND TREATMENT PLANNING

One goal of the first phase of EMDR treatment is conducting a treatment plan. This process typically takes place over the first few sessions. First, assessment and history taking allow the therapist to develop an understanding of the past traumatic events and the symptoms interfering with the client's functioning. Based on this understanding, the therapist and client collaboratively come up with specific ways to reduce and/or alleviate problematic symptoms. These actions form the basis for the treatment plan, which concretizes these steps into date-specific and achievable goals. Treatment plans often suggest a different future by using words such as decrease, increase and reduce to describe changes in the client's symptoms, but they fall short of motivating the client to believe that positive change is within reach. Clients are seeking answers to their problems, but are also seeking hope that they can have a fulfilling life (Tschudy, 2010). The goal with this intervention is to elicit high levels of positive emotions, such as hope and excitement, to allow clients to "see" themselves living the life they desire, therefore increasing motivation to follow the treatment plan. Hope is especially important in trauma treatment (Lambert, 1992), as clients with trauma histories often struggle to imagine a future life without these symptoms. Hope can strengthen a client's commitment to therapy and participation in future goals (Stotland, 1969; Ward and Wampler, 2010) and experiencing positive emotions is shown to be linked to recovery and learning new skills, behaviors and ways of thinking (Frederickson & Joiner, 2002).

Engaging the client in future-oriented goal-setting conversations can be a challenge. The client may feel that their present symptoms, hardships and struggles are being dismissed. It becomes a delicate balance to acknowledge the hardships and painful symptoms in the client's life, while also assisting them in achieving change by identifying a goal and a plan to reach that goal. Despite a therapist's best intention of instilling hope, the client's strong irrational beliefs can interfere with setting up goals and tasks for the treatment planning process. The client may feel the therapist is insensitive and that the therapist doesn't "get" them, which can cause a rupture in the early relationship of establishing safety and building trust. The risk of not obtaining a passionate future vision is that clinical treatment can fail when the client cannot connect to their future vision on a felt-sense, bodily level, therefore lacking the motivation to work through painful past events.

Insurance companies and agencies require treatment plans for record keeping; therapists should aim to enhance this treatment plan by helping the client identify a deeper, meaningful goal for the client. This allows the client to feel hopeful and passionate regarding their life, providing them with a motivating "good ending" (Greenwald, 2015) that helps them stay committed to the steps along the way.

Presenting the "Future Self" Intervention

The "future self" intervention takes treatment planning one step further by encouraging the client to creatively envision who they can be without their problematic symptoms. Future

Self intervention should be dreamy and fun to create, and include all desires! It can be short term (six months to a year) or long term (e.g., five to ten years) in the future. It is the vision of "someday I want to be…" as the aim is for the client to see an attractive and compelling future (without their symptoms, or with the ability to manage chronic conditions differently), to describe that life in detail, be elated about this possibility and feel empowered to live the life they want! This intervention bridges the first phase of EMDR treatment to the second phase of preparation and resource development as the ability to dream about and believe in a future becomes a resource in and of itself.

This intervention is not a one-time intervention; it is a creative, engaging and interactive process, developed over several sessions and utilized throughout the eight phases of treatment. Ideally, it should be introduced as part of the treatment planning in Phase One, then prepared and enhanced as part of preparation in Phase Two. This is the cornerstone of a client's treatment plan and can keep the client hopeful as they work on their steps toward the future they want. Additional ideas or steps can be added over several sessions. It is suggested to first develop the narrative and then enhance the vision through creative expression such as writing, drawing, painting, collage, poetry, song, or by using a storyboard format (the Future Self Storyboard is available for use in a printable format on the EMDR and Creative Therapies website, www.emdrcat.com, accessible by scanning the QR code in the introduction of this book). Ideas and dreams can change over sessions which can keep the client actively engaged in the creation of the future. The process of revisiting the future self and identifying more details can only enhance the client's self-worth and strengthen their ability to dream.

FUTURE SELF IN PHASE TWO OF EMDR: PREPARATION

In Phase Two, preparation phase, therapists are teaching specific techniques such as Safe Place and Container to clients to help them manage emotional disturbances. These techniques were to increase feelings of calm to be able to engage in subsequent trauma processing sessions. As EMDR therapy progressed, many EMDR innovators developed different techniques to help clients connect to positive resources. The term Resource Development and Installation (RDI) was developed by Leeds and Shapiro (2000) to encompass all of these ego-strengthening techniques that used bilateral stimulation to enhance positive images, memories and symbols. RDI is a set of EMDR-related protocols which focus exclusively on strengthening connections to resources in functional (positive) "memory networks" (Korn & Leeds, 2002; Leeds & Shapiro, 2000; Shapiro, 2018). Forming a Future Self is an expanded RDI intervention that allows the client to identify, develop and enhance future positive images and symbols. The therapist can introduce Future Self in Phase One and then further explore it in Phase Two. It is possible and recommended to continue through all eight phases using different creative arts methods to enhance the positive image and somatic sensations as this can strengthen the client's desire to process their traumatic past. The therapist's role in Phase Two of EMDR is a delicate balance between providing a supportive and therapeutic space and challenging the client to learn new concepts, resources and coping strategies.

Window of Tolerance for the Future

When is the right time in therapy for a client to think about their future? Ideally, this occurs at the beginning of treatment, as part of treatment planning; however, the future can be triggering for some clients. Due to the lasting effects of traumatic histories, the concept of living a happier life is often met with resistance. As with Pierre Janet's phase-based approach to complex trauma treatment, safety and stabilization is the first goal (Herman, 1998). A future-self discussion can only be implemented when enough safety has been established to do so. For this reason, the therapist's role then includes assessing the window of tolerance (Siegel, 1999) for future planning, much like the therapist assesses readiness for addressing the past. Therapists must also engender hope (Snyder, 2002) and fully empower clients to have choice over their future and to be able to shape and form their future self. Clinical expertise of the therapist is necessary to determine the timing of this intervention and it should be introduced based on the client's affect tolerance of looking past their problematic symptoms. Some clients excitedly embrace this concept but others find it impossible to look at the future without it evoking the client's strong defenses, lack of self-worth and negative beliefs. Proceeding with this intervention may be perceived by the client as the therapist being insensitive and misattuned. If a client rejects the idea of a future self, a therapist can gently say: "We can look at this another time in treatment". The therapist will then work on increasing the window of tolerance for future-oriented thoughts and possibilities. In addition, the 2020 pandemic is a worldwide event that has caused significant change and disruption in everyone's life. The therapist should take into consideration that the COVID-19 pandemic has increased hopelessness among many clients (Abbott, 2021), making the future seem even more uncertain and daunting.

Future Self Concepts

Future movies: Greenwald (2015) developed "Future Movies" while working with outpatient and residential at-risk youth who struggled to see a possible future and who were highly resistant to trauma treatment. Future Movies (Greenwald, 2015) is the foundation for the creation of Future Self. "Future Movies" was designed to ask youth to consider what their life would be like in ten years and helped them design a future goal. Greenwald also specified obtaining steps along the way for youth to recognize what they needed to do to obtain their goal. Future Self was born out of Future Movies (2015) and enhanced by allowing different options to view the future such as through a vision, a movie or an author of a book. The intervention also encourages the use of somatic and creative modalities throughout the development of the future. It aims to support the client to develop an embodied, felt sense of their future which can lead to a greater outcome of success.

Hope: Snyder (2002) defined hope as "a positive motivational state that is based on an interactively derived sense of successful agency (goal-directed energy), and pathways (planning to meet goals)" (p. 287). Hope as a variant on effective therapeutic change has *been* studied since the late 1950s (Frank, 1968; Menninger, 1959). Beck (1963) research studies have shown that hopelessness is a significant risk factor in developing many psychological disorders. Having hope is considered one of the elements in clients improving in therapy (Snyder et al., 1999). Through extensive reviews of numerous empirical outcome studies, Lambert (1992) identifies that hope can account for some of the change that takes place in therapy.

Goals: Goals are a significant factor in "Hope Theory" (Snyder et al., 1991). It is formulating the future desired vision of the client's *life*: relationships, school, work and other important aspirations. Future Self offers the opportunity to fine tune the details of the future vision.

Pathways: Pathways are the process through which the therapist and client will collaboratively figure out how to make the future possible. In *Future Self*, this can take place through verbal exchange as well as the use of artistic and somatic approaches in order to help obtain the desired future.

Agency thinking: Agency thinking is the high-energy, motivational thinking that encourages the client to move forward. In Future Self, *when* the client reaches the implicit belief that I can do "I can do it", it leads the client to forming steps to making the futuristic thinking of "Who I want to be someday" actually happen. This can motivate the client to want to resolve their past traumatic events.

Felt sense: The concept of the felt sense was developed by Eugene Gendlin (1961), who developed the therapeutic process called Focusing. Gendlin characterized the felt sense as a combination of emotion, awareness, intuitiveness and *embodiment*, therefore enhancing the connecting between mind and body through the act of focusing. The Future Self intervention aims to support the client in developing an embodied, felt sense of their future. This proponent of therapy is enhanced through creative expressions.

Time, place and action: Time, Place and Action comes from Greenwald (2015) in his approach to directing clients to clarify specifics of their future to visualize its components and "see" their dream more clearly. In Future Self, we embrace this concept to solidify a vision of the future dream. For example, if a client defines a future moment of graduating, the therapist wants to elicit the specifics of the time, place, and action: June in one year (Time); on stage at college (Place); *Being* handed their diploma by the Dean of their department, and family and friends are cheering and clapping! (Action). Making the details clear and vivid in the client's imagination or through creative expression allows the client to engage more fully with their vision.

First time for future thinking: This type of conversation may be foreign and the first time that anyone is asking the client to consider a future. This is especially common in high-risk teenagers or adults who are engaging in criminal behaviors, aggression or *self*-harm. Often these clients are told they will "end up in jail" or "end up in a hospital" or "go away to a 'home' for troubled kids". It is possible that a client may never have considered something outside of what is occurring in their everyday life and may be surprised that the therapist is suggesting that they could have a positive and fulfilling life. The therapist may be in the position of explaining why they embody a different stance with the client and be in opposition of family members.

Unrealistic future plans: Sometimes clients, especially younger teens, may state an unrealistic future idea. For example, they may see themselves as a pro sports player and are not engaged in the sport formally. Therapists should move forward with the client's dream and strengthen the desire to live a different life. Often, these goals get altered along the way and if not, then the steps along the way are a key piece in this intervention to clarify to clients what is needed to reach their dream. For example, if a client states they want to be a pro sports figure, then the steps along the way include doing homework, graduating high school and making plans for college. Further explanation of the "steps along the way" is described later in the chapter.

High risk/violent future: Clients may state they want to have their future being a criminal and that includes stealing, gang leader, or harming others. This may be the case if the client is exposed to this type of behavior on a daily basis and sees the *benefit* of those behaviors. The therapist can reflect the skills of being a leader, a business person, going after the things they want and being admired by peers for their harmful behaviors. Skillfully, the therapist should acknowledge these skills, and discuss the possibilities of the bad ending. The therapist could say "with your talents, there are other ways to use your skills and get what you want. Can we explore this?" This is an opportunity for the therapist to ask the client to draw both possible future paths in a side-by-side comparison. The therapist can ask for the client to identify feelings and positive body sensations. Again, introducing a different pursuit of a future may be the first time someone recognizes their talents and sees their future differently. It is recommended to *not* continue this intervention if the client is only willing to consider a criminal or harmful life.

FUTURE SELF SCRIPT AND FACILITATION STEPS

The following section provides the outline for the Future Self intervention and Future Self storyboard as well as the explanation of the concepts behind each step of the process. The script is provided in italics. The full script and storyboard are also available for use in a printable format which can be accessed on the EMDR and Creative Therapies website, www. emdrcat.com, or by using the QR code in the introduction of this book. The therapist is encouraged to alter the script based on the needs of the client. The therapist should be open to many creative arts modalities to help the client connect into and enhance and deepen their vision of their future self.

Optional creative formats:

- Creative Art Supplies: colored pencils, markers, paint, clay, etc.
- Storyboards
- Collage materials
- Mind movie (option to create a digital video vision board: www.mindmovies.com)
- Canva (option to use an online graphic design platform: www.canva.com)

Distancing strategies: Distancing strategies are included in the script for clients who have low affect tolerance and struggle to actually experience positive emotion about a more content life. In this case, it is recommended that the therapist word the invitation to look into the future as seeing it through a third person; for example, "this 15-year-old girl can make her future anything she wants it to be. She is the designer of her future goals, creator of her dreams…"

STEP 1: INTRODUCING FUTURE SELF

Introduction: *In these last few sessions, I have gotten to know your strengths and your present struggles. We have talked about your thoughts and feelings regarding the past and things going on inside of your mind, heart and body. What if today we try something different and look into your future? I know it might be hard to think about that right now with everything going on in your life.*

This part should be done in a slow, steady, invitational voice, as a way to guide the client to begin to slow down, settle their nervous system and enter a comfortable place in their mind. This may take a few moments for the client to find comfort by adjusting their surroundings—for example, settling in their chair, having cushions, blanket, lying down, blinds lowered and taking some slow deep breaths. The client can hold a special item in their hand, smell soothing scents, and if possible lowering or closing their eyes. Or if desired, the client can be engaged in a grounding creative arts activity, such as drawing or coloring. Saying to the client "I know it might be hard to think about that right now with everything going on in your life" acknowledges the previous history-taking sessions and the identified symptoms and problem behaviors that interfere with daily functioning. If this is a brand-new client, this can be introduced at the time of the treatment plan and as an intervention that will be worked on over several sessions. A clinician needs to be attuned with the client and notice the non-verbal cues if the client is struggling to think about their future. This can be observed by the client hesitating in answering, looking down, eyebrows raised or changing the subject. The therapist is utilizing good clinical judgment about the client's window of tolerance and if it is appropriate to proceed.

> **Beginning to dream:** *I want to ask you about what your life might be like or could be like. Let's spend some time creating your dreams and future goals and steps along the way. Close your eyes, if this feels comfortable to you and begin to go inside. As you begin to dream, your future can be anything you want it to be. You get to be the designer of your future goals and a creator of your future dreams. You can manifest your future in any way you want!*

It is recommended to use a neutral tone with slight enthusiasm. There is suggested caution to the therapist about being too excited during this paragraph as many traumatized survivors cannot tolerate positive feelings. If the therapist observes the client tolerating positive affect, then the therapist can choose to emphasize this part with a positive tone.

> **Offering choice:** *Let's talk about how you want to design your future? We could explore your future vision by telling me the details, or you can be a filmmaker and imagine a movie or you can be a writer and an author of a book?*
>
> **Option 1:** *Let's imagine that I can see a vision of your future.* (Optional Distancing Strategy: *Let's imagine that I see the future of a _____ year-old.*)
>
> **Option 2:** *Let's imagine I am watching a movie about you.* (Optional Distancing Strategy: *Let's imagine I am watching a movie about a _____ year-old.*)
>
> **Option 3:** *Let's imagine I am reading a book about you.* (Optional Distancing Strategy: *Let's imagine I am reading a book about a _____ year-old.*)

Therapists and clients can make a choice as to how to proceed with the versions above. Three options are provided and one should be picked for consistency throughout the intervention. If a distancing strategy is used, continue to use it throughout the intervention for consistency. Exploring the options may take some time but offering choice is empowering for clients and will enhance the process throughout the use of this intervention.

> **Setting the time frame:** *I will need your help to fill in the details. Let's say that 6 months, (1), (2), (5), (10) years from now—how old will you be?*

The therapist should assist in deciding how many months or years in the future based on the client's issues and tolerance for thinking about the future. For example, during the pandemic, high school seniors were struggling to see their future of going to college or playing a sport in college. Developing a future vision in six months to one year made sense for many teenagers. For an adult in the process of divorcing their partner and encountering a contentious proceeding, it might make more sense to look two years into the future. For a teenager/young adult who is in trouble with the law, it might make sense to look ten years into the future.

STEP 2: THE CLIENT'S STRUGGLES

Past struggles: *Some difficult things have happened to this person. The _____ year-old is not doing well and having some struggles. What would these struggles be? You can tell me, write or draw what they would be. (Some examples might be traumas, family problems, issues at school or work, health or mental health issues, etc.) Write, draw or imagine the struggles they might be having.*

Add client's problem behaviors: *With all of this buildup of stress, this person starts to… (Some examples might be oversleep, overeat, overuse alcohol, drugs, have excessive use of TV/games/movies/social media, not doing college/school work, fighting with family, criminal behavior or have episodes of low motivation, anxiety, depression.)*

Add the client's beliefs: *They have all sorts of thoughts… (Some examples might be I am not good enough, smart enough, worthy, I cause problems…etc.) Write, draw or imagine the thoughts they might be having.*

Add the client's emotions: *They have all sorts of emotions… (Some examples might be like feeling worried, sad, anxious, angry, hopeless.) Write, draw or imagine the emotions they might be having.*

Add the client's body sensations: *They have all sorts of sensations in their body… (Some examples might be headaches, stomach problems, numbness.) Write, draw or imagine the body sensations they might be having.*

The script starts with "this person is not doing well". It is purposeful that the script stays in the third person as it can be difficult to hear negative things about yourself. It's an opportunity for the therapist to take notes and gather information for Phase One and if needed for the therapist to offer some examples in order to guide the client if they need prompting. The script invites the client to represent their struggles in any creative format that works for them and this is especially helpful for clients to feel seen, heard and understood. Feelings and experiences that clients may find hard to articulate and yet more easily can express these struggles, beliefs, emotions and sensations in other ways like drawing, painting, clay, collage and poetry. The therapist should observe closely and monitor if the client is becoming overwhelmed or affected by the future conversation. The creative modalities can help client's stay in their window of tolerance and make this process more tolerable as their story and struggles are externalized and contained through the creative expression, such as in images, symbols, colors and metaphors. The caveat is that this part of the intervention can cause more sadness about their present life. It is a balance of encouraging the client to acknowledge the present painful moments and moving toward the next section of seeing their future self.

STEP 3: THE FUTURE PART

Shifting to a positive outcome: *So, as the stress and feelings keep piling up inside, more bad things happen… they feel worse and worse and the future doesn't look so good for this person. It's hard to watch (a hard movie to watch, a hard chapter to read). I am not sure I can keep going… Then one* *day, something happens and this adult/teenager/character decides to dream again. They want good things and want a different life. They want to pursue their dreams and goals. In this vision/movie/chapter, they start doing some positive things. They do more and more good things that help them get to their future goals. And ___ years later they look back and can't believe what they went through! Their life is better and their dreams and goals are actually real!*

If you can, look through the eyes of the future self and tell me what you see? In ___ months/years, what is life like? What does your future self see you doing? (Distancing option: *What is the 25-year-old's life like?*)

If the client has a preliminary idea, the therapist should keep written notes on the Future Self script. If the client is struggling with identifying and verbalizing ideas, then the next step for the therapist is to move on to the optional questions.

Optional Questions to Strengthen Future Part

This section provides clinicians with optional questions to help clients get a stronger, more vivid image of their future self. Clients will likely need assistance to get the full details of their life in the future. These questions can help the client to start outlining their future. This list is not exclusive; therapists can formulate their own questions to support this process.

School/College
- *Are you graduating from high school/college? Is there a ceremony? A graduation party?*
- *What college are you going to? What is your major? Do you have an internship? Study abroad?*
- *What knowledge or skills have you gained?*

Career/Work
- *What would you be doing for a living? Are you self-employed? Do you have employees? What company/business/store/team are you employed with?*
- *What hours do you work? Do you work inside, outside, at different locations? Do you travel for work?*

Wealth/Finances
- *How much money are you making?*
- *What is your bank balance?*
- *What investments do you have?*

Living/Home/City/Car
- *Where are you living? On campus or off campus? Do you have roommates?*
- *In a city, country, suburbs?*
- *Do you live in your own house or an apartment? How many rooms? Can you describe it?*
- *How is your home decorated? Do you have plants, art?*
- *Do you take public transportation? Drive? What kind of car? What color?*

Relationships
- *What relationships do you have in your life? Who are the most important people in your life? Is anyone living with you?*
- *Who do you trust? Who do you feel comfortable with? Who do you have fun with?*
- *Do you have friends? What are they like?*
- *Do you have a spouse/romantic partner, then: what's he/she like? Are you married?*
- *If kids, then: how many? Boys or girls? What age?*

- *What is your relationship like with all of them? How do you act or show up?*
- *Do you have animals? What kind? How many? Names?*

Activities/Hobbies

- *How do you spend your time? How do you spend your money?*
- *Dinners with friends, travel, vacation, walk the dog, sports, etc.*
- *What else do you own? Camera, instruments, boat, motorcycle, skis, kayaks, bikes, second home?*
- *Do you make art? Write poetry? Make music?*

Physical Health

- *How is your health? How is your sleep? What kind of food are you eating?*
- *Are you exercising? Walk? Yoga? Weightlifting? Cycling? Sports? Gym? Run marathons?*
- *How do you take care of your physical health on a daily basis?*

Emotions/Mental Health

- *What is your emotional state of mind? What is your primary emotion?*
- *What are you doing for self-care? Coping skills? How do you take care of your mental health?*

Spirituality

- *What spiritual or religious practices support you? Prayer? Meditation? Reading? Singing?*
- *Are you part of a spiritual or religious community?*
- *Do you have a daily spiritual and religious practice?*

Service/Giving Back

- *How do you make the world a better place?*
- *Do you serve your community? Help others? Volunteer? Take action for a cause? Advocate? Protest?*

Storyboard

This is an opportunity for the therapist to introduce the storyboard format to clients (therapists can use the visual template and script available on the EMDR and creative arts therapies website, www.emdrcat.com, or using the QR code in the introduction of this book). Therapists can then use the Future Self script to record the details while clients use the storyboard to write down the ideas or draw in the storyboard to express their vision. The artistic expression of the future could be the entire therapy session and the rest of the script can be utilized in the next sessions. Possibly in a different session, a client can use Canva or Mind Movies, creative web-based programs to further develop and deepen these desires.

Overcoming Resistance in the Future Part

Sometimes this is where the client struggles and may say, "I don't know". The client may experience deeper feelings/thoughts of "this is not possible", "my therapist doesn't get my pain", "this will never happen" or "why dream, as only bad things happen to me". The therapist should expect this resistance and be prepared to sensitively discuss and normalize these strong irrational beliefs and thoughts. It is important for therapists to spend some time making sure the client feels understood and their pain is heard and recognized. This is also an opportunity to invite the client to express their resistance or negative belief barrier through art media.

Negative belief barrier: *Can you draw or write all the negative thoughts or strong emotions that are coming to your head right now?* Allowing clients to express their defenses often helps them to move forward with this intervention and for the therapist to ask questions about their future.

Responses to Resistance

The therapist should present with an open, calm attitude if defenses and resistance are presented by the client. The following examples can be helpful in reducing resistance:

- *Anything goes.*
- *We are just dreaming.*
- *We can work out the details—that comes later.*
- *Don't let your doubts hold you back right now.*
- *I imagine this is so hard to think about with everything you are struggling with, and it may take some time to get here.*

Example Responses

TEENAGE CLIENT: "I want a Porsche but that will never happen."

THERAPIST: "Anything goes. We are just dreaming right now. And you never know…"

TEENAGE CLIENT: My life is so crappy, none of this will ever happen.

THERAPIST: Life is definitely hard right now. It may take some time to get to this future vision. Don't let your doubts hold you back from seeing a possible future.

JUNIOR/SENIOR IN HIGH SCHOOL: "I don't know which college will offer me a scholarship."

THERAPIST: "Pick your top choice and make up the scholarship amount you hope they will give you. Anything can happen!"

ADULT CLIENT: "I never had a job while we were married and raising the kids. I have no education or skills."

THERAPIST: "Let's keep envisioning the future and we can figure out the steps along the way to get you to a job you feel good about…"

STEP 4: FINAL SCENE

- **Option 1—Vision:** *It's the final scene of your vision. I am looking at an impressive scene. I am thinking, "Wow, I am so happy it turned out this way!" What do I see? What are you doing? What is happening?* (Distancing option: *What would it be for that teen/adult in this vision?*)
- **Option 2—Movie:** *The movie is almost over, and we are getting to the last scene—you know the last picture, when the music's playing and the credits are rolling? —I'm smiling, and I am saying, "Wow, I am so happy it turned out this way!" So, tell me, if this was your movie and things go the way you wish they would, what would your life be like in that last scene?* (Greenwald, 2015) (Distancing option: *What would it be for that teen/adult in this movie?*)
- **Option 3—Book:** *We have come to the end of your book with only one chapter left, and I am smiling and saying "I am so happy at how it turned out this way!" What would the last chapter say? What would I be reading?* (Distancing option: *What would the last chapter be like for that teen/adult in this book?*)

The final scene, picture or chapter of the future self is the moment that stands out to the client that they have "made it". It depicts all of the hard work from the client from today to months/years into the future. It's the ending scene when the client knows/feels like they have accomplished their dream. This could be a graduation party and cutting their cake, a divorced client coming home from work and entering her new home, or a teen from an orphanage putting their own child on the bus for school.

Time: *What time of year is it? What is the season? What is the date? What time of day is it?*

Place: *Where are you? What is surrounding you? What do you see, smell, hear, touch?*

Action: *What are you doing? What are you feeling? What does your body feel like?*

Take some time and add this to your storyboard—you can then use any modality you would like to represent your good ending.

After the client has expressed their final scene, it's an opportunity to strengthen the vision by obtaining time, place and action. To have a felt sense of the final scene, these questions create a strong visual. Often clients are smiling, feeling enthusiastic and overall content as they enhance their dream with these details.

Integrating Creative Arts Expression

Allowing the client to artistically express themselves continues to provide an opportunity for the client to have a felt sense of the future and add more details to the final scene.

What words do you want to say to yourself, such as "I can do this", "It will happen", "I will make it", "My future self will come true"?

Positive Beliefs/Affirmations

Identifying a possible belief or affirmation is done twice in this intervention. This is the first time and it's an opportunity to help clients identify a positive statement, and it's quite possibly the first time the client is thinking about the future. This first time is a "light touch". Since many clients with trauma histories struggle with feeling, thinking or imagining positives, it is best to go with a gentler statement. Later in the intervention, this can be broadened with more options and a stronger positive affirmation. Possible options are "I can do it", "It will happen", "I will make it" or "My future self will come true".

STEP 5: INSTALLING THE VISION

Eye movements/butterfly hug/tapping in: *Okay, now I'm going to ask you to do a concentration exercise. I'll be asking you to concentrate on the final vision/scene in the movie/last chapter of the book. Notice the feelings, where you feel it and your positive statement. Ready? (BLS) Were you able to concentrate on everything? Okay, let's try again.* (Repeat another time or two until the client is able to hold the picture reasonably well.)

In this step, the final scene is installed with eye movements, hand/leg taps, butterfly hugs or another form of bilateral stimulation (BLS); this is at the discretion of the EMDR therapist and what is comfortable for the client. BLS can include 8–12 repetitions, and done twice to strengthen and deepen the resource. It's important to obtain the feeling, the body sensation and the positive statement to embody the felt sense of the future. All of these components increase the felt sense of the future self.

Pausing in the Intervention

If there is not enough time in the session to complete the steps along the way, this would be the ideal place to stop in the Future Self intervention until you see the client in the next session. You can start the next session by reviewing their final picture and details and then developing the steps to get to that dream. It is not uncommon that a client changes their future and dreams and wants to revamp their Future Self. If this happens, it is an opportunity for the client to expand upon their ideas and modify their dream. Sometimes clients have several different dreams or paths. Encouraging clients to map out both futures is ideal. It allows the therapist to work with the client to sort out emotions and body sensations that go with both dreams.

Negative Barrier Belief Arises

The therapist should be aware that if the client experienced much satisfaction and positive experience from the last session and then had a difficult week, they might feel hopeless and then do not want to continue the intervention. Therapists should be prepared for defense responses such as "this is stupid" or "it will never happen" come up in the next session. This is an opportunity to invite the client to express the negative belief barriers through an art modality.

STEP 6: STEPS ALONG THE WAY

This part of the intervention guides the client in identifying the next steps to reach their dream/goal. Getting steps along the way is critical for people to foster investment in their future goal. It allows the client to clearly view what needs to be done to obtain their desires. Developing this part can be difficult as the intervention asks what the client is doing tomorrow, next week, next month and next year to get to their future vision. The client is then brought back to their present problem behaviors and may return to the feelings of hopelessness and defeat and "this will never change". On the contrary, the client may feel highly motivated to change some of these behaviors. If the client is expressing frustration with overcoming problem behaviors, this is an opportunity for the therapist to provide psychoeducation on the traumatic experiences of the past and how they are holding the client back from being who they want to become for the future. Part of the next steps can be trauma resolution of traumatic experiences.

> The thing is, in the future vision/this movie/this book didn't just jump from the middle to the end; there were all these things that happened along the way to get there. So, tell me, if this was your vision/movie/book, what would need to happen for you to get to your dream? What would we see you doing tomorrow, next week, next month, next year?
>
> (Greenwald, 2015)

Recording Details of the Steps

It is suggested that the therapist record the details of the steps in a collaborative and visual format while the client speaks out loud. Options include writing down notes in the Future Self script, a blank piece of paper, using a computer to type out the details, a dry erase board, or a large paper posted on the wall. The therapist can, for example, write as the client speaks out loud, allowing for easier organization. The brainstorming part does not have to be in chronological order, but can be later organized into a clear timeline of tasks.

Organization and Timeline of Steps

It is recommended that after coming up with the steps along the way, the therapist and client find a way to put it in chronological order. The therapist and their client can also make movie frames, book chapters, timeline or collage using art supplies.

Unrealistic Vision

Steps along the way are important even if the dream is perceived as unrealistic. This can be the case of a teen wanting to be a pro sports figure. For these teens, it's about the steps they need to take to get to their dream. If a teen wants to be a pro basketball player, the steps along the way include getting up for class, finishing homework, graduating high school, and applying for and attending college. It is recommended to allow the client to go forward with their dream and the therapist work on developing strong and detailed steps along the way.

Example:

CLIENT: I have to graduate from high school as one of the steps to my future self.
THERAPIST: And what does that entail?
CLIENT: I have to pass chemistry which is so hard.
THERAPIST: Okay, I see and what do you have to do to pass chemistry?
CLIENT: I have to go after school to meet with the teacher three times a week so I understand the concepts.
THERAPIST: Is there anything that is blocking that from happening?
CLIENT: I have to tell my friends I will meet up with them after that. I can do that. It's only 45 minutes extra of class.
THERAPIST: You have said they tell you to blow it off. How can you handle that?
CLIENT: Tell them "Hey, I want to get out of high school and not be here forever! I will meet you in an hour at the pizza shop."

Another example:

CLIENT: I need to go to a two-year program to get a job as an administrative assistant. I don't have the money to do that. Once I am divorced, I will have less money.
THERAPIST: What if we explore options to go to school so you can get a job. Have you met with anyone at the college to talk about it or explore financial aid?
CLIENT: No... but you think I could get a scholarship?
THERAPIST: I don't know but what I do know is that colleges want folks to enroll and I wonder if you start there to explore options about scholarship, financial aid, and see what they offer.
CLIENT: You are right. I will set up an appointment and see my options for enrolling.
THERAPIST: When are you thinking of going for an appointment?

CLIENT: I am off Tuesday of next week and my mom can watch the children. I will call today and see if I can meet with someone at the college to discuss this further.

In both examples, the therapist is helping the client manage the overwhelmed feelings. Assisting the client to see the actual first steps and problem solving any obstacles gives clients a clear plan of what needs to be done.

STEP 7: EMBODIMENT OF FUTURE SELF

What positive words might fit best with your future vision? Maybe something like, I can do it, I will go after my dream, I am transforming my life, I am successful, I am in complete control of where my life goes, I am open to change, I deserve a good life, I am worthy, I can do it, I move closer to my goals every day, I am an inspirational example to others, or everyday, in every way, I am getting better and better.

Add Positive Cognitions and/or Affirmations

This is the second time that clients are asked to add a positive cognition and/or affirmation. It allows the client the choice of sticking with their earlier positive statement or offering a stronger more enriching message to themselves. The therapist can suggest the above statements or have the client look at the list of EMDR positive cognitions. The therapist and client can identify other affirmations by searching the internet.

What song reminds you of your dream?

Is there a physical posture that you can do to remind you of your dreams? For example, superwoman/ man, mountain pose (arms/hands straight up in the air), or any other posture or movement that fits best for you?

Is there an object and/or scent that can remind you of your dreams?

It is recommended to use additional sensorial information to reinforce the positive associations with the steps along the way and final Future Self. Song, posture, object and scent are optional and your client will choose the ones that work best for them. This is an additional opportunity to find an object or make an object with art materials. If the therapist or client is familiar with utilizing scents, this can be an option to link the smell with the future vision. The client can be encouraged to associate their future every time they hear the song, hold the object or smell that scent. Therapists can encourage the client to do the physical pose every morning before they leave for work or school.

STEP 8: THE WHOLE VISION

The whole vision with BLS: *While I am doing (BLS) I want you to view the whole vision/ movie/book through the eyes of your future self. Looking through the eyes, see your future from today all the way to that good end. You can say it out loud, or to yourself. Remember to say your positive statement. How did it go? What happened in the vision?* (Repeat the process of viewing the whole vision two times.)

For additional strengthening options, the client can look at the storyboard, watch the Mind Movie, hold posture, hold the object, smell the scent or sing/hum their song.

Strengthening the Final Vision

The therapist can continue to strengthen and boost the steps along the way and the final version of future self over the course of treatment. For example, the client can complete the storyboard and then in additional sessions, using art supplies the client can make a timeline, collage or use Canva or Mind Movies to further enhance the future self vision. With each additional creation, installing the vision with BLS is recommended.

STEP 9: CONNECTING PRESENT SELF TO FUTURE SELF

Can you and your future self have a conversation? What does your future self want to say to you to encourage you toward your goals? What can your future self say to you when you are discouraged, or doing a behavior that might get in your way?

This is an invitation for the two selves to meet and have a discussion. No doubt that the steps along the way can be very daunting. The client may get depressed, sad, hopeless and struggle to see the future. If the future self can offer some positive and uplifting statements in these hard times, then the therapist can remind the client of these statements in the future. It is advisable that the therapist encourages the "future self" to say uplifting and encouraging words and not critical statements. Examples include:

What not to say: Don't mess up your life. Don't be an idiot and just follow the plan.

What to say: "You might make mistakes, and fall back into old habits, it's okay, just get up and go toward your goals".

Example:

CLIENT: Every day more and more stress and problems come into my life. I feel so over-whelmed. I can't imagine my future will ever happen.
THERAPIST: Do you remember what your future self said to you knowing you might feel this way?
CLIENT: Kind of... you wrote it down, can you read it?
THERAPIST: Your future self said "there is nothing easy about the road ahead. Take small steps and notice your progress. You being aware of your problems and taking actions are big steps. Don't stay defeated but go on to the next step. It will take time but you can do it".
CLIENT: Wow, what good advice... (chuckles). It's true, I have made big progress.

STEP 10: FOLLOW-UP (IF NECESSARY)

Identifying strengths and skills: *What sills, strengths, supports, successes or talents do you have to make your future happen?*

Challenges and obstacles (the old you): *What is limiting you and getting in the way of your future self? In the movie, what gets in the way of you going toward his dream? What's the biggest worry/challenge? Let's look at your attitudes, your beliefs, patterns, emotions, struggle with self-care, sabotage?*

This is an optional section for therapists to decide if a client needs these additional questions and discussion. If the client has high risk behaviors and/or strong irrational negative beliefs and the intervention was a struggle for them to participate in, this last section of the script can be utilized. The therapist and client can dialogue about the problem behaviors and negative thinking that get in the way of the client becoming the future self. It is also an opportunity for the therapist to help the client identify past successes and what skills, strengths, talents, supports and positive attributes that have helped the client in other ways to reach a goal or manage a difficult situation.

CASE EXAMPLE OF FUTURE SELF: 16-YEAR-OLD TEENAGER

THERAPIST: Hi Lila, I wanted to try this Future Self Intervention today. You up for it?

LILA: Sure. (Yawns.) I am tired. Do I have to think a lot?

THERAPIST: (Chuckles.) This is a fun kind of thinking! (Starts script) Lila, in these last few sessions, I have gotten to know your strengths and your present struggles. We have talked about your thoughts and feelings regarding the past and things going on inside of your mind, heart and your body. What if today we try something different and look into your future? I know it might be hard to think about that right now with everything going on.

Future Self Introduction

THERAPIST: In these last few sessions, I have gotten to know your strengths and your present struggles. We have talked about your thoughts and feelings regarding the past and things going on inside of your mind, heart and body. What if today we try something different and look into your future? I know it might be hard to think about that right now with everything on in your life. You have a lot of things going on with your family.

LILA: (Nods).

Beginning to Dream

THERAPIST: I want to ask you about what your life might be like or could be like. Let's spend time creating your dreams, future goals and steps along the way. If you feel comfortable, close your eyes and go inside.

LILA: If I close my eyes, I will fall asleep.

THERAPIST: Okay, no problem, keep them open. Ready to continue? (Client nods) Your future can be anything you want it to be. You get to be the designer of your future goals, a creator of your future dreams. You can manifest your future in any way that you want!

LILA: (Rolls her eyes but is smiling. Therapist makes a decision to continue.)

Offering Choice

THERAPIST: How do you want to design your future? We could explore your future vision by telling me the details: you can be a filmmaker and imagine a movie or you can be a writer and an author of a book?

What format do you want to use?

LILA: I guess… a movie.

Time Frame

THERAPIST: Let's imagine I am watching a movie about you. I will need your help to fill in the details for me. Lila, how far into the future do you want to think about? I was thinking when you are out on your own, and have independence. So maybe a bunch of years into the future?

LILA: Yeah… let's say 10 years. I will be out of that shithole house and away from the parents for sure.

THERAPIST: Okay, 10 years from now—how old will you be?

LILA: This is a lot of brain power… umm… 26? Yeah… 26.

Client's Struggles

THERAPIST: In this movie, some difficult things happen to this person like traumatic things when she was a child and having family problems. The movie starts with this 16-year-old not doing well and having some struggles. What would they be? We can talk about it or you can draw if you want.

LILA: You mean draw the beatings by mom and the drunkenness of my Dad? (Laughs.) I will just talk about it… that is too much work right now to draw, paint or whatever you are suggesting.

THERAPIST: *(Add Problem Behaviors)* With all of this buildup of stress, this person starts to… for example, get depressed, be nervous, struggle to complete homework. What do you think?

LILA: Sleep all day, cry, feeling like they wish they weren't here… (Laughs.)

THERAPIST: *(Add beliefs)* They have all sorts of thoughts, like…

LILA: *(Interrupts.)*…Like, my life sucks, I hate myself, I am a horrible person.

THERAPIST: *(Add in Emotions)* And this young person has all sorts of emotions…

LILA: Like sad, angry at how stupid her family is, frustrated a lot…. Is that enough? I could keep going if you want? (Laughs.)

THERAPIST: *(Add in Body Sensations)* And this young person has some sensations in their body like….

LILA: Stomach aches, headaches, vomiting–umm… we don't have time for me to list all of the things wrong with me.

Vision Continues

THERAPIST: So, as the stress and feelings keep piling up inside, more bad things happen…they feel worse and worse and the future doesn't look so good for this person. It's a hard movie to watch. I am not sure I can keep going… (Therapist's voice is slightly hopeful.) Then, one day, something happens and this adult/teenager decides to dream again. They want good things and want a different life. They want to pursue their dreams and goals.

In this movie they start doing some positive things. They do more and more good things that help them get to their future goals. And ten years later they look back and can't believe what they went through! Their life is better and their dreams and goals are actually real! If you can, look through the eyes of the future self and tell me what you see. In ten years, what is life like? What does your future self see you doing in the movie?

LILA: Living in a psychiatric facility as my parents drove me to complete insanity. (Laughs out loud)

THERAPIST: I know this is hard… life is really hard right now, but it won't always be that way. You *will* get out of this situation. Let's just dream… anything goes… (Therapist is considering offering the client to talk more about the negative belief barriers and waits to see what the client responds.)

LILA: Okay… this is hard but you are right... I am *for sure* not staying in that hell forever. So sometimes I dream of having a bakery. I want to be a baker and I want to live in a state like Connecticut! It's far enough away.

THERAPIST: Wow, I had no idea this is what you wanted to do. Umm. What are you baking me if I come to you? (Therapist is being playful in hopes the client keeps going as now the client is fidgeting, and looking around the room which could mean the client doesn't like thinking about the future.)

LILA: (Pauses for a bit.) So, if you come to my store… it will have vegan, gluten free stuff and peanut free. And it will taste damn good! (Client laughs.)

THERAPIST: (laughs) I will be coming to your store weekly! (Starts writing down details.) Tell me more about this store… I am intrigued, and now hungry.

LILA: I am teaching my staff how to make gluten free scones! We are chatting, and happily greeting customers. (Pauses.) I can't believe I said I was happily talking to anyone! (Fidgeting is increasing.)

THERAPIST: Okay, this sounds cool... can I ask more questions?

LILA: Yeah. But now I am hungry as we talk about cookies.

THERAPIST: (Hands client some chocolate.)

Optional Questions

THERAPIST: So, before the store, you graduated from high school?

LILA: (Chewing.) Yep, and the day after graduation I left my house to get away from those crazy people.

THERAPIST: (Decides not to pursue questioning about graduation celebration due to family situation.) So… Prior to owning the bakery, how did you learn to bake?

LILA: I bake all the time. It's how I keep my sanity. When my grandmother was alive, she taught me so many things. I want to go to the Culinary School in New York.

THERAPIST: Oh wow, and how long was that schooling?

LILA: I don't know.

THERAPIST: Let's check. (Therapist and client check the website.) Two to four years it says.

LILA: Let's say two years to three years, I can't handle much more than that.

THERAPIST: Did you do a certain track in the program? (Shows her the website to encourage the conversation)

LILA: Yep, pastries, cookies, cakes.

Storyboard Introduction

THERAPIST: Hey can I give you this Storyboard and you can write some of this down so we don't forget. (Client takes it and starts writing.) How did you end up owning your own store?

LILA: I have been saving all of my money from my job right now at the coffee shop and I will continue to do so. I have $3,000—did you know that?

THERAPIST: (Surprised.) No, I didn't... wow! Okay, and you're planning to keep saving from your job?

LILA: Yep, absolutely, right up until I graduate. And my grandfather already said he will give me money when I get out of this hell. He will help with college and the store. (Pause) I never told anyone what I wanted to do. This is kinda fun, you aren't a bad therapist after all... (laughs).

THERAPIST: (Laughs.) Glad to have scored some points today... With all this money, is it in the bank? Will you be investing it in stocks?

LILA: Hmm, that's a good idea. Can you believe my mother actually helped me with a bank account? Don't faint as I said a positive thing about her... I can talk to my grandfather about investing the money so it grows while I am at culinary school.

THERAPIST: What was it like at the culinary school? You lived on campus or off campus?

LILA: I think off campus. And I am rooming with another pastry person... and (she is thinking), she might be my business partner in the store...

THERAPIST: Oh, ok. So, a business partner sounds ideal so you can split the costs and the responsibilities.

LILA: (Claps her hands in excitement.)

THERAPIST: At the time you own the store, you are living where? NY? Or Connecticut?

LILA: Connecticut. NY is too expensive to live there!

THERAPIST: Okay Connecticut. With a business partner? Apartment? House?

LILA: Oh, separately. We ain't that close! For me, it would definitely be a house, small house, maybe upstairs of the bakery? Or next door? I don't want to be driving every day to the store for like 30 minutes.

THERAPIST: So, no car?

LILA: Yeah, I need a car to get supplies but just want to be close to the bakery.

THERAPIST: Okay house, bakery in the front. You live upstairs or next door. And who do you live with?

LILA: Uh, nobody... no way! So, what I can meet a boy who is like my father... no way! So alone with me and two dogs. My business partner is around a lot.

THERAPIST: What about friends?

LILA: Yes, lots of friends. We have fun, go to restaurants. There are restaurants who have my cakes, cookies and scones on their menu! We go on trips around the world - not only for pleasure but to sell my baked goods to places too. My cookies are famous!

THERAPIST: Wow, didn't know you wanted to travel! What is your ideal place for your cookies?

LILA: All the eastern states surrounding Connecticut. I would have to look at a map but like New York.

THERAPIST: How many employees?

LILA: These are hard questions! Slow down woman! (Laughs and thinks...) Maybe 5 people. That is enough. I don't trust too many people.

THERAPIST: How much are you making a year?

LILA: 75,000! But also I go to restaurants and get free meals as they have my cookies, cakes on their menu. So, lots of perks.

THERAPIST: Very very nice! So, you are 26, have a business partner, own a bakery, have friends, travel, eat out, make good money... (pauses and allows the client to see it visually) What else do you own?

LILA: A sailboat. I miss my grandfather taking me out on his. He is too old now and he sold it.

THERAPIST: That sounds nice… very nice. What will you name it?

LILA: (Pauses.) Same as Grandpa's. "Whatever way the wind blows." (Laughs.)

THERAPIST: (Laughs.) What about relationships? Significant other? Kids?

LILA: Kids will come when I am in my mid-thirties. Maybe two? Not sure how I am having them… maybe a restaurant owner will be the father. (Client is serious and contemplating this and then starts fidgeting.) And when I need therapy or we need therapy, I can fly you out to take care of me! (Laughs.)

THERAPIST: (Laughs. Pauses for a bit and decides not to pursue since this is the first time the client has talked about having a relationship and she is fidgeting and clearly agitated.) Of course, you can pay me in baked goods! (Both laugh.)

Let's go to some other questions. What is your emotional state of mind…

LILA: Happy… happy, peaceful, and content. You will come and see me and be shocked at how happy and calm I am.

THERAPIST: I never doubt that is the real you. Lila, I can see now you have a dream. A dream that I have no doubt will happen.

LILA: I never say it out loud as I don't know if I can get there.

THERAPIST: Yes, I can understand but wow you have some pieces worked out already. You already know the details of it. Can we continue with a bit more? (Client nods) The movie is almost over, and we are getting to the last scene—you know the last picture, when the music's playing and the credits are rolling? I'm smiling, and I am saying, "Wow, I am so happy it turned out this way!" So, tell me: If this was your movie and things go the way you wish they would, what would your life be like in that last scene?

LILA: I am in the bakery, handing large boxes of cookies and cakes to two restaurant owners, and at the same time, greeting my regulars.

THERAPIST: Wow… love it. Lila, look at all the details you wrote down in the Storyboard! Do you want to draw this, paint it? Or, do Mind Movies?

LILA: I want to make a collage.

THERAPIST: Love it… let me get the materials.

(Client completes a collage on a large poster board. It's a picture of a baker from a magazine and two other people. She writes "employees" above their pictures. Client writes out the cookies that will be on the menu.)

Time, Place and Action

THERAPIST: So, Lila, as you look at your collage, what is the time of the season?

LILA: June.

THERAPIST: And this is the bakery? (Client nods.) What are you doing?

LILA: Teaching employees how to bake gluten free, dairy free scones.

THERAPIST: (Smiles.) What are you feeling? What does it feel like in your body?

LILA: (Starting to tear up.) I feel so good… right in my chest. That horrible anxiety is gone.

THERAPIST: Yeah… nice good feeling. Show me with your hand. (Pause.) What words do you want to say to yourself? Such as "I can do this", "It will happen", "I will make it" or "My future self will come true".

LILA: My future dream will come true. I will have the life I want. (Sounds determined and proud.)

THERAPIST: (Eye Movements/Butterfly Hug/Tapping In) Okay, Lila, now I'm going to ask you to do a concentration exercise. I'll be asking you to concentrate on the final scene in the movie. Also, notice the feelings, where you feel it, and your positive statement.

Ready? (BLS) Were you able to concentrate on everything? Okay, let's try again. (Repeat another time or two until the client is able to hold the picture reasonably well.)

LILA: Wow... I need to go home... this is too much positive! (Laughs nervously). Session ends.

Next Steps to Reach Dream/Goal

THERAPIST: Hi Lila, can we continue from last week?

LILA: Yeah, thought about it all week. I am going to get there.

THERAPIST: (smiles and gives thumbs up) The thing is, this movie, this book didn't just jump from the middle to the end; there were all these things that happened along the way to get there. So, tell me, if this was your movie, what would need to happen for you to get to your dream? What would we see you doing tomorrow, next week, next month, next year? Let's start with tomorrow and next week. In your storyboard, you can write the details.

LILA: (Takes the storyboard and starts writing.) I need to count the number of days left to finish high school. (Starts calculating in her brain.) Every day I need to get up and go to school and mark off that day and say at the beginning of school: "this is one step closer to getting out of this hell life".

THERAPIST: (Writing down details in future self script.) Okay, sounds good. What else, Lila?

LILA: I am going to stay after for biology help with the teacher. I asked her yesterday and she was totally fine with it. I need to do my homework after school and mark off the day on my paper calendar. And say the same thing to myself in my bedroom—"one step closer to getting out of here". By the way, I put a piece of paper in my closet that says "One step closer". I know what it means. If my mother sees it, she won't get it.

THERAPIST: Okay, these sound like good steps.

LILA: I am going to get a second job during the summer so I can save more money. I am going to apply to a bakery! (Both client and therapist are writing, then begin talking about the local bakeries in the client's town and how to approach the owners.)

LILA: And, I already started looking at the culinary school website to see what else I will need to apply to there. I need better grades for sure. I am going to start taking pictures of my baking and creating my... hum?

THERAPIST: Portfolio?

LILA: Yeah, that's it.

THERAPIST: Wow you did all this over the past week? (Client nods). Okay all of this sounds good. (Therapist and client talk details about the portfolio).

THERAPIST: Lila, I know you want to leave right after graduation. What do you want to do about transportation? Do you need a car or would you just move when it is time to go to culinary school?

LILA: Yeah, I have not figured that out. I don't want to use my money to buy a car but I don't think I have a choice. I think I will ask for graduation money to put it down to get a car. Then pay a monthly fee. (Therapist and client talk details about leasing a car.)

THERAPIST: Okay, is there anything else?

LILA: Yeah, I need you to get this crap out of my head that spins, and spins around.

THERAPIST: You mean the bad stuff that happened? You mean trauma therapy? EMDR?

LILA: Yeah...

THERAPIST: Okay we can start working on some of the memories. I do think this will help. (Client was very resistant to ever considering EMDR prior to this intervention".

THERAPIST: *(Add in Positive Belief/Affirmation)* What positive words might fit best with your future vision? Maybe something like, I can do it, I will go after my dream, I am transforming my life, I am successful, I am in complete control of where my life goes, I am open to change, I deserve a good life, I am worthy, I can do it…

LILA: Slow down there, lady. That is a lot of positives! My brain can't take all of that. (Laughs.)

THERAPIST: (Smiles.) Want to hear the rest? (Client nods.) I move closer to my goals every day, I am an inspirational example to others, every day, in every way, I am getting better and better. And, you can choose something different and none of those!

LILA: Every day I am getting better and better.

THERAPIST: *(Song)* Is there a song that reminds you of your dreams?

LILA: Oh yeah… Calvin Harris Feat. "Let's go." His video is all about getting off the couch and making your dream happen!

THERAPIST: *(Posture)* Is there a physical posture that you can do to remind you of your dreams? (Therapist stands up and poses like superwoman.)

LILA: (Laughing.) Now that is weird… (Therapist motions to try it.) Let's do Warrior 2 pose. (Therapist and client both stand in warrior 2 pose.)

THERAPIST: (In pose.) I am getting better and better every day… (Client repeats and the therapist and client stay in pose for half a minute, then both sit down.) *(Object)* Is there an object you have that you can hold to remind you of your dream?

LILA: My grandma's picture... for sure…

THERAPIST: Would you be willing to bring it next time? (Client shows a picture on her phone of her grandma and her.)

THERAPIST: *(Scent)* What about a scent? No wait, you get headaches from scents... Forget it! (Client nods.) Okay, I am going to do eye movements while you view the whole movie through the eyes of your future self. Looking through the eyes, see your future from today all the way to that good end. You can say it out loud, or to yourself. Do you want to hold your grandma's photo or do you want to be in Warrior 2 pose? Or play that song?

LILA: (Client finds the song on her phone, puts it on, and goes into the Warrior 2 yoga pose.)

THERAPIST: Don't forget your positive phrase of I am getting better and better every day. (Therapist stands in front of the client as she is in Warrior 2 pose.) *(BLS)* (Does a set of 8 eye movements.) How did that go?

LILA: I didn't have time to get through all of it. Go more and slower. (Therapist complies.)

THERAPIST: How did that go?

LILA: Good… really good. (Client is singing the song.)

Future Self to Present Self Conversation

THERAPIST: Can you and your future self have a conversation? What does your future self want to say to you to encourage you towards your goals?

LILA: You got this.

THERAPIST: What can your future self say to you when you are discouraged or doing a behavior that might get in your way?

LILA: Don't let those people get you sad and depressed. And then tell me to turn on my song!

(In future sessions, Lila did Mind Movies with the therapist. It took two full sessions to get her mind movie completed. She then had a movie version that she watched every day for over a month.)

CONCLUSION

Future Self is an intervention that helps clients acknowledge their potential and self-worth. Oftentimes, clients have dreams and future goals that they think about but they don't talk about due to fear of shame and failure. This intervention can help them overcome the phobia of future-oriented thinking. Negative beliefs often get in the way of the client believing it could ever be true. If the intervention is well timed, and the client's tolerance of the future can be managed, this intervention can be life changing for the client. As in the future movies script, it can be pivotal in changing the direction of the client's life, and provide a hope and motivation that alters the course of the therapeutic process.

REFERENCES

Abbott, A. (2021). COVID's mental-health toll: How scientists are tracking a surge in depression. *Nature, 590*(590). https://doi.org/10.1038/d41586-021-00175-z

Beck, A. T. (1963). Thinking and depression. *Archives of General Psychiatry, 9*(4), 324. https://doi.org/10.1001/archpsyc.1963.01720160014002

Embodied Situated Cognition/The Felt Sense. (2020). Embodiment.org.uk. http://www.embodiment.org.uk/topics/felt_sense.htm

Fletcher, K. E. (1996). Childhood posttraumatic stress disorder. In Mash, E. & Barkley, R. (Eds.), *Child psychopathology* (pp. 242–276). Guilford.

Frank J. (1968). The role of hope in psychotherapy. *International Journal of Psychiatry, 5*(5), 383–395.

Fredrickson, B. L., & Joiner, T. (2002). Positive Emotions Trigger Upward Spirals Toward Emotional Well-Being. *Psychological Science, 13*(2), 172–175. https://doi.org/10.1111/1467-9280.00431

Gendlin, E. T. (1961). Experiencing: A variable in the process of therapeutic change. *American Journal of Psychotherapy, 15*(2), 233–245. https://doi.org/10.1176/appi.psychotherapy.1961.15.2.233

Greenwald, R. (2015). *Treating problem behaviors: A trauma-informed approach.* Routledge.

Herman, J. L. (1998). Recovery from psychological trauma. *Psychiatry and Clinical Neurosciences, 52*(S1), S105–S110. https://doi.org/10.1046/j.1440-1819.1998.0520s5s145.x

Korn, D. L., & Leeds, A. M. (2002). Preliminary evidence of efficacy for EMDR resource development and installation in the stabilization phase of treatment of complex posttraumatic stress disorder. *Journal of Clinical Psychology, 58*(12), 1465–1487. https://doi.org/10.1002/jclp.10099

Lambert, M. J. (1992). Psychotherapy outcome research: Implications for integrative and eclectic therapists. In Norcross, J. C. & Goldfried, M. R. (Eds.), *Handbook of psychotherapy integration* (pp. 94–129). Basic Books.

Leeds, A. M., & Shapiro, F. (2000). EMDR and resource installation: Principles and procedures for enhancing current functioning and resolving traumatic experiences. In Carlson, J. & Sperry, L. (Eds.), *Brief therapy with individuals & couples* (pp. 469–534). Zeig, Tucker & Theisen.

Menninger, K. (1959). The Academic Lecture: Hope. *American Journal of Psychiatry, 116*(6), 481–491. https://doi.org/10.1176/ajp.116.6.481

Mind Movies – Positive Daily Affirmations & Digital Vision Boards. (n.d.). www.mindmovies.com. Retrieved from https://www.mindmovies.com

Schore, A. (2012). Playing on the right side of the brain: An interview with Allan N. Schore. *American Journal of Play, 9*(2), 105–142.

Siegel, D. J. (1999). *The developing mind: Toward a neurobiology of interpersonal experience.* Guilford Press.

Shapiro, F. (2018). *Eye movement desensitization and reprocessing (EMDR) therapy: basic principles, protocols, and procedures.* Guilford Press.

Snyder, C. R. (2002). Hope theory: Rainbows in the mind. *Psychological Inquiry, 13*(4), 249–275. https://doi.org/10.1207/s15327965pli1304_01

Snyder, C. R., Michael, S. T., & Cheavens, J. S. (1999). Hope as a psychotherapeutic foundation of common factors, placebos, and expectancies. In Hubble, M. A., Duncan, B. L., & Miller, S. D. (2004). *The heart & soul of change: What works in therapy* (pp. 179–200). American Psychological Association.

Snyder, C. R., Harris, C., Anderson, J. R., Holleran, S. A., Irving, L. M., Sigmon, S. T., Yoshinobu, L., Gibb, J., Langelle, C., & Harney, P. (1991). The will and the ways: Development and validation of an individual-differences measure of hope. *Journal of Personality and Social Psychology*, *60*(4), 570–585. https://doi.org/10.1037//0022-3514.60.4.570

Stotland, E. (1969). *The Psychology of Hope*. Jossey-Bass.

Terr, L. C. (2003). Childhood traumas: an outline and overview. *American Journal of Psychiatry*, *148*(1), 10–20. https://doi.org/10.1176/ajp.148.1.10

Tschudy, J. (2010). Finding, Nurturing, and Instilling Hope in Family Therapy. *All Graduate Theses and Dissertations*. https://doi.org/10.26076/7cae-3b53

van der Kolk, B. A., Pelcovitz, D., Roth, S., Mandel, F. S., McFarlane, A., & Herman, J. L. (1996). Dissociation, somatization, and affect dysregulation: the complexity of adaptation of trauma. *The American Journal of Psychiatry*, *153*(7), 83–93. https://doi.org/10.1176/ajp.153.7.83

Ward, D. B., & Wampler, K. S. (2010). Moving up the continuum of hope: Developing a theory of hope and understanding its influence in couples therapy. *Journal of Marital and Family Therapy*, *36*(2), 212–228. https://doi.org/10.1111/j.1752-0606.2009.00173.x

CHAPTER 11

WORK IN PROCESS
Expressive Arts Therapy Solutions for EMDR Therapists

Irene Rodriguez and Jamie Marich

In expressive arts therapy, *process* is both a noun and a verb. When one engages in an expressive arts process (the noun), they are intentionally linking together two or more art forms or creative practices and being open to what the interplay may reveal. For example, a person *in process* may first engage in some creative movement or dance while listening to a playlist that they created along a certain theme. Then, after this movement, they take it to the page with some freewriting or poetry. They may conclude the process by engaging in some free-form gush art, or even making a sculpture or carving. *Processes* can utilize a variety of expressive forms and be tailored to whatever length of time works for the individual. The key is that the individual engaging in the process, or the facilitator guiding them, is not fixated on just one expressive form. One becomes open to what the larger process of life—and the various ways it can express itself—may reveal.

As a verb, *process* or *being in process* has a similar quality to how EMDR therapists might define *process* or *processing*. Process is about not forcing an outcome, rather "going with that" and noticing the connections that emerge. Expressive arts therapists will often say that engaging in practice is about *process over product*. When one dives into the expressive arts as a practice, the goal is not that you will create a museum-quality piece of artwork or perform your dance on a stage (although if this should happen, great!... *go with that*). Rather, one is encouraged to express themselves with the simple intention of freeing what may have been long buried inside. And true expressive arts therapy will provide people with a variety of avenues by which they can express themselves and hopefully make larger connections that impact the process of living life.

EXPRESSIVE ARTS THERAPY OVERVIEW

If the ideas that we presented in the opening paragraphs resonate with you, then you are well on your way to either becoming an expressive arts therapist or at least embracing the spirit of expressive arts therapy in your work. As your guides for this chapter, we hope to share our passion for expressive arts therapy with you and how this beautifully fuses with our passion for EMDR therapy, ultimately helping us to facilitate transformative experiences for our clients. As trainers in both approaches—expressive arts therapy and EMDR therapy— we firmly believe that the two cannot be separated at this point because of that powerful common element called *process*. Before we paint this picture of fusion further in this chapter, which includes breaking down how we might use expressive arts interventions in each phase of EMDR therapy and providing you with some practical exercises in the course of case studies, let's start with some fundamentals of expressive arts.

THE BUFFET: EXPRESSIVE ARTS THERAPY'S MULTI-MODAL AND INTERMODAL NATURE

Our creative natures brought us directly to the *buffet* that is expressive arts therapy. Neither of us are just one thing—we dance, we enjoy music, we make art, we write, we do theater

DOI: 10.4324/9781003156932-12

and improv. Expressive arts therapy honors our *all of the above* natures. Why choose just one expressive or creative form to use with clients when you can present them with an entire buffet of possibilities?

Consider the metaphor of the buffet—there are numerous flavors and dishes that one can sample. While there may be an occasional person who just piles their plate with one dish (no judgment to you chicken wing fans out there), most of us, when approached with a buffet, sample several things. Perhaps we go back for more of the dish that really appealed to us. Or perhaps we approach the buffet with adventure, using it as an opportunity to at least sample those foods we'd never considered trying before.

As a discipline, expressive arts therapy functions similarly. Expressive arts therapists use all creative forms that are available to them and to their clients. As facilitators of expressive arts, we can adopt an attitude of *meeting people where they are at* and encouraging them to start where they are comfortable or with the practice that most appeals to them. The hope is that people will eventually feel safe enough in the process of expressive arts to sample the practices that they might most resist. These practices typically have the most to teach us about ourselves and how we interact with the unknowns of life.

Here is a short list of some expressive practices that might appear on the buffet:

- Dancing and mindful movement (includes yoga, *Tai Chi*)
- Visual arts (painting, drawing, collage, mixed media, pottery, sculpture)
- Writing (short stories, novels, other fiction, poetry, scenes, memoir, other non-fiction)
- Music (drumming, playing an instrument, songwriting, making playlists, and listening to music)
- Drama and spoken word performances
- Stand-up comedy and comedic storytelling
- Improv
- Play
- Meditation and guided visualization
- Photography
- Filmmaking (yes, this includes TikTok)
- Fashion design and hair design
- Cooking, baking, and other forms of food styling
- Gardening
- Perhaps think of any that you consider to be an expressive practice for you that did not end up on this list…

Any practice that gives us a channel for expressing ourselves to the world, or expressing what we have kept locked tightly inside, has merit as an expressive art form. One of the Latin root words from which we get the English word "express" is the same root from which we get the word *press*, as in the process of extracting juice from a hardened fruit through a device called a press. We press the fruit to get the delicious and nutrient-packed juice, and the pulp from the rest of the fruit can be used in other recipes (Marich, 2019).

So yes, make sure that you sample the juice bar as well the next time that you walk through the buffet line!

THE HISTORICAL AND PHILOSOPHICAL ROOTS OF EXPRESSIVE ARTS THERAPY

The formal field of expressive arts therapy and education is currently regulated by an organization called the International Expressive Arts Therapy Association (IEATA), founded in 1994. Many of the original founders were trained in the singularly focused creative art forms (e.g., art therapy, dance-movement therapy) and became frustrated with what many call the *silo* mentality. In addition to the singular focus, that silo mentality in certain creative arts communities can put unnecessary barriers up around ordinary clinicians who may not have the time or resources to pursue further training being able to responsibly learn and implement creativity into their practices. Focus on what certain leaders founded or published can also be unattractive, especially when the roots of creative and expressive arts as healing run much deeper than modern psychotherapy. Such barriers can fly in the face of cultural humility and honoring the origins of creativity as healing in the first place.

IEATA recognizes that no one person invented expressive arts therapy. Indeed, the 2017 IEATA conference was even themed *The Indigenous Roots of Expressive Arts Therapy* to honor the people of our first nations as the ones who identified practices like drumming, dancing, storytelling, song, meditation, and ceremony as healing. Such practices form the basis for what we know as expressive arts therapy today (Marich, 2019). Expressive arts therapy recognizes that the current discipline comes from indigenous roots, and a variety of different voices, scholars, perspectives, and academic traditions fused together to create our evolving discipline.

One such influence in the development of expressive arts therapy is Angeles Arrien. Arrien, a cultural anthropologist who studied the healing arts of indigenous peoples, authored the classic *The Four Fold Way: Walking the Paths of the Warrior, Teacher, Healer, and Visionary* (2013). In a popular passage from this book that we use in our expressive arts teaching, she explains the concept of the four, universally healing salves—storytelling, singing, dancing, and silence. Gifted healers are empowered to restore the soul by using these healing salves, for at the root causes of distress and *dis-ease* are when we:

- stop singing
- stop dancing
- are no longer enchanted by stories
- become uncomfortable with silence

As EMDR therapists, we may also take pause at this point to consider how these healing salves show up in EMDR therapy. Our organization teaches more boldly now that Dr. Shapiro, while we can respect her study and research that emerged from her famous *walk in the park*, didn't really invent anything new with EMDR therapy. Rather, she developed something and brought it together (and researched it) in a systematized way. The ingredients of EMDR therapy—especially the bilateral qualities of dancing, drumming, and singing (yes, singing creates a natural bilateral stimulation between the hemispheres of the brain)—have been there all along. EMDR's emphasis that much can *come up* when we just silently sit with or *go with* something, or that we can transform the telling of our stories, are inherent to indigenous healing and form the basis of expressive arts therapy.

Expressive arts therapy blends well with any form of psychotherapy that emphasizes introspection and transformation. Another leader in the expressive arts therapy field, Natalie Rogers, literally grew up at the feet of her father Carl Rogers as he developed person-centered therapy. Many of the person-centered psychotherapy principles for which Carl Rogers is well known (e.g., empathy, congruence, unconditional positive regard) were adopted by Natalie in her expressive arts therapy training programs.

As Natalie Rogers (1993) explains in *The Creative Connection: Expressive Arts as Healing*, a landmark text in the expressive arts therapy field, there are three main conditions that foster creativity within an individual:

- **Psychological safety:** We experience such safety when, as an expressive arts practitioner, we are accepted as being of unconditional worth. We can also experience this safety when external evaluation of our work is absent, and when we feel understood in a spirit of empathetic connection.
- **Psychological freedom:** This is a state that can result in expressive worth when we are given many options for exploration. Freedom can also result when we are invited, rather than commanded, to try out new things.
- **Engage in experiences that stimulate us and challenge us:** Expressive arts work naturally facilitates this phenomenon because we are invited to explore, to the degree we are willing and able, those practices and processes that may feel outside of our comfort zones when we begin. Yet engaging in the practices that bring up some discomfort is often what we need the most in our healing journey.

In the mini-expressive arts process that follows, we will be inviting you into an experience where you can begin playing with some of these concepts explained by Rogers.

OPENING MINI-PROCESS

A hallmark of trauma-informed practice is that how you implement it is open to adaptation and variation based on your audience. In building expressive arts processes, you may have an hour or more to link six or seven separate practices together. If you'd like to see some examples of these longer processes, consider checking out Jamie's 2019 book *Process Not Perfection: Expressive Arts Solutions for Trauma Recovery*. In clinical work, especially if you are operating within the standard clinical hour, these shorter processes consisting of two to three short practices may be all that time allows. Or you may work on only one to two practices in the session, and invite the client or student to experiment with another practice on their own, if appropriate.

To get you into the vibe of expressive arts, we'd like to start you out with a much smaller process, consisting of three separate practices. The intention of this practice is to help you identify which expressive forms appeal to you, notice which ones you tend to resist, and perhaps find a practice in the middle that can serve as an effective translator. We recommend that you at least have some paper or pens and pencils nearby. If you have other art materials at your disposal, or a phone or a computer from which you can play music, you may elect to use those to enhance your experience.

PRACTICE 1: WORD CHAIN

- Take a few moments to ground in whatever way feels appropriate for you, and take a few natural breaths with the intention of tuning in and listening to gut-level responses at the level of your body. We're about to ask you a question and encourage you *not* to overthink the answer.

- Which of the expressive practices that you've read about in the chapter thus far appeals to you the most? Go ahead and write down the name of that practice or activity at the top of a page.

- Give yourself three to five minutes (we suggest setting a timer) and write down any words that come to mind as a free association. Bring in the spirit of *go with that*, and let the words keep flowing on the page, even if they are nonsense and even if one doesn't seem to connect to another. Release any tendency to censor yourself.

- After the timer rings, put down your writing instrument and be still for a moment. Take a breath, and notice whatever you notice in your body.

- Now it's time for the second question: which of the expressive practices that you've read about in the chapter thus far do you dislike or resist the most? Go ahead and write down the name of that practice or activity at the top of a page. If you truly feel you like and use all of them already, consider using the one that you traditionally struggle with the most or engage in the least.

- Give yourself three to five minutes (we suggest setting a timer) and write down any words that come to mind as a free association. Bring in the spirit of *go with that*, and let the words keep flowing on the page, even if they are nonsense and even if one doesn't seem to connect to another. Release any tendency to censor yourself.

- After the timer rings, put down your writing instrument and be still for a moment. Take a breath, and notice whatever you notice in your body.

PRACTICE 2: ALTERNATING GESTURES

- Come to a standing position if that is available in your body, or you can always modify by sitting or lying down.

- Skim over (without analysis) your first list connected to the practice that most appeals. Which word on the list is most standing out to you or *sparkling* in this moment? Go ahead and circle that word.

- Now, express that word in a gesture (with your hands only) or with a fuller body movement. Once you come into the position, take three to five breaths and hold as still as possible in the movement.

- Release that gesture or movement and come back to your lists. Look at the second list connected to the practice you most resist, skim over it (without analyzing), and circle the word that most stands out or sparkles for you.

- Express that word in a gesture (with your hands only) or with a fuller body movement. Once you come into the position, take three to five breaths and hold as still as possible in the movement.

- Now, transition your gesture and/or movement back to the first gesture or movement that your body made.

- You are now invited to flow back and forth between the two gestures or movements for the next three to five minutes. You are encouraged to set a timer. You can engage in this flow in silence, or put on a piece of music that you choose.

- As you move back and forth between these shapes in your body, feel free to *go with it* and follow the natural prompting for other movements or expressions that you might be receiving. This improvisation is optional; you can continue to stay with the two main gesture or movement patterns for the duration of the practice.
- When the practice feels complete (you are certainly free to move longer than three to five minutes), return to a sitting position and take a few breaths in the stillness. Notice whatever you are noticing in the physical body and in your experience overall.

PRACTICE 3: BEGINNING A VISUAL JOURNAL PAGE

- Staying in the spirit of being *in process* and noticing whatever you notice, you are now invited to go to the page. You may use a single sheet blank page, or if you have an art or writing journal of any kind, go ahead and open that up.
- For the next five to ten minutes (you can set the timer based on the time availability that you have for this particular process), uncensor yourself on the page. You have complete permission to use your pens, pencils, or any art materials that you have nearby.
- Consider using some of the words that emerged in your Word Chain practice together with any shapes, images, colors, or other visual expressions that may flow.
- You may continue in this practice for as long as feels appropriate, or you may always follow the prompting to start another page.
- The decision is totally yours if you want to keep this page to yourself or share it with someone else. Some people even elect to destroy it in some way (e.g., burning, shredding) if that symbolizes some type of release or transformation. Avoid the tendency though to just throw it away if you're stuck in a rut of self-judgment.

OFFERING FEEDBACK IN EXPRESSIVE ARTS THERAPY

If you elect to share your process with a colleague, your own therapist/healer, or a trusted friend, consider following these general conversation starters for giving feedback and offering reflections in expressive arts therapy. If you are practicing for yourself and do not have someone with whom you can share at this time, these questions can also be useful as journal prompts for your own written reflections. These questions, whether you are facilitating group therapeutic processes or individual therapeutic sessions, also apply when working clinically. Expressive arts therapy feedback and reflections is never about psychological analysis or performance critique. You can think of these questions and conversation starters. In the language of EMDR therapy, they can be woven in as resources or interweaves depending on how and where you are using them in the overall EMDR therapy process. They are useful to promote conversation and reflection on the work in a way that is likely to further open the individual's own organic processing.

- Describe your personal experience with the process.
- What did you discover in your process?
- What did you learn about yourself in the process?
- What did you notice about judgment or self-criticism during the process?

- What role did the different styles of creative forms play in discovering what you discovered in your process?
- Which of the skills explored in this process can be applied to your overall trauma recovery or wellness plan?

If offering reflections or feedback to another, please avoid using any language that can be construed as judgment. Even a comment like "That's beautiful" or "Such powerful work!" can potentially come with an air of judgment. Rather, focus on reflecting how a certain part of the work might make you feel, or, if appropriate, comment on how you are relating to what the individual expressed. You can certainly use the language of observation such as "I notice that you use a lot of green in this one section." The point is not for that to be analytical or to make some deep interpretation into it. Rather, see what yields conversationally from you making that observation. We've both had expressive arts facilitators invite us to "Tell me more," about this one part of the work, and from there an entire golden web of connections can emerge.

We hope that you are noticing how such approaches can be valuable throughout the phases of EMDR therapy. What an individual expresses can reveal a treasure about their internal world that can never be put into words unless gently invited to the surface with expression. Before moving on to the next section and reading about how we approach the natural fusion between expressive arts therapy and EMDR therapy, perhaps take a few moments to reflect on how you've brought expressive practices into the phases of EMDR before. What have you noticed so far? What intention can you set for what else you might like to learn?

BLENDING EXPRESSIVE ARTS THERAPY WITH THE STANDARD EMDR PROTOCOL

Many clinicians trained in EMDR are technical purists, only having experienced or heard of the strict "protocol" that EMDR therapists must learn in training, are surprised to hear that the work we do is even possible. Yet Dr. Shapiro gives more permission than ever for the fusion of expressive modalities in the latest (2018) version of her core textbook, especially when EMDR therapists are well trained to use them. EMDR therapists know that if a client gets stuck in the traditional flow of applying eye movements or other bilateral/dual attention stimulus like audio tones or tactile sensations, clinicians are allowed to use prompting questions, often called cognitive interweaves, to move the processing along in as natural a way as possible. Like many EMDR therapists who have come before us, we've leaned into using the word "interweaves" only to describe these proactive measures that we can take, since they can be more than cognitive (Shapiro, 2018). They can be somatic. They can be emotional. And yes, they can be expressive. Interweaves can also present the perfect opportunity to use free-form gush art with materials available, or inviting movement (e.g., dance, yoga, free-form organic expressions) by literally moving the stuck energy out of the body when a client is blocked or otherwise has difficulty processing. Once the expressive art practice employed reaches a natural completion or seems to have gotten the energy point moving or otherwise dislodged, the transition back into the standard EMDR protocol can be seamless.

In this section, we present each phase of EMDR therapy (handling Phases Three to Six together as the *reprocessing phases*) and provide insight into how you can bring the expressive arts mindset into EMDR therapy sessions. Specific practices and processes will follow, woven in with case studies, into the following section. The phase-based list that follows is not intended to be formulaic. Like with any EMDR strategy or clinical approach you learn, implementing it is an art that must be felt out on a case-by-case basis. In keeping with the metaphor that we used earlier in the chapter, what we offer you here and in the section to follow is a buffet. Some of these strategies you may be eager to sample as they will make sense to the way that you do EMDR therapy already, and others may feel a bit uncomfortable or unfamiliar. As with expressive arts therapy overall, consider starting where there is the most resonance and then once you feel more secure with these approaches, perhaps try something new from the buffet. Please remember to sample that practice yourself first before sharing it with clients. Above anything else, we believe that the willingness to practice expressive arts yourself is imperative for being successful in sharing them with any kind of client, especially those highly impacted by the legacy of trauma.

Phase One: Client History There is no set way to take a comprehensive client history in EMDR therapy. Yes, different trainers have their preferred methods that they emphasize in basic training, and Dr. Shapiro made some suggestions about how client history can be taken. Yet even the tone of her 2018 book suggests that you have options and the EMDR International Association standards are very permissive about letting trainers teach Phase One in whatever way that they see fit. There are two basic purposes of Phase One. The first is to get a comprehensive picture about the client, their overall presentation, and any concerns that may need to be noted so that more protective factors can be implemented. The aim of determining any complicating features to the case, like a high dissociative profile, pregnancy, or living in a high-risk environment, is never to *rule out* doing EMDR therapy with a client, although a great deal of myth, misinformation, and consultant's opinions that they can pass off as fact still abounds. We believe that any client can be appropriate for EMDR therapy as long as their case is properly conceptualized and the client is equipped with adequate preparation skills in Phase Two.

A great deal of rapport building and general human connection is also important in Phase One. Creative practices can help to enhance a budding therapeutic relationship, especially if the client is open to exploring their own expression and creativity as part of the healing process. While some posit that a relationship is not critical for successful EMDR to take place, our artistic souls and clinical experiences teach us the opposite—the relationship can be essential, especially when leading a client through target selection. The process of target selection in EMDR therapy helps the EMDR clinician and client to determine, in collaboration, where the arrow of the work will be pointed or targeted once the client is prepared for the reprocessing phases. There are many methods in the EMDR community that are used for getting at potential targets. Something as standard as an Adverse Childhood Experiences (ACE) inventory can be used, or a classic method of listing one's ten best and ten worst memories.

In our program, we teach a method called "Thematic Client History." Because unhealed complex trauma can impact a person's sense of chronology or keeping details of a story straight, we've generally found that it is impractical or sometimes too activating to take too detailed of a history at first. We like to tell our clients that we can *do a lot with a very little* in EMDR therapy, and that EMDR does not badger one with narrative. When you engage in target selection through a theme, the clinician listens to the client's presentation about their presenting problems or goals for being in treatment. In doing that, a clear theme or series of themes will likely emerge about what is blocking that client from attaining their goals for treatment or for life. Some classic examples of themes include low self-esteem, hopelessness, perfectionism, "the mother" or "father" wound (or other attachment-related themes), inadequacy. From identifying the core themes we can then guide the client into identifying some negative cognitions that are associated with those themes and then engage in a series of questions to get at some of the touchstone memories or clusters. We prefer a modification of the full floatback technique by asking, "Thinking back over the course of your whole life, when is the (first/worst/most recent) time you believed that *I am not good enough*" (as an example) to get at an initial series of memories for reprocessing. A full floatback technique may also be an option, especially when the client is immediately prepared to move into Phases Three to Six.

Theme is a strong component of expressive arts therapy, and consider how the questions for reflections and feedback presented in the previous section can help you and the client engage in dialogue that can help reveal themes, negative cognitions, and targets. We've both had clients present for EMDR therapy who are not so keen on telling us their story, especially at first, yet they are willing to show us some artwork or writing that they've done. In our experience, this is generally all the opening that you need. Language and visual images can be seen as co-facilitators in the AIP model. Clients who experience negative or oppressive cognitions, blocking beliefs, may feel stuck in a storyline. Their sense of understanding and willingness to work with those stuck points may be enhanced through use of images or other expressive pieces.

Phase Two: Preparation We hold steady to the belief that in working with any type of EMDR client, especially those impacted by complex trauma and dissociation, a wide variety of preparation skills must be offered to the client and implemented. One *Calm Safe Place* exercise is not going to cut it, and with some clients, they cannot even engage that exercise or it may promote more dissociation than might be helpful. Our approach to preparation is, in addition to giving clients a place of retreat when they need to stop or pause the flow of reprocessing sessions, to begin widening their capacity for affect and multi-channel sensory experiences. While a plethora of well-adapted mindfulness skills can be beneficial in this process, expressive arts practices can provide an avenue for more fully and accessibly practicing mindfulness. As long as clients are willing to engage with expressive practices (or at least give the ones that most appeal a try), you have a variety of skills that you can mix and match to meet the client where they are at. Moreover, orienting them to the expressive arts mentality of *process over product* and being with something without judgment can set them up to be more effective processors of information when the time arrives for Phases Three to Six.

During Phase Two it is important to facilitate clients' connections with their bodies. This is especially critical for clients with complex trauma because their internal system protects them through disconnection and dissociation. Encouraging interventions that aid defragmentation, connection with parts of the body, and activation of sensations is unpredictable for successful reprocessing. The therapist does not interpret the client's process or product. The therapist facilitates the exploration process by inviting the client to feel during the creation experience and to witness their own process. The therapist can ask the client to observe how the images feel in his body, where he feels them, and even observe if the feelings and emotions that arise have characteristics such as color, shape, and texture.

Here are some specific strategies that an EMDR therapist can implement during Phase Two work especially, using a variety of media and creative forms:

- Physical, not just imaginary, creation of a container and other objects that can serve as a container, such as envelope, movement/gesture, diary, and visual diary.
- Looking at the pictures can also become a meditation. The more we look, the more we see, and the more the image influences consciousness.

- Suggest creating an altar where the client can place objects and messages that can serve as a safe/quiet place also using images of their own arts. While you may teach this strategy in Phase Two, it can be especially vital for in-between session linking and management of affect. Place objects that can serve as grounding reminders or facilitate a positive response with your messages: picture of a quiet place, create the protective figure, rock painted with images of trees or messages that include positive cognitions.
- Use the voice of the client to remember instructions, visualizations, or positive quotes/affirmations. Encourage them to actually say what applies aloud. These activities can be started or completed during the session, and if positive/adaptive information is available, it should be strengthened with slow bilateral DAS.

Providing positive expressive arts experiences can also help with frontloading and adapting many of the classic EMDR therapy practices, like Calm/Safe place, to better serve the clients' needs. For clients who cannot visualize optimally, give them a chance to engage in free-form artmaking, or gush art, while facilitating the visualization. You may invite them to do it with their eyes open or closed while exploring different materials. For any images that are expressed, you may invite your client to observe the feelings and emotions that emerge and where they are located in the body.

The client may have learned that it is not safe to feel relaxed or calm. In what ways can I encourage the client to explore places where she may begin to feel calm? Which modality works best for my client? You may be the first person to truly model safety in expression for them by giving your clients options and opportunities to express themselves in an environment where they are respected. We need to start where they are and provide the tools to make the connection between their bodily sensations, emotions, and feelings. Each client is different, each session must be adapted to their needs. The creative process is the portal that will provide us with information that would not otherwise be available. Give opportunities for the clients to honor their experience. The therapist's role is to provide the space for the story to unfold from the somatic experience. It is an opportunity to invite the client to sit down with the experience.

At times, the therapist may feel the need to use many artistic modalities or creative forms in the same session. Although expressive arts therapy encourages multi-modality and inter-modality, being excessive with the number of forms used can backfire because it takes time for the client to establish the flow of the process and integrate the experience. Conventional 50-minute sessions may also not allow for adequate time for full exploration and integration.

Another avenue that you can explore in Phase Two Preparation for further building the therapeutic relationship is a process that we refer to as *Call and Response* expressive arts therapy. While there are many ways to practice *Call and Response*, a simple practice in which you can engage is to provide a client with a blank piece of paper, or have them open to a page in a journal that they might be keeping. For timed intervals (anywhere from one to three minutes), you and the client go back and forth creating whatever comes up for you on the page. Have the client go first, unless they are too bashful to start, then you can go first. During the time when the person who is drawing, painting, or using whatever materials are available in the book, the other person is invited to sit quietly and observe. Then, when it is the next person's turn, they take the page and respond on the same page in whatever way feels appropriate. If you both feel it's appropriate, you can also elect to turn away while the other person is doing their one to three minutes of work to truly practice not anticipating, and responding in the moment. Please refer to a video resource that we provide at the end of this chapter (via YouTube) for more ideas on Call and Response, and how you can use this practice as a springboard for connection and possibly working through difficulties in communication.

Phases Three to Six: The Reprocessing Phases Every phase of the *heart of EMDR* that we generally refer to as the reprocessing phases can be delivered within the standard protocol while also bringing in expressive practices if needed to further engage the client. Consider how, in Phase Three, instead of asking the client to describe an image, we could ask them to draw (or form with clay or sandtray) an image, or express the worst part of that scene using a gesture or movement. With the telehealth revolution showing EMDR therapists just how effective self-tapping can be in Phase Four, consider how the client's own, organic bilateral movements can be implemented into overall reprocessing. Both of us have seen clients, in Phase Four, make organically bilaterally gestures or movements on their own that can facilitate greater depth to reprocessing. It really is like a dance!

A major aspect of using expressive arts interventions in Phases Four to Six is to adapt *go with that* very liberally. If, in their Phase Four work, a client starts making natural gestures or movements, encourage them to not censor themselves and go with those. From here an entire dance or movement sequence may evolve. Whether it evolves on its own, or you invite the use of such expressions as interweave, you have endless possibilities at your disposal. We recommend at the very least that all EMDR therapists, whether you have formal training in expressive arts or not, keep some scrap paper and markers, crayons, or other drawing materials in your office. If you are seeing a client over teletherapy, encourage them to keep something to draw with nearby. If a client is stuck at any point in their reprocessing in Phases Four to Six, you can invite them into a process of free-form drawing or *gush art* for one to three minutes. Another good place to use this *gush art* interweave is when a client's SUDs is close to 0 but not moving down, you can offer the prompt: "What keeps the SUDs from being a 0?" and *go with that* via gush art on the page. If the SUDs is still rather high, you can keep the invitation more general: "What keeps the SUDs from going lower?"

We often tell our clients, "It doesn't matter if you scribble in red crayon for three minutes, just go with it. Express with your body, use as many colors as you want."

The creation of images as a form of non-verbal expression makes it easier for the client to feel more secure to express strong emotions connected with unconscious information. In expressive arts therapy, like in EMDR, the therapist refrains from giving meaning or interpretation to the images. By interpreting colors as depressive or aggressive, for instance, we lose the opportunity to let the client explore for themselves and *go with it*. Often, after this period of *gush*, a client is able to get back into the flow of where they were at in their reprocessing, or you can check back in with the target to reactivate. Like any good interweave, the purpose of using gush art within EMDR therapy is to facilitate the client's own organic processing by providing a gentle assist to move through a block.

Phase Seven: Closure Phases Two and Seven are linked in a great dance of fusion (to use expressive arts, specifically *Dancing Mindfulness* language). If you and your client have done your work well in Phase Two and maybe have even added to a person's collection of resources as they've navigated challenges in the reprocessing phase, what you need for effective Phase Seven closure is already there. These collections of skills can include more standard visualizations like Calm Safe Place or Light Stream that are well known in the EMDR community, standard mindfulness skills, or expressive arts skills. As discussed in our section on Phase Two, expressive practices can be brought in to make the visualizations more real for people, such as having them draw their Calm Safe Place, or do a movement-based Light Stream (see Jamie's chapter on Dancing Mindfulness in this volume for a breakdown of this exercise, called *Painting Light*).

In EMDR therapy closure, therapists alert their clients that processing may continue after the session ends, so it is important to have a collection of skills that they can use for managing affect, or having some kind of way to make note of what they may need to in-between sessions. Conventional journaling that is more verbal in nature, or using other logs like a TICES grid or diary card (popular in DBT) have always been honored options within EMDR therapy. However, we'd now like you to consider how the expressive arts, specifically the practices of visual journaling and making playlists, can enhance how clients can safely and effectively link their sessions. Please also refer to Jamie's Dancing Mindfulness chapter in this volume for more on making playlists and the role they can play in linking sessions.

Phase Eight: Re-Evaluation Re-evaluation is the art of checking in on progress from previous sessions and planning the next move. In EMDR therapy, re-evaluation has a micro-level (checking on progress from session to session) application and a macro-level (reviewing the treatment plan overall) application. Expressive arts interventions can be used to assist with both.

When a client comes in for a new EMDR therapy session, EMDR therapists will commonly ask clients what they've noticed since the last session. Whether they've been keeping a visual journal, a traditional writing journal, or some combination of the two, having them share what they want to from their in-between session work can be a phenomenal bridge to the session that's about to happen. Playlists that a person assembles can even take on a similar quality and can add to the potential of the check-in.

For clients who end up taking to the overall spirit of expressive arts therapy in their work (as opposed to just drawing on some of the practices from it), you find yourself engaging with them in language of creativity and the expressive arts. In formal expressive arts therapy supervision, it's commonplace for us to ask our supervisees, "Where are you at with your process this week?" or "What has your personal practice shown you this week?" These questions, if a client is willing to engage them, may assist you with the broad quality of Phase Eight, which is determining what treatment intentions or goals the client wants to go next. For many, their expressive arts processes will show them where they need to work on through EMDR therapy targeting and reprocessing in order to realize these intentions. Trust that the creative process will take the client where they need to go, just as we EMDR therapists teach with the AIP model.

CASES STUDIES AND EXPRESSIVE ARTS PROCESSES

Many expressive arts therapists are intuitive creatures, so it can be difficult to break down and systemize exactly what we do in sessions. For both of us, interweaving expressive arts therapy into EMDR therapy is a natural flow that is facilitated by our own deep engagement in expressive arts processes. When each client comes into our space, as part of Client History and general assessment, we regularly ask ourselves:

- What does the client bring to the therapeutic space regarding existing resources, interests, or, if applicable, spiritual practice?
- What does this client need?
- What gaps might exist in the client's willingness and ability to practice resources for the purposes of adaptive self-soothing, affect management, and, in general, coping with life?
- What might the client need to learn to continue along the path of a healing process?

What follows are some examples of how Irene specifically implemented interventions from her own understanding of expressive arts therapy, as she asked herself these questions with the following clients.

ANDREA: TEN-YEAR-OLD

Andrea is a ten-year-old bilingual Latinx girl who presented with symptoms of anxiety related to school. She overall had a supportive maternal presence who was engaged in the therapy. Irene determined that it was necessary to use the AIP model to help both Andrea and her mother understand the source of her anxiety, and the reasons why she couldn't just "stop it" until certain material was reprocessed or dealt with. For Irene, it was very natural to turn to the triune brain coloring page used in our training program. (See attached if you wish to make use of it as a coloring page with your clients, or in the manner that Irene used it, integrating clay.)

Here are the general steps that Irene took with integrating the coloring page and clay work with Andrea and her mother to explain the AIP model and the general principle of the triune brain:

1. Get out a blank copy of the triune brain coloring page, where the reptilian, mammalian, and neocortex brains are depicted.

2. Use three different colors of clay (as depicted in the attached image) to explain dynamics according to your understanding of the triune brain. We generally recommend that the therapist chooses a color to represent a bridge (i.e., the neurofiber bridge that connects the limbic brain with the neocortex). In this case, Irene chose brown. Then you can have the client choose one color to represent unpleasant memories that can stay stuck in the limbic brain (i.e., pink in this attached image), and the other to represent pleasant sensations or adaptive information (i.e., yellow in the attached image).

3. Both therapist and client play with the clay. Let the client lead the therapist and guide them on how they want the shape of the unpleasant feelings or memories to be.

4. Repeat the same process with the pleasant ones.

5. After the pleasant and unpleasant sensations have been given shape, guide the client in placing them on the triune brain picture: place the unpleasant shape on the limbic, and the pleasant in the neocortex. Then, after the bridge has been given shape by the therapist, place the bridge over the brain's picture and explain how memories get "stuck" in the reptilian and limbic system and need to be processed so the positive feelings/memories can be available. Explain that the bilateral dual attention stimulus component of EMDR at this point as a process that can widen the bridge, and when our aim is to work with unpleasant memories, the stimulation can let the information pass over the bridge more quickly and link up with the pleasant material. At this point you may need to model eye movements or tapping if they are not clear on what is meant by bilateral stimulation.

6. Allow the client to play with the clay by moving the positive and negative memories over the bridge.

7. Explain that sometimes we don't have time to complete the reprocessing in a single session and the upsetting feelings can be placed in a box. See attached image for an example of how you can play the clay structure made here in a literal container.

8. Once the client verbalizes understanding about why we are using DAS and how it may help process the unpleasant sensations or memories causing the anxiety symptoms, the client was encouraged to share what she learned with her mother.

Andrea had a solid understanding of why they were using the tappers (for bilateral dual attention stimulus) in EMDR therapy. Andrea's having an understanding of what was happening in her brain with her anxiety symptoms, and the impact of EMDR reprocessing on the related memories, seemed to connect her further to the process. Irene set up a more present-prong target using her typical anxiety in the morning, transitioning from the car to the school, and then being in class with an English teacher who frightened her. There did not seem to be any antecedent memories to the anxiety, so this present focus was appropriate. Both targets resolved to an adaptive resolution.

LOURDES: 17-YEAR-OLD

Lourdes is a 17-year-old Caucasian young woman who also presented with anxiety symptoms. She did not want to be in therapy and refused to identify any treatment goal. After several years of ongoing treatment, the client reported that she was "done with therapy." Her parents were granting her a weekly allowance with the condition of participating in therapy. During Phase One, the client stated that she likes music and often uses a journal to vent feelings. After getting the client's consent to use music and other art modalities, Irene

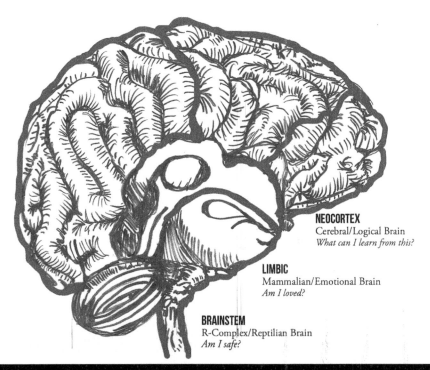

NEOCORTEX
Cerebral/Logical Brain
What can I learn from this?

LIMBIC
Mammalian/Emotional Brain
Am I loved?

BRAINSTEM
R-Complex/Reptilian Brain
Am I safe?

Figure 11.1 Triune brain coloring page.

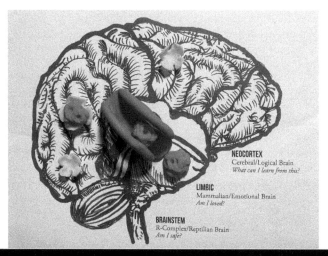

Figure 11.2 Triune brain coloring page with clay pieces.

Figure 11.3 Container image with clay pieces.

consistently made art material available for Lourdes to use. In this skill, we will describe how you can use collaging to identify treatment goals.

1. The therapist provides white paper and collage materials (magazines, pictures, glue, scissors), and invites the client to go over the magazines and choose any images that may get their attention. The client was invited to refrain from overthinking and just select the pictures that got her attention.
2. The therapist sits quietly, witnessing the client's process. At some point, ask the client what they are noticing as the images reveal themselves. You can also ask, are there any images that you like more than others? Are there any images about which you feel indifferent or neutral?
3. Through this process, notice if the client voices anything that can be shaped into a treatment goal.
4. Encourage the client to actually make the collage, giving them assistance only if they ask.
5. Invite the client to notice what is happening while they make and perhaps talk about their collage.

Lourdes could not identify any somatic responses but agreed to continue therapy to focus on her anxiety symptoms as they related to driving. This insight emerged from the collage work and became a doorway through which therapy could begin.

In moving to Phase Two, Lourdes was not able to create a conventional Calm Safe Place. For the client to create a safe enough place, Irene was able to meet her at a beach. Activities such as walking barefoot in the sand, creating mandalas with shells, and using the senses helped develop and install a safe place. Lourdes also responded to gush art, doodling, and creating self-portrait about how she was feeling on any given day. Playing music of her preference (in her case, Billie Eilish) facilitated a greater sense of conversation and connection by asking the client questions like "What do those lyrics mean to you?" In many cases, the client will be open to hearing the therapist's interpretation or impression of the lyrics as well. In the case of Billie Eilish, Lourdes reported how impressed she was with Billie's resolve to be herself and to express herself, and Billie became a protective figure they were able to tap in as a resource. Any time the reported adaptive information in these art sharing processes, bilateral DAS was used to strengthen the connection.

Those activities helped build a therapeutic relationship, help the client start connecting to her body sensations, and make the transition to Phases Three to Six. Lourdes used Phases Three to Eight to be able to target her anxiety around driving. She successfully passed her driver's test and completed her high school diploma.

LESLIE: 43-YEAR-OLD

Leslie is a 43-year-old first-generation Hispanic woman who presented with a sense of low self-esteem in her professional life. Her primary negative cognitions were that "I can't have what I want," and "I cannot speak my voice/I am invisible." During an EMDR reprocessing session, she reported seeing a little girl between six and eight years come into her awareness. In this scene, her parents were saying that she was different from white people because of her skin color. And this scene proved to be a sticking point for her in moving forward.

Irene then moved into exploring several different options for interweave. Irene asked if the girl had a negative cognition, and Leslie reported, "I'm different." The client was invited to *notice that*, and after several sets of bilateral DAS, the target was clear. In Phase Seven Closure, Leslie cried because she felt a connection with the little girl. They closed the session by having Leslie write a letter to the girl about all the things that make her unique, and everything she can now have. The following week, the target was still clear, and the positive cognition of "I can be myself" was still a VOC of 7. For the rest of the session, Irene helped the client to build a playlist focused on the theme "I can be myself," and they engaged in some mindful movements. The client was invited to notice sensations and feelings coming up and bilateral dual attention stimulus was added to strengthen the continual emergence of more adaptive information.

Leslie then had the playlist as a reminder and a reinforcement if she needed it on her own at home. The playlist could also be used as a resource for her after therapy concluded.

PAUL: 35-YEAR-OLD

Paul is an African American 35-year-old male. He presented with a history of complex trauma, and was nervous about engaging in any kind of trauma work. He initially expressed concerns that Irene didn't seem to "get him." In attempting to bridge the gap of understanding, Irene learned that the client enjoyed cooking and baking cakes. She used metaphor and storytelling to describe the treatment process using the example of baking a cake, which eventually convinced him to give EMDR therapy a try. Using metaphors that work with the client's worldview and areas of interest is a splendid skill to have at your disposal as an EMDR therapist. In our experience, being engaged in the expressive arts yourself allows you as the therapist to go with this flow.

Here is how Irene explained how EMDR therapy is similar to what he does when he bakes a cake:

1. Decide which kind of cake you want to bake, identifying the ingredients you have available and which ones you need to buy. These steps, like Phase One and Phase Two, ensure that you have the necessary quantities and all the tools (e.g., oven, container).
2. Ask the client to identify what resources and strengths they have, and others needed that may help them to achieve their treatment goals (e.g., getting the ingredients and tools).
3. As a resource, invite the client to recall a time when they felt good while baking. Use bilateral dual attention stimulus to strengthen the adaptive responses. Proceed to mix the ingredients while the oven is preheating. Once the oven is at the proper temperature, put the mixture in the oven for as long as necessary. During this time, the oven does not open because it would lose the temperature it needs to cook properly (e.g., Phases Three to Six).
4. Once the mixture is cooked, allow time for it to cool and to settle (Phase Seven), so that you can decorate as however you wish (Phase Eight).

Many artistically inclined and creative EMDR therapists regularly use metaphors to assist their clients in understanding elements of their treatment journey. What are some of your favorite metaphors that you have used in your practice of EMDR therapy? Moreover, consider how many of these metaphors emerged through direct collaboration with your clients and meeting them where they are at. This collaborative process is a prime example of how EMDR therapy and a person-centered expressive arts mindset can fuse beautifully.

CULTURAL ADAPTATIONS

The expressive arts in their various forms are cultural universals. Even though all of the cultures on our planet have their uniquely beautiful manners through which people can practice expression, the existence of the various practices can be found everywhere. Think back to what we taught you about *the four healing salves* as identified by Arrien (2013) in our opening section and the connection is clear—the expressive arts have been here forever. Certainly a lot longer than "professional" psychotherapy!

Whenever you are handling something as ubiquitous as the expressive arts, you have a unique opportunity to work with your clients in the level beyond or below (if thinking neuroscientifically) language. This opening is not only vital in working with trauma, it's also critical in working with people who come from cultures other than your own (as the therapist) or whose first language may be different than their therapist's native language. Because in the expressive arts process, words take a back seat to the organicity of one's own holistic expression and experience. Although some writing forms can be used in expressive arts processes, and music can certainly contain meaningful lyrics, words are just one channel through which an individual may communicate. And why limit people to just one channel? Especially people who come from cultures where white, colonial constructs of black/white, good/bad, right/wrong are not in the norm and, in many cases, seen as bizarre in working with human beings.

For many of the same reasons that we adore the expressive arts for its ability to bridge understanding between people who may be divided by language, we also like EMDR therapy. Narrative detail is not so important. Even if you, as the EMDR therapist, do not speak or understand the client's native language, you can give them permission to reprocess (i.e., *go with that*) in their native language or a mixture of the languages that they speak. Remember as the EMDR therapist, you do not need to know every little detail of their process. Allowing them to work in their mother tongue, sometimes called "the language of feelings," even if you don't fully comprehend the small details of their experience is possible in EMDR therapy.

We'd like to share some of our best practices for working specifically with Spanish-speaking clients (which is Irene's primary basis of expertise as a native Spanish speaker) and clients whose language and perhaps cultural background is different from the EMDR therapist. Even though we initially developed these practices for the EMDR therapists whom we trained, we make some commentary on where expressive arts can be brought in for a further assist. And if you find these skills useful in enhancing your EMDR therapy practice, they can also be used if you are practicing expressive arts therapy as a stand-alone modality.

RELATIONAL

In establishing a connection, understanding language changes, phrases, and words will help increase confidence and strengthen the therapeutic relationship. The use of sayings (*dichos*) is common in Spanish and many other languages. Such sayings can help you better understand the client and their circumstances. Moreover, the use of sayings can signal cultural sensitivity toward the client and strengthen the relationship. Even if you do not speak or understand the native language of the client, taking the time to learn how they speak, especially key phrases or slang, can make a significant impact on the client. Consider how listening to one of their playlists or having them share a favorite song with you from their native language might give you this needed linguistic insight; especially if they are willing to share with you what the song and its content means to them. For some clients, it may also feel organic to share with you some dances or movements that accompany the song.

Like any other social identity, language expresses itself as a place of privilege or oppression in a given place and time in history. A person's social identity will add to their experience of belonging, feeling understood, having a sense of value, safety, choices, or being invalidated, excluded, rejected, or misunderstood. Studies have documented that the client uses the second language when expressing unpleasant emotions to distancing themself from the memory (Santiago-Rivera et al., 2009). Being aware of the combination of verbal and non-verbal language is important. Observe the pauses, gestures, and tone of voice. Expressive arts work throughout the therapeutic process may help to further attune you to these non-verbal aspects of communication.

Clients will switch between Spanish and English (or any other languages) if they know that the therapist is bilingual or multilingual. This makes it easier for the client to use language to express emotions and memories accurately. In this process, they create what is in essence a unique *third language* by which they conduct therapy and the connection can be even more personal and intimate. In the case where the therapist is not bilingual, consider how the expressive arts, especially collaborative practices like *Call and Response*, may serve as a third language of sorts for bridging the gap of understanding. And every opportunity for building bridges must be embraced in any type of trauma work, especially when clients may view themselves as inferior to their therapist.

In the United States where we practice, we've observed that if Spanish-speaking clients have a white therapist from the dominant culture, they may be navigating a fear that the therapist perceives them as dumb or uneducated because they cannot pronounce certain words. They may also perceive the white therapist in a position of greater power or intelligence, which can have an impact on blocking beliefs (e.g., "I'm not as good as a white person"). The therapist may be the one who needs to address the proverbial *elephant in the room* and create a judgment-free dialogue to create space for communication to flow. This discussion can include an open dialogue about limitations and how to ask questions (or bring in music or other expressive practices) if either party feels stuck with communicating.

ATTUNEMENT IN THE PHASES OF EMDR THERAPY

Once the therapeutic relationship is established, clients can feel more comfortable in beginning the processing of the trauma. The therapist can be more sensitive and validate the experience of the bilingual client without it having to be constantly explained or translated. Use Phase One to develop a compassionate relationship to understand your client within the social, cultural, and economic context. Avoid making broad-sweeping assumptions (e.g., "Because that person is from Puerto Rico, they must be..."). Explore how the client perceives the therapeutic process and honor the level of disclosure that the client feels comfortable with from the trauma-informed approach and considering cultural elements. In conducting Phase One, proverbs and sayings can help clarify the issues and how the client views themselves and the world, and they may connect to the themes and negative cognitions. Allow for songs, dances, poems, photographs, or other pieces of artwork to be used in this process if it feels organic to the client.

Whether you identify direct negative cognitions as part of Phase One work or wait to bring them up in Phase Three (depending on your EMDR therapy approach), consider exploring how the client feels to repeat negative cognitions in Spanish (or their native language) versus a second language. Also, consider that stigmatization and racism can be connected to negative beliefs or blocking beliefs. What message did the client receive about the dominant culture when growing up? What message(s) did they receive about their relationship to the dominant culture growing up? If it's too painful or not possible for the client to put their gut-level answers to these questions into words, consider how any of the expressive practices described in this chapter can be used as a medium for that expression.

All of the strategies that we covered in Phase Two earlier in the chapter are rather broad-reaching and universally applicable, as long as you're addressing any language or relational issues that may emerge as you teach them. Phase Two also offers an excellent opportunity for clients to bring in figures, stories, legends, songs, and other aspects of their native culture as resources that can be strengthened with bilateral DAS. A client may even be open to engaging in an expressive arts process that engages all of these aspects, which can set an ideal foundation in Phase Two. When frontloading material as part of Phase Two, the struggles that they've overcome by coming to their new country can be leveraged in the resourcing process. You can ask a client what positive cognitions or sensations come up when they consider what they've overcome. All of these noticings can be strengthened as resources.

In the reprocessing phases, we've already established that clients are free to reprocess internally or externally in their native language or in a combination of languages—whatever makes the most sense for them. There are a few other matters to consider as you navigate the expressive art that is language. Be curious about how the client uses their first language. You may ask questions like, "How do you say that in Spanish?" If you said that in Spanish, how would it feel different? Can you say the same in Spanish and notice what is different this time? Consider how these questions and the space to be answered can begin to repair experiences of discrimination and oppression by language barriers, such as teasing for having an accent or use of *Spanglish*. Even therapists who do not speak the client's native language can use these strategies as *interweaves* assuming that a solid therapeutic relationship and understanding about communication is established.

When working with families and a family member who do not speak English, you cannot exclude them from the session. This situation can happen when the parent's primary language is Spanish (or another language), and the minor or identified client speaks English. Consider having psychoeducational material in both languages and having the family members translate to each other. Including a few coloring pages or images in these materials can be helpful. If you need to use an interpreter, it is your responsibility to guide the interpreter on the therapeutic process and especially on EMDR therapy, or EMDR and expressive arts therapy in combination. The interpreter must understand their role during therapy and its impact on the therapeutic relationship. In all of these relationships, consider how any of the expressive practices covered in this chapter may be incorporated in building that beautiful bridge of understanding.

A final note that is important to cover in setting up an office space that is conducive to culturally attuned expressive arts therapy practice. While we do not expect therapists of any kind to break their budget in obtaining only the highest quality of materials, please also be mindful of your material quality overall. Making materials available to your clients that are only cheap or of low quality may reinforce messages of not being good enough. You may certainly have materials of various qualities available, especially to experiment with sensation and differences in texture. Yet bear in mind that the experience you provide your client to begin or to continue their journey in expressive arts can be a tremendously reparative experience to them. Making good materials and enriching experiences available, whether you are simply witnessing their process or engaging with them in process, can show your clients that they are worthy of nourishing themselves with expression and creativity.

FUTURE DIRECTIONS AND CONCLUSIONS

Take a moment to consider what you've learned about expressive arts therapy in this chapter. Perhaps you already came in with some understanding of expressive arts therapy specifically, or other creative arts. How has that understanding been amplified by reading through this chapter, and hopefully engaging in some of the processes that we recommend? And how can this power of process improve your effectiveness and overall enthusiasm as an engaged, intuitive EMDR therapist?

A common question that we both get from our students is how *exactly* to weave expressive arts therapy into EMDR therapy. The short answer is that we cannot give you a formula. Sure, we can give you general best practices, as we've covered in this chapter, of how expressive arts practices and processes can be integrated into all eight phases. Yet we encourage you to think beyond the simple technique and steps. Your own expressive arts practice positively impacts your enthusiasm for connecting with your clients and using every possible channel of experience to help them to resource and to engage. In the indigenous origins of expressive arts therapy, expressive healing was understood as a community endeavor, and you can become a vital part of that client's community for healing.

Another question we entertain that has not yet been directly addressed in this chapter is whether or not you, as the EMDR or general therapist, ought to engage in the practices and processes with the clients, or if you ought to simply observe, perhaps asking occasional questions if they need an assist. In sum, elicit feedback from the client and then "go with that." Many of the practices are collaborative, like *Call and Response*, and using client's sharing of music or preferred metaphors for connection (both described in this chapter). Some will want you to make art or move with them as it might make them feel less judged, whereas others find nourishment in simply being witnessed. When you can show them the power of witness, they can in turn be inspired to sit back and witness what they may have just created. The power of witness, or *noticing without judgment*, is an imperative component of EMDR therapy as we encourage people to *go with that…* not judging, not commenting, just noticing. Expressive arts processes can remove the veil that allows for deeper experiences of what the yogis call witness consciousness.

While EMDR therapy is one of the most important innovations in the history of modern psychotherapy, the existence of books like this one shows that the technical protocol may not be enough for working with many clients. There is a craving for connection and expression that so many people experience, especially in modern times where people are increasingly cut off from community and living their fullest expression of self. You can be respectful of the EMDR therapy standard protocol while also realizing that there is more to healing than technique, and by recognizing that EMDR *plays well with other therapies*, especially in your Preparation and Closure/Re-Evaluation work. The technical method, mechanism, and model of EMDR can help a person work through blocks, especially those caused by trauma, preventing people from living in their fullest expression. As a metaphor, we often refer to Phases Three to Six as "Shapiro's Special Sauce" (Marich & Dansiger, 2022). Hopefully Paul, Irene's client who likes to bake, approves of that one! There is a beautiful alchemy that can happen in these core phases of EMDR by following that recipe, yet the nuance of applying that recipe varies from client to client and situation to situation.

The two practices—expressive arts therapy and EMDR therapy—can work together, and we are excited to see how blending of the modalities will continue to occur as EMDR therapists feel a greater sense of empowerment to be more innovative. And we also hope that a healthier crop of EMDR therapists emerge and grow who are committed to their own expressive arts therapy processes. Let the processes nourish you because you are worthy and deserving of being nourished! From this place, you will then be able to best share your practice…

REFERENCES

Arrien, A. (2013). *The four fold way: Walking the paths of the warrior, teacher, healer, and visionary.* Harper Collins.

Marich, J. (2019). *Process not perfection: Expressive arts solutions in trauma recovery.* Creative Mindfulness Media.

Marich, J. & Dansiger, S. (2022). *Healing addiction with EMDR therapy: A trauma-focused guide.* Springer Publishing Company.

Rogers, N. (1993). *The creative connection: Expressive arts as healing.* Science & Behavior Books, Inc.

Santiago-Rivera, A., Altarriba, J., Poll, N., Gonzalez-Miller, & Cragun, C. (2009). Therapists' views on working with bilingual Spanish-English speaking clients: A qualitative investigation. *Professional Psychology Research and Practice, 40*(5), 436–443. https://doi.org/10.1080/14753630412331313695

Shapiro, F. (2018). *Eye Movement Desensitization and reprocessing [EMDR] Therapy* (3rd ed.). The Guildford Press.

RESOURCES

"Call and Response" Expressive Arts Process. (2018). Featuring Jamie Marich, Stephen Dansiger, and Michelle Tompkins. Available at: https://www.youtube.com/watch?v=ZUSkPfG5Ww8

INDEX

Note: **Bold** page numbers refer to tables and *italic* page numbers refer to figures.

Milton Keynes UK
Ingram Content Group UK Ltd.
UKHW021020140124
435956UK00017B/190